MEDIEVAL YORK

MEDIEVAL YORK

600–1540

D. M. PALLISER

OXFORD
UNIVERSITY PRESS

OXFORD
UNIVERSITY PRESS

Great Clarendon Street, Oxford, OX2 6DP,
United Kingdom

Oxford University Press is a department of the University of Oxford.
It furthers the University's objective of excellence in research, scholarship,
and education by publishing worldwide. Oxford is a registered trade mark of
Oxford University Press in the UK and in certain other countries

Published in the United States of America by Oxford University Press
198 Madison Avenue, New York, NY 10016, United States of America

British Library Cataloguing in Publication Data
Data available

Library of Congress Control Number: 2013947865

ISBN 978–0–19–925584–9

As printed and bound by
CPI Group (UK) Ltd, Croydon CR0 4YY

In Memory of
Edward Miller 1915–2000
and
Philip Stell 1934–2004

Preface

Those familiar with the voluminous literature on medieval York might reasonably ask whether a new survey is needed. Yet, though it was throughout the Middle Ages one of the largest and most important English towns, satisfactory overviews are few. There are excellent studies of particular periods, themes, or buildings, but a reliable book-length survey covering most aspects has been lacking.

Edward Miller's 'Medieval York' in the *Victoria County History*'s volume on the city was written in the 1950s and published in 1961. It is still one of the finest histories in print of any English medieval town, but it was confined mainly to documentary sources, for he wrote before the large-scale archaeological excavations which began in the 1960s, before the publication of the massive inventory of the city's buildings by the Royal Commission on Historical Monuments, and before the huge increase in coin finds which have clarified so much of the early story. He was also constrained by the volume's format to the time between 1100 and 1509, reinforcing a too-widespread tendency to use the term 'medieval' for the period after the Norman Conquest of England.

Here, I use the term to cover the millennium or so from the fall of the Western Roman Empire to the sixteenth century, a usage widely accepted on the Continent and one officially endorsed by the Society for Medieval Archaeology. I therefore prefer 'early medieval' to 'Anglo-Saxon' for the five or six centuries before the Norman Conquest, and 'later medieval' for the time after 1066 or 1100. I have tried to avoid 'Celtic' and 'Anglo-Saxon' altogether, preferring 'British' and 'English', and though I use 'Vikings' as useful shorthand for the invaders of the ninth to eleventh centuries, I prefer 'Anglo-Scandinavians' for the people under their rule. It would be pedantic to avoid the popular terms altogether, but they are inexact and anachronistic ways of describing ethnically and culturally mixed populations of natives and invaders.[1]

---

1. See esp. Susan Reynolds, 'What do we mean by "Anglo-Saxon" and "Anglo-Saxons"?', in her *Ideas and Solidarities of the Medieval Laity* (Aldershot, 1995), III; Bryan Ward-Perkins, 'Why did the Anglo-Saxons not become more British?', *EHR*, 115 (2000), 513–33.

Inevitably, the nature and interpretation of source material varies greatly over the *longue durée* covered here, more archaeological for the earlier centuries and more documentary later, though material evidence remains important throughout. What perhaps should be emphasized, for those most familiar with later medieval or post-medieval sources, is the sheer scarcity of early medieval evidence of any type, which can lead to unwarranted deductions. A classic example occurs in the first edition of Richard Hodges' very stimulating *Dark Age Economics*, where he argued that there could have been no major trading settlement (*emporium*) at York in the eighth century, despite the explicit testimony of Alcuin. 'At some stage', wrote Hodges, 'one has to accept the power of this kind of negative [archaeological] evidence.' Yet, only three years after those words were published, exactly such evidence was unearthed at 46–54 Fishergate. And much the same can be said of the scanty documentary evidence for the early centuries. To argue against the importance, or even existence, of early kings and dynasties 'on the ground that we have no record of such importance', says James Campbell, 'is to argue, not from the silence of sources, but from their absence'.[2]

The literature on medieval York is enormous; most of what I have gratefully drawn on is listed in the footnotes and bibliography. The York volume of the *Victoria County History* is excellent on the period after 1100, thanks largely to Edward Miller's chapter; the brief pre-1100 account has worn less well because of the huge increase in archaeological evidence, much of it now published in the fascicules of the York Archaeological Trust (YAT) under the general title *The Archaeology of York*, and in Volume I of *Excavations at York Minster*, as well as online. For later medieval York there are now many specialized studies in print, as well as the five volumes of the RCHM's *Inventory* of the Historical Monuments in the City of York, which covers the entire city except for the Minster and its Close. The Corpus Christi plays have generated a huge literature, while the equally important corpus of surviving stained glass in the Minster and parish churches is being published by the CVMA.

One of the YAT fascicules deserves separate mention here, David Rollason's splendid *Sources for York History to AD 1100* (*AY* 1, 1998), which includes almost all key texts both in original languages and in translation. My usual practice is to cite key documents from either the original manuscripts or standard printed editions, but in the minefield of early sources it seems best to draw on Professor

---

2. Richard Hodges, *Dark Age Economics* (London, 1982), 73–4; James Campbell, *Essays in Anglo-Saxon History* (London, 1986), 90.

Rollason's edition as the first port of call. I would also like to make special acknowledgment of the work of Professor Philip Stell, who after a medical career used his retirement to produce an impressive body of published records and databases relevant to the medieval city.

Valuable secondary sources have been published in periodicals or booklets not readily available outside major libraries, but fortunately many have been reprinted in recent collected volumes, notably by the publishers Ashgate (Variorum) and Hambledon. I have chosen where possible to cite articles in this form rather than in the original journals and booklets, noting only if there are significant differences between the two. So, for instance, many of Barrie Dobson's valuable contributions are cited from his *Church and Society in the Medieval North of England* (Hambledon, 1996) and *The Jewish Communities of Medieval England* (Borthwick Publications, 2010), while my own essays relevant to York are cited for preference from *Towns and Local Communities in Medieval and Early Modern England* (Variorum, 2006). I have listed in the bibliography those works I have found most useful and relevant and which were published before the end of 2010, together with a few more recent publications.

A few points about transcription, terminology, and dating may be helpful. In transcribing from manuscripts, I have made no alterations beyond silently expanding contractions, modernizing the use of capitals, and standardizing 'u' and 'v' in accordance with modern usage. In referring to persons, I have modernized first names and standardized surnames to the most widely used contemporary forms. The early Middle Ages are more problematic: I have generally followed the *Oxford Dictionary of National Biography*, but I have arbitrarily used Erik, not Eric or Eirikr, for Scandinavians, and for 1066 have distinguished Harold of England from Harald of Norway to avoid confusion.

I have cited weights and measures as used in medieval England, usually with metric equivalents in brackets: helpful tables are given in Edward Miller's and John Hatcher's *Medieval England: Towns, Commerce and Crafts 1086–1348* (1995), xi, xii.[3] Sums of money are also expressed in contemporary terms, with 12 pence (*d.*) to a shilling (*s.*), 20 shillings to a pound sterling (£), and 13*s.* 4*d.* to a mark. The value of money is not easily translated into modern terms, since prices have changed at widely differing rates over the centuries, and any attempt here to give modern purchasing equivalents would be quickly outdated.

---

3. I have explained elsewhere why the widespread preference of British archaeologists for citing only metric equivalents can be misleading, especially with regard to the obsolete rod, pole, or perch, which was a common module in laying out defences, houses, and building plots: *Towns and Local Communities*, II, 24.

As for chronology, all dates cited in this book except one postdate the time of Christ, with no need to qualify any of them as AD (or CE). All are also, where possible, cited in New Style, with the year starting on 1 January and not 25 March: this means that occasionally my dates differ from those in older York histories and texts. The earliest document in the city's register, for example, is dated by its editor 1376, but refers to the year starting on 25 January 1376 O.S., i.e. 1377 N.S. The invaluable first register of freemen admissions is also a source of much confusion, given the simultaneous use of regnal years alongside the years in office of mayors and chamberlains: in consequence, the dating in Francis Collins's edition is slightly over a year out. Two alabasterers, for instance, were enfranchised in the year 1458–9, but Collins dates the entries 1457, while recent scholarly studies of the alabaster industry give 1457–8 and even 1456.[4]

A final point about chronology is the obvious necessity of organizing any long-term study like this by periods as well as by themes. For the early medieval centuries, invasions and conquests make natural breaks; but from 1066 I have subdivided the long periods between Norman Conquest and Black Death, and between Black Death and Reformation, partly by reigns. This may seem old-fashioned to those approaching urban history from a social or economic perspective, but 'the Crown was not only the provider of a uniform currency and a uniform law, but also the guarantor of the peace, the supervisor of the roads and bridges on which trade depended, and a constraint on the aristocratic terrorism which elsewhere in Europe could reduce a flourishing countryside to a wasteland.'[5] A monarch had the power also to give or withdraw urban privileges by royal charter, or to favour alien merchants against natives in return for favours. No study of any English town can afford to minimize the role of the monarchy, at least before 1688.

I am grateful to the Universities of Birmingham, Hull, Keele, and Leeds for support during the long preparation of this book, and to the kindness and helpfulness of the staff at many libraries and Record Offices, especially the Borthwick Institute, the National Archives, York City Archives, the York Company of Merchant Adventurers, and York Minster Library, as well as the staff of the Centre for Medieval Studies and the Department of History at the University of York, and of the York Archaeological Trust.

4. YF, I, 177; J. Blair and N. Ramsay, eds, *English Medieval Industries* (London, 1991), 34; Francis Cheetham, *English Medieval Alabasters* (Woodbridge, 2005), 15.
5. J. R. Maddicott, 'From wool to cloth', *Times Literary Supplement* (7 June 1996), 32.

I am indebted to numerous scholars, friends, and former colleagues for help over many years, including Peter Addyman, Lorraine Attreed, Bernard Barr, Richard Beadle, John Blair, Richard Britnell, Peter Brown, James Campbell, Wendy Childs, Peter Connolly, Claire Cross, Barrie Dobson, Rita Freedman, Mary Garrison, Jeremy Goldberg, Dawn Hadley, Richard Hall, John Harvey, Rosemary Horrox, Alexandra Johnston, Jennifer Kermode, Simon Keynes, Christian Liddy, John Maddicott, Ailsa Mainman, Michael Metcalf, Richard K. Morris, Pamela Nightingale, Christopher Norton, Mark Ormrod, Patrick Ottaway, Gordon Plumb, Tony Pollard, Sarah Rees Jones, Susan Reynolds, Julian Richards, Dick Reid, David Rollason, David M. Smith, Philip Stell, Joanna Story, Anne Sutton, Meg Twycross, Chris Webb, and Ian Wood. At a late stage, I benefited from the informative and encouraging comments of the publisher's anonymous reader. None of these, of course, is responsible for any errors I may have made in incorporating their references or suggestions. I would also like to thank the staff at Oxford University Press with whom I have worked over the years, including Emma Barber, Seth Cayley, Rupert Cousens, Anne Gelling, Stephanie Ireland, Ruth Parr, Cathryn Steele, and Christopher Wheeler.

Finally, I am grateful to Richard Palliser for his editing and computing skills; to Lisa Liddy for her word-processing and copy-editing; and especially to my wife Mary for her support, patience, and wise advice.

David Palliser

Contents

List of Maps

List of Plates

List of Abbreviations

AASRP	*Associated Architectural Societies' Reports and Papers*
ANS	*Anglo-Norman Studies*
Antiq J	*The Antiquaries' Journal*
ASC	*The Anglo-Saxon Chronicles*, cited sub anno (s.a.), where necessary with ref. to D. Whitelock, D. C. Douglas, and S. I. Tucker, eds, *The Anglo-Saxon Chronicle: A Revised Translation* (Cambridge, 1961) and M. Swanton, ed., *The Anglo-Saxon Chronicles* (London, 2000)
ASSAH	*Anglo-Saxon Studies in Archaeology and History*
AY	The Archaeology of York: series published by CBA for YAT in fascicules. Footnote references are to volume, fascicule, and page
AY 1	D. W. Rollason et al., *Sources for York History to AD 1100* (1998)
AY SS 1	The Archaeology of York Supplementary Series, I: The Pictorial Evidence (4 fascicules to date, 1998–)
Aylmer & Cant, eds	G. E. Aylmer and Reginald Cant, eds, *A History of York Minster* (Oxford, 1977)
BAA	British Archaeological Association
BAR (BS)	British Archaeological Reports (British Series)
Bartlett, 'Economy of York'	J. N. Bartlett, 'Some aspects of the economy of York in the later Middle Ages, 1300–1550', Univ. of London PhD thesis, 1958

Bartlett, 'Expansion and decline'	J. N. Bartlett, 'The expansion and decline of York in the later Middle Ages', *Econ HR*, 2nd ser., 12 (1959), 17–33
BBC	*British Borough Charters*, 3 vols (Cambridge, 1913–43: for details of each volume see Bibliography under Ballard; Ballard and Tait; and Weinbaum)
BIA	Borthwick Institute for Archives, University of York (formerly Borthwick Institute of Historical Research)
BJRL	*Bulletin of the John Rylands Library*
BL	British Library
BNJ	*The British Numismatic Journal*
BP	Borthwick Papers (University of York: nos 1–26 were styled St Anthony's Hall Publications)
BTC	Borthwick Texts and Calendars
BTS	Borthwick Texts and Studies
C & M	B. Colgrave and R. A. B. Mynors, eds, *Bede's Ecclesiastical History of the English People*, OMT (Oxford, 1969)
CBA (Res Rep)	Council for British Archaeology (Research Reports)
CCR	*Calendar of Close Rolls*
CChR	*Calendar of Charter Rolls*
CPR	*Calendar of Patent Rolls*
CR H III	*Close Rolls of the Reign of Henry III*
Cubbin, ed.	G. P. Cubbin, ed., *The Anglo-Saxon Chronicle: A Collaborative Edition*, VI: *MS D* (Cambridge, 1996)
CUHB I, II	*The Cambridge Urban History of Britain*, I: *600–1540*, ed. D. M. Palliser (Cambridge, 2000); II: *1540–1840*, ed. Peter Clark (Cambridge, 2000)
CVMA	Corpus Vitrearum Medii Aevi (Great Britain: British Academy Series)
Econ HR	*Economic History Review*
EEA	English Episcopal Acta (British Academy Series)
EETS	Early English Text Society

EHD	*English Historical Documents*, ed. D. C. Douglas: volumes cited are I: *c*.500–1042, ed. D. Whitelock (2nd edn, 1979), and III: *1189–1327*, ed. H. Rothwell (1975)
EHR	*English Historical Review*
Elenchus	Susan Reynolds and W. de Boer, eds, *Elenchus Fontium Historiae Urbanae*, II, pt 2 (Leiden, 1988), 1–153
EYC	*Early Yorkshire Charters*, 12 vols: I–III, ed. William Farrer; IV–XII, ed. C. T. Clay (YASRS Extra Series, 1914–65)
EYM	*Excavations at York Minster*, I, ed. D. Phillips and B. Heywood, RCHME (London, 1995); II, ed. D. Phillips, RCHME (London, 1985)
FYMAR	Friends of York Minster Annual Reports
GDB	Great Domesday Book (refs followed by folio and column, i.e. a–d, not r & v)
Gross/Graves	Charles Gross, *A Bibliography of English History to 1485*, ed. E. B. Graves (Oxford, 1975)
HAEY	S. Neave and S. Ellis, eds, *An Historical Atlas of East Yorkshire* (Hull, 1996)
HANY	R. A. Butlin, ed., *Historical Atlas of North Yorkshire* (Otley, 2003)
HBC	E. B. Fryde et al., eds, *Handbook of British Chronology* (Cambridge, 3rd edn 1986)
HCY	*Historians of the Church of York and its Archbishops*, ed. James Raine, 3 vols (RS, 1879–94)
HE	Bede, *Historia Ecclesiastica Gentis Anglorum*, usually cited here by book and chapter (e.g. I. i). Where needed, refs are given to the edns by Plummer (1896), Colgrave and Mynors (see C & M above), and McClure and Collins (1994)
HKW	R. A. Brown, H. M. Colvin, and A. J. Taylor, *The History of the King's Works*, I–II (London, 1963)
HMS	Harlaxton Medieval Studies

HP 1386–1422	J. S. Roskell, ed., *The History of Parliament: The House of Commons, 1386–1422* (Stroud, 1992)
HP 1509–1558	S. T. Bindoff, ed., *The History of Parliament: the House of Commons, 1509–1558* (London, 1982)
HR	*Historical Research* (formerly *Bulletin of the Institute of Historical Research*)
Irvine, ed.	*The Anglo-Saxon Chronicle: A Collaborative Edition*, VII: *MS E*, ed. Susan Irvine (Cambridge, 2004)
Med Arch	*Medieval Archaeology*
Miller, 'Medieval York'	Edward Miller, 'Medieval York', in *VCHY*, 25–116
NH	*Northern History*
NS	New Style
ODNB	*Oxford Dictionary of National Biography*, ed. H. C. G. Matthew and Brian Harrison, 60 vols (Oxford, 2004)
OMT	Oxford Medieval Texts
ON	Old Norse
OS	Old Style
Palliser, *Towns and Local Communities*	D. M. Palliser, *Towns and Local Communities in Medieval and Early Modern England* (Aldershot, 2006)
Pipe R.	Publications of the Pipe Roll Society
P&P	*Past & Present*
PROME	*Parliament Rolls of Medieval England*, ed. C. Given Wilson et al., 16 vols (Woodbridge, 2005)
RCHMY	Royal Commission on Historical Monuments (England), *An Inventory of the Historical Monuments in the City of York*, 5 vols (London, 1962–81)
REED: York	*Records of Early English Drama: York*, ed. Alexandra F. Johnston and Margaret Rogerson, 2 vols (Toronto and Manchester, 1979)
Rees Jones, 'Property, tenure and rents'	S. R. Rees Jones, 'Property, tenure and rents: Some aspects of the topography

	and economy of medieval York', D.Phil. thesis, University of York (1987)
RLC	*Rotuli Litterarum Clausarum*, ed. T. D. Hardy, 2 vols (London, 1833–4)
RMY	*Records of Medieval York: City, Church and Crown*, ed. Debbie Cannon, BTC (York, forthcoming)
RRAN	*Regesta Regum Anglo-Normannorum*: volumes cited are I, ed. David Bates (1998) and III, ed. H. A. Cronne and R. H. C. Davis (1968)
RS	Rolls Series
RSEH, NS	British Academy, Records of Social and Economic History, New Series
SCBI	*Sylloge of Coins of the British Isles*
SS	Publications of the Surtees Society
TE	*Testamenta Eboracensia*, 6 vols, various editors, SS vols 4, 30, 45, 53, 79, 106
TJHSE	*Transactions of the Jewish Historical Society of England*
TNA	The National Archives (formerly the Public Record Office)
TR Hist S	*Transactions of the Royal Historical Society*
UH(Y)	*Urban History (Yearbook)*
VCH	*The Victoria History of the Counties of England*; *VCH Yorks.*, general Yorkshire volumes: *VCHER*, East Riding; *VCHNR*, North Riding
VCHY	*VCH, The City of York*, ed. P. M. Tillott (1961)
YAJ	*Yorkshire Archaeological Journal*
YAS	Yorkshire Archaeological Society
YASRS	Yorkshire Archaeological Society Record Series
YAT	York Archaeological Trust
YAYAS AR	*Annual Reports of the Yorkshire Architectural and York Archaeological Society*
YCA	York City Archives
YCR	*York Civic Records*, ed. Angelo Raine, 8 vols, YASRS vols 98, 103, 106, 108, 110, 112, 115, 119

YF   *Register of the Freemen of the City of York*,
                                    ed. Francis Collins, 2 vols, SS vols 96,
                                    102 (1897, 1900)
YH   *York Historian*
YHB   *York House Books 1461–1490*, ed. Lorraine
                                    C. Attreed, 2 vols (Far Thrupp, 1991)
YLP   The Latin Project, Centre for Medieval
                                    Studies, University of York, ed. Ann
                                    Rycraft (2000–)
YMB   *York Memorandum Book*, I–II, ed. Maud
                                    Sellers and III, ed. Joyce Percy, SS vols
                                    120, 125, 186
YML   York Minster Library (including Dean
                                    and Chapter Archives)

York's Name and Status[1]

It may help in reading the following text to know the successive names and titles of the city from Roman times onwards, as an important piece of what might be called linguistic archaeology: they are a reminder of the elements of continuity and change in the inhabitants' culture and languages. It was recorded under a succession of names which had elements in common: Roman *Eburacum* or *Eboracum*, Old Welsh *Cair Ebrauc*, Old English *Eoforwic*, Old Scandinavian *Iorvik* or *Jorvik*, and Middle and Modern English *York*. There are at least two possible ways of interpreting them: as a series of gradual shifts in pronunciation as successive settlers tried to copy and adopt the previous name, or as a new coinage by each wave of invaders, using terms with a meaning in their own tongue but which sounded like the old name.

The Romans almost certainly adopted the former strategy, for it is generally agreed that *Eburacum* derived from a previous British name something like *Eburacon*, probably meaning 'place of yew trees' or 'estate of Eburos'. However, whatever its origin, it may eventually have come to be understood by its inhabitants to include a word for 'boar', and a boar appears, apparently as a pun for York, on a Latin inscription of 237. If so, it might have caused the English incomers of the fifth or sixth centuries to coin *Eoforwic*, 'boar town', though it may equally be that, regardless of the Roman past, the English called it that because of the 'unusual prevalence of pigs' in a farming phase on the site of the later cathedral. Alternatively, the English could simply have been trying to copy the Roman name: although *Eoforwic* was the usual written form, a variant *Eforwic* exists, and in one unique annal of about 900 the Emperor Severus is described as having died in *Efforica*. Other scholars interpret *Eoforwic* as a new coinage, 'the trading settlement

---

1. Based largely on A. L. F. Rivet and Colin Smith, *The Place-Names of Roman Britain* (London, 1979), 355–7; Cecily Clark, 'Historical linguistics—linguistic archaeology', in *Words, Names and History*, ed. Peter Jackson (Cambridge, 1995), 92–4; and Gillian Fellows Jensen, 'The origin and development of the name York', in *AY* 1, 226–37.

[*vik, wic*] on the river Ure [Ouse]'. Nevertheless, Fellows Jensen and Clark concur that in each period conquerors of York rendered in their own language what they thought the inhabitants were saying: a splendid example, if they are right, of fundamental continuity of settlement through all the conquests and invasions.[2]

There are similar problems with the descriptive terms used for York over the centuries. Since the fourteenth century it has officially been the *city* of York, but the distinctions between cities, towns, and boroughs, peculiar to England, raise questions of shifting and imprecise terminology. Roman York was possibly a *municipium* and certainly, by 237, a *colonia*, the highest level in the urban hierarchy. Bede, who was scrupulous in distinguishing different categories of settlement, always called York a *civitas* (city) and never *urbs* (town); the Old English translation of his *History* usually calls it by the equivalent *Eoforwicceastre*.[3] Later usage was more variable. A saint's life of about 950 calls Leeds a *civitas* (in the wider Roman sense of a town and its dependent territory) but York *urbs*, while Domesday Book makes no attempt at consistency. It uses *civitas* twelve times for York and *urbs* four times; and though it never calls it *burgus* (borough), it normally calls its inhabitants *burgenses* (burgesses) and only once *cives* (citizens). Not until the late Middle Ages did the Crown become consistent in calling some towns cities and not others. I have therefore normally called York a city but with no attempt at consistency; and I have preferred 'townspeople' for the whole population, reserving 'citizens' or 'freemen' for those residents (usually male) who were legally, politically, or economically privileged.

2. 'Prevalence of pigs': I. N. Wood, 'Turning a fortress into a cathedral', *British Archaeology* (Sept. 1995), 7. *Efforica*: D. N. Dumville, 'A new chronicle fragment of early British history', *EHR*, 88 (1973) 312–14.
3. James Campbell, *Essays in Anglo-Saxon History* (London, 1986), 99, 100n., 117; *AY* I, 170; D. M. Palliser, *Domesday York*, BP 78 (1990), 8.

Introduction

A city in time and space

The importance of York as a historic English city needs little urging. Since the 1970s it has become England's most successful town in promoting its past, especially its medieval past. It is easy to see why it should often be thought of as—even today—essentially 'medieval'. It includes a nearly intact (if heavily restored) circuit of medieval defences; the largest medieval cathedral in Europe north of the Alps and Pyrenees; nineteen parish churches; four medieval guildhalls; and very many medieval houses, including the earliest datable timber-framed row in England. The classic tourist image of a thousand postcards—the Minster (cathedral) viewed from the city wall near the railway station—combines the two most striking survivals from the thirteenth century, the Minster as rebuilt from the 1220s and the stone walls from the 1250s (Plate 1).

Impressed by all this, it is easy to forget that much else has been destroyed, and that what survives owes as much to the poverty and decline of post-Reformation York as to the achievements of the medieval builders (Plates 2a, 2b). Furthermore, as Barrie Dobson points out,

> It might be even more hazardous still to assume that because York is now so regularly publicised as a uniquely medieval city it was similarly *sui generis* in medieval England itself. All allowances made for the very distinctive features of its history ... [medieval York] deserves our attention most because of the way in which it so often exemplifies ... the universal aspirations and preoccupations of medieval English townsfolk everywhere.[1]

1. R. B. Dobson, 'The city of York', in B. Ford, ed., *The Cambridge Guide to the Arts in Britain*, II (Cambridge, 1988), 201.

The lack of focus in the popular view of York extends not only to its physical fabric but to its political context, in viewing it as throughout history *England's* second city. When in 2006 York commemorated the acclamation of Constantine as emperor in the city 1700 years before, a poster depicted him as deciding to 'control all England' from York. That, of course, is to ignore the fact that there was no kingdom of England until the tenth century, a kingdom which did not finally incorporate York until about 954. If we start with a broad British perspective, and look at the shifting powers of the island between the fifth and tenth centuries, then the emergence of York as a northern outpost of a kingdom centred on Winchester and Westminster is seen as by no means inevitable. As the historian of the British navy puts it well:

> Nothing is pre-ordained in history...York is well placed to be a national capital of Britain, and if Æthelstan had lost the battle of Brunanburh [937], the Viking kingdom of York with its mixture of Norse, Celtic and English elements might have made a logical centre for a strong island kingdom.[2]

Indeed, much the same could be said of the pre-Viking kingdom of Northumbria. In its heyday, between the 630s and the 680s, its kings ruled most of central Britain between the Trent and the Forth; and they were at times overlords of most of the other English kingdoms to the south, as well as of many Britons, Scots, and Picts to the north.

That said, however, the poster of Constantine did grasp an essential truth: that York was a Roman foundation which fixed once and for all the site of the modern city; and it was their English successors who deliberately chose to build on their location. So, in covering York's story over the 'long' Middle Ages, from the fifth century to the sixteenth, I would wish to emphasize at the outset its position as a fixed point in a fluid and shifting political landscape. For perhaps three hundred years the city was an important 'central place' (one cannot speak of a 'capital' at that period) of successive Northumbrian states, and then for a further century it played a similar role for Viking rulers. In the 950s York was absorbed into the new kingdom of England, though even a century after that Edward the Confessor was sometimes styled 'King of the English *and the Northumbrians*'. Effectively, what is now northern England then became the frequent victim of a power struggle, as the emerging states of England and Scotland contested it.[3]

2. N. A. M. Rodger, *The Safeguard of the Sea: A Naval History of Britain, 660–1649* (London, pb. edn 2004), 48.
3. Frank Barlow, *Edward the Confessor* (New Haven and London, 2nd edn 1997), 136. For the slow English absorption of the north in a British perspective, see R. R. Davies' brilliant *The First English Empire* (Oxford, 2000), especially pp. 55–6, 63–5, 71–2, 77 (quotation from p. 55).

England was, after all, 'a country created in the south', and in the eleventh century it usually took between two and three weeks to travel from Winchester to York. In contrast, the Scottish border was relatively close to the city. Until 1092 the Cumbrian kingdom formed a salient thrusting deep into English territory, so that Cumbrian kings—and their Scottish successors—could muster troops 'within two days' ride of York'. Not until the 1160s were Northumberland, Durham, and even parts of Yorkshire firmly under English control; only in 1237 was most of the present Anglo-Scottish border confirmed (appropriately by a treaty signed at York); and as late as 1319 Scottish forces almost reached the walls of York, and slew the mayor and other citizens at Myton-on-Swale.[4]

It was against this backdrop of state formation and warfare that York developed, and I make no apology for constructing much of this book chronologically by conquests, dynasties, and even (for the Normans and early Angevins) by the reigns of individual monarchs. Of course, much of the city's life moved at the generally slower pace of economic, social, technological, religious, and cultural change; and much was at the mercy of forces beyond human control, such as climatic change, harvest failure, and epidemic disease. Nevertheless, York's history was heavily constrained by political power, law, justice, and warfare. James Campbell has demonstrated that by the tenth century England was already a centralized and much-governed state; and given the well-recorded actions of Old English and Norman kings, and the lack of much detail for the lives of individual citizens before the thirteenth century, a regnal approach seems the most sensible one.

A final reflection on York's situation within changing states and boundaries is prompted by the two conquests of England in the eleventh century. Alfred's successors had not long conquered the Viking 'kingdom of York' before all England was overrun by foreign invaders, firstly by Swein and Cnut of Denmark (1013–16) and then by Duke William of Normandy (1066). In both cases York's traders had the opportunity to operate within new maritime empires, especially between 1066 and 1558 when much of France was ruled by the same person who was also king of England. York's earliest royal charter confirmed to its merchants those trading privileges in England and Normandy which they had enjoyed before 1135; the second earliest granted them further privileges throughout England, Normandy, Aquitaine, Anjou, and Poitou. Most of the French territories were lost to

4. G. W. S. Barrow, 'The Anglo-Scottish border', *NH*, 1 (1966), 21–42 (quotation from p. 25). Journey time from Winchester: Richard Fletcher, *Bloodfeud* (London, 2002), 31.

the English Crown in 1204–5, but much more was conquered after 1337. One fixed point was the great wine-exporting port of Bordeaux, which attracted English merchants, including men from York and Hull, throughout the period of English rule (1154–1453). Another was Calais (1347–1558), where the post of Mayor of the Staple of wool merchants was more than once filled by a York man.

One reason why kings, rebels, or invaders wished to control what became the city was its strategic position in the Vale of York (Map 1), which provides a much broader and easier land route between England and Scotland than the Lancashire plain. Equally, the Vale and its surrounding hills made for centuries a contrast between uplands which could shelter rebels, freebooters, and outlaws—what Kapelle characterized as a 'free zone'—and the more easily governed lowlands. York was therefore a natural target in any armed conflict, and it is no coincidence that—in addition to sieges of the

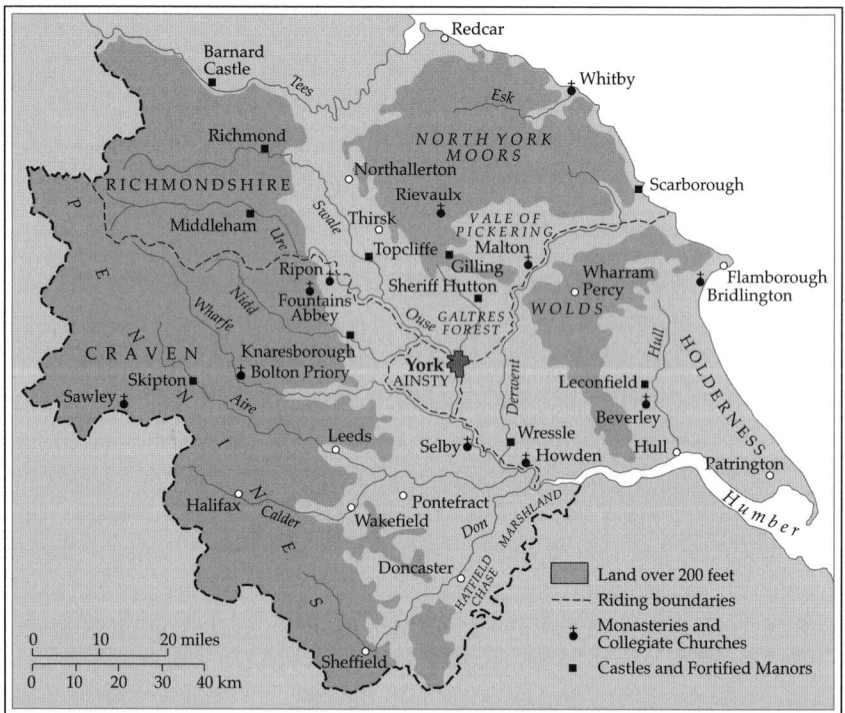

Map 1. Yorkshire in the later Middle Ages, c.1100–1540
The outer border is that of the historic (pre-1974) county. Pecked borders are those of the wapentake of Ainsty and of the three Ridings.

city itself—several key battles were fought within 20 miles (32 km) of it, including Fulford (1066), Stamford Bridge (1066), Myton (1319), Towton (1461), and rather later Marston Moor (1644), while the Battle of the Standard (1138) was fought only a little further north. Less often emphasized, but equally tokens of the city's situation, are the many lesser skirmishes and riots in its immediate hinterland. For example, the series of eleventh-century massacres and murders brilliantly evoked by Richard Fletcher began and ended close to York; in 1453–4 another feud (between Percys and Nevilles) triggered 'battles' at Heworth and Stamford Bridge in which York men were involved; in 1489 the fourth Percy earl of Northumberland was murdered by rebels at his lodge north of the city; and in 1504 his successor came close to being assassinated at Fulford by servants of the archbishop.[5]

However, there was much more to the region than its military attractions. What made York desirable to the Romans and their successors was a combination of defensibility and access: what gave it long-term viability as a major town was the richness and variety of its surrounding landscapes, farming regions, and communications by land and water. The Vale itself begins in the North as the narrow Vale of Mowbray before widening south to form the Vale of York proper, a spacious lowland some 60 miles (97 km) from north to south and in most places 30 miles (48 km) broad. To its west are the Pennines, a chain of bleak hills, mostly moorland and upland pasture, though intersected by fertile and low-lying dales (valleys). To the east, the Vale of Mowbray is bordered by the tabular upland now known as the North York Moors; south of the moors is the Vale of Pickering; and south of that again the Yorkshire Wolds, northernmost outlier of that chain of chalk uplands radiating from Salisbury Plain. Finally, the Vale at its southern end merges imperceptibly into the Midland Plain, the junction being marked by wide expanses of fen and marsh around the intersection of the rivers Ouse, Derwent, Humber, and Trent.

What gave York a great advantage in exploiting and marketing the produce of a very varied hinterland was, indeed, its position on a major river system. 'Rivers were', it has been well said, 'the lifelines of early and high medieval England'. York's trade depended not merely on the Ouse, but on its powerful tides, which until 1757 (when Naburn lock was constructed) extended above York to Poppleton; and even above that the river Ure was accessible to small boats as high as Boroughbridge. The Romans had secured

5. W. E. Kapelle, *The Norman Conquest of the North* (London, 1979), 7, 128–9, 131–3, etc. Fletcher, *Bloodfeud, passim.* Events of 1453–4, 1489, and 1504: see Ch. 7.

a double advantage when they founded *Eburacum*—locally, in finding a defensible place at the confluence of Ouse and Foss, and regionally, in giving access by water to much of the North and Midlands. That advantage they increased by digging two canals, the Foss Dyke from the Trent at Torksey to the Witham at Lincoln, and the Car Dyke connecting Lincoln with the Wash, canals which were periodically renewed well into the Middle Ages. It was possible to sail inland from York to Boston, Ely, or Cambridge: hence the note in Domesday Book that if the king's messengers came to Torksey, 'the men of the same town should conduct them to York with their ships'.[6]

The corollary to York's riverside situation was its liability to flood, especially after heavy rain or melting snow in the Pennines. The Vale of York covers some 1,000 square miles (2,590 km²), and much of it lies under 50 feet (15 m) above mean sea level. More importantly, the total catchment area of the Vale is 3,447 square miles (8,927 km²). There are almost no written records of flooding in the city before the fourteenth century, but there may have been extensive flooding in the post-Roman period, and it is a reasonable assumption that Yorkshire floods mentioned in chronicles, such as around 1130 and in 1236, would have struck the city. The chronicle of St Mary's Abbey noted a severe flood in 1315, high enough to fill half the abbey courtyard, which must have reached some 33 feet O.D. (10 m). Nearly as devastating must have been the floods of 1328, which disrupted all road traffic north of York at Skelton. And at the end of 1348, the Ouse flooded at Ouse Bridge as far as the crossroads of Micklegate and North Street.[7]

There are fewer records of floods between 1350 and 1550, perhaps because of an increase in retaining riverbank walls, piled housing, and a slow accumulation of domestic refuse which has raised the present occupation level

6. The best source for the transport history of the Ouse is B. F. Duckham, *The Yorkshire Ouse* (Newton Abbot, 1967), supplemented by Colin Briden, 'York as a tidal port', *YAJ*, 69 (1997), 165–71. For flooding: J. Radley and C. Simms, *Yorkshire Flooding: Some Effects on Man and Nature* (York, 1971). For bridges: D. F. Harrison, 'Bridges and economic development, 1300–1800', *Econ HR*, 2nd ser., 45 (1992), 240–61, and his *The Bridges of Medieval England* (Oxford, 2004), esp. pp. 13, 16, 22, 138; B. Wilson and F. Mee, '*The Fairest Arch in England*': *Old Ouse Bridge and its Buildings*, AY SS 1, fascicule 2 (York, 2002), *passim*. Valuable recent research on medieval water transport in the York area is included in several essays in *Waterways and Canal-Building in Medieval England*, ed. John Blair (Oxford, 2007). Citations from the volume include Della Hooke, 'Uses of waterways in Anglo-Saxon England', at p. 37, and James Bond, 'Canal construction in the early Middle Ages', at pp. 167, 175–6. Domesday Book: GDB, fo. 337.
7. Jeffrey Radley and Colin Simms, *Yorkshire Flooding: Some Effects on Man and Nature* (York, 1971), 1–16 (1625 map on p. ii); H. H. E. Craster and M. E. Thornton, eds, *The Chronicle of St Mary's Abbey, York*, SS 148 (1934), 67; W. R. Childs and John Taylor, eds, *The Anonimalle Chronicle 1307 to 1334*, YASRS 147 (Leeds, 1991), 88–9; HCY, II, 418.

in the city by up to 20 feet (6 m) above the natural ground level. Nevertheless, major floods in 1565 and 1625 show that the danger had not vanished.
That of 1625 reached some 35 feet O.D. (11m), and a hypothetical mapping
of the vast area it covered probably gives a fair idea of the scale of the worst
medieval floods. It also acts as another indication of why the Romans sited
Eburacum where they did: the city would have been at the northern extrem-
ity of the worst flooding, and close to the glacial moraine giving a raised
routeway across the Vale, suggesting that they found it the best place for land
communication across Yorkshire from west to east.[8]

The primacy of rivers as 'lifelines' did not mean that roads were unimportant, though the combination of flooding, permanent marshland, and
unfordable rivers meant that the major overland routes passed either side of
the Vale where possible. Of the two main Roman roads north from Lincoln,
one ran along Lincoln Edge to cross the Humber by ferry, before skirting
the Wolds east of York. The other diverged west to join the Great North
Road, passing through Doncaster, Castleford, Tadcaster, Aldborough, and
Catterick. York was reached by transverse linking roads (running where
necessary over causeways), which explains some of the oddities of its plan.

Throughout the Middle Ages and beyond, the Roman network survived
little modified. English kings, for instance, usually approached York via Doncaster, turning north-east at Tadcaster and along what is now the A 64,
entering the walled city at Micklegate Bar. This is to speak only of major
routes; Roman York was at the hub of at least eight roads, and in the Middle
Ages the five main gates (bars) and six postern gates gave access to ten or
more approach roads.

The integration of road and river transport required, of course, river
crossings, whether fords, ferries or bridges; and York's position was crucially at what was until 1792 the lowest bridging point on the Ouse. The
Romans built the first Ouse Bridge on a line approximately between Tanner Row and the Guildhall; their crossing-point, and possibly their bridge,
was still in use in Anglian times, judging from the alignment of Anglian
structures excavated in Micklegate. However, by Anglo-Scandinavian
times the crossing-point shifted some 270 yards (250 m) downstream; the first
bridge on the present site can be dated by dendrochronology to about 980.[9]
No other York bridge spanned the Ouse until the 1840s, though the smaller

---

8. Radley and Simms, *Yorkshire Flooding*, 13; *RCHMY* IV, pp. xxvi, xxvii.
9. Wilson and Mee, *'The Fairest Arch in England'*, 26–8.

river Foss carried three, if not four, medieval bridges, of which Foss Bridge, the most important, was in existence by the 1140s.

Equally vital for York and its hinterland were the bridges and causeways which gave road access to the city. By about 1540 there were at least thirty bridges over the three main rivers (Swale, Ure, and Nidd) which merged above York to form the Ouse, eleven over the Wharfe, and nine across the Derwent. These are based on firmly dated records, but their compiler, David Harrison, points out that most were probably in existence by 1350. This is certainly the case on the lower reaches of the Ure and Ouse: four are recorded between Ripon and York before 1350, and no others were built over this stretch of water until about 1800. The crucial role of bridges and causeways in trade is attested by frequent bequests from York merchants for their building and repair. An especially generous benefactor was Nicholas Blakburn senior (d.1432), who was apparently responsible for building or rebuilding four bridges, at Catterick and Thornton on the Swale, and nearer York at Skip Bridge on the Nidd and Kexby on the Derwent.[10]

York was accessible both for bulky or fragile cargoes by river, and for quicker access overland by horse—quicker, that is, by medieval standards. Around 1300 a royal clerk estimated that it took three days to travel from York to Warwickshire or Leicestershire, and six to London. It was probably written at a time when the royal administration was shuttling between Westminster and York, and the writer perhaps hoped to show that administration from London was cheaper. Four days' riding from Westminster, he calculated, brought 27 shires within reach: from York, an equivalent time could reach only 15. All of these estimates assumed men on urgent Crown business employing frequent changes of mount; most travellers needed longer, though generally less by road than by water. In 1319 two groups of Cambridge scholars travelled to York to attend the king's Christmas feast there. One party travelled overland in five days; the other went by boat and took nine, arriving three days too late.[11]

10. Harrison, *Bridges of Medieval England*, 13, 16, 22. Blakburn's bridges: *CCR 1422–29*, 473; L. F. Salzman, *Building in England Down to 1540* (Oxford, 1952), 497–9; Harrison, *Bridges of Medieval England*, 131–4, 163, 196; A. Rycraft, ed., *The Blakburns in York*, YLP (York, 2006), 20–1, 24, 32–3.
11. W. M. Ormrod, 'Competing capitals? York and London in the fourteenth century', in S. R. Rees Jones et al., eds, *Courts and Regions in Medieval Europe* (Woodbridge, 2000), 94–6; Bond, 'Canal construction in the early Middle Ages', 204. Cf. Michael Prestwich, *Plantagenet England 1225–1360* (Oxford, 2005), 25, for other examples.

One feature of York's hinterland, unique among English provincial cities, was its control of the fertile Ainsty wapentake to its west—the entire tract of countryside almost enclosed by the rivers Ouse, Nidd, and Wharfe. Other cities like Norwich held adjacent rural manors from the Crown, but there seems no parallel to control of a whole subdivision of a county (hundred or wapentake). How the Ainsty came into York's hands is not clear. Domesday Book records it as one of the wapentakes of the huge West Riding, but with no indication of any special link with the county town.[12] By 1218–19, however, royal justices found York in possession of the Ainsty, claiming it as an 'appurtenance' of the city and therefore covered by John's charter of liberties to York. That charter, however, made no mention of the Ainsty, which was more than once seized back by the king. From 1283, for whatever reason, the king accepted York's jurisdiction over it; and from 1449 until 1836 the mayor and aldermen were *ex officio* justices of peace for the Ainsty as well as the city. Altogether, the city fathers seem to have governed the Ainsty without any formal representation by its inhabitants; and even voting by the Ainsty freeholders in parliamentary elections was not fully allowed until 1736.[13] It is not possible in this book to treat the Ainsty in its own right, but it should be borne in mind that for centuries it was treated by the Crown as 'the county of the city of York'. That was why monarchs entering York in late medieval and early modern times were met by the city sheriffs at Tadcaster Bridge on the Wharfe, or at Skip Bridge on the Nidd, as the limits of their jurisdiction.

York lay within easy reach of a varied range of farming regions, making it a natural entrepôt. The Vale itself has long been a zone of mixed husbandry, though woodland, scrub, and marsh were also extensive; as late as the twelfth century, a thumbnail sketch of the wealth of English towns singled out York for its woodlands.[14] To the north, Bulmer wapentake was largely covered by Galtres Forest, though it was not all woodland; to the

---

12. GDB does record, separately from the rest of the Yorkshire description, 13 holdings, one 'within the circuit of the city', one in the East Riding, and the other 11 in the North Riding, identifying them collectively as an 84-carucate territory which gelded (paid tax) with the city; but it was completely distinct from the Ainsty.
13. Francis Drake, *Eboracum* (London, 1736), 381–2 and App. p. lxiii; *VCHY*, 318–19; D. M. Palliser, *Tudor York* (Oxford, 1979), entries indexed under 'Ainsty'.
14. Diana Greenway, ed., *Henry, Archdeacon of Huntingdon: Historia Anglorum*, OMT (Oxford, 1996), 20. This might seem vague and trivial, but Henry's very next example, 'Exeter for its bright metal' [tin] has been shown to have a solid basis in fact: J. R. Maddicott, 'Trade, industry and the wealth of King Alfred', *P&P*, 123 (1989), 25.

west, the Ainsty comprised fertile arable and pasture; to the south-east, Ouse and Derwent wapentake was also mostly fertile, though more low-lying and liable to flood; and further south, the lower Vale was largely marsh and fen. West of the Vale, the Pennines were mostly upland pasture, raising cattle and sheep, and including productive lead mines; to the east, the Moors and Wolds specialized in sheep, Wolds wool being particularly fine. And beyond the Wolds, the flatlands of Holderness and north Lincolnshire were major sources of grain when it was scarce in York.

It would be wrong to consider York's region solely in terms of geograph-ical constraints. Clearly climate, contours, soils, and fertility were fundamen-tal, as was the presence of lead and other minerals; but Yorkshire, like any other English region, had varied patterns of landownership and settlement which were not geographically determined. A widely held generalization makes the medieval Vale a zone of nucleated villages and open fields, and the uplands areas of scattered settlements and open pasture, but that is only partly true. Classic nucleated villages are certainly characteristic of parts of the Vale, but they were also common on the Wolds until the late Middle Ages, when many were depopulated, including the classic type-site of Whar-ram Percy. Wharram has become the best-studied medieval settlement in England; and although its investigation started by proving what might have been expected from the documents (its desertion in the fifteenth and six-teenth centuries), it ended more unexpectedly by showing that it had prob-ably become a nucleated village only around the tenth century, something which has since been established for other English villages. Eastern and central Yorkshire formed, in fact, part of a central English belt which under-went a 'village revolution' between about 850 and 1200, which was probably connected to major changes in farming practices.[15]

The nucleated villages, even after the tenth century, were never the norm, but coexisted alongside scattered settlement in the Vale (especially in wood-pasture areas) as well as in the open pastures of the Pennines and Moors. And at the other end of the settlement spectrum there were towns as well. Admittedly, York was almost the only substantial town north of the Humber in the early Middle Ages, but there were small towns serving some greater

15. Christopher Dyer, *Making a Living in the Middle Ages: The People of Britain 850–1520* (New Haven and London, 2002), 18–24; D. M. Palliser, *Towns and Local Communities in Medieval and Early Modern England* (Aldershot, 2006), II, 5–7. The literature on Wharram is now considerable: the latest survey is S. Wrathmell, ed., *Wharram XIII: A History of Wharram Percy and its Neighbours* (York, 2012).

churches and monasteries by the eleventh century, notably at Beverley, Ripon, Selby, and Whitby (as well as Durham), and by the twelfth century many more small towns had sprung up in Yorkshire and further north. Some were deliberately planted as 'new towns', and two twelfth-century foundations, Newcastle-upon-Tyne and Wyke (later Kingston) -upon-Hull, overtook York as ports in the later Middle Ages. Fourteenth-century tax returns confirm that York was still the largest and wealthiest town in the North, but that others had joined it in the upper ranks. The 1334 lay subsidy puts York as the third richest town in England, with Newcastle fourth, followed at a distance by Beverley (20th), Hull (34th), and Scarborough (35th). By numbers of taxpayers in 1377, York was second after London, Beverley eleventh, Newcastle twelfth, with well behind them Hull (24th) and Scarborough (31st).[16]

The rise of the east coast ports is a reminder of the importance of the North Sea to trade. Indeed, York's entire medieval story can be seen as one where its position turned its interests east as much as inland. Like other great towns of eastern England—like Lincoln or Norwich—it was originally a major port, and even when coastal ports eclipsed them in terms of shipping, they remained the dominant partners at one remove. Like much of eastern England, it was accessible as much to Scandinavia and the Low Countries as to western England. Historians of early medieval culture have repeatedly noted that East Anglia, Lincolnshire, and Yorkshire often had more in common with parts of Scandinavia than with Wessex, despite their absorption into a kingdom of England.

16. Alan Dyer, 'Appendix: Ranking lists of English medieval towns', in *CUHB* I (2000), 755–8.

I

Origins and myths

Eburacum and its successors

A history of medieval York could begin with its shadowy British occupation in the fifth and sixth centuries, with the arrival of the English invaders, or with the rebirth of recognizably urban life in the seventh and eighth centuries. It would be, however, misleading to omit some account of the previous Roman occupation. So far as we know at present, it was the Romans who first settled York, at a well-defended site which proved to be permanent, even though *urban* life temporarily ended in the fifth century. It was the Romans who created a network of metalled roads linking York with the higher and drier land to west and east, a network which conditioned the medieval route system and which still partly survives; and it was they who initiated York's role as a centre for control of what became northern England, a role it retained until the seventeenth century. It was the Romans also whose defences, street lines, and former buildings still influence today's cityscape. It is fitting and not surprising that York's medieval inhabitants looked back with pride to their Roman past.

Roman York

There is no evidence for any permanent occupation at York before the Roman Ninth Legion arrived about the year 71, when they 'probably encountered a pleasant meadowland environment not unlike that on the upper reaches of the Ouse today'. The one hint of a possible pre-Roman settlement is that the invaders gave the site the name of *Eburacum* (*Eboracum*), which, as we have seen, perhaps meant 'place of yew trees' or 'estate of Eburos', a personal name known from Roman Gaul. It was that name which lay behind a persistent medieval myth that York had been founded by a British king called Ebraucus.[1]

The absence of pre-Roman settlement would fit with the marginal nature of the district before the Romans, when the Vale formed a generally marshy and lightly settled frontier zone between the Parisi to the east, and the Brigantes who controlled most of what is now northern England. The Brigantian tribal centre was probably the vast fortified settlement at Stanwick, north of Richmond, which the Romans replaced by *Isurium Brigantum* (Aldborough). The Parisian tribal centre has not been located, but the Romans governed them from *Petuaria* (Brough) on the Humber.

It was, therefore, the Romans, with their 'unerring talent for assessing a site's potential', who, in or around the year 71, chose the confluence of the Ouse and Foss for their legionary fortress, quickly followed by a civilian town. This is, in fact, to confirm what was said nearly three centuries ago by Francis Drake, who in his pioneering history of the city, significantly entitled *Eboracum*, dismissed the legend of King Ebraucus still current in his day, urging that 'in all probability' York was 'first planted and fortified' by the Romans.[2]

It was the Romans who combined defence and accessibility by siting the fortress on rising ground in the angle of the rivers, and by linking it with roads across the Vale of York to their two main north–south highways; and it was they who made it central to their control of northern Britain. It was entirely appropriate that when the province of *Britannia* was divided during the reign of the emperor Caracalla (211–17), York was made the capital of *Britannia Inferior* (Lower Britain). Later, Britain was further subdivided into four and finally into five provinces, but York seems always to have retained its status as a provincial capital. That status was enhanced when, perhaps in Caracalla's reign also, it was raised to the rank of *colonia*, the highest level in the imperial urban hierarchy, and when in the fourth century it became the seat of a Christian bishop, one of three British bishops who attended the Council of Arles in 314.[3]

1. Quotation: Patrick Ottaway, *Roman York* (Stroud, 2nd edn 2004), 26. Place name: see the earlier section 'York's name and status'.
2. Ottaway, *Roman York*, 24, 31; Francis Drake, *Eboracum* (London, 1736), 8.
3. This brief account relies chiefly on the latest edition of Patrick Ottaway's excellent *Roman York*; the older and more detailed survey by the RCHME (*RCHMY* I, 1962) is still valuable. For more recent archaeological evidence see also the fascicules in *AY* 3–6, and for the key texts for 211, 306, and 314, see AY 1, 40–1, 43–4, 92–3, 108–10.

In terms of surviving documentary history, the centuries of Roman rule in York are poorly recorded, but sufficiently to emphasize its crucial military importance, both to defend the province from attacks by tribes north of Hadrian's Wall, and as a launch pad for campaigns north of it. From 208 until his death in 211, the emperor Septimius Severus made York his home while campaigning against the Caledonians; he died in York and was cremated there, the ashes being taken to Rome. A century later, the Emperor Constantius crossed to Britain with his son Constantine; he defeated the Picts somewhere in northern Britain before dying at York on 25 July 306. On the same day the troops in York hailed Constantine as emperor, a successful usurpation which Constantine followed up by defeating his rivals in west and east, reuniting the whole empire by 324. Constantine's other achievements, for which posterity called him 'the Great'—notably his conversion to Christianity and his creation of a new Christian capital called Constantinople—go far beyond the scope of this book, but it was entirely right that medieval Englishmen long remembered that his reign had begun in York. Had Constantine not been there with his father, he would not have secured the succession in Britain which he was able to use as a springboard for conquering the rest of the empire.[4]

The primary nucleus of *Eburacum* was the fortress, occupied successively by the Ninth and Sixth Legions. It covered a rectangle of about 50 acres (21.5 ha), two sides of which remained standing well after the Roman period to become the core of the medieval city defences. First of earth and timber, the defences were rebuilt in stone over the course of the second century; then the south-west wall, facing the road to London, was given great projecting towers designed to impress, possibly during Severus' residence in 208–11. If this dating is correct, it shows York setting a trend in late Roman military architecture in Britain; and the western angle tower, the so-called Multangular Tower, still survives above ground to a height of 19 feet (5.8 m), capped by a medieval superstructure. The defences were maintained to the very end of the Roman occupation or even beyond: a tower plugging a gap in the north-west wall has been tentatively dated to the late fourth or early fifth century (Plate 3).[5]

4. Elizabeth Hartley et al., eds, *Constantine the Great: York's Roman Emperor* (York, 2006), *passim*.
5. The western towers and wall are often dated late third or early fourth century, but Ottaway makes a strong case for the early third: *Roman York*, 63, 75. Dating of 'Anglian' Tower: see this chapter, Appendix I.

Civilian settlement of an urban character started in the second century: it lay partly around the fortress, but more important was a large rectangular zone across the Ouse, probably including most of the major public buildings, and linked to the other bank by a substantial bridge. It is likely that this south-western civilian town (the *colonia* proper) was defended by the Romans on the same line later followed by the medieval city wall. Outside the main urban areas, scattered evidence for Roman settlement has been found in a zone about two miles (3 km) across, which also included extensive cemeteries. A particular feature of late Roman York is a series of gypsum burials, which may be those of Romano-British Christians.[6]

Physically, *Eburacum* had a permanent influence on the topography of medieval and modern York. Although almost nothing of its fabric survives above ground except for the Multangular Tower, we have to picture an Anglian, Viking, and even Norman York where much Roman work still stood, enough to condition the layout of the new city from the seventh century. Writers from Alcuin to William of Malmesbury imply considerable Roman survivals, and most stone building in early medieval York, even as late as the lower stages of the Norman cathedral, was constructed of reused Roman stone. Only from about 1100 did it become necessary to turn to freshly quarried supplies.[7]

The northern half of the fortress defences and the probable *colonia* wall survived to become the base of much of the medieval walled circuit, and the two principal streets within the fortress continued into the Middle Ages as Petergate and Stonegate. The fortress was aligned, however, at an angle of 42° to due east, whereas the huge cathedral cuts across it due east-west. In the civilian town there is less correspondence between Roman and later streets, except for the Coney Street–Nessgate–Castlegate line, partly because the shift from Roman to medieval bridging-point over the Ouse distorted the pattern within the *colonia*. Beyond the built-up area, however, the main roads to Tadcaster, Malton, and Catterick still follow approximately the Roman routes.

For a long time after the Romans, indeed, it was the very existence of the vast ruined city that conditioned all later settlement. It could readily be

---

6. C. Sparey-Green et al., 'Where are the Christians? Late Roman cemeteries in Britain', in Martin Carver, ed., *The Cross Goes North: Processes of Conversion in Northern Europe, AD 300–1300* (York, 2003), 93–107, 292–3.

7. R. K. Morris, 'Churches in York and its hinterland: Building patterns and stone sources in the 11th and 12th centuries', in John Blair, ed., *Minsters and Parish Churches: The Local Church in Transition 950–1200* (Oxford, 1988), 192–5.

made defensible again, both as a centre of power and as providing 'a legitimacy to lordship which harked back to an earlier era'. It was surely choice,
and not accident, that placed York's cathedral, like the church of St Cadoc
in the legionary fortress of Caerleon, directly over the *principia* of the fortress, 'where the legionary standards were displayed, and the images of the
Roman Emperors venerated'.[8]

Even the type of urban life was not so very different in *Eburacum*
from that in its successor. It has been fashionable to stress the contrasts
between Romano-British towns and their medieval successors. The former
have been seen as alien Mediterranean imports, flourishing only as political
and social centres; but 'much of what went on in Roman towns was what
went on in later towns: commerce and manufacture'. Lunaris, probably a
merchant, who dedicated an altar at Bordeaux in 237 in fulfilment of a vow
'on starting from York', was perhaps not very different in spirit from the
late-medieval Yorkers who shipped wine from Bordeaux. Much, perhaps,
depends on *Eburacum*'s size. The legion numbered 5–6,000 men, so that if
the town never exceeded 3,000 civilians, they might simply have serviced
the garrison, whereas if they totalled 10,000 or more, that would imply a
major economic centre.[9]

Nevertheless, there must have been real discontinuity between *Eburacum*
and medieval York. Under the stress of a major Germanic invasion of the
western Roman Empire, the British army rebelled in 406 and set up their
own emperor, Constantine III. Instead of defending the island, he took the
army to Gaul in 407, leaving Britain denuded of defence. The whole machinery of imperial rule—army, civil service, taxation, and even the circulation of
coin—ground to a halt. Matters might have been less desperate had power
been devolved to local people, but the collapse of a highly centralized regime
made the condition of Britain 'much worse after the termination of Roman
rule than before its start. The problem was, in short, not too little integration
but too much'. Or, as another scholar has put it, 'post-Roman Britain . . . sank
to a level of economic complexity well below that of the pre-Roman Iron

8. D. M. Hadley, *The Northern Danelaw* (London, 2000), 123–4; Jeremy Knight, 'Basilicas and bar-
rows: Christian origins in Wales and Western Britain', in Carver, ed., *The Cross Goes North*, 119.
9. James Campbell, 'The end of Roman Britain', in James Campbell, ed., *The Anglo-Saxons*
(Oxford, 1982), 10; John Wacher, *The Towns of Roman Britain* (London, 2nd edn 1995), 177–9;
Ottaway, *Roman York*, 128. Ottaway suggests a maximum population of 3,000 civilians, based on
a comparison with London and assuming a London maximum of 10,000; but Campbell ('The
end of Roman Britain', 10) suggests that Roman London might have had 30,000 people, and
other large towns 10–15,000.

Age', recovering to those levels only around AD 700 with the return of a wheel-turned pottery industry, silver coinage, and the emergence of coastal trading towns like Southampton and London. As we shall see, York was also in those ranks by 700 as a major inland port, but only after two or three centuries without urban life.[10]

Sub-Roman York

The end of direct Roman rule in Britain, conventionally dated to 410 but really a drawn-out process between 406 and 411, was not a sharp break: Roman attitudes and law were still to be found in the 420s and probably the 430s. For York itself, however, the end of Roman government and organization simply cannot be dated. There is no reliably established event for York between 314 and 627, and for much of that time even its regional context is a blank.

> There is, for example, no information whatsoever as to any post-Roman kingdom . . . of which York might have formed part . . . The suggestion that York in the post-Roman period might have been the political centre of the British tribe of the Brigantes is pure speculation; and the suggestion that the Coel Hen whose name occurs in the Welsh genealogies might have ruled from York is entirely conjectural.[11]

Nevertheless, archaeology indicates that *Eburacum* was not entirely deserted: there continued to be life in the town, if not town life. With its defences and major buildings standing, it was a natural choice for any local leaders wanting a fortified base. Evidence for occupation includes post-Roman activity round the *principia* in the fifth century; a timber building in the *colonia* probably of the same time; and some scattered sub-Roman pottery. There is also evidence for an Anglian (English) presence in the mid/late fifth century, in the shape of cremated burials of warriors in extramural cemeteries on the Mount, at Heworth, and possibly at two other sites: their location suggests occupation of both fortress and *colonia* at that time.[12]

---

10. Peter Salway, *The Short Oxford History of the British Isles: The Roman Era* (Oxford, 2002), 236; Bryan Ward-Perkins, *The Fall of Rome and the End of Civilization* (Oxford, 2005), 118.
11. David Rollason, in AY 1, 45.
12. I. M. Stead, 'An Anglian cemetery on The Mount, York', *YAJ*, 39 (1958), 427–35; Rosemary Cramp, *Anglian and Viking York*, BP 33 (York, 1967), 2; *RCHMY* IV, pp. xxvii, xxviii; M. O. H. Carver, 'Roman to Norman at York Minster', in *EYM*, I, 187–91; Dominic Tweddle, 'The Anglian city', in AY 7/2, 167–77, 190, 208.

Presumably the inhabitants were Romanized Britons, and the Germanic soldiers may not have been invaders but allied troops (*laeti*) often paid by late Roman and post-Roman leaders to protect them. There has been much speculation about who those leaders might have been, derived from fragments of later Welsh verse and annals. Coel Hen was not the only one: there was also a Peredur map Efrawc Iarll whose father's name suggests a link with York, and who might have been the same Peredur who died in battle in 580. He has been seen as the last British king of York, killed by invading English, but the evidence is much too slight to justify John Morris's claim that York was captured by the English in 580. Others have identified sub-Roman 'kingdoms' of Elmet, Craven, and Yrechwydd north and west of York, and speculated that a king called Gwallawg attacked York in the 580s, presumably because it was then in English hands; but again the evidence is tenuous in the extreme.[13]

Another possible scenario is major flooding in the Vale of York owing to a rise in sea level. Ramm suggested in 1971 that much of *Eburacum* was destroyed by flooding between the late fourth and late sixth centuries, flooding so serious that it would have made uninhabitable all areas below the then 35 ft (11 m) contour. No conclusive archaeological proof has been found and Ramm's suggestion was largely dismissed. However, recent work on the Vale and on the Humber wetlands has confirmed the existence of a major marine transgression in the second half of the fourth century, resulting in severe flooding, though probably not as far upriver as the York area. If the district remained in British hands throughout the fifth century, that may have owed as much as anything to 'the unattractiveness of flooded York' to the English invaders.[14]

Flooding or no, there is another indicator that much of York ceased to be occupied. As in London, Canterbury, and other major towns, Roman levels are in many areas overlain by 'dark earth', a dark, silty deposit including what

13. John Morris, *The Age of Arthur* (London, 1973), 54, 118, 214, 233–4, 513, 515; M. L. Faull, 'Roman and Anglian settlement patterns in Yorkshire', *NH*, 9 (1974), 23; G. R. J. Jones, 'Early territorial organization in Gwynedd and Elmet', *NH*, 10 (1975), 10–12; A. C. Breeze, 'The kingdom and name of Elmet', *NH*, 39 (2002), 157–71; David Rollason, *Northumbria, 500–1100* (Cambridge, 2003), 40, 85–7, 103; A. C. Breeze, 'Yrechwydd and the river Ribble', *NH*, 47 (2010), 319–28; Mike McCarthy, 'The kingdom of Rheged: A landscape perspective', *NH*, 48 (2011), 14.
14. H. G. Ramm, 'The end of Roman York', in R. M. Butler, ed., *Soldier and Civilian in Roman Yorkshire* (Leicester, 1971), 181–3; *RCHMY* IV, pp. xxvi, xxvii; Faull, 'Roman and Anglian Settlement patterns', 23; *HANY*, 23–4, 65; Robert van de Noort, *The Humber Wetlands* (Macclesfield, 2004), 109, 127, 153; Patrick Ottaway, pers. comm.

seems to be the result of refuse disposal: broken pottery, animal bones, and so on. This can be interpreted as evidence of absence of occupation, coupled perhaps with reworking of the soil by agriculture; but it might indicate reduced occupation, involving lower living standards, and a tendency to dump rubbish near housing.[15]

In any case, there are sufficient hints that York remained an attractive strong point for local rulers, rather than an empty shell; and that this attraction lay behind the reuse of York under the early English kings. 'That York remained some sort of authority centre ... would explain both why there are fifth- and sixth-century cemeteries grouped around it, and King Edwin's determination to have himself baptized there' in 627. Edwin may well have been attracted by the protection of the Roman walls: Alcuin describes his baptism as taking place under 'the still lofty walls of the city'. Edwin's baptism, to which we shall return, was indeed a key moment in the revival of York as a centre of power; but it may have happened less because of Edwin's need for a defensible base—evidence for an early royal capital is, as we shall see, slight—than because of the choice of York by Bishop Paulinus as a suitable location for an episcopal church.[16]

Early history and myth

Paulinus was one of the Roman monks sent to England in 601 by Pope Gregory I; he came to York as an escort for Edwin's bride, a Christian Kentish princess, and in the hope of converting the king and his court. He must have been aware of Gregory's intention that the English kingdoms, if converted, should be grouped under two archbishops, at London and York. The plan seems to have been based on knowledge at Rome of past imperial geography rather than current conditions, and if so, the choice of York—so important for the future of the city and of the whole north— was based on memories of *Eburacum*'s former greatness rather than its condition around 600.

---

15. Ottaway, *Roman York*, 146–8.
16. D. A. Hinton, 'Decay and revival: Early medieval urban landscapes', in Philip Waller, ed., *The English Urban Landscape* (Oxford, 2000), 62; Peter Godman, ed., *Alcuin: The Bishops, Kings and Saints of York*, OMT (Oxford, 1982), 20: *Celsis etiam sub moenibus urbis*. Godman does not translate *etiam*, but Ramm translates it as 'still' (*RCHMY* IV, p. xxviii).

Certainly that Roman greatness had not been forgotten. York's medieval clergy and citizens knew that two emperors had resided and died there; that Constantine had been proclaimed emperor there; and that Bishop 'Eborius' of York had attended the Council which Constantine had summoned to Arles. These memories, however, were entangled in myth, especially with regard to Constantine's parents, Constantius I and (St) Helena, the latter an early Christian and allegedly the discoverer of the True Cross at Jerusalem. The belief that Constantine was born to Helena in Britain was already current around 700, and by 1066 there was a belief that Helena was the daughter of a British king, Coel of Colchester. However, there was also a northern and Welsh cult of Helena as daughter of a British emperor, Magnus Maximus, and the two legends seem to have merged. English churches dedicated to St Helen were especially numerous in York and Yorkshire, and she was depicted in glass in the Minster and at least two other churches.[17]

At some point the northern tradition came to see Constantine as not only proclaimed in York but also born there, an argument seriously advanced by the English delegates to the Church Councils at Constance (1414) and Basel (1431). The latter delegation even supplied his birthplace as being *Peterna*, apparently the Bedern. That precinct lay just within the former Roman fortress, but it may also have been hit upon because it was close to St Helen-on-the-Walls. St Helen's, Camden was informed in the 1580s, was the first burial place of Constantius; and excavations in 1973–4 showed that the first church had been built directly over a Roman mosaic with a central female head, possibly interpreted as Helen by the founders. That church was probably founded in the tenth century, but if a burial of 680–890 came from the lost St Helen's church in Fishergate, the cult of Helen at York may antedate the Viking conquest.[18]

Beyond this embroidered but genuine Roman past, most citizens seem also to have believed Geoffrey of Monmouth's less credible stories of York before and after the Romans, as laid down in the 1130s in his *History of the Kings of Britain*. These include the existence of a King Ebraucus who had founded the city sometime around 1000 BC, which he named Kaerebrauc

17. C. Davidson and D. E. O'Connor, *York Art*, Medieval Institute Publications (Kalamazoo, 1978), 159–60; J. M. Cooper, 'Medieval Colchester', in *VCH Essex*, IX (1994), 19–21; Sarah Brown, *'Our Magnificent Fabrick': York Minster: An Architectural History c. 1220–1500* (Swindon, 2003), 119.
18. D. M. Palliser, 'Location and history', in AY 10/1 (1980), 5, 6; John Blair, *The Church in Anglo-Saxon Society* (Oxford, 2005), 380n.; C. A. Spall and N. J. Toop, 'Before Eoforwic', *Med Arch*, 52 (2008), 13–18.

after himself, a city which was to be the scene of important events down to the Roman invasion. After the Romans, said Geoffrey, York was seized by the English leader Hengist in the fifth century; retaken by the British king Aurelius Ambrosius, who made Samson its archbishop; seized again by English forces under Octa; and recaptured by King Arthur. Though much of Geoffrey's 'history' was quickly doubted by contemporary scholars, it was widely welcomed by a less critical readership. It may well be, for instance, that York's St Sampson's church, first recorded in 1154, acquired its dedication from a belief in Geoffrey's archbishop. A Latin poem of about 1190, based on Geoffrey, was apparently written especially to celebrate York's legendary origins, and it ended with a couplet on Ebraucus:

> He founded York, which from him took its name,
> Eboracum, and he adorned it well.

Such beliefs understandably appealed to the citizens, and they proved hardy. Two fourteenth-century chronicles of the Church of York developed further Geoffrey's tales of Ebrauk, Samson, and others. As late as 1486, Henry VII was welcomed to the city by an actor personifying 'the begynner of the same [citie] callid Ebrauk', and from about the same time an 'ymage of Ebrauk' was publicly displayed on a prominent site. It might seem trivial to recall such obviously fictional beliefs, but they clearly had a wide appeal to the citizens as validating their importance and their inheritance.[19]

Appendix I: The 'Anglian Tower'

The so-called Anglian Tower (Plate 3) is a structure of crude rubble construction built into the fortress wall near the Multangular Tower. It was unearthed by accident in 1839 and promptly reburied; in 1969 it was professionally excavated by Jeffrey Radley, who was, tragically, killed during an extension of the excavation in 1970. In 1970–1 the tower and adjacent fortress wall were permanently exposed, with a plaque affixed to the tower calling it 'The Anglian Tower'.

19. A. G. Rigg, *A History of Anglo-Latin Literature 1066–1422* (Cambridge, 1992), 98 and n.; *HCY*, II, 446–87; Angelo Raine, *Mediaeval York* (London, 1955), 59, 60; *YHB*, II, 482–3; *YCR*, II, 171; Palliser, *Towns and Local Communities*, X, 79.

The dating was suggested by Radley in his posthumously published excavation report. He thought it post-Roman because of its position (blocking a gap in the fortress wall), its construction, and its similarities to Anglo-Saxon structures. He considered that Edwin's reign (616–33) or its aftermath was the most plausible period for its building, possibly as an attempt to repair the defences against an attack from the British kingdom of Elmet. Even at that time, however, R. M. Butler supplied a prescient note to the report, pointing out that a late Roman date was also possible. Since then, a consensus has emerged for the late Roman as the most likely period, though any date down to the ninth century is possible.[20]

20. *RCHMY* II, 111–15; AY 3/3, 273, 287; AY 7/2, 189–90; J. Radley, 'Excavations in the defences of the city of York: An early medieval stone tower and the successive earth ramparts', *YAJ*, 44 (1972), 38–64; P. C. Buckland, 'The "Anglian" Tower and the use of Jurassic limestone in York', in P. V. Addyman and V. E. Black, eds, *Archaeological Papers from York* (York, 1984), 51–7; *EYM*, I, 8–9; Ottaway, *Roman York*, 142–3.

2

One York or several?

The city resettled[1]

It is hard to know, or even guess, what happened to York in the three centuries between 400 and 700. Urban life certainly shrivelled in the fifth century, as we have seen, but that does not mean that *Eburacum* was totally deserted, and sub-Roman 'kings' or warlords may well have found its walled site a useful strongpoint. By the late sixth century, immigrants from across the North Sea, calling themselves Angles or English, had taken over the York district, imposing their rule and their language, and perhaps, like their displaced predecessors, finding the still-standing Roman walls of fortress and *colonia* useful for defence. One of their rulers, Edwin, king of Northumbria, was certainly in York at Easter 627, when he was baptized a Christian in a new church, probably located within the fortress walls. That does not necessarily mean that York was a town again by that date, still less that it was in any sense a royal 'capital'; not until the 670s or 680s can we be sure that urban life was being revived (Map 2).

Before plunging into this most obscure period of York's history, it helps to consider what types of evidence do survive. Written records mentioning the city are absent before 601, and remain scarce until well after the Danish conquest of 866–7. Much of what is considered in this chapter has to rely on just two writers, Bede (*c*.673–735) and Alcuin (*c*.740–804), and it must be remembered that for all early English history huge numbers of important documents have been lost. This can easily lead us into one of two traps. One is to confuse absence of evidence with evidence of absence: we might have

---

1. Chapters 2 and 3 are much indebted for York's regional context to N. J. Higham, *The Kingdom of Northumbria AD 350–1100* (Stroud, 1993) and David Rollason, *Northumbria, 500–1100: Creation and Destruction of a Kingdom* (Cambridge, 2003). I am also indebted to John Blair, Mary Garrison, and Michael Metcalf for comments on earlier drafts of both chapters.

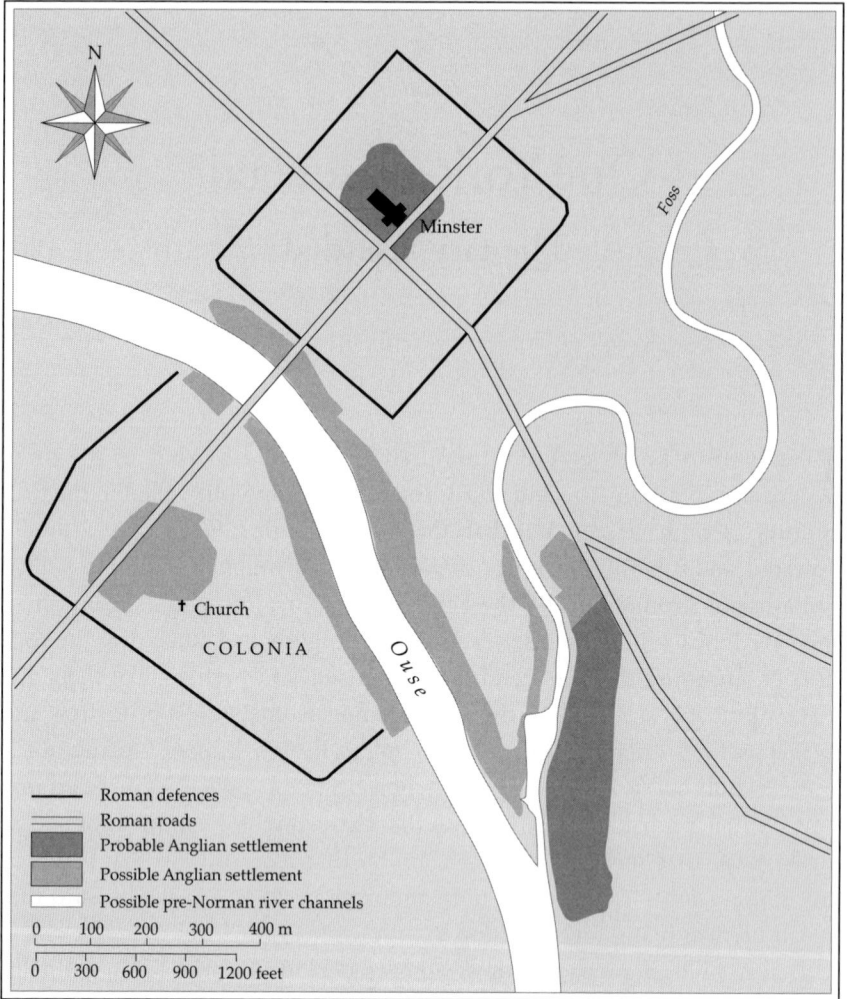

Map 2. Anglian York, *c.*700–866

A speculative interpretation of the current archaeological evidence, superimposed on the modern plan.

Source: R. A. Hall, '*Burhs* and boroughs: Defended places, trade, and towns', in H. Hamerow, D. A. Hinton, and S. Crawford, eds, *The Oxford Handbook of Anglo-Saxon Archaeology* (Oxford, 2011), 603. Reproduced by permission of Dr Ailsa Mainman and the York Archaeological Trust.

lost the record of an important event, and those sources which do survive might simply not have been interested in what we would like to know. 'Then, as now, those who recorded the news gave prominence to the sensational. The burning of York was noted, but not the building of the new cathedral church.' The opposite trap is to seize upon something which *was* recorded, and to place more weight on it than it will bear. For instance, the mention of a Frisian merchant killing a Northumbrian, causing the Frisians to flee England, is often cited as evidence of a Frisian merchant colony in York, a deduction well beyond the evidence.[2]

Material evidence has different strengths and weaknesses. Excavations can establish important points not recorded in documents, such as the position of a ninth-century graveyard, as well as the post-1066 cathedral, directly over the Roman fortress headquarters. It can also confirm literary evidence which has been doubted, as when the trading settlement on the river, mentioned by Alcuin, was discovered in 1985–6, a clear warning against assuming the absence of an *emporium* site, as had been argued by a distinguished archaeologist only three years earlier.[3] Perhaps more importantly still, archaeology can establish facts probably never considered worthy of recording, such as evidence for urban diet. On the other hand, it cannot (apart from dendrochronology) furnish exact dates, so that finds, or layers of destruction and burning, can rarely be tied to specific events in chronicles.

Nevertheless, it is archaeology in its broadest sense which has transformed our knowledge of the early English ('Anglian') period and of the Anglo-Scandinavian ('Viking') age which followed. In particular, the excavations beneath the cathedral in 1967–73, and the work of the York Archaeological Trust since 1972, have allowed us a far more detailed picture of York between 400 and 1066 than was previously possible, work drawn on repeatedly in this and the next chapter.[4] By archaeology I include all material evidence, whether excavated or not, including sculpture and coins. Sculpture has been well surveyed by Lang, while coins have been intensively studied by Metcalf, Booth, Pirie, Blackburn, and others. Thanks to them, we

2. Quotation: P. H. Blair, *Northumbria in the Days of Bede* (London, 1976), 55. Frisians: Susan Reynolds, *An Introduction to the History of English Medieval Towns* (Oxford, 1977), 26; AY 1, 131–2.

3. James Campbell, 'Production and distribution in early and middle Anglo-Saxon England', in T. Pestell and K. Ulmschneider, eds, *Markets in Early Medieval Europe* (Macclesfield, 2003), 14.

4. That is not to belittle valuable pre-1967 work carried out with much smaller resources, especially D. M. Waterman, 'Late Saxon, Viking and early medieval finds from York', *Archaeologia*, 97 (1959), 59–105, and Rosemary Cramp, *Anglian and Viking York*, BP 33 (York, 1967).

can appreciate that numismatics is not simply of antiquarian or artistic interest; coinage was, after all, a necessary lubricant for the growth of medieval towns and trade.

Romano-Britons and English: *c.*500–618

With these considerations in mind, what can we piece together of the transition from Roman *Eburacum* to English *Eoforwic*? Some of the shadowy evidence has already been touched on: the possible existence of a British kingdom of Elmet which might have included the city; fifth-century burials of Germanic soldiers just outside York; the slight hints from later poems that the Britons were driven from the city by the 580s; and the possibility that much of *Eburacum* might have been made uninhabitable by flooding. There is also the widespread existence of a layer of 'dark earth' sealing late Roman sites, a feature of many Romano-British towns, but one which does not necessarily mean total abandonment of settlement. More controversially, there are current theories of a major climatic catastrophe throughout the northern hemisphere in the 530s, which might have caused a breakdown in society and an inability to withstand invaders.[5]

The coming of the English is equally obscure, and what really happened will never be known. All we can be certain of is that pagan Germanic peoples, mostly from parts of northern Europe which had never been Roman, invaded eastern England. The best early account is that of the Northumbrian monastic scholar Bede, writing in and before 731. He probably visited York; he was certainly in touch with its clergy and scholars, and had access to more distant sources of information; and he gives a detailed account of the Northumbrian kings from their conversion to Christianity in the 620s and 630s. Given that, it is disappointing that he tells us so little of their kingdoms before that time, and he gives no hint that many of the northern Britons they conquered may have been Christians. He provides only one firm date—and that an afterthought—for any pagan Northumbrian king: '547. Ida began his reign, from whom the Northumbrian royal family trace their origin'.[6] Bede does, however, describe another pagan,

---

5. Chris Wickham, *Framing the Early Middle Ages* (Oxford, 2005), 549n., citing A. Arjava, 'The mystery cloud of AD 536 in the Mediterranean sources', *Dumbarton Oaks Papers*, 59 (2005).
6. Bede, *Historia Ecclesiastica* (hereafter *HE*); the 547 date is in V. xxiv. Earlier than Bede was Gildas, but Gildas's account is vague, hard to date, and has no reference to northern England.

Ælle, as king of a Northumbrian people called *Deiri*, and elsewhere he implies that Ælle was reigning in 597, when the first Roman Christian mission arrived in England. And a morsel more is supplied by a later tradition that King Ida had fortified Bamburgh, suggesting that his main stronghold was there rather than further south.[7]

None of this may seem, at first sight, relevant to York—Bede mentions nothing of it before 601—but it is important to try to understand who were the Northumbrians and how, if at all, York might have played a part in their developing kingdoms. Bede is explicit that in his time the people living in what is now north-east England and south-east Scotland—between Humber and Forth—considered themselves English (*Angli*), a Germanic people who had invaded and conquered it all and created a Northumbrian kingdom. That need not mean that they massacred, drove out, or enslaved the native Britons. A persuasive case has been made (for England as a whole) that Britons continued to form the mass of the people, but subordinated to the invading minority, and largely adopting their language and culture. This has been corroborated by recent genetic analyses, which suggest that English male immigration was on a scale of not more than 10 to 20 per cent, and perhaps as low as 5 per cent, of the native population. The distribution was, however, highest in an eastern coastal zone including much of Yorkshire.[8]

Equal uncertainty surrounds the nature and extent of the early chiefdoms or kingdoms which merged to form Northumbria. Bede seems to describe two rival dynasties, the *Bernicii* and *Deiri*, who at times ruled separate states, and at other times were forcibly united under one or other. The Bernician line finally triumphed as rulers of all Northumbria, though they permitted separate sub-kings for the *Deiri* until 679. The usual reading of Bede and other sources is that there were two separate kingdoms of Deira and Bernicia (though Bede never uses those terms), probably divided along the Tees, 'the former with its capital at York, the latter at Bamburgh, with its related religious site of Lindisfarne'. Certainly, Bede was explicit that Ælle ruled over the *Deiri*, and that his son Edwin was baptized at York.[9]

7. AY 1, 45; *EHD*, I, 12, 13.
8. Bryan Ward-Perkins, 'Why did the Anglo-Saxons not become more British?', *EHR*, 115 (2000), 513–33; Stephen Oppenheimer, *The Origins of the British* (London, pb. edn 2007), 398–443; Heinrich Härke, 'Anglo-Saxon immigration and ethnogenesis', *Med Arch*, 55 (2011), 1–28. Oppenheimer's and Härke's figures are based on Y-chromosome rather than mitochondrial DNA, thus reflecting male immigration.
9. Quotation from I. N. Wood, 'Monasteries and the geography of power in the age of Bede', *NH*, 45 (2008), 11–25, at p. 11.

It may not, however, have been so straightforward. The *Anglo-Saxon Chronicle* rightly or wrongly made Ælle son to Ida of Bamburgh; and Ian Wood has persuasively argued for two rival dynasties not ruling within fixed frontiers, but with different heartlands. The Bernician kings focused their burials and family commemorations in a group of monasteries on the lower Tyne, and the Deirans in another group in and around the Vale of Pickering, together with an outlying royal monastery at *Streanaeshealh*. Apart from that, it may have been the monasteries of the Vale of Pickering—rather than York—which were dominant in the region of the *Deiri*, at least until the eighth century.[10]

Whatever our interpretations of this slippery evidence, Bede's mention of Ælle as king of the *Deiri* in the 590s is generally accepted, partly because he appears also in an anonymous *Life of Gregory the Great* written at *Streanaeshealh*, apparently independently of Bede. Both authors relate a story that St Gregory (Pope Gregory I) was inspired to convert the English to Christianity by finding slave boys for sale in a Roman market, and being told that they came from the land of the *Deiri* in Britain, whose king was Ælle. The story may not be authentic, but we do know that in 595 Gregory was concerned to educate English slave boys in Rome, and that it was in 596–7 that he sent out missionary monks under Augustine, men who first landed in Kent, but whose successors in the second generation reached Northumbria.[11]

When Ælle died, York may still have been in British hands; the evidence for pagan English settlers (chiefly burials) is largely confined to eastern Yorkshire, the Wolds, and the Vale of Pickering. The *Deiri* were then conquered by the Bernician king Æthelfrith, and Ælle's son Edwin fled into exile, returning to kill Æthelfrith in battle. And it was in Edwin's reign as king of a united Northumbria (616–33) that York was unquestionably under English rule, as when he was baptized in 627 by Paulinus, it was in the city. It is also clear that by then his authority reached well to the west, for when Paulinus had baptized him, he built a church at the Roman *Cambodunum* (a lost site in the Leeds area), and performed open-air baptisms at another Roman site, Cataractonium (Catterick). Both were places described by Bede as royal centres 'in the territory of the *Deiri*' and there is later evidence for

10. Wood, 'Monasteries and the geography of power', *passim*.
11. Bede, *HE*, II. i; B. Colgrave, ed., *The Earliest Life of Gregory the Great* (Cambridge, 1940, repr. 1985), 10; R. A. Markus, *Gregory the Great and His World* (Cambridge, 1997), 177–8, 185–6.

Catterick as a royal vill. For those and other reasons, it is no longer thought likely that Edwin needed to protect York from a hostile British attack from the west, as was believed when the so-called Anglian tower was excavated.[12]

What can be said of English settlements before 627, both in the city and its hinterland? The best evidence so far is from West Heslerton in the Vale of Pickering, where Powlesland's excavations have demonstrated the existence of a substantial rural settlement with an accompanying cemetery. It was clearly planned, with separate areas for housing, crafts, and agricultural processing, and it was occupied between about 450 and 650. It is too early to say how typical this may have been, but it seems that York itself and its immediate environs included agricultural settlements nearer subsistence level, even in the heart of *Eburacum*. The final use of the *principia*—just before or just after the English takeover—was, according to its excavators, a 'small subsistence farming unit' concentrating on pig rearing, though another interpretation sees the bones found (of piglets and lambs) as the residue of royal feasts on special occasions. Certainly there was hand-to-mouth farming just outside York: a settlement on Heslington Hill established around 550 seems to have lived at subsistence level.[13]

In a broader context, the York area can be contrasted with the upland, pastoral parts of Northumbria. Here the key excavation is that of Yeavering, a major royal 'palace' still occupied in Edwin's reign. Its careful planning and impressive timber buildings give some idea of how grand the king's power-centres could be. What would we not give to have a similar picture of Edwin's palace on the Derwent—or, for that matter, a Northumbrian royal tomb to match Sutton Hoo? Yeavering is also a reminder that we should not antedate the rise of York to be again—as it had been under the Romans—the dominant centre for what is now northern England. The baptism of Edwin at York has led, from Alcuin's time onwards, to a tradition that sees York as a natural royal and ecclesiastical centre for Northumbria from 627 onwards. Yet Bamburgh and Lindisfarne were slow to yield place to it, and with good reason. The power and wealth of Northumbrian kings

---

12. Bede, *HE*, II. xiv; P. R. Wilson et al., 'Early Anglian Catterick and Catraeth', *Med Arch*, 40 (1996), 1, 2; D. M. Hadley, *The Northern Danelaw* (London, 2000), 254. For the 'Anglian' Tower's date, see Chapter 1, Appendix I.

13. D. J. Powlesland and C. Haughton, *West Heslerton—The Anglian Settlement* (Yedingham, 2000); D. J. Powlesland, in *HANY*, 62–7. York *principia*: *EYM*, I, 554–5; D. A. Hinton, 'York', in P. Waller, ed., *The English Urban Landscape* (Oxford, 2000), 62. Heslington: C. A. Spall and N. J. Toop, 'Before Eoforwic: New light on York in the 6th and 7th centuries', *Med Arch*, 52 (2008), 4–13, 18, 19.

came above all from their successful military expansion from about 600 to
750, which meant that at its greatest extent 'the Northumbrian empire may
have comprised rather more than a third of modern Scotland' as well as all
northern England. Royal wealth over this vast territory was built especially
on an abundance of silver and cattle, as well as on trade with Ireland. In that
context, York was rather peripheral, and it is perhaps the success of the city
in eclipsing Lindisfarne that needs explaining. After 1014, on the other hand,
with Scottish expansion to the Tweed, and York firmly part of a new English
state, York was in a very different geopolitical situation.[14]

Before we consider Edwin's baptism at York, it should be stressed that
before his reign it was almost certainly not a town in the modern sense.
It is all too easy—as with other former Roman cities like London, Winchester, or Canterbury—to glide from Roman to medieval urban life and
to assume some (unrecorded) continuity. This has not, however, yet been
demonstrated for *any* town in the Roman province. As far as the archaeological evidence goes, there was life in towns but no longer town life:
walled cities like York were decaying shells in the fifth and sixth centuries, utilized perhaps as 'central places' rather than towns, whether by
kings, warlords, or pagan priests, but with little economic function. For
Britain, as for the north-western Roman provinces as a whole, we must
think of a rebirth of towns from the seventh century, rather than of
continuity.[15]

King, bishop, and cathedral: *c.*618–85

Late Roman *Eburacum* had been officially Christian, with its own bishop,
but the location of his cathedral is not known, nor whether a British Christian church survived long after 409. The English invaders were pagan, and
their conversion was owing to two initiatives, Gregory's mission from Rome,
carried out under Augustine of Canterbury from 597, and an Irish mission
from Iona which reached Northumbria in the 630s. That, at least, is the
picture given by Bede; but recent research has shown that he not only

14. B. Hope-Taylor, *Yeavering: An Anglo-British Centre of Early Northumbria* (London, 1977);
    J. R. Maddicott, 'Two frontier states: Northumbria and Wessex, *c.* 650–750', in J. R. Maddicott
    and D. M. Palliser, *The Medieval State* (London, 2000), 25–45 (quotation from p. 26).
15. R. Hodges and B. Hobley, eds, *The Rebirth of Towns in the West AD 700–1050*, CBA Res Rep 68
    (1988), *passim*.

ignored other missions to the English (especially by other Irish and by Franks), but also understated the importance of the fact that much territory conquered by the English was already Christian.

Gregory's aim, described in a letter of 601, was to convert the various English kingdoms and to group them into two ecclesiastical provinces of London and York. However, his plan probably 'owed more to the ancient administrative geography of Roman Britain than to any grasp of sixth-century political realities', and in the event Augustine and his successors remained in Canterbury. York did not attain metropolitan status until 735, and later popes mostly upheld a primacy of Canterbury over York which had not been Gregory's intention, and which caused centuries of friction.[16]

The Roman mission's first success was the conversion of King Æthelberht of Kent, whose daughter Æthelberg (Ethelburga) married the still-pagan Edwin of Northumbria in 618–19. She was escorted north by Paulinus, one of the Canterbury monks, who was consecrated a bishop before the journey (see Appendix II). Thereafter the course of Edwin's conversion, if we follow Bede's account, centred on the Vale of York. At Easter 626 the king was staying at a royal palace or vill (*villa regalis*) east of York, by the Derwent, when he narrowly escaped assassination; and at some point in the following twelve months he called a council to discuss whether he should accept Paulinus' urgings that he should become a Christian. Bede does not name the location; but since the council assented, and the decision was emphasized by the ritual destruction of a royal pagan temple at Goodmanham east of the Derwent, the assembly very likely took place either in York or at the *villa regalis*.[17]

Bede is very specific in relating the sequel to Edwin's conversion:

> He was baptized at York on Easter Day, 12 April [627] in the church of St Peter the Apostle, which he had hastily built of wood . . . He established an episcopal see for Paulinus, his instructor and bishop, in the same city. Very soon after his baptism, he set about building a greater and more magnificent church of stone . . . in the midst of which the chapel which he had first built was to be enclosed.

16. Bede, *HE*, I. xxix; *AY* 1, 46; Marion Gibbs, 'The decrees of Agatho and the Gregorian plan for York', *Speculum*, 48 (1973), 213–46; quotation: Markus, *Gregory the Great*, 180.
17. Bede, *HE*, II. ix, xiii; John Blair, 'Anglo-Saxon pagan shrines and their prototypes', *ASSAH*, 8 (1998), 22, 23.

Some scholars have read this passage in conjunction with another story in the anonymous *Life of Gregory*, and with the findings of the Minster excavations of 1967–73. They suggest that York was already a royal centre before 627, and that when in the city Edwin resided in a palace converted from the Roman *principia*, which lay partly beneath the present cathedral. If so, it would have been an obvious location to offer Paulinus for an episcopal church. The anecdote in the *Life of Gregory* certainly depicts Edwin, preparing for baptism, hurrying to the church from the hall (*aula*) where Paulinus had been instructing him, and across a *platea populi*, translatable as a public square, courtyard, or street. Since the author linked the story to Edwin's baptism, he probably intended the location as York, and if his *aula* meant the cross-hall (*basilica*) of the *principia*, and if *platea* meant courtyard, it could all fit the topography of the fortress.[18]

This, however, is to put much weight on an incident which (if it happened at all) need not have occurred in York. Furthermore, the jury is still out on the implications of the Minster excavations. On one reading, the fortress *basilica* remained roofed and usable until the ninth century; on another, it might have collapsed between the sixth and eighth centuries or even earlier. In any case, there need not have been any royal palace alongside which to site a cathedral; for, as we have seen, it was Gregory and his Roman missionaries who chose York. It was surely, therefore, Paulinus rather than Edwin who fixed a site for the episcopal church, following a pattern in the Roman conversion of England whereby bishops often seated themselves within walled towns of Roman origin. Whether Edwin and his successors chose to align themselves with that Mediterranean urban tradition, by residing at least periodically in York, is not clear. It has usually been assumed that they did, but two distinguished historians have recently pointed out that there is no evidence for a royal palace in York before the tenth century.[19]

Most early medieval kings were peripatetic, and had no fixed capital in the modern sense. It is true that Bede calls Canterbury the capital (*metropolis*) of Kent, and London that of Essex; and in James Campbell's view 'it is likely that York occupied a similar position in relation to Northumbria'. Alcuin certainly understood Bede to mean that Edwin's baptism took place

18. Bede, *HE*, II. xiv (trans. from C & M, 186–7); AY 1, 132–4; Colgrave, ed., *Earliest Life of Gregory the Great*, 96–9. For differing interpretations of the anecdote in the *Life*, see C. Daniell, 'York and the Whitby author's Anonymous Life of Gregory the Great', *NH*, 29 (1993), 197–9; AY 1, 127–9; Rollason, *Northumbria, 500–1100*, 77–8.
19. Date of basilica collapse: *EYM*, I, 69, 187–95. Royal palace: Rollason, *Northumbria, 500–1100*, 202–7; John Blair, *The Church in Anglo-Saxon Society* (Oxford, 2005), 271 and n. 112.

'under the lofty walls of the city', as though he resided periodically in the fortress. There is also the scrappy and late suggestion of a possible royal residence outside the walls in the area called *Earlsburh*; and the fact that the street between *Earlsburh* and the main river crossing had the pre-Viking name of Coney Street (King's Street). Nevertheless, the limited evidence suggests that we might envisage Anglian York as more an episcopal than a royal city, comparable to Metz or Trier, as David Rollason argues.[20]

Having said that, almost nothing is recorded of the city or its bishopric between 633 and 664—less, it seems, because the evidence has gone, than because Edwin's successors deliberately shifted power north. After Edwin's death in battle, Paulinus fled back to Kent with the king's widow and children. The next Christian ruler, Oswald, made Bamburgh his centre of power, and brought Aidan from Iona to be bishop of all Northumbria, with his cathedral on nearby Lindisfarne. York's fledgling ecclesiastical status was in abeyance for a generation, which would be appropriate for Aidan's tradition: Iona's Irish monks were accustomed to rural centres and not the urban bishoprics of the Roman world.

However, in 664, events unfolded in quick succession which were to be crucial for York, for Northumbria, and ultimately for all Christian England. Firstly, Oswald's successor Oswiu, the most powerful English king of his age, summoned a Church council to meet in the monastery of *Streanaeshealh* (possibly Whitby) of which Edwin's great-niece Hild (St Hilda) was abbess.[21] It was a decisive meeting at which Oswiu ruled in favour of Roman rather than Irish or British ecclesiastical practices. Secondly, a severe epidemic (probably of bubonic plague) struck England that year, and reached Northumbria by the autumn. And thirdly, whether connected with that disruption or not, the see of York was revived after the Synod, but in a confused way: both Chad and Wilfrid were separately appointed to York as bishops, a situation not fully resolved until 669, when Wilfrid came into unchallenged possession, found the cathedral derelict, and restored it. All we know of the restoration is that he improved the church with lead roofs, glass windows,

---

20. J. Campbell, 'Anglo-Saxon courts', in C. Cubitt, ed., *Court Culture in the Early Middle Ages* (Turnhout, 2003), 156; Peter Godman, ed., *Alcuin: The Bishops, Kings and Saints of York*, OMT (Oxford, 1982), 20; *AY* 1, 125–6; Rollason, *Northumbria, 500–1100*, 205, 207.

21. The 'Synod of Whitby' is therefore what it is almost always called, though Bede's *Streanaeshealh* has never been conclusively identified. A recent argument that it might equally have been Strensall near York is ingenious but controversial: P. Barnwell et al., 'The confusion of conversion: Streanaeshalch, Strensall and Whitby . . .', in Martin Carver, ed., *The Cross Goes North* (Woodbridge, 2003), 311–26; J. Campbell, review of Carver, ed., in *EHR*, 120 (2005), 107.

and rich furnishings; from his surviving work elsewhere, at Ripon and Hexham, there is no reason to doubt that his York work would have been impressive.

York under Wilfrid regained its ecclesiastical pre-eminence, for there is a break in the succession of bishops of Lindisfarne from 664 to 678. In the latter year Wilfrid was expelled from York, and his huge diocese divided into four, including Lindisfarne. The next manoeuvrings about bishoprics coincided with another plague, which struck Northumbria around 685–7. At Easter 685 Archbishop Theodore of Canterbury came to York, where he consecrated Cuthbert as bishop of Lindisfarne in the presence of King Ecgfrith. So much is attested by Bede; but a much later account reports that just after his consecration, Cuthbert was granted by king and archbishop all the land in York 'from the wall of the church of St Peter as far as the great gate on the west side, and from the wall of the church of St Peter as far as the wall of the city on the south'.[22]

How far this preserves the essence of a genuine grant of 685, and what area of the former fortress was involved, are both disputed. If it was genuine, why should the king have made so generous a grant in the heart of York to a bishop of Lindisfarne? A recent ingenious solution proposes that Ecgfrith and Theodore made Cuthbert bishop jointly of York and Hexham as well as Lindisfarne, thus placating York by increasing its status as an episcopal residence. If this was so, it held for only a year or so, for Ecgfrith died in battle later in 685, Cuthbert resigned his see in 686–7, and Wilfrid was reappointed briefly to York, which was once more a separate bishopric.[23]

Urban life reborn

So far, seventh-century York has featured as a central place but not a town. The Roman fortress walls survived, and the crucial crossing-point over the Ouse remained at or near the Roman bridgehead until at least the ninth century. Within the fortress, however, there was seemingly little settlement. Abandonment of the Roman layout is indicated by a disregard for the

22. Gibbs, 'The decrees of Agatho and the Gregorian plan for York', 229, 242; J. R. Maddicott, 'Plague in seventh-century England', *P&P*, 156 (1997), 13, 14; AY 1, 140–1; David Rollason, ed., *Symeon of Durham: Libellus de Exordio . . . Dunhelmensis Ecclesie*, OMT (Oxford, 2000), 46–7. I have preferred Rollason's latter translation to that in AY 1.
23. Christopher Norton, 'The Anglo-Saxon cathedral at York and the topography of the Anglian city', *JBAA*, 151 (1998), 28–35.

pattern of some streets and *insulae*, and the creation of two new roads diagonally across the fortress to link adjacent gates. This would have happened at some time between the fifth and ninth centuries.

By about 700, however, craft and trading activity was reviving, if well outside the old Roman centre. Indeed, it might go back well before that. A dozen small gold coins (*thrymsas* or *tremisses*) have been so far found in Yorkshire or not far beyond, three of them at York itself. First dismissed as forgeries, but now accepted as genuine, they are the only known group of early English gold coins outside the south east. However, most were found east of York, and previous suggestions that they were minted in the city now look less probable, as does the early date of *c.*640 proposed for them (the 650s or 660s are now favoured). More significantly, Yorkshire just came within the range of gold coins from the Rhine mouth area circulating in England: of seven *tremisses* found in England and minted at the great continental *emporium* of Dorestad, two have been found in Yorkshire, one at Cawood on the Ouse only nine miles south of York.[24]

The next type of coin struck in southern Northumbria is the silver *sceat* (pl. *sceattas*), a predecessor of the penny, of the reign of Aldfrith (685–*c.*705). Here we are on firmer ground: Aldfrith's Northumbria was then, remarkably, 'the only kingdom in northern Europe issuing an overtly regal coinage'. They bear out the same point, however, that York was probably not yet the main economic centre. No coin of Aldfrith has yet been found there, and the main concentration lies in the East Riding. Three are from North Ferriby, which might have served as an *emporium* and mint before York; and Aldfrith died at Driffield, where other early *sceattas* have been found.[25]

The real revival of York as a major economic centre began, it seems, in his reign. In 1985–6 excavations at 46–54 Fishergate revealed part of a trading and craft settlement, which seems to have begun around 700 and which flourished until the 860s or 870s. It has been plausibly identified as part of the trading settlement alluded to by Alcuin when he called York *emporium terrae*

24. D. M. Metcalf, *Thrymsas and Sceattas in the Ashmolean Museum Oxford* (London, 1993–4), 49–51, and pers. comm. from Dr Metcalf (2009). Dorestad coins: J. Naylor and A. Cooper, note on the Cawood find, in *Med Arch*, 52 (2008), 331–2. The terms *thrymsa/tremissis* and *sceat* have been used since the 17th century to denote early Anglo-Saxon gold and silver coins respectively: P. Grierson and M. Blackburn, *Medieval European Coinage 1: The Early Middle Ages (5th–10th Centuries)* (Cambridge, 1986), 157.
25. Grierson and Blackburn, *Medieval European Coinage 1*, 158, 166, 182; C. P. Loveluck, 'The development of the Anglo-Saxon landscape . . .', *ASSAH*, 9 (1996), 44; D. M. Metcalf, 'The coinage of King Aldfrith . . .', *BNJ*, 76 (2006), 150–1. On Aldfrith, see now Barbara Yorke, *Rex Doctissimus: Bede and King Aldfrith of Northumbria*, Jarrow Lecture (Newcastle upon Tyne, 2009), esp. pp. 14, 15.

commune marisque, 'a general seat of commerce by land and sea alike'.[26] Since Old English *wic* was the equivalent of *emporium*, this helps to explain the name *Eoforwic* as 'the trading town on the Ure' or Ouse. York was apparently similar in its trading functions to Ipswich, *Hamwic* (Southampton), and *Lundenwic* (just west of Roman London). The four are now recognized as a group, the largest known English settlements of the period, with Ipswich the earliest, from about 600, and the others all founded between about 650 and 700, corresponding to their main continental equivalents, Quentovic, Dorestad, and Domburg. York took its place as one of a series of major 'gateways' through which overseas trade was funnelled between the seventh and ninth centuries, all located near coasts or on navigable rivers, and in most cases apparently allowing kings to control and tax trade. Not everyone is persuaded that we can call such places towns: they often comprised, like York, a cluster of settlements with separate functions—a royal centre, a major church, craft and trading zones—which would later merge into true multi-functional towns, places often called proto-urban for want of a better term. They were also a varied group: in both London and York the new *emporia* were started outside the Roman walls, before settlement moved back inside them in the Viking period. Southampton was similar, in that a new *emporium* was created outside Roman *Clausentum*, but distinct in that the eventual medieval walled city was on a third site. Of the four main *wics*, only Ipswich was a truly new, unfortified coastal centre.[27]

York was clearly a thriving trading port well before the Viking conquest of 866–7. Its story forms part of a major shift in the economy of north-west Europe between about 700 and 850, an economy once thought to have reverted to near-subsistence level, but now seen as one of expanding trade and manufacturing. By the eighth century York was within an 'English zone' using Ipswich pottery as well as local ware, while by the ninth it was integrated into a wider European zone using pots manufactured in the Rhineland.[28] York was well placed for North Sea trade, trade that was then

26. R. L. Kemp, *Anglian Settlement at 46–54 Fishergate*, AY 7/1 (1996), 66; though Dominic Tweddle, in AY 7/2 (1999), 193, suggests the site 'was active from the mid 7th century'. Alcuin: Godman, ed., *Bishops, Kings and Saints of York*, 4. Alcuin here repeats almost word for word Bede's characterization of London (*HE* II. iii) but it has not, I think, been previously noticed that Bede may have taken the phrase from Orosius's description of Corinth as *emporium commune Asiae atque Europae* (Migne, *Pat. Lat.*, vol. 31, col. 923), a reference I owe to Dr J. W. Binns.

27. The literature on the *emporia* is now considerable; for useful summaries, see e.g. *CUHB* I, 32–4, 218–21.

28. M. McCormick, *Origins of the European Economy* (Cambridge, 2001), 657; Wickham, *Framing the Early Middle Ages*, 811; AY 16/6, 568–83.

largely in the hands of Frisians; and though their presence is not as well recorded for York as for London, the story already mentioned—of a Frisian merchant or merchants probably in York in 773—does suggest that. We simply do not know what such merchants might have exported from Northumbria through York, but both slaves and wool (or even woven cloth) are possibilities.[29]

A commercializing economy could not have been based solely on a handful of major ports; and the *wics* were apparently at the apex of a hierarchy of craft and trade centres, the so-called 'productive sites' of recent archaeological literature. Fishergate should, therefore, be set in its regional context before returning to its importance within York. To the east, other than North Ferriby, 'productive sites' have been identified at Cottam and South Newbald: Newbald has so far yielded at least 173 coins and 114 other metal items datable between the 650s and 850s. Across the Humber was Flixborough, discovered in 1989–91, and clearly a smaller member of the same group of riverine craft and trade centres as *Eoforwic*. More such sites must still await discovery: another, this time north-west of York, was discovered in 2007 in the Boroughbridge/Thirsk area. Fishergate was clearly no isolated entrepôt, but part of a trading and manufacturing network.[30]

Once established, Fishergate grew, with many buildings clearly extending beyond the excavated limits. Metals, wood, antler, and bone were all worked there, and furs, skins, and leather prepared; pottery was imported from other English sites and from overseas, as were glass and quern-stones. Growth must have been rapid, for of the thirty-four pre-867 coins found there, almost half date from before 737. Its inhabitants may have been almost exclusively traders and craftsmen, for animal bone evidence indicates that meat, mostly beef, was supplied to them ready jointed. They may have had their own church, for a later excavation has taken in more of the settlement, locating a cemetery (probably that of St Helen, Fishergate) with at least one burial datable between 680 and 890. The *emporium* might well have covered between 60 and 160 acres (25 and 65 ha), comparable in size to the other three English *wics*.[31]

It seems on present evidence that the Fishergate *wic* was not a commercial extension of an existing town, but a separate component of a polyfocal, proto-urban settlement. Just before the *wic* was discovered, I had suggested

29. *EHD*, I, 788–9; AY 1, 131–2.
30. e.g. Pestell and Ulmschneider, eds, *Markets in Early Medieval Europe*, chs 12, 13.
31. AY 7/1, *passim*; 7/2, 193, 205–6; AY 15/4; Spall and Toop, 'Before Eoforwic', 13–18.

that the medieval city had formed from the fusion of 'at least two urban or pre-urban nuclei', based on evidence for separate early English settlements within the former fortress and *colonia*. To those can now be added Fishergate, and possibly others still to be found; and the polyfocal model has now been refined and revised by others. We can now, therefore, envisage the Roman fortress as a fortified episcopal and (possibly) royal enclave; an unfortified commercial *wic* near the junction of Ouse and Foss; and the *colonia* as a third settlement dominated by the Church. The dedication of St Gregory's church might suggest a foundation of the conversion period, and it apparently had early burials on a Roman alignment; Alcuin mentions a church of St Mary which might have been one of the Bishophill churches; and there is much sculptural evidence for an early foundation of both St Mary Bishophill churches, of Holy Trinity and of St Martin's. There may also have been a royal presence on the south-west bank of the Ouse, as there certainly was by 1065–6: a cross-head comes possibly from a chapel on Toft Green connected with a royal residence.[32]

The evidence of coin finds confirms York's active commerce in the eighth century. The opening series of what numismatists call secondary *sceattas* (from *c*.705–10) includes a small hoard from Fishergate. It was followed by Series J from about 720, finds of which are centred on York—though, tellingly, with a strong presence also around the Rhine estuary, near the Frisian *emporia* of Dorestad and Domburg. Metcalf is confident that these were York coinages 'with strong Frisian connections', though Booth is less sure that they were minted in York. Some Series J coins were issued in the king's name, others jointly for the king and archbishop (the king's brother). Perhaps the church was as much involved in the profits of trade as the Crown; and these are certainly the earliest known English coins struck by an identifiable ecclesiastical authority. Yet whoever most benefited—kings, churchmen, merchants, or consumers—the city undoubtedly prospered from what Maddicott has aptly called 'the period of monetary "take-off" in the first half of the eighth century' when literally millions of coins were struck from Wessex to Northumbria.[33]

32. D. M. Palliser, 'York's west bank', in P. V. Addyman and V. E. Black, eds, *Archaeological Papers from York* (York, 1984), 101–8; R. K. Morris, 'Alcuin, York and the alma sophia', in L. A. S. Butler and R. K. Morris, eds, *The Anglo-Saxon Church*, CBA Res Rep 60 (1986), 80–9; J. Lang, *Corpus of Anglo-Saxon Stone Sculpture*, III: *York and Eastern Yorkshire* (Oxford, 1991), 80–95; AY 1, 171, 187; AY 7/1, 3, 82.
33. Metcalf, *Thrymsas and Sceattas*, 341–2, 359; D. M. Metcalf, 'The beginnings of coinage in the North Sea coastlands', in B. Ambrosiani and H. Clarke, eds, *Developments around the Baltic and*

The evidence for York's urban rebirth is therefore mostly archaeological and numismatic. Bede says nothing of the city or cathedral after the 670s, and Alcuin did not write on either until the 780s, though a little can be gleaned from some lost 'Northern Annals' of 732–c.806 preserved in later compilations. The level of detail about York and the apparent influence of Alcuin on their style suggest that they were written in the city, and some prefer to call them the York Annals. Their entries are not without problems, however; for instance, MSS D and E of the *Anglo-Saxon Chronicle* report laconically that in 741 'York was burnt down', whereas the more specific entry in the Northern Annals has it that on 23 April 741 'the *monasterium* in the city of York was burnt'. Was it the cathedral that burned, or—as Bullough thought—an episcopal monastery on another site? Certainly Alcuin, who knew the cathedral from the 740s, mentions no recent destruction or rebuilding. The 741 annal reminds us that we shall never know much of any major York church, even the cathedral, without more archaeological investigations. And even more problematic is the annal for 764, asserting that in that year six named 'cities', including London, York, and Winchester, 'and many other places', were burned. It is an entry preserved in only one version (unlike the 741 annal) and is hard to take literally.[34]

A further thought about York and Northumbria in the first two-thirds of the eighth century is that the gloomy picture often assumed from Bede's attitude to his own time, and thereafter from fragmentary annals, need not be given too much weight. Such sources have been read to depict a kingdom almost continuously in decline from the death of Aldfrith (c.705). Yet York, at least, flourished economically, and the reign of Eadberht (737–58) was seen at the time as a golden age of strong and just rule. It is true that his death was followed by several short reigns, often ending in abdication, exile, or murder, yet that does not seem to have interrupted the cultural and economic flowering of city and kingdom.

North Sea in the Viking Age (Stockholm, 1994), 205; James Booth, 'Northumbrian coinage and the productive site at South Newbald ("Sancton")', in H. Geake and J. Kenny, eds, *Early Deira* (Oxford, 2000), 84; J. R. Maddicott, 'Prosperity and power in the age of Bede and Beowulf', *Proc. British Academy*, 117 (2002), 52. Dr Metcalf kindly informs me that Series J *sceattas* at York seem to date from c.720 at the earliest.

34. *EHD*, I, 265, 267; AY 1, 17, 18, 59, 60, 144; Rollason, *Northumbria, 500–1100*, 15, 16; Donald Bullough, *Alcuin: Achievement and Reputation* (Leiden, 2004), 156, 167–8. The 'York Annals' are sometimes called the 'First Set of Northern Annals' to distinguish them from a second set of 888–957 drawn on in Chapter 3 in this volume.

If there is one reason above all why York was not only reborn as a city, but prospered so much in its first two centuries, it might be the coming of Christianity and the whole Mediterranean cultural package that it entailed, including 'literacy and books and the Latin language...; Roman notions about law, authority, property and government; the habits of living in towns and using coin for exchange...[and] new architectural and artistic conventions'.[35]

Alcuin's York

One striking example of the impact of Christian culture in York is the career and literary output of Alcuin, who was born around 740 and sent as a small child to be educated in York's cathedral school. Its master at that time was Ælberht (Æthelberht), and when he became archbishop in 766/7 Alcuin succeeded him as master. Altogether, Alcuin resided in York for some forty years, attracting students from as far afield as Ireland and Frisia. It may have been his growing international reputation which led the Frankish king and emperor Charles the Great (Charlemagne), the most powerful ruler in western Europe, to persuade Alcuin to join his court in the 780s. There he became a leading light of the Carolingian Renaissance before revisiting England (790–3) and then retiring to end his life as abbot of Tours on the Loire (796–804). Because of his international career, his life and writings go far beyond the scope of this book, but he does record much of value about York's cathedral and diocese, even if he tells us much less of the city than we would wish.[36]

His most relevant work is the long poem which later editions have entitled *Poem on the Bishops, Kings and Saints of the Church of York* (hereafter the 'York Poem'), written in the 780s or 790s. This, a metrical version of parts of Bede's *History* with additions, includes lengthy accounts both of Ælberht's teaching programme and of the books he collected for the cathedral library. They demonstrate that by the 760s York had become a major centre of the Northumbrian Renaissance and a source from which Alcuin was able to draw in inspiring its Carolingian equivalent.

35. Richard Fletcher, *The Conversion of Europe: From Paganism to Christianity 371–1386 AD* (London, 1997), 2.
36. See Appendix III in this chapter, 'Alcuin's life and works'.

The York Poem is primarily about the history of Christian Northumbria, particularly the see of York. It is evident that a key figure in the growing importance of see and city was Bishop Egbert (Ecgberht, 732–66), who received the *pallium* at Rome in 735, and thus became the first archbishop of York. Crucially, he was of the royal line, and his brother Eadberht was king from 737/8 to 757/8. 'The consequences were unmistakeable,' said Bullough; 'both the ecclesiastical and political "capitals" of the kingdom were at York, not as they had once been... at Lindisfarne and Bamburgh'. Eadberht's reign was clearly prosperous for York: not only did Alcuin look back on it as a golden age, but the king struck fine silver coins which were probably minted in the city. It was under Egbert and his successor Ælberht that the School of York eclipsed Bede's Jarrow-Wearmouth to become the leading Northumbrian centre of learning. And it was the development of that school which led Alcuin, in his York Poem, to set down what Ian Wood calls 'a Deiran version of Bede, in which the bishops and archbishops of his city played the dominant role'.[37]

Why did the pope grant York metropolitan status at that time? It is often seen as a response by him to local pride and piety: Eadberht and Egbert certainly worked closely together for the mutual advantage of Church and State, and Eadberht finally abdicated to enter his brother's monastic church at York and to be buried there; it would be natural for the brothers to ask the pope to make good the promise to Paulinus a century before. However, it was also in the 730s that the Frankish Church was being reformed under the guidance of the Northumbrian Willibrord, based on the principle of a metropolitan province with dependent bishoprics. It might even be that Northumbria was not copying Frankish developments but vice versa, and that Willibrord was introducing to the Franks developments in his native land.[38]

Whatever, therefore, the Church of York had been in the seventh century, it was supreme in eighth-century Northumbria. The archiepiscopal title conferred not only prestige, but also oversight over bishoprics covering a huge area: under York's jurisdiction were the sees of Lindisfarne, Whithorn

37. Donald Bullough, 'Hagiography as patriotism: Alcuin's "York Poem"...', in [no editor named], *Hagiographie, Cultures et Sociétés*, Etudes Augustiniennes (Paris, 1981), 346; Wood, 'Monasteries and the geography of power', 25.
38. Joanna Story, *Carolingian Connections: Anglo-Saxon England and Carolingian Francia, c. 750–870* (Aldershot, 2003), 22–3, 41–50. Since this book was completed, Dr Story has taken the subject further in her 'Bede, Willibrord and the letters of Pope Honorius I on the genesis of the archbishopric of York', *EHR*, 127 (2012), 783–818.

(now in Scotland), and by 767 even Mayo in western Ireland. It was appropriate that the cathedral school and library were also distinguished. Indeed,
Ælberht's curriculum 'surpassed, in the range of subjects taught, all other
schools in England or continental Europe at that time', while his library,
along with those of Jarrow-Wearmouth and Canterbury, outshone most
libraries outside Italy. That library was sufficiently well-stocked for Alcuin in
the 790s to ask for copies of some of its books for Tours.[39]

Alcuin's York Poem opens with the earliest surviving description of the
city and its setting:

> ...My heart is set to praise my home
> And briefly tell the ancient origins
> Of York's famed city through the charms of verse.
> It was a Roman army built it first,
> High-walled and towered...
> To be a trading town [*emporium*] by land and sea alike...
> A haven for the ships from distant parts
> Across the ocean, where the sailor hastes
> To cast his rope ashore and stay to rest.
> The city is watered by the fish-rich Ouse
> Which flows past flowery fields on every side...

Bullough drily remarked that 'topography and buildings apparently do not
interest Alcuin very much', but that may be unfair. Alcuin was writing to
those known to him in York, and to describe the city would have been stat-
ing the obvious. At the least, this passage earns its place as the first surviving
description by a contemporary of *any* English town, and Alcuin may have
been inspired by the *laudatio urbis*, a literary form just then developing in the
Italian cities. And since in describing Edwin's baptism Alcuin refers to York's
'lofty walls' (*celsis...moenibus*), we may presume that Roman defences and
other buildings must still have been impressive.[40]

Later in the poem, Alcuin does—warmly if imprecisely—praise Egbert
and Ælberht for adorning various churches—possibly more than one of
them in York—and for giving splendid ornaments to the cathedral. His

39. *EHD*, I, 201; Helmut Gneuss, *Books and Libraries in Early England* (Aldershot, 1996), II, 652;
Mary Garrison, 'Alcuin', in E. Hartley, ed., *Alcuin & Charlemagne: The Golden Age of York* (York,
2001), 6. The best account of the library is now Garrison, 'The library of Alcuin's York', in
Richard Gameson, ed., *The Cambridge History of the Book in Britain* (Cambridge, 2012), I, 633–
64. I am grateful to Dr Garrison for allowing me to read it before publication.
40. The translation is based on Stephen Allott, *Alcuin of York, c.732 to 804 A.D.* (York, 1974), 157, with modi-
fications from translations by Godman, *Bishops, Kings and Saints of York*, 5, and from Garrison *Alcuin's
world through his letters and verses* (Cambridge, forthcoming). Quotation: Bullough, *Alcuin*, 155.

longest description, however, is puzzling: he relates how he and Eanbald (archbishop 779/80–96) built for Ælberht a new church (*basilica*) 'of wondrous design' dedicated to Holy Wisdom (*Alma Sophia*), which he describes at length. No such church was ever mentioned again, and scholars are divided on whether it adjoined the cathedral or whether it was a quite distinct episcopal church, possibly on the other bank of the Ouse.[41]

Not only do we not know the location of Holy Wisdom, but—as with all periods between 627 and 1069—we are not certain where even the cathedral stood. The long tradition that it was on the present Minster site was apparently disproved by the excavation of 1967–73, though the Anglo-Scandinavian cemetery with high-status graves found beneath the south transept suggests that the cathedral was probably nearby (see Map 4 in Chapter 4). Even that evidence, however, barely goes back before the Viking conquest: the earliest evidence seems to be a single pair of charcoal graves with radiocarbon dates centring on 790 and 820, dates mentioned, oddly, in the excavation report on the Norman Minster but not in that on the pre-Conquest building, where no dating seems to be given for the start of the cemetery except for the finding of York ware pottery in the latest floors of part of the Roman *principia*.[42]

However, we need not rely on Alcuin alone for evidence of the economic and artistic wealth of York in his day. Fine eighth-century crosses and tombstones have been found both under the cathedral and also in and around Holy Trinity, Micklegate (Richard Morris's suggested site for Alma Sophia). Possibly the cathedral was a secular church and the other an episcopal monastery: the evidence for whether York was staffed by secular clergy, monks, or both is thin and ambiguous.[43] Altogether, enough sculptures, luxury goods, and dress items have been found to justify Alcuin's praise of York. One example is the Ormside bowl, a highly decorated vessel possibly made there, and finer still is the York Helmet, unexpectedly discovered in 1982 and dating from about 750–75. Lavishly decorated, it bears a Latin Christian

---

41. Godman, ed., *Bishops, Kings and Saints of York*, 98–101, 118–21; AY 1, 142–4, 155–7; Morris, 'Alcuin, York and the alma sophia', 85–6; Norton, 'The Anglo-Saxon cathedral at York', 14, 15; Bullough, *Alcuin*, 320–6, 333–6.

42. *EYM*, II, 46; *EYM*, I, 81.

43. Bullough was certain that the cathedral community in Alcuin's time was secular, and the fact that the cathedral before 1066 had been termed *monasterium* or *mynster* does not, of course, prove Benedictine monasticism. Harder to explain away is the fact that the request for the loan of York books by the abbot of Ferrières in 852 was to *Abbot* Ealdsige of York, though his other letter of that year was to the *archbishop* (*EHD*, I, 215–16).

inscription mentioning Oshere, presumably its owner and possibly, judging from his name, from one of the Northumbrian royal families.[44]

The helmet's inscription has a convoluted word order forming a cross, of a type Alcuin is known to have used. One possible reading is 'In the name of our Lord Jesus Christ and of the Spirit of God, let us offer up Oshere to All Saints. Amen.' The helmet had been buried close to the church of All Saints, Pavement, which was already known from the evidence of sculpture and high-status tiles to date back well before its first recorded mention in Domesday Book. The inscription may add to the speculation that here was another major church in Alcuin's time. It is a reminder that many of the parish churches of medieval York, though recorded only after the Norman Conquest, may have originated in Anglo-Scandinavian or even Anglian times. The possible cases of Holy Trinity, Micklegate, the Bishophill St Mary churches, and St Gregory's have already been mentioned, as has the church of St Helen near the Fishergate *emporium*, while a group of churches surrounding the cathedral (St Michael-le-Belfrey, St Sepulchre, St John-del-Pyke, and St Mary-ad-Valvas) are also suggestive of early origins, as are the six churches confirmed as capitular property by the pope in 1194.[45]

Yet again, some of the best evidence is numismatic. Rigold's Series Y *sceattas* (Y stands for York) were issued in the names of kings (or sometimes king and archbishop jointly) between 738 and 788; nearly 200 have so far been studied and published. They were struck—almost certainly in York—in very large quantities (the surviving coins were struck from an estimated 1,070 upper dies). They were also of a volume and perhaps of fineness which 'outmatched, in mid-century at least, any coinage produced in the south'.[46]

The evidence therefore justifies a view of York as both important and prosperous in Alcuin's lifetime. The one apparent pointer in the opposite

44. Dominic Tweddle, *The Anglian Helmet from Coppergate*, AY 17/8 (1992). Ormside bowl: Tweddle, 'The catalogue' in Hartley, ed., *Alcuin & Charlemagne*, 24–5, 30.

45. J. W. Binns, E. C. Norton, and D. M. Palliser, 'The Coppergate helmet inscription', *Antiquity*, 64 (1990), 134–9; Laurence Keen, 'Pre-Conquest glazed relief tiles from All Saints church, Pavement, York', *JBAA*, 146 (1993), 67–86. 1194 is of course late evidence for churches of early origins, but one of the six, at St Mary Bishophill Junior, existed by 866 judging from sculptural evidence. I owe to the late H. G. Ramm the suggestion that they were the churches associated with the six canons of the pre-Conquest cathedral.

46. J. Booth, 'Sceattas in Northumbria', in D. Hill and D. M. Metcalf, eds, *Sceattas in England and on the Continent*, BAR (BS) 128 (1984), 71–97; Grierson and Blackburn, *Medieval European Coinage 1*, 173, 182, 189, 297; Metcalf, *Thrymsas and Sceattas*, 576–93; quotation: Maddicott, 'Two frontier states', 29.

direction is a relative decline in the numbers both of foreign imports and of coins recorded at Fishergate. The first stage of settlement there (c.700–40) was deliberately demolished, levelled, and then reoccupied on a reduced scale. Coin finds were far fewer after 737 and the proportion of imported pottery much lower. Indeed, Mainman and Kemp have argued that international trade was therefore less important. However, that decline may have been caused not by a decline in the volume of York's international trade, but by a shift in trading activity to other parts of York.[47]

English York after Alcuin: 786–866

Northumbria's story after 793 is often dismissed as that of a once-powerful state in terminal decline, an issue very relevant because of its implications for what was certainly, by Alcuin's time, the chief urban settlement of the kingdom if not its settled capital. The pessimistic narrative is based on the supposed effects of Viking raids, on an unstable and divided monarchy and aristocracy, and on a poorer coinage of small, dumpy, debased pennies. How far is that true?

Alcuin was still at Charlemagne's court when he learned of the Viking sack of Lindisfarne in 793, followed the next year by a raid on another Northumbrian monastery, *Donamuthe* (possibly Jarrow). These attacks are often seen as the beginning of the kingdom's decline, a tradition going back to Alcuin himself. He had already sounded a nostalgic note in his York Poem in praising the joint rule of the brothers Eadberht and Egbert:

> These were fortunate times for the people of Northumbria, ruled over in harmony by king and bishop…

On learning of the sack of Lindisfarne, Alcuin wrote at once to King Æthelred and others, interpreting it as God's judgement on rulers and people. He seems to have had in mind the rivalries of aristocratic families, which led to a succession of depositions and murders of kings from the 760s. It is true, for instance, that Alcuin's correspondent Æthelred was murdered in 796.[48]

Nevertheless, it will not do to confuse prophetic judgements with sober history; and the little we can learn from documentary sources (even the

---

47. AY 7/1, 63; AY 16/6, 570; John Moreland, 'The significance of production in eighth-century England', in I. L. Hansen and C. Wickham, eds, *The Long Eighth Century* (Leiden, 2000), 79.
48. *EHD*, I, 193–4; Allott, *Alcuin of York*, letters 12, 13; Godman, ed., *Bishops, Kings and Saints of York*, 100–1.

York annals come to an end by 806) can be read another way. King Eard-wulf was expelled in 806, but took refuge at Charlemagne's court and may possibly have been restored with the emperor's help. Certainly the family of Eardwulf then occupied the throne until at least 848, refashioning a more stable monarchy, especially under the thirty-year reign of Eardwulf's son Eanred. And, fortunately, ninth-century Northumbrian coins are now as abundant as written records are scarce, and can be used to suggest the state of trade, as well as to amplify and correct the names and dates of kings.

There may well have been a short crisis in the 790s as Viking raids dis-rupted trade by striking at east coast shipping. The *sceattas* were replaced from that decade by smaller coins of lower silver content called *stycas*, and these in turn by copper-alloy *stycas* from the 830s; both have been seen as indicating political and economic decline, especially as southern kingdoms adopted broader flan pennies of good fineness. Yet distinguished scholars have taken issue with this, seeing the *stycas* as evidence of efficient royal control of the economy and of a public confidence which could accept brass coins as of equal value with silver. It must also have helped that Viking raids on Northumbria apparently ceased between the 790s and 860s, though admittedly surviving annals are very sparse for that time.[49]

This necessary preamble fits with what non-documentary evidence we have for York. For example, coins found at Fishergate increase to a level almost as high as a century before. Of all coins struck between 600 and 867 found there, 35 per cent date to the 840s and early 850s, while for all other York sites, the proportion is 45 per cent, the highest in the whole two-and-a-half centuries. The bulk of coins found are Northumbrian, but among other finds on York sites was one hoard of mostly ninth-century coins from the Carolingian mint at Dorestad. There is also the converse, of York-minted coins found elsewhere. These include twenty-two coins (datable to *c*.837–51) found in the London *wic* district, 'possibly the property of a North-umbrian traveller', and buried in a purse around the time of a Viking raid on London in 851.[50]

49. Grierson and Blackburn, *Medieval European Coinage 1*, 296–303; D. M. Metcalf and J. P. Northover, 'The Northumbrian royal coinage in the time of Æthelred II and Osberht', in D. M. Metcalf, ed., *Coinage in Ninth-Century Northumbria*, BAR (BS) 180 (Oxford, 1987), 212; E. J. E. Pirie, *Coins of Northumbria* (Llanfyllin, 2002), 18.
50. AY 7/2, 205–7; Michael Dolley, 'New light on the pre-1760 Coney Street (York) find of coins of the Duurstede mint', *Jaarboek voor Munt- en Penningkunde*, 52/53 (1965/6), 1–7; E. J. E. Pirie, 'The purse-hoard of Northumbrian stycas', in G. Malcolm et al., *Middle Saxon London: Excavations at the Royal Opera House 1989–99*, MoLAS Monograph 15 (London, 2003), 278–84.

It is true that the Fishergate site was seemingly less densely settled in the early ninth century, but that may reflect a broader spread of trading and crafts within the polyfocal city. It has been much argued in the last twenty years that Viking attacks on the *emporia*—not only at York—led to shrinkage, reduced trade, and finally desertion, but this can now be questioned for all four English *wics*. As Richard Hall put it, 'Change there certainly was; but change does not necessarily equate with decline. Rather...there was a broad continuity of commercial and manufacturing activities at and around these sites.'[51]

Sculptural evidence points the same way. Lang lists twenty-nine stone carvings datable to before 866: many cannot be closely dated, but at least four cross shafts or arms are definitely ninth century, and eleven others could be ninth century or earlier. Much the most accomplished is a fragment carved with a vine-scroll inhabited by an animal and a bird: it seems to have been rejected before it was finished, yet its design and technique are of high quality. Similarly, a handful of eighth- or ninth-century glass fragments were found under the cathedral, which indicate something of the establishment's wealth; one, an imitation jewel, was probably designed to be inlaid in metal work such as a cross or book cover.[52]

As for casual finds of coins, sculpture, pottery, and other artefacts, there is a 'very steep increase' in ninth-century finds over those of the eighth, concentrated in the Minster, Coppergate, and Fishergate areas. The Coppergate finds are especially interesting, implying settlement preceding the well-known tenth-century activity under Viking rule. It seems that the fortress wall may have been deliberately breached to allow settlement to the south, and that the new district may have been served not only by All Saints' church but also by a St Peter's church, later named St Peter-the-Little to distinguish it from the cathedral.[53]

Yet our knowledge of life in *Eoforwic* is still patchy. No domestic buildings, and little even of the more durable churches and defences, have survived to match the volume of artefacts. We can, however, glimpse the appearance of at least two prosperous townsmen of around 850 carved on a cross-shaft and seemingly an attempt at realism: one wears a belted gown and carries a horn, while the other, cloaked, has a sword. There are also hints of urban

51. R. A. Hall, 'The decline of the *wic*?', in T. R. Slater, ed., *Towns in Decline AD 100–1600* (Aldershot, 2000), 133.

52. Lang, *Corpus of Anglo-Saxon Stone Sculpture*, III, 53–114; *EYM*, I, 433–67, 481–3; L. Webster and J. Backhouse, eds, *The Making of England: Anglo-Saxon Art and Culture AD 600–900* (London, 1991), 146–7.

53. AY 7/2, 211–12.

diet. Alcuin's favourite food and drink when in Francia—porridge and ale as well as wine—seem to echo his York background rather than the privileged diet of a senior churchman; and more interesting is the increasing evidence from environmental archaeology for the lay population. The largest pre-Viking sample of bones so far, from Fishergate, suggests that the commonest meat was beef, followed by mutton and pork; domestic fowls were scarce, but there was abundant fish, especially herring and eels. This is, however, evidence from only one—possibly specialized—district, and may not have been typical of most townspeople's diet.[54]

We are equally ignorant of the rural context of *Eoforwic*. We might expect a major trading town and inland port to require a productive hinterland from which to draw food supplies, but we know little yet of farming and settlement in the Vale of York before the tenth and eleventh centuries. There is some evidence from the Wolds, where Cottam and Wharram Percy have both been investigated. In both there was still dispersed settlement at little more than subsistence level; the nucleated villages, with their open fields and productive mixed farming, were not established until Anglo-Scandinavian times or even later. That would fit well with Julian Richards' suggestion that not more than one in twenty of the Northumbrian people lived in York, and that, judging from animal bone, 'the restricted nature of its food supply . . . indicates that there was only limited contact with the hinterland.'[55]

There is still much to learn of York before 866, but it was clearly flourishing. Even the cathedral and associated monastery, often pictured as in decline after Alcuin's time, were sufficiently active for Abbot Lupus of Ferrières to request copies of four specified books in 852. And it was at that time that Archbishop Wigmund, one of Lupus's correspondents, issued a large and heavy gold coin in Carolingian style, much superior to the staple products of the York mint. Grierson saw it as a special issue from a southern mint in Wigmund's honour, intended only as an ornament, but Story is prepared to accept that the archbishop's aim was 'to initiate a serious commercial coinage'. Altogether, there are enough hints from our meagre sources to suggest a proto-city with a thriving economy and culture on the eve of the Viking conquest.[56]

54. Lang, *Corpus of Anglo-Saxon Stone Sculpture*, III, 83 and plate 216; AY 15/4, 282, 286.
55. J. D. Richards, 'Anglo-Saxon settlements of the golden age', in J. Hawkes and S. Mills, eds, *Northumbria's Golden Age* (Stroud, 1999), 44.
56. *EHD*, I, 216; Grierson and Blackburn, *Medieval European Coinage 1*, 330; Story, *Carolingian Connections*, 243.

Appendix II: Northumbrian dates to 627

Before 616, dating is very uncertain, and Bede's date of 547 for Ida may be too early, while his implication that Ælle was still reigning in 597 has also been challenged. However, Barbara Yorke believes that from the reign of Æthelfrith Bede's dates for the reigns of the Northumbrian kings may be accepted as they stand. Suggestions by Kirby and others that Bede misdated several key events, including Edwin's York baptism, have not found general favour; and Wood and Yorke accept Bede's date of 12 April 627 for the baptism, though Wood is in error in calling that day Easter Eve; it was, as Bede said, Easter Day.[57]

There is, however, one crucial event for York which Bede probably misdated by several years. He assigned Paulinus's consecration as bishop to 625, but a good case has been made that he had travelled north with Æthelberg as early as 618 or 619. Another problem with Bede's account of Edwin's conversion is that it is implicitly contradicted by a later claim by 'Nennius' that Edwin was baptized not by Paulinus but by Rhun from Rheged, implying conversion via Iona rather than from Rome or Canterbury. It may or may not be true, but there are other indications that the royal houses of Rheged and Northumbria had relationships not mentioned by Bede.[58] For an excellent setting of Edwin's conversion in a European context, see Richard Fletcher's *The Conversion of Europe* (London, 1997), 2–5.

Appendix III: Alcuin's life and works

Donald Bullough's massive *Alcuin: Achievement and Reputation* (2004) contains his posthumously published Ford Lectures but does not amount to a biography, though he did write a very useful entry for the *Oxford Dictionary of National Biography*; a new study by Mary Garrison is forthcoming. Peter Godman's edition of the York Poem includes an excellent 100-page

57. D. P. Kirby, 'Bede and Northumbrian chronology', *EHR*, 78 (1963), 514–27; Susan Wood, 'Bede's Northumbrian dates again', *EHR*, 98 (1983), 280–96; Barbara Yorke, *Kings and Kingdoms of Early Anglo-Saxon England* (London, 1990), 72, 77.
58. James Campbell, *Essays in Anglo-Saxon History* (London, 1986), 8, 24; J. M. Wallace-Hadrill, *Bede's Ecclesiastical History of the English People: A Historical Commentary*, OMT (Oxford, 1988), 65; Caitlin Corning, 'The baptism of Edwin, king of Northumbria', *NH*, 36 (2000), 5–15; S. D. Church, 'Paganism in conversion-age Anglo-Saxon England', *History*, 93 (2008), 176 and n.

introduction, and also valuable is *Alcuin & Charlemagne: the Golden Age of York*, ed. Elizabeth Hartley (2001), which includes scholarly essays by Garrison, Nelson, and Tweddle and the catalogue of a York exhibition, one of a series of European exhibitions commemorating Charlemagne (who became emperor in 800) in 2000–1. Alcuin's works other than his York Poem are drawn on in this chapter only when they include relevant information on York and Northumbria, but they were much more extensive and important. 'A recurrent problem for historians (not always recognized) is that the only letters to survive in any number from the two decades 790–810 are Alcuin's—in the years 795–802, indeed, almost a letter a fortnight.' Two at least of the surviving collections of letters were probably compiled at, or kept at, York. The letters were edited by Dümmler (1895), and there is a selection in English translation by Allott (1974).[59]

It should be noted that uncertainty surrounds the chronology of Alcuin's life and writings. His year of birth is unknown—it is often assumed to have been sometime in the 730s, or as Bullough prefers, *c.*740; a modern attempt to arrive at a date in the late 740s is in his view 'demonstrably mistaken'. His departure from York for the Frankish court is usually dated 781/2, though Bullough opts for 786; and the date of composition, or at least revision, of the York Poem, is equally controversial. (It is usually dated to *c.*780–2, a dating accepted by Garrison, though Bullough prefers the late 770s and Godman a much later date, perhaps as late as 792/3.)

59. Quotation: D. A. Bullough, 'Was there a Carolingian anti-war movement?', *Early Medieval Europe*, 12 (2003), 373. Letter collections at York: Bullough, *Alcuin*, 85, 88, 93, 101–3. Ernst Dümmler, ed., *Epistolae Karolini Aevi*, Monumenta Germaniae Historica, Epistolae 6 (Berlin, 1895), 1–49.

3

Anglo-Scandinavian York

866–1066

'Viking' York, or *Jorvik*, to use its contemporary name, has long attracted attention.[1] Whereas 'Anglian' York barely registered in the popular image of York's medieval past before the Fishergate excavations of 1985–6, it did not need the equivalent (and more spectacular) Coppergate excavations to remind citizens that theirs had been a great Viking city (Map 3). 'Danish coins struck at York' were collected and discussed in the eighteenth century; and a century ago W. G. Collingwood was studying the city's Anglo-Danish sculpture, while George Benson was recovering important finds from Viking buildings in Coppergate and High Ousegate. By the time that Waterman, Cramp, and Radley published their surveys of Viking York, such finds were abundant. However, a turning point was reached in 1972–3 with the excavations at 6–8 Pavement, which demonstrated that much Anglo-Scandinavian organic material was preserved in the damp and anaerobic soil, material which would long before have turned to dust on dry sites. That lesson was reinforced by Richard Hall's much larger excavation at nearby 16–22 Coppergate (1976–81), and this chapter leans heavily on its results.[2]

1. Early accounts of the conquest of 866–7 do not call the invaders Vikings, but 'heathens' or 'pagans'. Most modern discussions of Anglo-Scandinavian archaeology in York called them Danes until D. M. Waterman, 'Late Saxon, Viking and early medieval finds from York', *Archaeologia*, 97 (1959), 59–105. Nevertheless, 'Viking' is now a useful shorthand term which avoids the dubious distinction still often made between 'Danes' after 866 and 'Norwegians' from *c.*914. Cf. G. Fellows Jensen, 'To divide the Danes from the Norwegians', *Nomina*, 11 (1987), 35–60.
2. Waterman, 'Late Saxon, Viking and early medieval finds from York'; Rosemary Cramp, *Anglian and Viking York*, BP 33 (York, 1967); Jeffrey Radley, 'Economic aspects of Anglo-Danish York', *Med Arch*, 15 (1971), 37–57. Coppergate: Richard Hall, *The Viking Dig* (London, 1984); Richard Hall, *English Heritage Book of Viking Age York* (London, 1994); R. A. Hall et al., *Aspects of Anglo-Scandinavian York*, AY 8/4 (2004); and others as cited below.

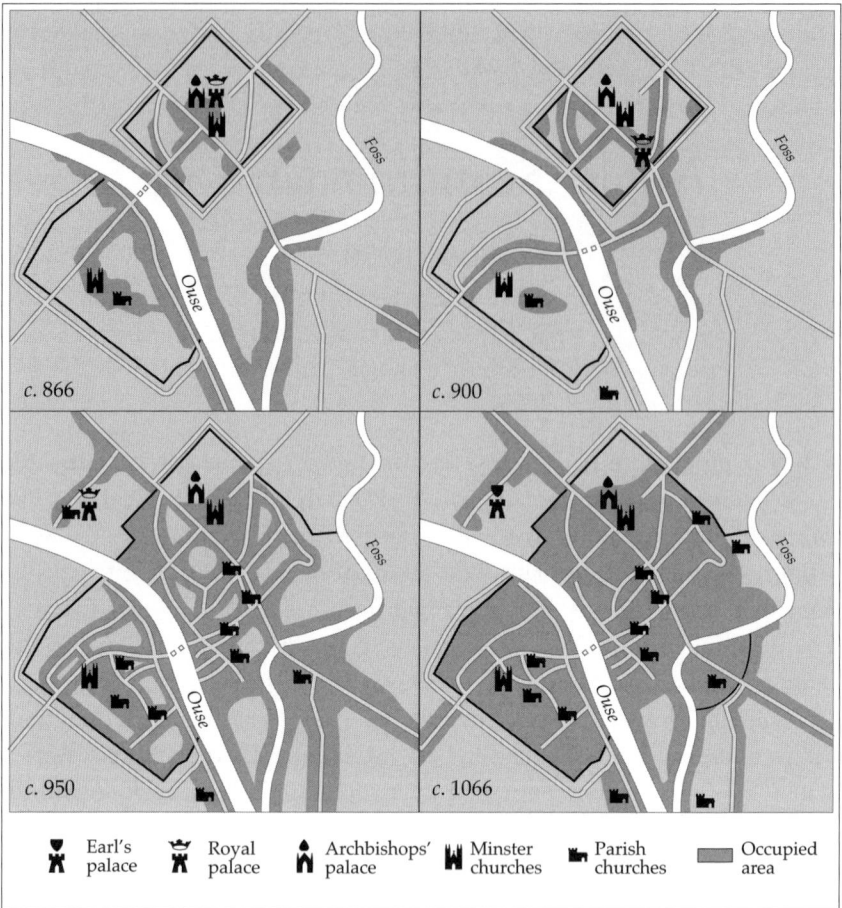

Map 3. Anglo-Scandinavian York, *c.*866–1066

A hypothetical reconstruction of the city's development between the Danish and Norman conquests, based on archaeological research to 1994. The picture has not been greatly altered by more recent work except in the Hungate area.

Source: Richard Hall, *Viking Age York* (B. T. Batsford/English Heritage, 1994), 32. Reproduced by permission of Dr Ailsa Mainman and the York Archaeological Trust.

A context is needed, however, before the archaeological evidence is considered—the relatively well-documented capture of York in 866–7. A 'Great Army' (*micel here*) landed in England in 865 under the command of the brothers Ivarr, Halfdan, and Ubba. After overwintering in East Anglia, they invaded Northumbria, where King Osberht had been supplanted by Ælle, and civil war was raging. Possibly the three brothers had prior knowledge of a kingdom ripe for conquest (the later story that their motive was revenge for Ælle's having killed their father Ragnall in a snake-pit in York is colourful fiction). The Great Army captured York on 1 November 866 and advanced to the Tyne, only to find that the rival kings had joined forces against them. Osberht and Ælle 'attacked the [Viking] enemy in York, and broke into the city', probably on 21 March 867, but both were killed together with many of their followers, 'and the survivors made peace with the enemy'.[3]

Doubtless the two battles for York entailed destruction and humiliation, and one price of peace may have been slaves: Ivarr is recorded as having taken many English slaves to Dublin in 871. Symeon of Durham related that the Great Army 'destroyed monasteries and churches far and wide with sword and fire', but this is a much later account which in any case seems to relate to their advance from York to the Tyne. Had they left the city a blackened shell, it is hard to see why they should have resettled it so quickly; and furthermore no destruction layer has been found. Disruption is certainly implied by two coin hoards hidden near Bootham Bar, the dating of which suggests deposit by townspeople fleeing the invaders, and by a plausible tradition that Archbishop Wulfhere fled York to take refuge at Addingham in Wharfedale.[4]

Disruption may have been only short term, given the evidence of thriving trade and crafts before 900. In the early years of the Jorvik Viking Centre (opened in 1984 on the site of the Coppergate excavation), visitors were greeted by a display panel on 'rape and pillage', which was later—significantly—removed. The jury is still out, however, on the scale of the initial destruction. Lapidge's re-examination of English manuscripts between the 830s and 880s convinced him that there could have been no wholesale destruction of York's cathedral library, but Mary Garrison is almost sure that there was, and Campbell is equally sure that Viking destruction of documents and libraries was widespread in the north.[5]

As with Northumbria before 866, so with the two centuries following, the survival and interpretation of sources are crucial. No original chronicle

3. Translation from *EHD*, I, 191; cf. *AY* 1, 71; David Rollason, *Northumbria, 500–1100: Creation and Destruction of a Kingdom* (Cambridge, 2003), 212. For the snake-pit legend, see A. P. Smyth, *Scandinavian Kings in the British Isles 850–880* (Oxford, 1977), ch. III.
4. Smyth, *Scandinavian Kings*, 154, 182; *RCHMY* IV, p. xxx; S. D. Keynes, 'The additions in Old English', in Nicolas Barker, ed., *The York Gospels*, Roxburghe Club (London, 1986), 89; David Rollason, ed., *Symeon of Durham: Libellus de Exordio . . . Dunelmensis Ecclesie*, OMT (Oxford, 2000), 96–7.
5. 'Rape and pillage': J. L. Nelson, 'England and the Continent in the ninth century: II', *TR Hist S*, 6th ser., 13 (2003), 4 n. 14. Destruction of books and charters: M. Lapidge, *Anglo-Latin Literature 600–899* (London, 1996), 426–32; Nelson, 'England and the Continent in the ninth century: II', 7; Mary Garrison, 'The library of Alcuin's York', in Richard Gameson, ed., *The Cambridge History of the Book in Britain* (Cambridge, 2012), I, 635.

compiled in the Anglo-Scandinavian north seems to survive, but fortunately
(as with the earlier Northern Annals) there are later sources preserving valuable material. The group of seven manuscripts known, misleadingly, as '*the
Anglo-Saxon Chronicle*' includes three versions (MSS D, E, and F) apparently incorporating material from a lost 'Northern Recension'. Whitelock
believed that the common source from which D and E derived was compiled in York, though their latest editors are less certain of that. More recently,
Pauline Stafford has suggested that it was produced by or for the archbishop
of York some time after 956.[6] Once more, an invaluable complement to
written evidence is that of coins, fortunately the subject of much recent
research, including a masterly survey of York's Viking coinage by Mark
Blackburn. There is also the evidence of inscriptions; of the names of the
city's streets and lanes; of the known personal names of citizens and moneyers; and of all the evidence usually grouped as 'archaeological'.[7]

Yet the most intriguing problem about *Jorvik*, as about *Eoforwic*, remains
unsolved. We know something of the Viking kings and of daily life under them,
but we are ignorant of the ethnic composition of their subjects. The proportion
of Scandinavian personal and place names suggests that immigration was considerable; and the old orthodoxy, voiced by Sir Frank Stenton, was that such
indicators throughout the Danelaw (roughly eastern England between Watling
Street and the Tees) were best explained by 'an intensive Danish colonization'.[8]
However, since those words were first penned in the 1940s, Peter Sawyer has
argued that Viking armies were numbered in hundreds rather than thousands,
though if so—his critics retorted—an initial conquest by small numbers must
have been followed by a larger, secondary migration. Does any evidence from
the York area help to resolve this problem?

Research on indicators like DNA and blood groups has not yet settled
the issue either way. Oppenheimer's survey of male gene type markers suggests a 'Viking' intrusion of about 5.5 per cent to the population of the

6. Dorothy Whitelock et al., *The Anglo-Saxon Chronicle: A Revised Translation* (London, 1961), p. xiv;
Cubbin, ed., pp. lvi–lxvi; Irvine, ed., pp. xxxvi–lxxv; AY 1, 19; Pauline Stafford, 'The Anglo-Saxon
chronicles, identity and the making of England', *Haskins Society Journal*, 19 (2008), 42–9.
7. Mark Blackburn, 'The coinage of Scandinavian York', in AY 8/4 (2004), 325–49, repr. in his
Viking Coinage and Currency in the British Isles (London, 2011), 281–307; Gillian Fellows Jensen,
'The Anglo-Scandinavian street-names of York', in AY 8/4, 357–71.
8. F. M. Stenton, *Anglo-Saxon England* (Oxford, 3rd edn 1971), 521, but the words appear in earlier editions. The Danelaw is a useful but imprecise term, first used in legal compilations of
Archbishop Wulfstan II of York to distinguish areas under Danish law (*Dena lage*) from those
under English law, but now conveniently extended to cover all areas under Danish control
between 865 and 954.

British Isles, though the proportion rises to a maximum 'in York and around the Wash'. Another approach is to measure skull types: a recent comparative study of burials in York and Wharram Percy found the proportion of crania of Norwegian type greater in the city than in the Wolds village—perhaps because York was more heavily settled by Vikings than its hinterland? Other indicators, such as place names and personal names, may reflect 'acculturation' by natives to Scandinavian culture, rather than population replacement. Even the names of the three founders of St Mary's church, Castlegate, recorded on its dedication stone, can be regarded by some experts as all Old Norse, while others are sceptical. By 1066 many York townspeople had undoubtedly Scandinavian names, but it could well be that Northumbrians were simply giving their children fashionable Norse names (much as their descendants adopted French names after 1066).[9]

It is certainly noteworthy that little of the abundant evidence from *Jorvik* is specifically 'Viking' in style. The timbered houses are paralleled in contemporary English towns and display no obviously Scandinavian characteristics; 'purely Scandinavian artefacts seem to be few in number'; and textiles manufactured in the city are much closer to earlier Anglo-Saxon fabrics than to contemporary Scandinavian ones.[10] And yet, whatever the scale of the Norse settlement in York, many of the conquered Northumbrians quickly came to identify with their Danish conquerors against West Saxon expansion from the south.

The Viking kingdom: *c.*867–954

The Great Army, having kept its grip on York in 867, installed a puppet-king, moved to Nottingham, returned to York in 868–9, and then went back south to conquer East Anglia. Ivarr, meanwhile, who may have come to

9. Stephen Oppenheimer, *The Origins of the British* (London, pb edn 2007), 444–63 (quotation from p. 455); Simon Mays, 'Wharram Percy: The skeletons', *Current Archaeology*, 193 (2004), 48. St Mary's dedication names: the extensive literature includes James Lang, *Corpus of Anglo-Saxon Stone Sculpture*, III: *York and Eastern Yorkshire* (Oxford, 1991), 99–101, and refs there cited; AY 1, 176–7; AY 8/4, 353–5.

10. AY 17/5, 418; AY 17/11, 1859; R. A. Hall, 'Anglo-Scandinavian attitudes: Archaeological ambiguities in late ninth- to mid-eleventh-century York', in D. M. Hadley and J. D. Richards, eds, *Cultures in Contact: Scandinavian Settlement in England in the Ninth and Tenth Centuries* (Turnhout, 2000), 315; D. M. Hadley, *The Vikings in England: Settlement, Society and Culture* (Manchester, 2006), 152.

York from raiding Ireland, probably returned there. Indeed, Alfred Smyth has shown that Ivarr's family ruled both Dublin and York, together or separately, for much of the next eighty years. Ivarr was very likely the same man who in 873 was called in the Annals of Ulster 'King of the Norsemen of all Ireland and Britain', while some later kings of both cities were called in Irish sources 'grandsons of Ivarr'. There was a regular route across the Irish Sea, up the Ribble or Mersey, and over the Pennines to York, though Smyth argues that the more regular route was via the Clyde-Forth isthmus. The later-recorded name of a York quay, *Divelinestaynes*, 'Dublin Stones', may well be a reminder of trade between the two cities.[11]

With the Great Army away after 869, 'the Northumbrians' rebelled in 872, expelling both their puppet king and also Archbishop Wulfhere, who had clearly returned from Addingham to make his peace with the Vikings: for when part of the Army returned to York in 873, they reinstated Wulfhere. It is even possible that the archbishop was in charge of the city under the conquerors, and this raises important questions. Was there an entity we can call 'the Viking kingdom of York', was York its capital, how far and how quickly did the Vikings reach an accommodation with the Church, and indeed were the archbishops the real rulers of the city?

The usual view of the period from the 870s to the 950s is that there was indeed a 'Viking kingdom' centred on York, with known borders and with an organized administration. The undoubted facts that York grew rapidly and spectacularly by around 900, and that regal coins were again struck there from the 890s, have been read as evidence for the Viking kings as sophisticated rulers who rapidly adopted literacy, Christianity, and advanced methods of government. However, David Rollason has recently presented an alternative picture, both in his history of Northumbria and in a survey of the historical sources for Anglo-Scandinavian York. Aristocrats and churchmen were, in his view, the dominant figures under the Viking kings, who may not have ruled from York or even resided there. We have seen his suggestion that *Eoforwic* could have been essentially an ecclesiastical city ruled by its archbishops, and his view of *Jorvik* is similar.[12]

11. A. P. Smyth, *Scandinavian York and Dublin* (Dublin, 1975), I, 22, 35–6; Smyth, *Scandinavian Kings*, 234–5; D. M. Palliser, 'The medieval street-names of York', *YH*, 2 (1978), 9; biography of Ivarr: *ODNB*; Fiona Edmonds, 'Barrier or unifying feature?', in John Blair, ed., *Waterways and Canal-Building in Medieval England* (Oxford, 2007), 30–1, 33.
12. Rollason, *Northumbria, 500–1100*, 205, 207; Rollason, 'Anglo-Scandinavian York: The evidence of historical sources', in AY 8/4 (2004), 305–24; Blackburn, 'The coinage of Scandinavian York', 328–32 (= reprint 2011, 284–8).

Certainly the kings must have ruled with the support of the Church as well as their leading aristocrats: how else can we explain the two periods in the 920s when regal coinage gave way to St Peter pennies, or the fact that in 947 it was Archbishop Wulfstan and 'all the Northumbrian council [*witan*]' who negotiated with the English King Eadred? And there is no doubt that Viking royal rule was disrupted and intermittent, with no established line of succession. Nevertheless, the clear evidence of coins is against minimizing royal power. 'The York regal coinage is remarkable . . . for its size, complexity and sophistication', and it was intended to emphasize royal power, for over 90 per cent of the York coins prominently display the king's name.[13]

It is also necessary for the context of the Viking kingdom to appreciate that the conquest of 866–7 was not a straight takeover of Northumbria, but a shattering of that kingdom into a series of 'successor states', a dismembering which opened a way for the growing powers of England and Scotland to swallow them piecemeal over the following centuries. The Viking 'York' kingdom did not include ancient Bernicia north of the Tees, where two separate but linked powers emerged: the ecclesiastical liberty of St Cuthbert between Tees and Tyne, and between Tyne and Forth at least three English kings 'whose identity beyond their names is utterly obscure', followed after 900 by a dynasty of earls ruling from Bamburgh. Meanwhile Hiberno-Norse Vikings settled much of Lancashire and southern Cumbria around 900, and north of them British rulers calling themselves kings of Cumbria held sway.[14]

The evidence for the rump 'York' kingdom itself is thin, and much of it is not directly relevant to a history of the city; indeed, the sources 'never use the expression "kingdom of York" in connection with the Viking kings'. We know, first of all, that from the mid-870s the Vikings abandoned puppet kings for direct rule. In 876 Halfdan, leading half of the Great Army, 'shared out the land of the Northumbrians', while in 877 other Vikings settled in eastern Mercia and based themselves in and around the 'Five Boroughs' of Derby, Leicester, Lincoln, Nottingham, and Stamford. This territory was sometimes controlled by the same Viking kings who held sway in York, and

13. *EHD*, I, 222; Cubbin, ed., 44; quotation: Blackburn, 'The coinage of Scandinavian York', 329. Rollason and Blackburn have disagreed over whether the St Peter issues were archiepiscopal or regal: AY 8/4, 313, 333; Blackburn, *Viking Coinage and Currency*, 33.
14. N. J. Higham, *The Kingdom of Northumbria AD 350–1100* (Stroud, 1993), 181, 183; Rollason, *Northumbria, 500–1100*, 211–55.

that is presumably why in 894 Alfred of Wessex sent an ambassador to York to negotiate with King Guthfrith (Guthred) over land west of Stamford. Guthfrith is the first of the Viking rulers with a definite York connection, since the same source notes that in 895 he was buried there 'in the high church [*basilica summa*]'.[15]

Of Guthfrith's successors, some are merely names, known almost entirely from their coins. The Vikings had come from homelands without coinage, and coins from the 860s to the 890s found in Viking Northumbria came from mints in southern England or Francia; but from the 890s there began the series of often fine coins minted at York both by kings and archbishops; the city thus resumed its position as the only mint north of the Humber. Indeed, whether or not the kings after Guthfrith often resided in York, it must have been perceived as the central place of their kingdom. Why else would the chronicle known as the Mercian Register have called their subjects the *Eoforwicyngas*? For the years around 900, the best evidence for the wealth available to York's kings is the huge hoard from Cuerdale, just within Danish Northumbria, and apparently deposited about 905. It comprised some 8,600 silver pieces in coin, hack silver, and bullion, including over 3,000 freshly minted coins struck at *Jorvik* for Kings Sigfrith and Cnut. It was a mixed hoard from York and Dublin, and could represent treasure accumulated by Norsemen expelled from Dublin about 902 and in close touch with York. Certainly it was deposited on the bank of the river Ribble, which formed part of the overland route between the two Viking cities.[16]

Soon after 910, and probably by 914, York was seized by an army from Ireland under Ivarr's grandson, Ragnall. Numismatic evidence, however, suggests a period of blurred or shared rule: York coins from about 910 replace

15. *EHD*, I, 195; A. Campbell, ed., *The Chronicle of Æthelweard* (London, 1962), 51; AY 1, 173; quotation: Rollason, *Northumbria, 500–1100*, 215.

16. P. Grierson and M. Blackburn, *Medieval European Coinage* (Cambridge, 1986), I, 318–20; C. E. Blunt, B. H. I. H. Stewart, and C. S. S. Lyon, *Coinage in Tenth-Century England* (Oxford, 1989), ch. 4; Blackburn, *Viking Coinage and Currency*, 33. *Eoforwicyngas*: Cubbin, ed., 40. Cuerdale hoard: Blunt, Stewart, and Lyon, *Coinage in Tenth-Century England*, 25–6, 33–5, 102–3, 248; J. Graham-Campbell, ed., *Viking Treasures from the North West: The Cuerdale Hoard and its Context* (Liverpool, 1992). (The 'Quentovic' coins in the hoard, with the name of King Cnut, persuaded Blunt and Stenton that Cnut had once ruled a cross-channel empire based on York and Quentovic, but that is now known to be erroneous: Blackburn, *Viking Coinage and Currency*, 11.) The definitive account of the hoard, published after this chapter was written, is J. Graham-Campbell et al., *The Cuerdale Hoard and Related Viking-Age Silver and Gold from Britain and Ireland in the British Museum* (London, 2011).

the king's name by that of St Peter; then Ragnall briefly issued coins in his own name; but from *c*.921 to 927 there was a second phase of St Peter coins, but this time with a sword and, in some cases, the pagan hammer of Thor.[17]

By then, however, the West Saxon rulers were pushing north in an attempt to conquer Viking Northumbria. In 907 Alfred's daughter Æthelflæd advanced to the border, occupying Chester, which was a key strongpoint between York and Dublin. In 918 she was allegedly promised that 'the people of York' (*Eoforwicyngas*) would accept her rule, but she died that year before any such agreement could take effect. In 920, according to the *Chronicle*, Ragnall accepted the overlordship of King Edward of Wessex, though that may be a propagandist reading of a more equal treaty between the two.[18] In 926 Ragnall's successor Sihtric I, who seems to have expanded his power as far south as Tamworth, certainly made a treaty with Edward's successor Athelstan; but on Sihtric's death in 927 Athelstan promptly seized his kingdom and, according to a later source, destroyed a Danish fortress (*castrum*) at York. He followed this up by meeting several northern and western kings later that year at Eamont Bridge (near Penrith), where he was acknowledged as overlord of all Britain. Significantly, at least two hoards of mixed Viking and English coins were deposited near York in, or just after, 927. One—the Vale of York Hoard, found in 2007—is the largest Viking hoard found in England since Cuerdale in 1840. Besides jewellery and silver bullion, it includes 617 coins, mainly of Edward and Athelstan, but also twenty-two York St Peter issues. Twenty-two others, also struck at York, are of a rare type issued by Athelstan: they depict a building, possibly a church, and were apparently issued to commemorate his conquest of Sihtric's kingdom. One of the latest is another coin of Athelstan, issued in 927–8, and inscribed REX TOTIUS BRITANNIAE (king of all Britain).[19]

17. Grierson and Blackburn, *Medieval European Coinage 1*, 322–3, 616; Blunt, Stewart, and Lyon, *Coinage in Tenth-Century England*, 103–6; AY 18/1, 34–7; C. S. S. Lyon, 'The coinage of Edward the Elder', in N. J. Higham and D. H. Hill, eds, *Edward the Elder 899–924* (London, 2001), 73. The traditional date of 919 for Ragnall's seizure of York is probably too late: D. M. Hadley, *The Northern Danelaw* (London, 2000), 12; B. E. Crawford, 'The Vikings', in W. Davies, ed., *From the Vikings to the Normans* (Oxford, 2003), 63.
18. *EHD*, I, 216; Cubbin, ed., 40; Hadley, *The Northern Danelaw*, 11; M. R. Davidson, 'The (non) submission of the northern kings in 920', in Higham and Hill, eds, *Edward the Elder*, 200–11.
19. Gareth Williams, 'The coins from the Vale of York Viking hoard: Preliminary report', *BNJ*, 78 (2008), 228–34; Gareth Williams and Barry Ager, *The Vale of York Hoard* (London, 2010).

927 was certainly a turning point in the long story of York:

> For the first time since the withdrawal of Roman power, it had fallen under the actual control of a ruler of southern Britain, who was linked by marriages and alliances with the principal continental states. The links which bound York and Northumbria to the south were the links which bound their new Anglo-Scandinavian society to the Christian civilization of western Europe. While he was at York in 936, for example, Athelstan received a Frankish embassy inviting Louis, son of Charles the Simple, to return as king of the Franks.[20]

In other words, Athelstan not only struck coins at York but held court there. The Frankish embassy is attested by a near-contemporary writer, while a later chronicler also has Athelstan have Norwegian envoys 'royally entertained' in York.[21] His power was further demonstrated in 934, when he led an army north to ravage Scotland, and again in 937, when he crushed an invading force of Scots, Britons, and Norse at an unidentified place called *Brunanburh*, possibly Bromborough in Cheshire, though in neither campaign is it clear how far his York base was involved.

927 was not quite the end of northern independence. After Athelstan's death (939) there followed a series of power struggles between English and Viking rulers, poorly documented but now clarified by studies of the coinage.[22] In 939 York was seized by Olaf Guthfrithson, king of Dublin, who then took over the Five Boroughs to the south. After Olaf's death (941) the English king seized the Five Boroughs and then (in 944) York. His successor Eadred (946–55) was at first accepted in York, but in 947/8 Archbishop Wulfstan I and the northern nobles turned to Erik 'Bloodaxe', exiled king of Norway. Eadred drove out Erik, but in 952 the men of York submitted to Olaf Sihtricsson, only to expel him in 952 and return to Erik. Wulfstan may have been the instigator again; certainly, when he was unwise enough to travel south, probably in 953, Eadred imprisoned him, and Wulfstan was never able to return north, though he remained titular archbishop until his death.

---

20. A. G. Dickens, 'York before the Norman Conquest', in *VCHY*, 12.
21. AY 1, 166–7; AY 8/4, 312; Patrick Wormald, *The Making of English Law: King Alfred to the Twelfth Century*, I: *Legislation and its Limits* (Oxford, 1999), 432; J. R. Maddicott, *The Origins of the English Parliament, 924–1327* (Oxford, 2010), 17.
22. Especially Blunt, Stewart, and Lyon, *Coinage in Tenth-Century England*, 211–34 (with table on p. 220); Blackburn, 'Coinage of Scandinavian York', 282, 335–8 (= reprint 2011, 282, 291–4).

For this last Viking reign at York, there survives a thirteenth-century saga which may incorporate a genuine account of Erik's court by his enemy Egil Skalagrimsson. Egil described himself as brought before Erik in his hall

> Where the king kept his people cowed
> under the helmet of his terror.
> From his seat at York he ruled unflinchingly
> over a dank land.[23]

But his rule by terror—if such it was—did not last. Eadred invaded Northumbria again, probably in 954; Erik was driven to the border of his kingdom, at Stainmore, where he died in battle.

Well before 954, the Dublin–York axis had been weakened by the growing power of the English kings in north-west England, and especially their erection of a major port and mint at Chester. By Athelstan's reign, much Chester pottery was exported to Dublin, and Irish coin hoards attest 'that Chester, ahead of York, was the principal trading partner for tenth-century Dublin'. After 954 the political links between Dublin and York were snapped, and what trade continued between them was probably at one remove. The discovery at Coppergate of a lead customs tag produced at the Chester mint in Eadwig's reign (955–9) may suggest York imports of Irish goods via Chester, though this interpretation has been queried.[24]

From 954 onwards, English kings were realistic enough to accept that Northumbria could not be controlled directly from Winchester or London, and they installed a succession of earls as their viceroys, sometimes one each for Bernicia (the earls of the house of Bamburgh, of royal descent) and for Deira (York), and at other times a single earl for both. Northern separatism, however, was slow to vanish. Some charters of King Eadred distinguish between 'Anglo-Saxons' and 'Northumbrians', the former apparently including the 'Danes' of the Five Boroughs and East Anglia but not those of York. And many Northumbrians remained ready to rebel against West Saxon rule for another century.[25]

---

23. Translation from Richard Fletcher, *Bloodfeud* (London, 2002), 42.

24. A. T. Thacker, 'Early medieval Chester, 400–1230', in *VCH Cheshire*, V pt. 1 (2003), 21; AY 8/4, 340; David Griffiths, 'Exchange, trade, and urbanization', in Davies, ed., *From the Vikings to the Normans*, 102.

25. *EHD*, I, no. 105; Simon Keynes, 'King Alfred and the Mercians', in M. A. S. Blackburn and D. N. Dumville, eds, *Kings, Currency and Alliances* (Woodbridge, 1998), 38–9 and n. 167.

York under English and Danish earls: 954–1066

There is much more to be said of Viking York, especially from the recent massive increase in archaeological information. Yet much of that evidence is not closely datable either side of 954, while no York street names (almost all of them Norse) are recorded before 1086. It therefore makes sense to continue the narrative to 1066 before turning to the city's society, economy, and culture over the two centuries 866–1066 as a whole. That does not mean, however, that the conquest of the Viking kingdom and its incorporation into a new *Englalond* was unimportant. Eadred (946–55) and his successors, especially Edgar (957/9–75), intended from the start to impose effective rule on their new northern subjects. The first indication was that when Archbishop Wulfstan I died in 956, already stripped of real power, the West Saxon kings appointed successors from among their own subjects, who were installed at York while retaining their southern bishoprics—Osketel of Dorchester (956–71) and then three successive bishops of Worcester (971–1023), thus helping 'to peg York's loyalties firmly to the south'. Indeed, it is likely that these prelates deliberately manipulated the past to encourage 'a remaking of the Northumbrians as English', by sponsoring the Northern Recension of the *Anglo-Saxon Chronicle*: it seems to have been intended as consciously 'assimilationist history'.[26]

The next step was to ensure the loyalty of the northern earls. King Erik had been betrayed in 954 by Earl Oswulf of Bamburgh, whom King Eadred had rewarded by making him earl of all Northumbria. King Edgar, however, clearly found his reliability suspect. In 963 or 966, in an important but ill-recorded episode, Edgar held court at York, the first English king to do so since Athelstan. At the same time he replaced Oswulf by the more trusted Oslac (963–c.975), and made generous grants of Yorkshire estates to local supporters.[27] After that, we know little of the Yorkshire earls between about 963 and 1006, except that Earl Thored is said to have despoiled York Minster

26. Fletcher, *Bloodfeud*, 43, 69; Stafford, 'The Anglo-Saxon chronicles', 42–9. Wulfstan II is usually said to have resigned Worcester in 1016, but there are grounds to think that he held both sees until he died in 1023: Patrick Wormald, 'Archbishop Wulfstan: Eleventh-century state-builder', in Matthew Townend, ed., *Wulfstan, Archbishop of York* (Turnhout, 2004), 12.
27. Oswulf's deposition is usually dated to 966, but Simon Keynes argues for c.963, and for the 'unusually large meeting' of royal councillors as held probably at York: 'The additions in Old English', 87n. Cf. Wormald, *Making of English Law*, I, 442n.; Maddicott, *Origins of the English Parliament*, 26 and n.

of its estates around the 980s. We do not even know whether they based their rule in York, as later earls did. Nevertheless, it is clear that Edgar kept a tight grip on Northumbria and had ambitions beyond it. That was signalled in 973, when he was crowned at Bath in a delayed ceremony (attended by Archbishop Oswald of York) and then led an army to Chester, where six or more British kings and princes promised to serve him.[28] And it can be no coincidence that in the same year he initiated a major reform of the coinage, uniformly struck at numerous mints of which York was the only one north of Humber. The coins, with his title *rex Anglorum*, 'King of the English', circulated in Northumbria as in all other parts of his kingdom.

In or before 1006 King Æthelred II reunited the Northumbrian earldom (which had been divided again) under Uhtred of the house of Bamburgh, who that year defeated an invading Scottish force at Durham. Before long, however, Northumbria and all England faced a more formidable opponent, Swein of Denmark, who invaded in 1013, basing himself at Gainsborough on the Trent. He was readily accepted as king by the leaders of Yorkshire and the Five Boroughs, but died on 3 February 1014 just as his rule was being accepted by the other English. He was buried in York, presumably in the Minster and if so, surely with the consent of the archbishop. It is usually accepted that Swein had died at Gainsborough, so why was he buried in York?

A plausible case has been recently made for the context in terms of the actions of Archbishop Wulfstan II (1002–23). He had been trying for some time to reform the English state in the face of the renewed Viking attacks, and his 'Sermon to the English' was delivered in 1014. Jonathan Wilcox has suggested that it was delivered at York on 16 February at a meeting of the national council or *witan*. If so, it follows that the council had already assembled there before Swein's unexpected death; that it met to acknowledge—or even crown—Swein there; and that his burial there may imply that he had already reached the city before he died. When the plans had to change, it was Wulfstan who negotiated the return of King Æthelred; and after Æthelred's death he worked with Swein's son Cnut for reconciliation between Danes and English. He can be seen as an 'eleventh-century state-builder', one who helped to re-establish an enduring English kingdom after its near-collapse in 1013–16.[29]

This, however, is to anticipate. When Cnut conquered England rapidly and ruthlessly in 1015–16, Northumbria was destabilized. Firstly, the two 'chief

28. *HCY*, I, 436–8, for Oswald's attendance at Bath.
29. Townend, ed., *Wulfstan, Archbishop of York*, esp. Wormald, 'Archbishop Wulfstan', 9–25, and J. Wilcox, 'Wulfstan's *Sermo Lupi ad Anglos* as political performance', 380–3.

thegns belonging to the Seven Boroughs' (which probably included York) were murdered during a meeting of the *witan* in Oxford.[30] Secondly, when Cnut invaded and advanced rapidly on York, Earl Uhtred decided to submit, and came to Cnut under promise of safe conduct at a place near the city called *Wiheal* (probably Wighill in the Ainsty). There he and his retinue were massacred in Cnut's presence, presumably with his connivance, though it was apparently part of a vendetta between Uhtred and a rival Northumbrian called Thurbrand. Thus began what Stenton called 'the most remarkable private feud in English history', a blood feud lasting until the 1070s. Its grim unfolding took place elsewhere in Yorkshire and need not detain us, especially as it has been superbly retold by Fletcher, and it led to no immediate crisis in the York area. Cnut replaced the murdered Uhtred by his own brother-in-law Erik of Hlathir, and then by Siward, probably also a Dane, and the first earl firmly recorded as residing in York.[31]

By then York was undoubtedly a centre for secular administration under the English kings. The Midlands and north were being reorganized into shires on the West Saxon model, and though Yorkshire is not recorded until about 1050, it is likely to have been created by around 1000. However, its enormous size suggests that before 1066 it was primarily a military zone under the earl, rather than a smaller unit under a sheriff (shire reeve) on the southern pattern. And the scanty evidence suggests that Siward's earldom consisted primarily of a greater Yorkshire, the historic county together with what became south Lancashire, and (from 1041) Durham and Northumberland.[32]

Siward's power certainly seems to have been centred on York. Soon after Duncan, king of Scots, was murdered (1040), his heir—and Siward's nephew—Malcolm took refuge at the earl's court in York, and it was from there that Siward mounted a successful invasion to put Malcolm on the throne in 1054. We can even guess the location of his court, thanks to an entry in the York-connected version of the Anglo-Saxon Chronicle:

> In this year [1055] Earl Siward died at York, and he lies at *Galmaho* [*Galmanho*] in the minster which he himself had built and consecrated in the name of God and Olaf.[33]

30. *EHD*, I, 247 and n.
31. Stenton, *Anglo-Saxon England*, 390n.; Fletcher, *Bloodfeud*, *passim*.
32. Stephen Baxter, 'Edward the Confessor and the succession question', in Richard Mortimer, ed., *Edward the Confessor* (Woodbridge, 2009), maps between pp. 116–17.
33. AY 1, 175.

Galmanho was near Bootham Bar, an early name for which was *Galmanlith*, and Siward's minster was almost certainly the predecessor of St Olave's church and St Mary's Abbey. Later tradition assigned the name Earlsburgh to the St Olave's/St Mary's precinct, perhaps reflecting a genuine memory of where Siward's palace had stood.[34]

On Siward's death, King Edward (1042–66) gave the earldom to Tostig Godwinsson, the first southerner appointed to the office. He proved unpopular with the northern nobles, two of whom he had killed in his York hall in 1063; and in 1065 his rule provoked a revolt which precipitated a national crisis. On 3 October, in Tostig's absence, three thegns led an armed band to York, killed many of his retainers, and plundered his treasury. That triggered a rising of Mercians as well as Northumbrians, a collapse of royal resistance, and the installation of the Mercian Morcar as earl. Tostig fled abroad; the king died on 5 January 1066, his end apparently hastened by the humiliation; and Tostig's brother Harold seized the throne. That, in turn, provoked coordinated plans by Tostig, King Harald of Norway, and Duke William of Normandy to invade England.

In September, Norwegian forces under Harald and Tostig sailed up the Humber and Ouse, disembarked at Riccall, and marched on York. On the 20th they crushed Northumbrian and Mercian forces at Fulford and entered the city without resistance: twelve male skeletons with weapon injuries, all buried in one York churchyard near the battle site in the later eleventh century, may have been casualties from Fulford.[35] However, the English King Harold moved rapidly north, passed through York on the 25th to take the Norwegians by surprise, and decisively routed the invaders at Stamford Bridge seven miles east. Among the slain were Tostig and King Harald, and the surviving Norwegians fled. Yet, while Harold was probably still resting his army in York, he learned of Duke William's descent on Sussex, and events moved rapidly to Harold's defeat and death near Hastings on 14 October.

Two lessons can be drawn from the Northumbrian revolt against Tostig. One is an instance of the law of unintended consequences: the crises and battles of 1066 'stemmed directly from the turbulent events which started to

34. Francis Drake, *Eboracum* (London, 1736), 256–8, 579; J. H. Harvey, 'A Bootham mystery— Galmanho, Kenningdike, Werkdike', *YH*, 1 (1976), 13–17; *RCHMY* IV, p. xxxv.

35. C. Daniell, 'Battle and trial: Weapon injury burials at St Andrew's church, Fishergate, York', *Med Arch*, 45 (2001), 220–3. Fletcher points out that York evidently surrendered on terms, and that the citizens were apparently willing to march south with the invaders: *Bloodfeud*, 167.

unfold at York on 3 October 1065'. The Northerners had found Tostig's rule oppressive: they were soon to find the yoke of the new Norman king much heavier. The other is that the Northumbrian thegns were seeking reform, not secession. Their revolt did not 'seriously threaten the integrity of the English state. Few English kings frequently visited the north, but their northern rule was not marginal.'[36]

Life in *Jorvik*: Topography and economy

The first point to make about *Jorvik* is its size and wealth. The conquest of 866–7 was followed by a boom; like Dublin, York was one of the most success-ful urban enterprises of the Viking period. *Eoforwic* had been a polyfocal place, with scattered zones of occupation and little settlement between them. Under the Danes, not only were the fortress and *colonia* more densely peopled, but a large commercial zone was developed between the fortress and the two rivers. And the key turning point seems to have been not immediately after 867, but about thirty years later. It was around 900–10 that Coppergate and the houses along it were laid out, then that the earliest settlement occurs at Hungate to the east, and then that the Fishergate *wic* was abandoned. By about 980 at latest, a new bridging point over the Ouse replaced the Roman one, permanently changing the topography of the city centre. The extent of occupation can be roughly gauged by pottery finds. York ware (*c.*850–950) is found in all parts of the later walled city, as is Torksey ware (*c.*950–1050). So from being 'a series of shifting foci around churches, elite halls and wharfage', York became, for the first time since the Romans, 'something approaching an entity'.[37]

This would all suggest a denser, more compact city in place of a polyfocal scatter, but at the same time *Jorvik* seems to have spawned satellites, some of them commercial. Old Norse *thorp(e)* means a dependent settlement: and apart from Layerthorpe east of the Foss, there was a whole clutch south of York and close to the Ouse—Clementhorpe, Middlethorpe, Bus-tardthorpe, Bishopthorpe, Dringthorpe, and Copmanthorpe. The last ('ham-let of the *kaupmanna*', chapmen or merchants) lay close to the main road south, but most of the others can be seen as satellite harbour settlements.

---

36. Quotations: Fletcher, *Bloodfeud*, 162; Wormald, *Making of English Law*, I, 360.
37. York and Torksey ware: AY 8/4, 460–2. Quotation: P. C. Buckland, 'Ragnarok and the stones of York', in J. Sheehan and D. Ó'Corráin, eds, *The Viking Age: Ireland and the West* (Dublin, 2010), 56.

That would imply a large population, which is just what a contemporary, Byrhtferth of Ramsey, attested. Writing sometime between 995 and 1005, he said that York's 'multitude of people' numbered no fewer than 30,000 adults. The figure, like many medieval statistics, may be much too high; but at the least we might envisage a pre-1066 maximum of 10–15,000 or more. Domesday's incomplete figures for housing in 1066 imply a total of over 9,000, and considerably more if there were several houses on each 'messuage'. An ingenious and very different calculation, based on 'the volume of faeces preserved by waterlogging' at Coppergate, gives a minimum of 6–10,000, and that should probably be increased, since it assumed a much lower multiplier than is usually taken to convert medieval households to total population.[38]

The growth in York's size and prosperity after about 900 seems to have been accompanied by a transformation of the countryside, as new patterns of agriculture and settlements led to greater productivity. In what Dyer has called a 'village revolution', scattered settlements were gradually replaced by nucleated villages, which were accompanied by a replanned landscape of arable open fields. It was not confined to the areas of Danish conquest, covering a broad zone from Dorset to Northumberland; but Yorkshire and County Durham especially had large numbers of well-planned villages and field systems. And although 'revolution' might exaggerate the speed of change—the process occurred roughly between 850 and 1200—some East Yorkshire studies do suggest that it began in the Anglo-Scandinavian period. On the Wolds, Wharram Percy became a nucleated village in the tenth century, in a period of change accelerated by the Scandinavian settlement.[39]

The 'village revolution' may well have been stimulated by York's growth. It is likely that the rapid development of London, Southampton, Ipswich, York, and other towns contributed to a reorganization of rural settlement, 'so that production of an agricultural surplus could be more vigorously pursued, and new land brought into cultivation'.[40] Certainly by 1066 parts

38. Byrhtferth: *HCY*, I, 454; AY 1, 171–2; Fletcher, *Bloodfeud*, 48. Domesday: D. M. Palliser, *Domesday York*, BP 78 (York, 1990), 12, 13; AY 8/4, 321. Coppergate: AY 8/4, 395, 500.
39. Christopher Dyer, *Making a Living in the Middle Ages* (New Haven and London, 2002), 17–26; Palliser, *Towns and Local Communities*, ch. II; B. K. Roberts, *Landscapes, Documents and Maps: Villages in Northern England and Beyond AD 900–1250* (Oxford, 2008). I owe confirmation of the likely 10th-century dating of Wharram Percy to Prof. J. D. Richards. Professor John Blair, however, is sceptical as to whether Wharram—or any other planned, nucleated village—can be dated before *c.*1100 (pers. comm.).
40. D. A. Hinton, *Archaeology, Economy and Society: England from the Fifth to the Fifteenth Century* (London, 1990), 58.

of central and eastern Yorkshire were among the most productive and
populous parts of England, and comparable to East Anglia. Another parallel
with East Anglia was the primacy of one very large town. The conventional
wisdom is that a major city needs to have headed a hierarchy of second-
order towns, but until the eleventh century there were virtually no towns in
Yorkshire except York itself, just as Norwich was the only large town in East
Anglia except for Thetford and Ipswich: in neither case did it inhibit major
growth in the countryside. The uniqueness of York is emphasized by the
fact that tenth-century English kings expected every market town to have
a mint, and that York was the only mint town north of Humber until after
1066. By that time, however, there was incipient urban growth outside the
county town, notably at the archbishop's estates of Ripon and Beverley.

Was the rural and urban flowering a result of the stimulus provided by
Viking rulers and settlers, or simply part of an expanding West European
economy that coincided with it? Certainly the place name evidence suggests a major Viking impact: the names of nearly all York's streets, and of
many of the nearby villages and hamlets, are Old Norse in origin. Of some
1,830 Yorkshire settlements named in Domesday Book, two in five (41 per
cent) have Scandinavian or hybrid (Anglo-Scandinavian) names, the commonest being those with the suffixes *-by* and *-thorp(e)* for larger and smaller
settlements respectively. Many others have a Norse prefix followed by the
Old English *tun*, which may be interpreted as 'evidence for the taking over
by the Danes of English settlements'.[41]

In the city itself, the influence of Danish nomenclature was even greater.
Almost every York street likely to have existed by 1066 has the Old Norse
suffix *-gata*, 'street', while many lanes were called *-gail* (ON 'narrow alley').
There is plentiful Middle English evidence for citizens using Old Norse
terms for features like 'kirk' (ON *kirkja*) for church, or 'beck' (ON *bekkr*) for
a stream. And, as we have seen, Old Norse personal names were common in
tenth- to twelfth-century York: for instance, 'uniquely at York, about three-
quarters of the moneyers' names are Scandinavian'. All of this must suggest
that many, at least of the dominant townspeople, spoke Old Norse; whether
it proves a mass influx from Scandinavia is another matter. At the very least,
however, it seems reasonable to accept the argument of the leading expert

41. Gillian Fellows Jensen, *Scandinavian Settlement Names in Yorkshire* (Copenhagen, 1972), 169;
    Gillian Fellows Jensen, 'Scandinavian settlement in Yorkshire', in B. E. Crawford, *Scandinavian
    Settlement in Northern Britain* (London, 1995), 185.

on York's street names for 'a greater number of Scandinavian settlers and longer-lasting Scandinavian occupation there than further south'.[42]

Much of our knowledge of the life of the townspeople, whether English or Viking, inevitably derives from the large-scale excavations at 16–22 Coppergate in 1976–81, which extended over about 1,200 square yards (1,000 m²). They revealed parts of four tenth-century house plots, and in total produced over 40,000 individually recorded objects, a quarter of a million pottery sherds, and some five tons of animal bones. Precisely because the site has yielded so much, it is tempting to see its buildings and artefacts as a typical sample area of *Jorvik*. It needs to be remembered, as its excavator modestly observed, that the four tenements amount to only 'about 0.025 per cent (one four-hundredth) of the town itemized in *Domesday Book*'—and even less of the whole city, since Domesday's figures for housing are manifestly incomplete. Fortunately, an even larger excavation at Hungate (2006–11), completed as this was being written, promises more valuable information.[43]

What the Coppergate excavations have revealed is remarkable. *Jorvik* was clearly importing a wide range of goods, including Rhenish pottery (probably originally containing wine) and quernstones, honestones (for sharpening) from Shetland or Scandinavia, clothing pins from Ireland, amber from the Baltic, and cowrie shells from the Red Sea or the Gulf of Aden. There were twenty-three pieces of silk, deposited *c*.930–70, probably from Constantinople or Western Asia; and there was a contemporary forgery of an Islamic coin from Samarkand. The importance of trading is indicated by the fact that more tenth- and eleventh-century weights and balances have been found in York (mostly at Coppergate) than anywhere else in England.

What crafts supplied the needs both of York's exports and of local consumers? There is now abundant evidence—mainly but not wholly from Coppergate and nearby sites—for metalworking (gold, silver, copper alloys, iron, lead, tin, and pewter); bone, antler, and horn working; pottery; leather crafts, including shoemaking; glassmaking; textiles (both woollen and linen cloth); and woodworking. One of two workshops on Coppergate Plot B was that of a wood turner, appropriately since Coppergate means 'street of the turners' or 'cup makers': at that time most domestic

42. D. M. Metcalf, *An Atlas of Anglo-Saxon and Norman Coin Finds 973–1086* (London, 1998), 197; G. Fellows Jensen, 'The Anglo-Scandinavian street-names of York', in AY 8/4, 367.
43. Coppergate: refs in n. 2 above, and YAT fascicules including AY 14/4, 14/7, 15/3, 16/5, 17/5, 17/6, 17/7, 17/11. Hungate: I am indebted to Peter Connolly for current information on the results.

cups, bowls, and dishes were wooden. Silverworking on two Coppergate tenements (C and D) seems to have included the minting of coin, since finds included two iron coin dies of the 920s and 930s, and three lead trial pieces for testing coin dies: the former are without parallel in the Viking world. There must also have been numerous masons and stonecarvers to account for the church fabrics and the numerous funerary monuments. Altogether, the quantities of finds suggest a manufacturing town of the first rank. Coppergate's is the largest assemblage of Anglo-Scandinavian textiles found in England, while 'in the British Isles only Dublin can rival the quantity and range of Viking age bone and antler material found in York'.[44]

Coppergate lay within a new zone of settlement south of the Roman fortress apparently laid out in the late ninth and early tenth centuries. It included Ousegate, Pavement, Nessgate, Castlegate, and the three water lanes. East of that, and a little later, from the 960s, another belt of regular plots was laid out along Hungate, though apparently for storage or warehousing rather than houses and workshops. The zone was linked to the west bank by a new crossing point replacing the Roman bridging point upstream. In short, Coppergate was part of a planned 'industrial and commercial quarter', a plan involving 'the diversion of the main street of the former *colonia* and of the river crossing to serve it'.[45]

If this is broadly correct, it would fit with hints of similar development in the former *colonia*: for rerouting the river crossing and the main road (Micklegate) leading to it went with a replanning of the Bishophill district. The streets south-east of Micklegate form a loose grid which may have been planned in the late ninth century, possibly under the sponsorship of the archbishop, who had extensive holdings in the area. The Queen's Hotel excavation of 1988–9 found Anglian buildings respecting the Roman street alignment, whereas tenth-century structures followed the present street line. The likelihood is that the road was diverted, and a first bridge on the present site constructed, sometime after 866, and certainly by about 980 judging by dendrochronology. By 1066 Yorkshire landholders (including the citizens) had the duty of keeping up the main bridge in York as one of the 'three works of the king'.[46]

44. Coppergate minting: Blackburn, 'The coinage of Scandinavian York', 33–43. Quotation: A. MacGregor et al., *Bone, Antler, Ivory and Horn from Anglo-Scandinavian and Medieval York*, AY 17/12 (1999), 1923.

45. Quotation: Rollason, *Northumbria, 500–1100*, 221.

46. GDB, fo. 298b; D. M. Palliser, 'York's west bank', in P. V. Addyman and V. E. Black, eds, *Archaeological Papers from York* (York, 1984), 105; B. Wilson and F. Mee, *'The Fairest Arch in England': Old Ouse Bridge, York, and its Buildings*, AY SS 1/2 (York, 2002), 28.

The growing, replanned city needed improved and enlarged defences. The fact that the English kings could break into the city in 867 suggests decayed fortifications, as Asser testified, and another source reports that once the Danes were in control they restored its defences (*moenia*). That would imply renewed earth-and-timber fortifications to both fortress and *colonia*: but later, the south and east fortress walls were demolished to link the older settlement to the new commercial quarter. There is as yet no firm date for this, nor for when the enlarged town was given new defences to the south-east. Older views about an intermediate wall between fortress and Foss were based on now-discarded interpretations of archaeological features, and the current view is that in the tenth century the fortress embankment was extended to the Foss at Layerthorpe Bridge. The Foss would then have formed the eastern defence, with possibly a defended bridgehead beyond it, where the rounded boundary of St Denys' parish looks planned: that would fit the pattern of defensible bridgeheads at many tenth-century fortified towns. And it must have been at the same period that a short rampart was added from the west corner of the fortress to the Ouse. Even if we discount the Micklegate area (as probably not walled) and the possible St Denys bridgehead, the defended area of *Jorvik* from the fortress to the two rivers was about 87 acres (36 ha), making it larger than even the major Scandinavian towns of Hedeby and Birka.[47]

The enlarged town probably had centres of authority for king and archbishop on both banks of the Ouse. The cathedral and its ancillary buildings were probably near the site of the present Minster, given the discovery of an important Anglo-Scandinavian cemetery below its south transept; and there was very likely a major episcopal church or monastery in the Holy Trinity precinct off Micklegate. That is suggested by Domesday's evidence for a well-endowed and highly privileged minster of Christ Church, possibly the direct successor of an episcopal *monasterium* founded in Alcuin's time. Similarly, there are indications that by the tenth century the kings, and their successors the earls, had residences or courts on each bank. One may have been adapted from the still-standing south-east gatehouse of the Roman fortress: there are later references to the site as *Kuningesgard* (ON *Konungsgarðr*, 'king's residence') and to the church near it as standing *in curia regis*. North-west of the fortress was *Earlsburh*, which may have been the location

47. AY 1, 164–5; AY 8/4, 491–3; J. D. Richards, *English Heritage Book of Viking Age England* (London, 1991), 46.

of Earl Siward's hall, while across the Ouse lay the King's Tofts and royal chapel, the centre of shire authority until the twelfth century.[48]

What of the houses and workplaces of the townspeople? Too little has yet been discovered (outside Ousegate, Coppergate, and Hungate) of the often ephemeral domestic and commercial buildings and markets which occupied most of the city. It must, however, have been in the tenth or eleventh century that large new marketplaces were created south of the putative royal palace in King's Square. The meat market with stalls mentioned in Domesday was seemingly part of a triangular marketplace (later infilled to create Colliergate and the Shambles), while south of that was the broad market of the Pavement. (The whole district, later called Marketshire, was probably one of the seven city 'shires' or wards of Domesday.) Nor need this have been the only market zone: fish markets may already have stood by Ouse and Foss Bridges, as they did later; and outside Bootham Bar may have already been an extramural street market, since the street name Bootham derives from the Old Norse 'at the booths'. Quays and warehouses must have lined the river banks: the civic quay by Ouse Bridge is not recorded early, but the three 'water lanes' leading to it all have names derived from Old Norse (Kergate, Thursgeil, and Hertergate). The one limited excavation so far on the Anglo-Scandinavian Ouse waterfront 'suggests the repeated stabilisations of a beaching area'; perhaps significantly, the site adjoined the quay called 'Dublin Stones'. Near the Foss, the Hungate excavation has located nine late-tenth-century buildings, all apparently intended for storage of goods. Trade was probably organized before 1066, as it certainly was later, by a guild merchant, and the mysterious *gildegard* recorded about the 1080s, somewhere on Bishophill, could have been its headquarters.[49]

As for the houses of the merchants and craftsmen, much the best evidence so far is again that from Coppergate, where the new street was created around 910 and, at the same time, new and regular building plots were laid out, with street frontages of 18 feet (5.5 m), but stretching back over 140 feet (43 m) to the river behind. The first buildings erected on the four excavated plots were fairly flimsy one-storey structures of post-and-wattle construction. This clearly planned section of townscape proved remarkably stable: the original structures were replaced in more substantial form around

---

48. *RCHMY* II, 8; III, 106; IV, p. xxxii; Palliser, 'York's west bank', 103; AY 1, 171.
49. Palliser, 'York's west bank', 107; Palliser, *Domesday York*, 12, 25; AY 1, 188.

973 (a date established by dendrochronology), but this and later rebuildings all took place within the original plot boundaries, which can still be seen unchanged on the Ordnance Survey plan of 1852. The houses of 973 had upright posts and horizontal planks, and their walls survived up to 6 feet (1.8 m) above the foundations, making them the most completely preserved wooden buildings of this period in Britain. The lower levels had survived because they were basement walls sunk into the ground, probably to support an upper storey.

The densely packed timbered houses and workshops, with latrines in their yards and with livestock on the site, made for a very squalid environment, both by Roman standards and by those of the twelfth century onwards. The state of the floors of the Coppergate houses was 'gross'; houses were infested with flies, lice, and other species, while the black rat was also common. The combination of decomposing wood, rubbish, and dung built up an organic layer at about an inch (25 mm) a year. Yet it would be wrong to assume that the whole city was equally filthy from one sample area; wrong, too, to suppose that the inhabitants of Coppergate were poor. Many were clearly prosperous craftsmen, and among the small finds recovered were an unusually large number of silk textiles, clearly luxury items, including a woman's headdress.[50]

The Coppergate middens provide much evidence for diet. O'Connor's report on the bones shows that beef was the staple meat, but that food also included pork, venison, horsemeat, wildfowl, geese, and some thirty-five different fish, both marine and freshwater. Taking this evidence together with O'Connor's later report on Fishergate suggests that the inhabitants of late-ninth-century Coppergate had a diet similar to pre-Viking Fishergate, whereas those of later Coppergate (c.975–1050) enjoyed a much more diverse diet. One element of that diversity was a huge increase in North Sea fish catches from about 975 or so, especially herring and cod, part of a 'fish event horizon' which has been detected on many other English sites. A herring-processing workshop has been excavated in the churchyard of St Mary, Bishophill Junior, its presence marked by a thick deposit of fish-scales.[51]

50. Quotation: AY 8/4, 384; 15/3, 189–92; 17/5, 360–82; T. P. O'Connor, 'On the lack of bones of the ship rat Rattus rattus from Dark Age York', Journal of Zoology, 224 (1991), 318–20.
51. AY 15/3; 15/4, 278; 8/4, 436–9; J. H. Barrett, 'Cod bones and commerce', Current Archaeology, 221 (August 2008), 20–5, summarizing his earlier work.

Like all large towns, York had to rely heavily on imported goods, raw materials, and manufactures as well as foodstuffs. Coppergate alone has testified to luxury goods from distant parts of Europe, the Mediterranean, and even central Asia and the Indian Ocean: and there would have also been perishable imports like wine and spices. Who brought them? Byrhtferth tells us that the city was 'enriched with the treasures of merchants, who come from all parts, but above all from the Danish people'. The counterpart was that men of *Jorvik* travelled widely. Sometime around 970 'merchants coming from York' were robbed of all their goods on the Isle of Thanet. For there was, as is to be expected, much trade with the rest of England: hence the presence in York of coins from all the other major mint towns, and of pottery from those towns engaged in mass-market production, including Stamford, Thetford, Torksey, and St Neots. This was all possible because *Jorvik* was an inland port, sited characteristically—like Cambridge, Ipswich, and Lincoln—at the lowest bridgeable point on a major river (ports on the coast or an estuary, like Hull, Boston, and Lynn, did not rise to prominence until after 1066). Nevertheless, much bulk trade must have been local and overland. The Northumbrian Priests' Law of the 1020s or later banned Sunday trading except that 'in case of hostility one may travel because of necessity between York and a distance of six miles'.[52]

One key English import was silver, whether acquired by trade or plunder. It was essential for trading, though not necessarily as coin. Even after the Viking kings started striking coins, hacksilver and ingots remained in use as alternative means of trading, as the hoards show. At Coppergate were found stone moulds for casting ingots, and there is evidence for a common unit of measurement. Lead weights found in Dublin, York, and Anglesey suggest a standard silver unit of 26.6 grams. What kings and archbishops relied on to exchange for silver, we do not know: possibly slaves, but very likely wool. It has been suggested that England was already exporting wool on a large scale by the later tenth century, sufficient enough to suck in 'the bullion demanded by its prodigious coinage'.[53]

As we have seen, silverworking, and even the minting of coin, have been identified as crafts at Coppergate: some sceptics have doubted whether coins

52. *EHD*, I, 284, 475; AY 1, 172; Fletcher, *Bloodfeud*, 28–9. The Priests' Law may be later than Whitelock suggested in *EHD*: Townend, ed., *Wulfstan, Archbishop of York*, entries indexed under 'Northumbrian Priests' Law'.
53. Lead weights: Griffiths, 'Exchange, trade, and urbanization', 79. Quotation: Patrick Wormald, *Times Literary Supplement*, 25–31 May 1990, 562.

were actually struck there, but in Blackburn's view there is little reason to doubt it. Wherever the York mints, royal and archiepiscopal, were located, they produced large numbers of coins. Of a hoard of over 800 English coins sent to Rome as a gift for the pope in the 940s, twenty-nine (3.5 per cent) were minted in York. Among English coins found in hoards in Scandinavia, the proportion is much higher: almost 40 per cent came from Danelaw mints, and a high proportion of those from York, very likely as a result of trade. The Danelaw can, indeed, be seen as involved in a triangular trade, enjoying a favourable balance with the near Continent, sucking in silver coin, and a negative balance with Scandinavia. York's role as a port must have been crucial in this trade: of the five leading mints under Ethelred II (978–1016)—London, Lincoln, York, Winchester, and Chester—only Winchester was not a port.[54]

Life in *Jorvik*: Christianization and society

Among the most striking survivals from *Jorvik* and its region are the numerous stone carvings. Over 400 complete pieces or fragments datable between *c.*876 and 1066 survive in Yorkshire, more than for any other English county, and they testify to artistic skill and to social ranking as well as to Christianization. J. T. Lang, the acknowledged expert on the subject, was in no doubt that the main reason for this artistic flowering was 'the growing prosperity of York as a commercial centre'. Whereas early English sculpture was mostly ecclesiastical, most tenth-century monuments were funerary, commissioned by 'prosperous land-holders anxious to display their prestige' and sometimes willing to commission secular and even pagan subjects. That would certainly fit the evidence of the Minster graveyard, where many of the funerary monuments may have been aristocratic, but in other districts merchants might have been the patrons. Stocker has suggested that the large number of grave-covers in the church of St Mary Bishophill Senior represents a new mercantile elite, the 'Hiberno-Norse trading community': and the concentration is certainly striking. Against the Minster's minimum of twenty-eight

54. Blackburn, 'The coinage of Scandinavian York', 341; D. M. Metcalf, 'The Rome (Forum) hoard of 1883', *BNJ*, 62 (1993), 73; D. M. Metcalf, 'Monetary circulation in the Danelaw, 973–1083', in S. Keynes and A. P. Smyth, eds, *Anglo-Saxons: Studies Presented to Cyril Ray Hart* (Dublin, 2006), 167–8.

Anglo-Scandinavian funerary monuments, St Mary's has fifteen, easily the second largest concentration in the city.[55]

Most of the sculptures are not closely datable, but two exceptions are fragments of a grave-cover carved with lively beasts, found in a stratified context at Coppergate of before *c.*960. Since it was a work of the same carver as other sculptures from Clifford Street and Newgate, 'the York Master', the workshop must have been active under, or just after, the Viking kings. Of other pieces, at least three from the Minster cemetery suggest paganism coexisting with Christianity, or at least some accommodation of Norse beliefs into it. Two are grave-slabs with scenes from the life of Sigurd, and the third is part of a cross-shaft depicting Weland the Smith. They are, however, a small proportion of the total: what should be emphasized about the Minster monuments as a whole is that they greatly increase our knowledge of sculpture in York, and allow the identification of a 'York Metropolitan School'.[56]

Undoubtedly the conquerors of York must have rapidly reached an accommodation with the Christian Church. There is no clear evidence of any break in episcopal succession at York, as there was in the other bishoprics overrun by the Vikings. Archbishop Wulfhere seems to have remained in post from 854 until his death, permitting King Guthfrith burial in the cathedral in 895. And from *c.*905 to 927 the pennies minted in York were nearly all the so-called St Peter issues, which certainly implies officially sponsored Christianity. We need, however, to distinguish between conversion and Christianization, the former covering baptism and formal acceptance of the new religion, the latter 'the process whereby Christian beliefs and practices penetrated into the converted society'. The frequent changes of ruling families meant that even kings could remain pagan very late. The rulers from Dublin after *c.*914 must have been heathen, since West Saxon kings expected their conversion as the price of alliance or submission: Sihtric (921–7), his son Olaf (941–52), and Erik Bloodaxe all accepted baptism in this way.[57]

55. J. T. Lang, 'Anglo-Scandinavian sculpture in Yorkshire', in R. A. Hall, ed., *Viking Age York and the North*, CBA Res Rep 27 (1978), 11; D. A. Stocker, 'Monuments and merchants', in Hadley and Richards, eds, *Cultures in Contact*, 203–5.
56. Lang, *Corpus of Anglo-Saxon Stone Sculpture*, III, 38–40, 53–78, 104; Hadley, *The Northern Danelaw*, 242; AY 8/4, 454.
57. Lesley Abrams, 'The conversion of the Danelaw', in J. Graham-Campbell et al., eds, *Vikings and the Danelaw* (Oxford, 2001), 31–44. Whether there was any break in episcopal succession depends on whether Wulfhere died in 892 or 900. Recent scholarship prefers 900 and makes him the archbishop who allowed Guthfrith's burial in the Minster in 895.

Yet, whether pagan or Christian, successive kings worked amicably with Archbishop Wulfstan I (931–56), and it was doubtless to ensure loyalty to themselves that, as we have seen, English kings made sure that his successors were southern men, mostly holding York in plurality with Worcester. The reasons often given for this pluralism were the poverty of the diocese of York and the paganism of its inhabitants, but both seem unlikely. 'In terms of territory and power the see of York', wrote Fletcher, 'did rather nicely out of the Viking invasions and settlements', and in tenth-century York any pagan beliefs and practices must have been much diluted. The reasons for believing that include not only the location of all Anglo-Scandinavian graves in Christian churchyards, often with an explicitly Christian message, but also the sheer number of new churches founded in both city and countryside, signs perhaps that 'Anglo-Scandinavian Christianity may not have been deep, but it was eager and it was pious'.[58]

None of this activity, of course, proves that paganism was extinct. The Northumbrian Priests' Law ordered clergy to guard against such heathen practices as sacrifices, divination, witchcraft; veneration of sacred stones, trees, and wells, 'or any such nonsense'. Whether the writer had in mind his cathedral city, or the perhaps more pagan countryside, he was clearly aware that Christianization was far from complete. It is not clear whether York had recovered its role as a nursery for scholarship and mission, as in Alcuin's time: the birth at York of St Sigfrid, who converted the first Christian Swedish king and may then have helped St Olaf, the first Norwegian Christian king, is only a late tradition. Yet York was undoubtedly still a major ecclesiastical centre. If it had as yet no strictly Benedictine monasteries, it had minster churches other than the cathedral—superior churches staffed by groups of priests. One was Domesday's Christ Church, Micklegate, already noted; another was possibly Siward's minster of St Olaf, predecessor of St Mary's Abbey and significantly dedicated to St Olaf of Norway. And a third might have been All Saints, Pavement, called a minster after 1066, but known to have been adorned with pre-Conquest tiles of a type usually found only in major Anglo-Saxon churches.[59]

58. R. M. T. Hill and C. N. L. Brooke, 'From 627 until the early thirteenth century', in Aylmer & Cant, eds, 16; Richard Fletcher, *The Conversion of Europe* (London, 1997), 394, 396.
59. Laurence Keen, 'Pre-Conquest glazed relief tiles from All Saints church, Pavement, York', *JBAA*, 146 (1993), 67–86.

The only pre-1066 parish church documented outside Domesday Book is St Mary's, Castlegate, because of the survival of its dedication stone; but eight other churches were named in Domesday as in existence before the Conquest, and one of them was All Saints, Pavement. In addition, recent excavations indicate or suggest other churches already founded but not yet documented, including All Saints, Fishergate, St Benedict's, St Helen-on-the-Walls, and probably St Clement's. Altogether, there are reasons to think that many of the final complement of forty-five or more city parish churches were founded before 1066; there could also have been 'lost' churches founded early which later disappeared, such as the one suggested by the name St Swithin's Lane. York fits well with Blair's model of an eastern England which, between 950 and 1100, was less like western England than like Denmark and southern Sweden, with its faster economic development and 'its teeming towns with their many churches'. Another distinction is of the independence of urban parishes in York as in the Danelaw generally: those early churches so far excavated had graveyards from the start, whereas most large towns in southern England and the West Midlands had a hierarchy of churches, with a cathedral or other major church having a monopoly of burial rights.[60]

Above the minsters and neighbourhood churches, of course, was the Minster with its ancillary buildings and institutions. Though we know too little of it before 1070, it was clearly very wealthy and a major pastoral, educational, and cultural centre. It had a community of seven canons on the eve of the Norman Conquest, living in common; in the 1060s Archbishop Ealdred built them a refectory, and they must also have had a dormitory. And there was almost certainly, as later, an attached hospital of St Peter for the sick and poor. We need not believe its traditional foundation by King Athelstan, but its generous royal endowment of 'Petercorn' from all arable land in the diocese does suggest a pre-Conquest foundation. Sadly, no sign of the cathedral foundations has yet been located, and of the two surviving treasures usually ascribed to it, one—the York Gospels—was probably made in Canterbury, while the other, the Horn of Ulf, may be of post-Conquest date (see Appendix IV). Nevertheless, there are hints that—as we would expect—the cathedral was indeed lavishly decorated and furnished

---

60. Palliser, *Domesday York*, 15, 21–2; AY 1, 207–10; Julia Barrow, 'Survival and mutation: Ecclesiastical institutions in the Danelaw . . .', in Hadley and Richards, eds, *Cultures in Contact*, 168; Barrow, 'Churches, education and literacy in towns', in *CUHB* I, 135–7; Blair, *The Church in Anglo-Saxon Society*, 422–5, 500 (quotation from p. 425).

in up-to-date style; and it enjoyed considerable privileges including (like its daughter minsters at Ripon and Beverley) extensive rights of sanctuary.[61]

York in the time of King Edward

We are fortunate to have, in the folios of Great Domesday Book, a description of the city in 1066. That text was compiled in or shortly after 1086, but it included an account of York not only 'now' but also 'in the time of King Edward', meaning before 5 January 1066. That is standard Domesday form, but since the intended descriptions of London and Winchester are missing, York is (with the possible exception of Norwich) the largest town described. To enhance its value further, the description can be read in conjunction with a slightly earlier text describing Archbishop Thomas's 'Rights and Laws' within the city and suburbs. It is close in date to Domesday, but much of it reads like a list of privileges enjoyed by Thomas's pre-Conquest predecessors, and the fact that it is written in Old English corroborates that.[62]

York, like most other shire towns in Domesday, was described separately at the head of the county section, before the accounts of the lands of the king and other lords. This was done not just because it was a shire town, but because it had what Maitland called 'tenurial heterogeneity': many houses there belonged to the king, but many others to churchmen and county landholders, so that the town did not fit neatly into either royal or seigneurial lands. Indeed, we can go further: the great men of the county, in 1066 as well as later, were expected to own houses in the county town, partly to play their part in the ancient duties laid on English landholders to maintain the 'three works of the king', two of which were to repair the defences of the town and to keep up its bridge.[63]

If we strip away all the Domesday evidence relating to c.1086, what picture does the survey give of York on the eve of the Conquest? First and foremost, it confirms York's position as probably second in size and wealth among English towns. It contained, at a minimum, some 1,900 *mansiones*

61. *HCY*, II, 107, 353; J. M. Cooper, *The Last Four Anglo-Saxon Archbishops of York*, BP 38 (York, 1970), 27; AY 1, 198, 223–4; Wormald, *The Making of English Law*, I, 394–6; Christopher Norton, 'York Minster in the time of Wulfstan', in Townend, ed., *Wulfstan, Archbishop of York*, 207–34.
62. GDB, fo. 298 a–d; YML, MS. L2 (1), pt. 1, fo. 61r, v. Both texts are translated in Palliser, *Domesday York*, 20–5, and edited in full in AY 1, 210–20; and both are discussed more fully in Ch. 4.
63. F. W. Maitland, *Domesday Book and Beyond* (Cambridge, 1897), 178–82, 186–7, 273–4; Robin Fleming, 'Rural élites and urban communities in late-Saxon England', *P&P*, 141 (1993), 3–37.

(tenements, messuages, or dwellings), a long way ahead of any other towns described in Domesday. It is not a record designed for like-for-like comparisons, but Norwich apparently came next with 1,320 burgesses and Lincoln third with 1,150 messuages. In terms of wealth, as measured by borough 'farms' payable to the king, York outranked all other towns in the Domesday record with the erratic exception of Droitwich, boosted by its lucrative salt industry. And we can derive a further indication of York's importance from another Domesday entry: Exeter, we are told, 'in the time of King Edward did not pay geld except when London, York and Winchester paid geld'.[64]

That almost casual reference implies, surely, something otherwise almost unrecorded before the twelfth century, the emergence of a body of men acting effectively as a town council, and working in consultation with a wider group—a town assembly or guild—both capable of common action to work for collective privileges. As Susan Reynolds remarks of the Exeter entry, 'collective responsibility and collective bargaining were...common enough for the news of a good deal to get around and be copied'.[65] What was the York group which might have been involved?

There are two clues in the York texts. One is the Domesday record that among those in the city specially privileged were 'four judges [*iudices*]'. They corresponded to similar bodies of judges or 'lawmen' recorded in Cambridge, Chester, Lincoln, and Stamford, and who probably took the lead both in the borough court and in a town assembly. Most were explicitly described as twelve in number, and York may also have had twelve, with the four singled out being specially privileged. The other clue is the mention in 'Rights and Laws' of a York *Gildegarde*: if this was the hall of a guild merchant, one of those shadowy bodies of urban traders emerging in the eleventh century, then that may have been linked to the lawmen. Certainly the spokesman of a jury of twelve in 1106 was Ulvet son of Forno, 'by hereditary right *lagaman* of the city, which in Latin may be translated lawgiver or judge', and in 1129–30 Thomas son of Ulviet, presumably his son, was made alderman of the York 'guild'. This may all seem thin evidence, but written records for York's government are meagre before 1066, and even in better-recorded

---

64. GDB, fo. 100a (Exeter); Palliser, *Domesday York*, 2, 10–14. Statistical tables are in Carl Stephenson, *Borough and Town* (Cambridge, Mass., 1933), 221 (size), and James Tait, *The Medieval English Borough* (Manchester, 1936), 184 (borough farms). The York figures T.R.E. are difficult: Stephenson reckons 1,890 *mansiones*, but H. C. Darby and I. S. Maxwell, eds, *The Domesday Geography of Northern England* (Cambridge, 1962), 154, have 1,875. York's figures would be higher if reckoned by the 'long hundred' (120) common to the Danelaw, as those at Lincoln were (GDB, fo. 336a).
65. Susan Reynolds, 'Towns in Domesday Book', in J. C. Holt, ed., *Domesday Studies* (Woodbridge, 1987), 307.

towns early guilds are shadowy: in Geoffrey Martin's words, 'it was the ubiquity of the gild, and its indispensable foundation as a means to common action... that accounts for the rarity of such references to it'. We might wonder if the organization implied by the planned streets and housing of the tenth century did not require some sort of council of elders even then.[66]

What else can we deduce about York in 1066 from Domesday? The king held the lion's share of urban properties, and his revenue from York totalled £53 a year, while one third of the city's revenues belonged to the earl of Northumbria. The city was divided into seven shires (*scyrae*), the equivalents of the later wards; six were in royal hands and one belonged to the archbishop, who also had a third of the revenues from one of the others. Domesday does not describe the boundaries of the shires, but a combination of 'Rights and Laws' and other sources allows us to deduce that the core of the archbishop's shire was the later cathedral close, together with sections of Petergate, Stonegate, and Goodramgate; while the shire in which he had 'a third part' was a broad zone straddling the rivers and the defences: it included parts of Bishophill, Clementhorpe, and Walmgate, as well as Monkgate and Layerthorpe. And the archbishop and Minster clergy, like the king and the city merchants, had their own courts and privileges, including a court for the canons, as well as extensive sanctuary rights. These, though not recorded before 1066, are unlikely to have been new in early Norman times.

With such documentation for the urban environment, it is a pity that lack of written evidence prevents us from attaching names, let alone personalities, to most of *Jorvik's* inhabitants. Rare exceptions are two short documents in Old English inserted on a blank folio in the cathedral's Gospel Book which do name names, but not necessarily those of citizens. Other than that, we are reduced to the bare names of moneyers on coins and of those commemorated on memorial stones and on the dedication stone at St Mary's, Castlegate: none can be convincingly linked to men and women named in other sources until we come to the better-recorded Domesday period. As a result, desperate measures are sometimes resorted to to identify clergy or citizens below the level of archbishops and earls. For instance, one of the wives of Earl Uhtred (d. 1016) was daughter to Styr Ulfsson, whom the chronicler calls *civis divitis*, literally 'a rich citizen'. In consequence, successive historians have cast Styr as a York 'citizen', even as 'the leader of the

---

66. Tait, *Medieval English Borough*, 43–4; G. H. Martin, 'Domesday Book and the boroughs', in P. H. Sawyer, ed., *Domesday Book: A Reassessment* (London, 1985), 161–2; Reynolds, 'Towns in Domesday Book', 307; AY 1, 186–7, 220–1.

Danes of York', but such a marriage alliance would have been very unlikely. *Civis*, to an eleventh-century writer, often meant a prominent landholder, in this case possibly the Styr of Stearsby, ten miles north of York.[67]

Nevertheless, identifying Styr as a rural landholder rather than a 'citizen' should not lead to making too sharp a separation between the two categories. There were many close ties—political, social, economic, and religious—between late Saxon rural elites and their local towns, including York. Domesday casually mentions that the holders of property in the city in 1066 included 'two reeves of Earl Harold', and that two Yorkshire thegns held 'two stalls in the meat market'. England was a state where, in Fleming's words, 'town and country were closely bound by a single élite, an élite intent on controlling them both'.[68]

Two final points may be made about Anglo-Scandinavian York. One is the very provisional state of our knowledge. The Minster and Coppergate excavations have provided vastly more information, but there has simply been no opportunity since 1981 for further large-scale excavation except for the Hungate discoveries of 2006–11. The priority remains to test the 'Coppergate model'. The second is that, nevertheless, the city's size and wealth are not in doubt: by the late tenth and eleventh centuries York was one of several towns, including Lincoln and Chester, flourishing more than those in southern and western England. Between 973 and 1066, almost a quarter (24 per cent) of surviving coins were struck at London (including Southwark), but the next largest numbers came from York (11 per cent) and Lincoln (10 per cent), and apart from Winchester the next in rank were all Danelaw towns.[69]

Appendix IV: Survivals from the pre-Conquest churches

In the absence so far of any trace of the foundations and fabric of the pre-Conquest cathedral (other than the graveyard beneath the present south transept), it has been well said that the destructive events of the 1060s and

---

67. Keynes, 'The additions in Old English', 97–9; W. E. Kapelle, *The Norman Conquest of the North* (London, 1979), 19; Fleming, 'Rural élites and urban communities', 34; Fletcher, *Bloodfeud*, 52–3; AY 8/4, 318.
68. GDB, fo. 298a; Fleming, 'Rural élites and urban communities', 8, 18, 37.
69. 'Coppergate model': Richard Hall, in *HANY*, 74. Mint rankings: Alan Dyer, 'Ranking lists of English medieval towns', in *CUHB* I, 750, from statistics by D. M. Metcalf.

1070s consigned the old cathedral to 'a historical black hole'.[70] In compensation, much has been made of three beautiful objects which survive among its treasures.

The York Gospels form the one book which has unquestionably been in the possession of the archbishop or the cathedral since the eleventh century; since the thirteenth century it has been used as an oath-book for the cathedral chapter and more recently for archbishops. There is general agreement that it was written and illuminated around the turn of the millennium, very likely at Canterbury, and that it was probably presented to Wulfstan II when he went to Canterbury in 1020 to consecrate Archbishop Æthelnoth. However, the fact that no other volume seems to have survived the catastrophes of 1069–75 gives pause for thought. Norton's radical suggestion is that the book survived because it was in the archbishop's hands during the devastation of 1069, not in the Minster library but at his nearby estate of Sherburn-in-Elmet.[71]

Furthermore, two treasures surviving in the crypt and Treasury have traditionally been dated to before 1066. One can be quickly dismissed, a very beautiful (though badly damaged) stone sculpture of the Virgin and Child. It was long thought to be eleventh century, but despite the archaic lettering of its inscription it is now generally dated *c.*1150. The other is the so-called Horn of Ulf, a decorated ivory horn probably from southern Italy. Camden (1586) was told that it had been given by Ulphus son of Thorald, a Deiran noble, as a token of his gift of estates to the cathedral; certainly much Minster property was in 1276 listed as 'lands of Ulf', and from about 1300 carvings of the horn feature prominently in the rebuilt fabric. There is no reason why the tradition should not be genuine; there was indeed a prominent landholder called Ulf who went on pilgrimage to Jerusalem in the 1060s and who might have been the donor; and Domesday records one manor (Stonegrave) as having been given by Ulf 'to St Peter'. The problem remains one of identifying Ulf (unfortunately one of the commonest male names in Scandinavian England) and of dating the horn. It has usually been ascribed to the tenth or early eleventh century, but recent art-historical scholarship prefers *c.*1080. There are similar problems with the one major standing building which has usually been dated as pre-Conquest, the massive tower

70. Norton, 'York Minster in the time of Wulfstan', 212.
71. Barker, ed., *The York Gospels*, *passim*; Wormald, *The Making of English Law*, I, 195–7; T. A. Heslop, 'Art and the man: Archbishop Wulfstan and the York Gospelbook', in Townend, ed., *Wulfstan, Archbishop of York*, 279–308; Norton, 'York Minster in the time of Wulfstan', 214–18.

of St Mary, Bishophill Junior (Plate 4). It was accepted as such by no less an authority than Harold Taylor. It has now, however, been re-examined using photogrammetry and petrological analysis. The conclusion is that it was probably built in a single phase of construction in the third quarter of the eleventh century: it is not clear whether it was before or after 1066.[72]

72. Ulf and the horn: William Camden, *Britannia*, ed. Edmund Gibson (London, 1695), col. 720; Drake, *Eboracum*, 479–81; Hill and Brooke, 'From 627 until the early thirteenth century', 39; Sarah Brown, *York Minster: An Architectural History c. 1220–1500* (Swindon, 2003), 90, 124–5, etc.; AY 8/4, 318, 457–8; Norton, 'York Minster in the time of Wulfstan', 211–13. St Mary's tower: AY 8/2, 146.

4

French conquest and lordship

1066–1215

York, in common with the rest of England, endured not one but two conquests in the eleventh century, but the Norman Conquest, unlike that of Swein and Cnut, endured; and Hastings marked much more than a change of dynasty. Duke William overturned the structure of power and landholding, imposing new French lords on town and countryside, and French bishops on the Church. If any date in English history marks a permanent and revolutionary break, it is 1066, even if—in York and the rest of Northumbria—the revolution did not take full effect until 1068–70. That said, the break with the past was not total. The invaders numbered at most 1 or 2 per cent of the English population and could not rule for long solely by force. Most people carried on under new masters, but with many of their familiar rights and obligations intact; and that was especially true of the government of towns. 'It is difficult to see any significant change in English urban institutions which can be attributed to the Conquest.'[1]

Taking the long view, what happened to York and its vast shire was the completion of a process begun by Athelstan, their assimilation into a powerful state based in Winchester and Westminster, which would have continued even if Harold had won at Hastings. William and his sons expanded royal authority both in the south and the north; there was a temporary reversal of the process in the 1140s, but from 1154 to 1215 'the pressure of royal authority upon the north . . . became ever more assertive, burdensome and chafing', so that by the time of Magna Carta the region was 'more effectively integrated into the English kingdom than ever before'.[2]

1. H. Härke, 'Kings and warriors', in P. Slack and R. Ward, *The Peopling of Britain* (Oxford, 2002), 162; quotation: S. Reynolds, *An Introduction to the History of English Medieval Towns* (Oxford, 1977), 42–3.
2. R. Fletcher, *Bloodfeud* (London, 2002), 202.

Norman and Angevin kings were not only taking a firmer grip on the north for reasons of internal control; they were also anxious to defend it against rival expansion by the Scots, whose kings had already seized Lothian from Northumbria and taken over Strathclyde. The dependent kingdom of Cumbria was now under their control, and though Earl Siward seems to have conquered southern Cumbria in the 1040s, Malcolm III recovered it, perhaps in 1069–70. Rufus in 1092 advanced north and took Carlisle, but the northern borders remained peripheral to the Norman kings with their cross-Channel interests. The Scottish kings were eager to retake Cumbria and to annex Northumberland, areas which they did seize in the 1140s during the English civil war. 'The Tyne, or even the Tees, and the Duddon, or even the Ribble, rather than Tweed and Solway Firth, could well have been the borders of the new Scotland.'[3] Indeed, at the height of David I's power and Stephen's weakness, the Scots controlled parts of Yorkshire. It did not last once the vigorous Henry II took the English throne: in 1157 he compelled David's grandson Malcolm IV to surrender the 'northern counties'—as they can henceforth be called—and the Anglo-Scottish boundary reverted to the Tweed-Cheviot line. The formal establishment of the border took place in 1237 by the Treaty of York, when Alexander II of Scots renounced his claim to Northumberland, Cumberland, and Westmorland, but this effectively only confirmed the settlement of 1157.[4]

The Norman Conquest: William I

Many of the crucial events which shaped later medieval York took place under the Conqueror; but they are often hard to decipher from surviving written records, though archaeology since the 1960s has done much to clarify the picture. MS D of the *Anglo-Saxon Chronicle* is helpful until 1069, but its northern interest vanishes after that, and in its present form it was not compiled until the twelfth century. Orderic's *Ecclesiastical History* is more detailed on Yorkshire until 1070, but he did not write that section until about 1125: he drew on a near-contemporary account by William of Poitiers, but William's crucial account of 1069 is now lost. Likewise, the *Historia*

3. R. R. Davies, *The First English Empire* (Oxford, 2000), 64–5.
4. G. W. S. Barrow, 'The Anglo-Scottish border', *NH*, 1 (1966), 21–42; G. W. S. Barrow, 'The Scots and the North of England', in Edmund King, ed., *The Anarchy of King Stephen's Reign* (Oxford, 1994), 231–53.

Regum (*History of the Kings*), attributed to Symeon of Durham, which also preserves information on York in 1069–70, is a later copy of a chronicle seemingly compiled about 1129. None of these sources, therefore, is strictly contemporary.[5]

The immediate results of 1066, at least, are unarguable. Many Northumbrians must have been killed or wounded at Fulford, Stamford Bridge, and Hastings, and the survivors were in no position to resist the French. In December the English leaders, including Earl Morcar of Northumbria, submitted to William at Berkhamsted; and on Christmas Day the duke was crowned king at Westminster by Archbishop Ealdred of York. Northumbria thus submitted to an invader exactly two centuries after the Danish conquest; but the region remained restive. In 1068 the Northumbrian nobles rose in support of Edgar Ætheling, one of the old royal family, but the revolt collapsed: William garrisoned York and built there one—possibly both—of the castles on either bank of the Ouse.[6] Northern rebels rose again, however, in January 1069, destroying a Norman force at Durham and moving south. Then, according to MS D of the *Anglo-Saxon Chronicle*,

> immediately after that the aetheling Edgar came to York with all the Northumbrians, and the citizens [*burhmenn*] made peace with him. And King William came upon them by surprise...and put them to flight; and then killed those who could not flee—that was several hundreds of men; and ravaged the town, and made St Peter's Minster a disgrace, and also ravaged and humiliated all the others.[7]

Orderic's more detailed account says that the royal castellan, William Malet, held out while the city fell until relieved by the king's arrival; and that the king then stayed on for eight days to build a second castle, leaving Earl William fitz Osbern as castellan, before returning to Winchester for Easter. After the king's departure, the rebels again attacked both castles, but were overwhelmed by Earl William in 'one of the baileys'.[8]

---

5. D. M. Palliser, 'Domesday Book and the "Harrying of the North"', *NH*, 29 (1993), 4, 5; AY 1, 18–19, 27, 31.
6. *ASC* MS D says that both were built in 1068; Orderic dates one to 1068 and the other to 1069. Rollason prefers Orderic and argues that MS D and other sources have telescoped two events: AY 1, 180–3.
7. AY 1, 188; but I follow D. Whitelock et al., *The Anglo-Saxon Chronicle* (Cambridge, 1961), 149, in translating *burhmenn* as 'citizens' rather than 'men of the stronghold'.
8. AY 1, 182–3. It has been pointed out that the castle built in eight days was probably a ringwork rather than a motte: Barbara English, 'Towns, mottes and ring-works of the Conquest', in A. Ayton and J. L. Price, *The Medieval Military Revolution* (London, 1995), 52.

Assuming that Orderic's narrative is preferred to the *Chronicle*, the king's strategy makes sense. In 1068, moving north, he ensured the submission of shire towns, including Nottingham and Lincoln, and established in each a castle, a fortress of a type almost unknown in England before 1066: and he repeated the tactic at York. When that failed to deter further revolts, he built a twin on the opposite bank of the river (it is not known which castle was built first). York was the only town (bar London) where he built two castles, and their positions were clearly designed to guard against an attack upriver (like that of the Norwegians in 1066), as well as to overawe the citizens.

If William still feared attacks on York upstream, he was right. In August or early September 1069 King Swein of Denmark sent a fleet to support another revolt under Earl Waltheof and Edgar Ætheling. The Danes sailed up the Humber and Ouse, attacked York in cooperation with the rebels, and on 21 September stormed both castles. Ten days earlier Archbishop Ealdred had died, leaving the city and Church leaderless. So much is clear: but again the sources differ. The *Chronicle* records the burning of the city [*burh*] and Minster as deliberate actions by 'the Frenchmen'. The *Historia Regum*, however, has the garrisons burn houses near the *castella* (usually translated 'castles'), a fire which accidentally 'seized on the whole city [*totam civitatem invasit*]', including the cathedral. This has been a puzzle, since no widespread destruction layer has been found archaeologically between castles and cathedral. The difficulty can be surmounted, as Norton points out, if *castella* is translated as 'fortifications'. He postulates a two-pronged attack, the Danes upriver and the rebels overland from the north; a fire started by the rebels near Bootham Bar could have leaped the city defences and reached the Minster without burning the whole city: *totam civitatem invasit* could be interpreted 'spread right into the city itself'.[9]

So far, and no further, the chronicles take us: but Domesday Book yields a little more. The royal castellan from 1068 and sheriff by 1069 was William Malet, who was captured by the rebels. Whatever his fate, he was replaced as sheriff by the end of 1069, and Domesday testifies that he lost all his Yorkshire estates, many of which lay within fifteen miles of York. It seems clear from Newman's careful study of the Malet fee that the city was until 1070 'a vulnerable outpost in hostile territory', in which Malet was given a bloc of lands to defend a 'salient', which Newman calls graphically 'Fortress York'.

9. AY 1, 184–5; Christopher Norton, *Archbishop Thomas and the Norman Cathedral at York*, BP 100 (York, 2001), 34 n. 2; Norton, 'York Minster in the time of Wulfstan', in M. Townend, ed., *Wulfstan, Archbishop of York* (Turnhout, 2004), 208 n. 2.

Only after the final defeat of regional revolts could the Normans expand their effective power further north.[10]

That final defeat came swiftly in the autumn of 1069. William moved north again against the invaders and rebels; he reached an unresisting York, leaving a force there to repair the castles. Then, says MS D of the *Chronicle*, he 'utterly ravaged and laid waste' Yorkshire, staying there all winter and holding his Christmas feast and council in York. Orderic accused him of having caused famine by a deliberate scorched-earth policy, so that over 100,000 men, women, and children died of starvation; the *Historia Regum* relates that the land was uncultivated for nine years, and that 'between York and Durham no village was inhabited'. These three sources do not specifically describe the fate of York itself, but Hugh the Chanter noted tersely that the city and its hinterland were 'destroyed by the French with the sword, famine, and flames'. These lurid if sub-contemporary claims have often been read in the light of the Domesday description of York—which describes the majority of its houses as 'empty' or 'uninhabited' in 1086—to suggest total catastrophe.[11]

Domesday includes many other entries which have been read in a similar light: references to rural manors in 1086 as 'waste' are more frequent in Yorkshire than anywhere else, and account for a third of all land in the county. They have often been interpreted as deserted land, and have been bracketed together with other Domesday manors not called waste but with no recorded population, and with the city's 'empty' and 'uninhabited' houses, to suggest massive depopulation. Yet there are real problems in making this common-sense assumption, and the entry for one manor at Warthill (just outside York) gives us pause: it was called 'waste', but the clerk added 'Nevertheless two villans have two ploughs and render 2s'. Some scholars believe that 'waste' meant simply land 'not yielding the usual dues and profits', for whatever reason.[12]

Altogether, as I have argued elsewhere, some scepticism about the severity of the 'Harrying of the North', as it is often called, is allowable. The chronicles, as Fletcher justly remarks, 'become more highly coloured the

10. J. A. Green, *English Sheriffs to 1154* (London, 1990), 89; C. R. Hart, 'William Malet and his family', *ANS*, 19 (1996), 126–9; P. R. Newman, 'The Yorkshire Domesday *clamores* and the "lost fee" of William Malet', *ANS*, 22 (1999), 266–74.
11. Palliser, 'Domesday Book and the Harrying', 3–4, with references.
12. Quotation from Barbara Harvey (pers. comm.). See D. M. Palliser, 'An introduction to the Yorkshire Domesday', in *The Yorkshire Domesday: Introduction and Translation* (London, 1992), 33–8; Palliser, 'Domesday Book and the "Harrying"', 8–14.

further they are removed in time from the events they describe', and it is 'impossible' to believe that the damage was as extensive as Orderic and the *Historia Regum* alleged. The archaeological evidence in York is negative, and 'the Norman Conquest is surprisingly hard to detect'. As for Domesday, even if the numbers of 'waste' and 'uninhabited' houses are taken at face value, York was nowhere near the worst-affected English town. Stephenson calculated that while York lost 30 per cent of its inhabited housing between 1066 and 1086, both Chester and Oxford lost 50 per cent and Ipswich an astonishing 86 per cent.[13]

Furthermore, the Conqueror's actions in November and December 1069 are eloquent: while still fighting the rebels, 'he sent to Winchester for his crown and other royal insignia and plate, left his army in camp, and came to York to celebrate Christmas'. As Maddicott points out, the return journey to Winchester—some 500 miles, and moreover in mid-winter—demonstrated the importance that the king attached to a ceremonial crown-wearing, 'perhaps conducted in the presence of English prisoners of war and certainly in hostile territory'. It also suggests, surely, 'that the city had not undergone the degree of destruction implied by the more lurid phrases of the chroniclers'. For these and other reasons, I stand by my view that York was treated harshly by William, 'but not more so than other major towns'.[14]

It is only just to add that historians are divided on the problem. One Domesday expert has taken issue with the argument presented here, calling the devastation 'appalling' and concluding that 'Yorkshire could well have been a desert in 1070', though others have taken a view similar to mine.[15] The Norman army must, at the least, have waged a campaign of deliberate devastation which shocked the chroniclers by going beyond what was accepted as legitimate strategic ravaging. One contemporary witness bears out the suffering entailed: distant Evesham Abbey (Worcs.) took in starving refugees from Yorkshire and other counties. And a near-contemporary account of the

---

13. Carl Stephenson, *Borough and Town* (Cambridge, Mass., 1933), 153, 221; Fletcher, *Bloodfeud*, 182; AY 8/4, 424.

14. J. R. Maddicott, *The Origins of the English Parliament 924–1327* (Oxford, 2010), 60; *VCHY*, 18; D. M. Palliser, *Domesday York*, BP 78 (York, 1990), 18.

15. J. J. N. Palmer, 'War and Domesday Waste', in M. Strickland, ed., *Armies, Chivalry and Warfare in Medieval Britain and France* (Stamford, 1998), 273–4, supported, e.g., by D. Carpenter, *The Struggle for Mastery: Britain 1066–1284* (Oxford, 2003), 77–8. In contrast: Paul Dalton, *Conquest, Anarchy and Lordship: Yorkshire, 1066–1154* (Cambridge, 1994), 23–5; AY 1, 189; Fletcher, *Bloodfeud*, 180–4; David Hey, *A History of Yorkshire* (Lancaster, 2005), 80–1. For a judicious summary of the debate: David Roffe, *Decoding Domesday* (Woodbridge, 2007), 250–6.

founding of St Mary's Abbey, York, has the Conqueror assent to it so that religion should be encouraged in that city, 'in which more blood had been shed than in the other cities of the English'.[16] Certainly some of York's wealthier inhabitants must have fled, whether to avoid robbery or death: there is a quite exceptional concentration of Yorkshire coin hoards ending with issues of c.1069–70, four of them from the city itself, comprising over 1,000 silver coins; and numismatic experts are convinced that they were associated with the 'Harrying'.[17]

Yet there are other reasons to doubt whether city and county, if badly ravaged, were a depopulated 'desert'. One is the rapid return of York's royal moneyers to strike coins for William. Of ten moneyers working before 1069 (all with Scandinavian names), five were striking coins again after 1070. Furthermore, four York moneyers issued coins of William's 'PAXS' type, datable 1083–6, and all four had Old Norse names.[18] It is impossible to trace the fate of the mass of the townspeople, but the fact that street names like Davygate and Castlegate were still being coined in Norse form after 1066 suggests a largely surviving population. So does the fact that a crowd of townspeople was able to testify in 1086 to pre-Conquest landholding arrangements: the Domesday commissioners heard evidence from 'many' present. And a revealing anecdote from 1101, when Henry I was embroiled in civil war, suggests that it was a very valuable royal city. One of the king's men advised him to buy support lavishly, even to the extent of giving away London or York.[19]

The city certainly had new masters who intended to exploit it. The lawmen and moneyers may still have been natives, but the real power lay with the conqueror's men, not all of them Normans. When William I issued a writ in favour of Archbishop Ealdred—significantly in English—at some point before the 1069 revolt, he forbade incursions on the archbishop's rights and possessions by 'any man . . . French or Flemish or English'. By 1086 all land was held either directly by the king or under him by the Church

16. W. D. Macray, ed., *Chronicon Abbatie de Evesham*, RS (London, 1863), 90–1; Christopher Norton, 'The buildings of St Mary's Abbey, York and their destruction', *Antiq J*, 74 (1994), 280.

17. Marion Archibald (pers. comm. 1989) told me she was 'confident that this is to be associated with the "Harrying of the North"', though the exact chronology of the early issues of William I is uncertain.

18. Information from Marion Archibald and the late Peter Seaby; also D. M. Metcalf, 'Notes on the "PAXS" type of William I', *Yorkshire Numismatist*, 1 (1988), 15, 18.

19. AY 1, 214; M. Chibnall, ed., *The Ecclesiastical History of Orderic Vitalis*, 6 vols, OMT (Oxford, 1969–80), V, 316–17.

and by a small number of Frenchmen; and the process must have started early, since William Malet had amassed many forfeited estates of Yorkshiremen before 1069, most close to York and some in the city itself. The pattern until about 1073 continued to be one of Normans given the confiscated lands of named Englishmen; after that, a single Norman was apparently allowed to seize almost all remaining English land in a given wapentake.[20]

By 1086 Robert, count of Mortain, was the chief landholder north and east of York, and Osbern d'Arches dominated Ainsty wapentake to the west. The king was careful to keep most of the city in his own hands, but nineteen 'Frenchmen' (*Francigene*) were listed in Domesday as holding 145 messuages, including Count Robert with a central block around Pavement and the Shambles. And the 'French' remained distinct for many years. When the 1106 inquest was held, attested by five French justices and twelve local jurors, all but one with Anglo-Scandinavian names, a local reeve had to act as interpreter. 'Forty years after the Norman Conquest, royal justices and the leaders of the local community could still not speak to each other directly.'[21]

The 'French' included the leading clergy as well as laity. When Ealdred died, William secured the appointment of a Frenchman, in this case Thomas, a royal chaplain and treasurer of Bayeux Cathedral. Thomas, who held the see of York for thirty years (1070–1100), is best remembered for his enforced obedience to the new archbishop of Canterbury, the Italian Lanfranc, but he deserves better. He exercised outstanding qualities of leadership in an unruly city and province, including a complete rebuilding of the ruined cathedral and a reorganization of its clergy.

Little is recorded of York between 1069–70 and the end of the reign, but it is clear that the city and county remained vulnerable. In 1070 Malcolm III of Scots raided north Yorkshire and carried off many inhabitants as slaves; and in 1075 another Danish force sailed upriver, 'travelled to York and broke into St Peter's Minster, and there took much property, and so went away'.[22] It was, perhaps, the damage they caused that spurred Thomas to undertake the rebuilding of his cathedral. And before William's reign was over, Benedictine monasticism was introduced to the city, another means by which the

20. *EYC*, I, no. 12; *RRAN*, I, no. 351; Robin Fleming, *Kings and Lords in Conquest England* (Cambridge, 1991), 153, 159–60; Newman, 'The "lost fee" of William Malet', with map on p. 266.
21. R. Bartlett, *England under the Norman and Angevin Kings 1075–1225* (Oxford, 2000), 503.
22. AY 1, 196.

conquerors sought to create sources of order and authority in restive Yorkshire.

For one of the features of the north which must have forcibly struck the Normans was the absence of monasteries under a strict Benedictine rule, a sharp contrast to Normandy and to England south of the Humber. Their first foundation was made close to York at Selby, in 1069–70, with the support of the new county sheriff Hugh fitz Baldric. The founder, Benedict of Auxerre, had unknowingly selected a site on royal land, but it was confirmed to him in person by the king, perhaps when he kept the Christmas feast of 1069 at York. At the same time another event led ultimately to the next two northern foundations, at Whitby and York. The inspiration came from Reinfrid, a soldier in William's army that autumn, who later became a monk at Evesham. Around 1074 Prior Aldwin of Winchcombe, reading Bede's *History* and realizing that the monasteries he described were now desolate, decided to visit them. He stopped at Evesham, where he met Reinfrid, and the two decided to journey north with another priest; the three paused at York to receive safe conduct from Sheriff Hugh. Their mission developed into an attempt to refound monasteries on their ancient sites, including Whitby about 1077: the first abbot, Stephen, later moved with some of the monks first to Lastingham and finally, by 1086, to York. The story of this, which became St Mary's Abbey, depends on the authenticity of an account by Abbot Stephen himself, famously dismissed by Dom David Knowles as 'wholly untrustworthy', but now accepted by most scholars as a genuine account compiled before *c.*1112.[23]

Domesday Book

The earliest evidence for the presence of the monks in York, as for much else already touched on, is Domesday Book. The date, purposes, and interpretation of that record have generated a huge literature, most of which need not concern us. What matters here is that in Domesday we possess an

23. Selby: R. B. Dobson, *Church and Society in the Medieval North of England* (London, 1996), ch. 2; Janet Burton, *The Monastic Order in Yorkshire 1069–1215* (Cambridge, 1999), 23–31; J. D. Hass, *Medieval Selby*, YAS Occasional Paper 4 (2006), 1–4. St Mary's and Whitby: Janet Burton, 'The monastic revival in Yorkshire', in D. Rollason et al., eds, *Anglo-Norman Durham 1093–1193* (Woodbridge, 1994), 41–51; Norton, 'The buildings of St Mary's Abbey', 280–2; Burton, *Monastic Order in Yorkshire*, 13–14, 32–44.

account of York both in 1066 and about 1086, and an account which makes
it the largest town described there with the possible exception of Norwich
(entries for London and Winchester are missing and that for Bristol is very
defective). Furthermore, there survives a separate survey of the archbishop's
rights in the city, close in date to Domesday, as well as a later inquest into the
rights of the cathedral chapter in 1106. Consequently, our knowledge of York
from 1066 to 1106 is better documented than for any earlier period.[24]

It is unnecessary to repeat what has been deduced from the Domesday
evidence for 1066, with the city's structure of wards, lawmen, and so forth,
but it may be remembered that the housing stock, or at least the number of
inhabited messuages, had been about 1,900. Since then there had been
much destruction, not least because one of the seven wards, Domesday tells
us, had been 'laid waste for the castles [*vastata in castellis*]'. The 1086 total is
not easy to arrive at, but possibly amounted to 1,000 or 1,200, excluding
those called 'empty' but not those described as 'not inhabited'—perhaps not
literally uninhabited, as they paid rent. The apportionment of revenues from
York was more in the king's favour than in 1066, when the earl of Northumbria had received one third of them; with no earl, William I took all the
profits except those of the archbishop, and he exacted a considerably
increased total: £100 a year instead of the £53 of 1066. That £100 was,
however, a total raised from thirteen outlying rural settlements as well as
from York itself, so the increase may not have been quite as large as the figures suggest.[25]

Domesday also provides incidental glimpses of some of the inhabitants and of their townscape. Most of those who held houses from the
king were great men with many estates elsewhere, but the careful enu-
meration of all the 'Frenchmen' included lesser figures who could well
have been residents, like Hamelin who held one messuage 'in the town
moat', or the sub-tenant Osbern son of Boso who held from Count Robert
fourteen messuages, 'two stalls in the meat market' (almost certainly the
Shambles), and the church of Holy Cross (St Crux). Few ordinary townspeople, French or English, were mentioned, though it might be noted that

24. Palliser, *Domesday York*; AY 1, 213–20; and for the two surveys of *c.*1080 and 1106, see Appendix
    V in this chapter.
25. House totals: Stephenson, *Borough and Town*, 221; H. C. Darby and I. S. Maxwell, eds, *The
    Domesday Geography of Northern England* (Cambridge, corrected edn 1977), 155; Palliser, *Domes-
    day York*, 13, 14. However, a maximum of at least 1,576 in 1086 is possible. The thirteen vills are
    mapped in Darby and Maxwell, *Domesday Geography*, 157.

the York entry is probably incomplete in its population figures. Domesday sometimes lists urban tenants under rural manors held by their lords (as with forty-eight burgesses described as 'in' the manor of Staines, but actually living in London). Possibly that could account for the curious reference to fifteen 'burgesses' in nearby Pocklington, not otherwise known to have had borough status; they could have lived in York as craftsmen but attached to that manor.[26]

Other than St Crux, seven parish churches are mentioned, six of them identifiable; but it was not the purpose of the survey to list streets or public buildings systematically. The eight churches were singled out because their ownership had changed since the Conquest, while but for Osbern's two stalls there is no mention of markets. The two Minster surveys are a little more informative about the extent of the archbishop's shire and of that other shire in which he enjoyed one third of the revenues, as we have seen. One rare piece of topographical information in the Domesday survey is the casual mention that William de Perci claimed to hold 'seven small messuages containing 50 feet in width', probably a row with seven-foot frontages for poor tenants; and another is a note that another messuage, which must have been larger, included four 'dings', apparently small shops or cellars for trading.[27]

Conquest consolidated: William II and Henry I

The reigns of the Conqueror's sons, William II 'Rufus' (1087–1100) and Henry I (1100–35), saw city and shire bound more firmly into a strong, centralized English state, as both granted extensive estates to loyal followers new to the county. By 1135, at least in lowland Yorkshire, these lords had in turn enfeoffed most of their chief tenants—in other words, they granted them land by hereditary fee in return for military service—and there developed a stable network of what we can begin to call a county gentry. Furthermore, both kings and lords founded monasteries and other religious institutions, bodies which were important in making the Norman settlement permanent. In all these directions, the role of the shire town was crucial.

26. F.W. Maitland, *Domesday Book and Beyond* (Cambridge, 1897), 111, 181; GDB, fo. 299c.
27. Palliser, *Domesday York*, 16, 21. *Dingis* has previously been taken as a mistranscription for *drengis*, i.e. a category of tenant: cf. AY 1, 187.

York's importance as a centre of northern power was emphasized by the two great building projects at the cathedral and St Mary's Abbey. Archbishop Thomas had probably planned his new cathedral before 1080, and it was certainly completed during Rufus's reign, since William of Malmesbury attests that it was finished before Thomas's death in 1100 (see Map 4). It was built on a vast scale, both longer and wider than Lanfranc's contemporary rebuilding of Canterbury, and it was surely a deliberate statement of the importance of the northern province. Eric Fernie has suggested that Anselm's extension of Lanfranc's cathedral was, in turn, a response to Thomas's work at York.[28]

Meanwhile, early in 1088 William II came to York and presided over the refoundation of St Mary's Abbey, in the presence of Thomas, three other bishops, and many nobles. The event has been downplayed, misdated, and even doubted altogether, since it was recorded only by Abbot Stephen, whose account has been unnecessarily doubted. Since he has now been rehabilitated as an authority, the problem disappears. As Norton puts it, 'what more natural than that the new king should have gone north to assure his hold on the very part of the kingdom which had caused his father so much trouble'. Stephen's monks had come to York by 1086, under the patronage of Alan the Red, earl of Richmond; but by granting them a new and larger site and cutting the first turf, Rufus formally made himself their founder. The abbey commended itself to him by becoming a loyal outpost in the north, and Stephen was relied on both by Rufus and by Henry I as a political supporter.[29]

About the time that Rufus refounded St Mary's, one of the leading Yorkshire barons, Ralph Paynel, refounded the pre-Conquest Christ Church as a Benedictine Priory of the Holy Trinity, while before 1100 the church of All Saints, Fishergate, was granted to Whitby Abbey and refounded as a Benedictine cell. With those, and with Selby only a few miles downriver, the

---

28. J. H. Harvey, *Cathedrals of England and Wales* (London, 3rd edn 1974), 85, 93, 94; *EYM*, I, 7, 209–13; E. Fernie, 'The effect of the Conquest on Norman architectural patronage', *ANS*, 9 (1986), 71–85; Norton, *Archbishop Thomas*, 28. Harvey estimates 59,000 sq. ft for York and 43,000 for Canterbury. For possible sources for Thomas's Minster, see E. Fernie, *The Architecture of Norman England* (Oxford, 2000), 122–4.

29. Norton, 'The buildings of St Mary's Abbey', 281; Burton, *Monastic Order in Yorkshire*, 41. Norton shows that the date 1089 often cited for Rufus's visit is an error; though there is no other evidence for his visit in 1088, the list of those present at the foundation ceremony makes a date after 12 March 1088 impossible. See also R. Sharpe, 'King Harold's daughter', *Haskins Society Journal*, 19 (2007), 4–6, 24, for estates held in 1086 by Alan and later donated to the abbey.

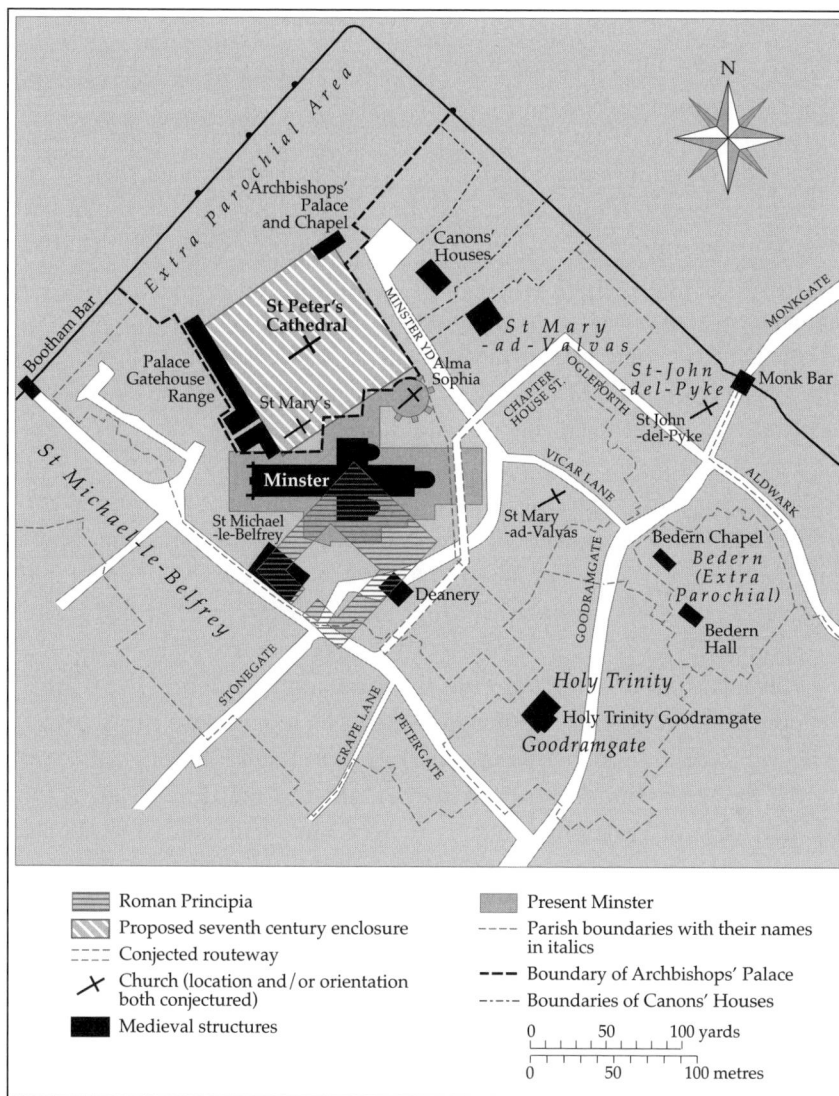

Map 4. The Minster area before and after the Norman Conquest
Some of the reconstruction is necessarily speculative, including the position of the pre-Conquest Minster, here labelled St Peter's Cathedral.

Source: Christopher Norton, 'The Anglo-Saxon Cathedral at York and the topography of the Anglian city', *Journal of the British Archaeological Association*, 151 (1998), 6. Permission given by the author and compiler, Prof. Christopher Norton.

York district was becoming an important monastic centre. Thomas of Bayeux, meanwhile, reorganized his cathedral clergy as a secular college or chapter on the lines which had become normal in northern France, with four senior officials (dean, precentor, treasurer, and master of the schools) and a body of canons each with his own house and 'prebend' or share of the cathedral revenues. It took effect sometime around 1090–1, but might have been planned some years earlier. Norton has plausibly suggested that Thomas's sustained opposition to the royal refoundation of St Mary's (which he maintained until 1093) stemmed from his fear that Abbot Stephen, Archbishop Lanfranc, or the king himself might have considered allowing the abbey to take over the Minster, thus turning it into a monastic cathedral, as had lately happened at Durham. It could have spurred Thomas to reorganize the Minster on secular lines, dividing the precinct between himself and the newly formed chapter of canons. The early history of the canonries or prebends is poorly recorded, but Sir Charles Clay gathered evidence that at least five were established by Thomas himself; and Hugh the Chanter testifies that Thomas also appointed the four senior officers once he had created the prebends.[30]

William II thus drew on vigorous northern leadership from the Church; but perhaps as important was his push north in 1092 against the Scots. He advanced to the Solway, refounding Carlisle as an English borough and ending the era when the Scottish territory reached to the Rere Cross, within two days' ride of York. Then in 1093 Robert Mowbray defeated and killed Malcolm III, whose son was installed (in 1097) as a client king. From the 1090s to the 1130s Scotland was a friendly, though not a subordinate, neighbour. Furthermore, Rufus seems to have reorganized landholding in Yorkshire as well as regions further north and west, forming strong lordships under reliable 'new men' on the potential Scottish invasion routes.[31]

'William Rufus had provided for the security of Yorkshire. It was to be Henry I and his "new men" who would consolidate his efforts.' Henry was lucky in being able to confiscate vast estates after a rebellion in 1101, allowing him to reshape Yorkshire lordships even more than his brother. They included many Ainsty manors west of York, and others further north and

30. Hugh the Chanter, *The History of the Church of York 1066–1127*, ed. C. Johnson, rev. M. Brett et al., OMT (Oxford, 1990), 19; R. M. T. Hill and C. N. L Brooke, 'From 627 until the early thirteenth century', in Aylmer & Cant, eds, 25–30; Norton, *Archbishop Thomas*, 6–9.
31. F. Barlow, *William Rufus* (London, 1983), 297–8, 316–18; Dalton, *Conquest, Anarchy and Lordship*, 82–7; Davies, *The First English Empire*, 5–7.

west, granted to Nigel d'Aubigny; estates east of the city acquired by Eustace fitz John; and the Helmsley lordship granted to Walter Espec. These three were the leading figures in northern government for much of the reign, helping to integrate Yorkshire peacefully into the national system of justice. One measure of Henry's success is that he could afford to delegate: after 1109 he visited the north only once or twice. However, it is possible that he chose to spend his birthday in York in 1122, and he was certainly an active patron of the Minster, St Mary's, Holy Trinity, and St Leonard's.[32]

More monastic foundations in Henry's reign brought further stability: St Clement's nunnery just outside the city walls, founded by Archbishop Thurstan about 1130 and probably incorporating an Anglo-Scandinavian church; and the Augustinian priory at Kirkham (c.1121) and Cistercian abbey at Rievaulx (1132), both founded by Walter Espec. The last provoked an unexpected consequence in the city: the monks who came from Clairvaux to found Rievaulx spent some months in York beforehand (1131–2). Their presence there fomented a revolt by some monks of St Mary's, who demanded reform of their own house from their elderly abbot. When he refused, the prior and thirteen monks seceded, and were protected by Archbishop Thurstan, who then granted them the site of Fountains Abbey near Ripon (1132). It was thus that the location of St Mary's, so accessible to visitors and to new ideas, was unwittingly crucial in creating what became the richest Cistercian monastery in Britain and a powerful neighbour to the city until 1539.[33]

Conflict, invasion, and civil war

Stephen's reign (1135–54) is familiar chiefly for his wars with rival claimants to the throne, his cousin Matilda and her son Henry. They have often received less prominence in histories of York than a 'conflagration' in 1137 which, on the usual reading of the chronicle evidence, must have destroyed almost the whole city. If, however, Norton's review of the evidence is correct, the fire

32. Dalton, *Conquest, Anarchy and Lordship*, 87–111 (quotation, p. 87); Judith Green, 'King Henry I and Northern England', *TR Hist S*, 6th ser., 17 (2007), 37, 49, 51–2.

33. D. Nicholl, *Thurstan: Archbishop of York* (York, 1964), 151–91; Burton, *Monastic Order in Yorkshire*, 103–7. The infamous assault on Thurstan at St Mary's, often misdated, occurred on 6 October 1132: C. Norton, 'Richard of Fountains and the letter of Thurstan', in T. N. Kinder, ed., *Perspectives for an Architecture of Solitude* (Turnhout, 2004), 10.

may be a myth based upon a misread text. It is perhaps unnecessary to rehearse his convincing argument at length, but it needs emphasis because even recent works of scholarship have drawn on the 'fire' to explain, for example, the rebuilding of much of the cathedral, without citing Norton's work or even showing awareness of it.[34] That aside, there are good reasons to give prominence to Stephen's reign. Both city and shire were heavily involved in the civil wars of 1138–53, and the king's problems were compounded when the man he selected to promote royal interests in Yorkshire came to act as an independent warlord. Furthermore, the civil wars became entangled with a conflict between rival claimants to the archbishopric; and finally, both struggles were complicated by an Anglo-Scottish tussle for control of the north.

David I (1124–53) was both an ambitious king of Scots and a leading English landholder; and the disputed English succession encouraged him to expand his territories by intervening on Matilda's side. Barrow has suggested that he aimed at a greater Scotland reaching to the Tees and the Ribble; others have gone further, seeing his aim as annexing the whole of Northumbria, to form a state with twin capitals at Edinburgh and York. In 1135–6 he crossed the border in force, prompting Stephen to come north and bring David to terms. The royal court of February 1136 at York was a significant one, involving homage to Stephen by David's heir, and also grants of privileges by Stephen to York Minster and to other great Yorkshire churches.[35]

In 1138 David invaded again, crossing the Tees and moving on York. Archbishop Thurstan rallied the county forces, who defeated the Scots near Northallerton at the Battle of the Standard, so called because the English rallied round a standard bearing the banners of St Peter of York and other great churches. The commanders included the young William le Gros, count of Aumale and lord of Holderness, who was rewarded by Stephen with the earldom of York and with supreme administrative power in Yorkshire.[36]

---

34. E. C. Norton, 'The York fire of 1137: Conflagration or consecration?', *NH*, 34 (1998), 194–204. Work published since 1998 but still assigning the 'fire' a role in Roger's reconstruction at the cathedral includes EEA 20 (2000), xxxiv, and Frank Barlow's biography of Roger in *ODNB*, 44 (2004), 833–4.
35. G. W. S. Barrow, 'David I', in *ODNB* 15, 285–8; Barrow, 'The Scots and the North of England'; Dalton, *Conquest, Anarchy and Lordship*, 204; K. J. Stringer, 'State-building in twelfth-century Britain', in J. C. Appleby and P. Dalton, eds, *Government, Religion and Society in Northern England 1000–1700* (Stroud, 1997), 59; G. J. White, *Restoration and Reform, 1153–1165* (Cambridge, 2000), 51; D. Crouch, *The Reign of King Stephen 1135–1154* (Harlow, 2000), 38n., 40–1, 322–4. For Stephen's grants in 1136, see *RRAN*, III, nos 99, 335, 716–17, 919, 975, 979.
36. R. H. C. Davis, *King Stephen* (Harlow, 3rd edn 1990), 31, 132. For William's career, see B. English, *The Lords of Holderness 1086–1260* (Oxford, 1979), 16–28; Dalton, *Conquest, Anarchy and Lordship*, 146–95; Dalton, 'William le Gros', in *ODNB*.

There was need for such a man, since Stephen had conceded Cumbria to King David in 1136, and in 1139 effectively surrendered Northumberland. It was doubtless the Scottish pressure that persuaded Stephen to give William powers previously exercised by the county sheriff, including control of the city of York, its castle, and its royal mint. Stephen's charter of 1140 for St Peter's Hospital is addressed to 'William earl of York and all his barons *and burgesses* of York' (my italics). In other words, York had joined Warwick and Leicester as a 'mediatized' county town, one whose immediate lord was not the king.[37]

York was in the front line for much of the civil wars. Stephen should have been able to rely on the earl, but William's private ambitions provoked a series of local conflicts which created near-anarchy in the county. For instance, the first recorded tournament in England—at York in 1142, between the men of Earl William and those of Earl Alan of Richmond—is documented only because Stephen intervened to break it up.[38] Furthermore, the experienced Thurstan had died in 1140, leaving a gap in northern ecclesiastical and secular leadership. The result was a further complication to the civil war, provoking a tussle between Stephen's candidate for the see, his cousin William fitz Herbert, and William's opponents in England and Rome. Matters came to a head in 1147 when the pope deposed William in favour of Henry Murdac, abbot of Fountains. Stephen refused to accept that, and the citizens of York were placed under papal interdict for preventing Henry from entering the city to be enthroned.

York in the 1140s has been called 'a frontier town...fiercely loyal to Stephen, but for much of the time left to its own devices, as its coinage clearly shows'. Its royal mint had long struck currency from punched dies distributed from London, but between about 1142 and 1150 its coins were all irregular issues of low weight (and some of Flemish style), struck from dies engraved locally. Of the ten York issues during those years, five bore Stephen's name, and the others those of 'Bishop Henry' (probably Henry Murdac), Eustace fitz John, Robert Stuteville, and the moneyer Thomas fitz Ulvieth, who was also alderman of the York guild merchant; all but Bishop Henry were closely associated with Earl William.[39]

---

37. *RRAN*, III, no. 991; Dalton, *Conquest, Anarchy and Lordship*, 153–4.
38. Bartlett, *England under the Norman and Angevin Kings*, 242.
39. Edmund King, *Medieval England 1066–1485* (London, 1988), 61; Mark Blackburn, 'Coinage and currency', in Edmund King, ed., *The Anarchy of King Stephen's Reign* (Oxford, 1994), esp. 182–7; Dalton, *Conquest, Anarchy and Lordship*, 161–2.

In 1149 Henry of Anjou, son and heir to Matilda, went to Carlisle to join his kinsman King David, together with Henry Murdac and Earl Ranulf of Chester. They planned to seize York and to rob Stephen of control of all northern England, under cover of installing Murdac as archbishop. However, warned by loyal supporters in York, King Stephen moved swiftly to secure the city and deter the assault. Nevertheless, his hold on Yorkshire remained insecure, and in 1151 he sought reconciliation with Murdac. Then in 1153–4 events moved rapidly. Murdac died in October; in November the civil war was ended by a treaty between Stephen and Henry of Anjou; and about the same time William fitz Herbert was re-elected archbishop. However, having returned in triumph for his enthronement in York in May 1154, he died suddenly within a month. In the summer Stephen made a military progress to the north, holding a great court at York, and demonstrating to Earl William and the other northern barons that 'they must forget the semi-independence some of them had assumed'. When the king died unexpectedly in October, Henry of Anjou succeeded him peacefully as Henry II (1154–89). Within a month of his coronation he marched north to secure the submission of Earl William at York, and to force him to disgorge the royal lordships he had held. The earldom of York was allowed to lapse.[40]

The early Angevins: 1154–1216

Henry's grip on the north was quickly demonstrated in other ways. In 1157 he compelled King Malcolm IV of Scots to surrender all land south of the Tweed and Solway; and it is striking that, unlike Stephen, he rarely needed to visit York. He was fortunate in that just before he took the throne, William fitz Herbert's death allowed for the promotion of Roger of Pont l'Evêque, who proved Henry's loyal servant during twenty-seven years as archbishop. A shrewd administrator and financier, he was able to fund a lavish rebuilding of the eastern arm of the Minster, as well as to build a great collegiate chapel of St Mary and All Angels north of the nave.

Only once was Henry's control of the north threatened, when rebels once more allied with a Scottish king, William the Lion (1173–4). One

---

40. W. L. Warren, *Henry II* (London, 1973), 36–7, 60; Stringer, 'State-building in twelfth-century Britain', 59; David Crouch, *The Normans* (London, 2002), 277.

regional magnate, Roger de Mowbray, persuaded many citizens to join the rising, as can be seen from the list of those later fined by the Crown. Roger aimed, according to one chronicler, to dominate Yorkshire by controlling 'the good city of York', and he may have appealed to those wealthy citizens chafing at control by the royal sheriff. As will be seen, it was either in 1173 or a little later that a group of them tried to set up a 'commune', or sworn association campaigning for corporate liberties, and Edward Miller certainly believed that Roger had 'a group of bourgeois retainers in York', one of them, Hugh son of Lefwin, who was among those heavily fined after the revolt collapsed. William the Lion was captured in battle, and in 1175 Henry summoned an assembly of nobles in York Minster, where William did him homage, leaving his breastplate, spear, and saddle on the high altar in token of submission.[41]

One other event of the reign was to have profound consequences for the city, the admission of Jews as residents. Henry II is known to have encouraged the spread of urban Jewish communities from about 1164, when he turned from Christian to Jewish creditors. Jews were under royal protection, at a price: the king could tallage (tax) them arbitrarily at any time. York was not one of the ten known Jewish settlements by 1159, but they were certainly present in the city by the 1170s, apparently at first as agents of a national syndicate dominated by Aaron of Lincoln.[42]

The first unambiguous references to resident Jews are from 1176, and it is from just that time that evidence also emerges of a curious turn in the city's Christian history. It was, seemingly, in 1177 that a cult of Archbishop William was initiated, apparently by his successor Roger. York Minster had never possessed a saint's shrine to rival those of Cuthbert at Durham, or John at Beverley; and the lack was keenly felt by the 1170s, when the cults of several major saints were promoted elsewhere, especially that of Thomas Becket at Canterbury. In that context, a series of thirty-three miraculous cures reported at William's tomb in Pentecost week 1177 can be seen as carefully 'orchestrated'. The cult has often been dated from William's canonization in 1226

---

41. Miller, 'Medieval York', 26; E. Miller, review of Mowbray charters in *NH*, 9 (1974), 173; Warren, *Henry II*, 138, 140, 185; Davies, *First English Empire*, 13, 14.

42. Previous studies of York's medieval Jews have been almost wholly superseded by the studies of R. B. Dobson, now usefully collected and reprinted as *The Jewish Communities of Medieval England*, ed. Helen Birkett (York, 2010). This is cited throughout this and the next chapter in preference to the original articles.

as St William of York, but the 1177 cases were only the most prominent of a series of miracles that preceded it.[43]

After Henry's death in 1189, the two sons who succeeded him had pressing reasons to raise money by selling charters of privilege to their leading towns. The Londoners led the way by taking advantage of Richard I's absence on crusade to form a commune under an elected mayor, and both Richard and John came to terms with them, John in 1215 recognizing the mayoralty if not the commune. York was not far behind, if inevitably the privileges granted were more modest than those of London. In 1189 Richard freed York from a wide range of charges on trade throughout his lands in England and France, in return for a substantial payment of 200 marks (£133.6s.8d.).[44] By Easter 1190 he went further, allowing the citizens to hold York in fee farm—that is, to bypass the county sheriff by themselves raising the various sums due to the Crown and to pay an agreed annual lump sum direct to the Exchequer. The latter privilege was, however, cancelled after only six months, perhaps as part of Richard's punishment of the citizens for the horrific events which had unfolded just before Easter.[45]

The notorious massacre of the city's Jews is well documented, especially by the chronicler William, a canon of Newburgh Priory fifteen miles (24 km) north of York. It was the worst of several urban massacres, triggered by crusading fervour, which had begun after Richard's coronation on 3 September 1189. Those who had tried to attend the coronation had included the two leading York Jews, Benedict and Josce; Benedict was killed, but Josce escaped home to York. Pogroms then spread to other towns, the last occurring in York in March 1190.

It was then that at least five Yorkshire barons in debt to Jewish moneylenders, led by Richard Malebisse, took advantage of the popular mood to burn Benedict's house and slaughter his family. The other Jews, led by Josce, took refuge in the royal castle under the protection of its constable. A tragic misunderstanding caused them to refuse him readmittance when he had gone out, and led to a siege by the county sheriff. Hopelessly trapped, most of the Jews committed suicide on 16 March, and next day the survivors were massacred as they emerged. Immediately after that, the conspirators (*conjurati*, as Newburgh called them) went to the cathedral to seize and burn

43. C. Norton, *St William of York* (Woodbridge, 2006), 150–64.
44. YCA, MS A2 (the original charter); *EYC*, I, no. 204; *CChR*, I, 379.
45. Pipe R. 2 Richard I, 59. J. Tait, *The Medieval English Borough* (Manchester, 1936), 179, notes the cancellation, but links it simply to lack of payment and an 'opportunist' Crown policy.

the Jewish bonds deposited there. The angry king ordered his chancellor, Longchamp, to punish the murderers, but the conspirators fled before he reached York with an armed force. In the event, Longchamp contented himself by arresting a hundred citizens, pending a trial (which never took place) and—as all the citizens denied involvement—imposing heavy fines in proportion to their wealth.[46]

The massacre, horrific though it was, resolved nothing, though its effect could still be seen in 1194, when York was conspicuously absent from the returns of a royal tax on English Jews. Nevertheless, within a year of the massacre, Benedict's sons were confident enough of their prospects to agree to pay the king 700 marks to inherit their father's lands and debts; and Jews returned to the city probably by 1195 and certainly by 1201.[47] Indeed, the York Jews were to become wealthier and more numerous in the thirteenth century than ever before.

The background to the Crown's weakness over the massacre, with hindsight, is that Richard's government in 1190 had no strong local support either in city, county, or archbishopric. The king's ill-judged decision in 1189 to nominate his quarrelsome half-brother Geoffrey as archbishop provoked continuing conflicts and local disorders for over twenty years, though Geoffrey's disputes with both Richard and John, and with many fellow clergy, have little relevance to the city's history, and they have fortunately been well told elsewhere. Secular government in the shire nearly received equally bizarre leadership in 1190 when Richard offered his nephew, Otto of Brunswick, the earldom of York, only to back down in the face of opposition from the Yorkshire barons: the evidence for the episode has been doubted but it seems reliable.[48]

In contrast to Richard I, his brother John (1199–1216) knew the city well, and visited it more often than any previous English king. He was there in 1200 for an abortive meeting with the Scottish king, and in 1201 when he

46. Dobson, *Jewish Communities*, 1–52; R. C. Stacey, 'Crusades, martyrdoms and the Jews of Norman England, 1096–1190', in A. Haverkamp, ed., *Juden und Christen zur Zeit der Kreuzzüge* (Sigmaringen, 1999), 248–50; M. J. Kennedy, 'William of Newburgh's writings on anti-Jewish violence', *ANS*, 25 (2003), 139–52. The documents about the massacre are almost all printed in E. Royle et al., *Clifford's Tower Commemoration 1190–1990* (York, 1990).

47. Bartlett, *England under the Norman and Angevin Kings*, 346–7; Dobson, *Jewish Communities*, 9, 25–6.

48. For Geoffrey: D. L. Douie, *Archbishop Geoffrey Plantagenet and the Chapter of York*, BP 18 (York, 1960); Marie Lovatt, ed., *York 1189–1212*, EEA 27 (Oxford, 2004). For Otto: A. V. Murray, 'Richard the Lionheart, Otto of Brunswick and the earldom of York: Northern England and the Angevin Succession', *Medieval Yorkshire*, 23 (Leeds, 1994), 5–12.

fined the citizens £100 for various offences. It was, however, the loss of
Normandy in 1204 which threw John back on his English resources; he was
in York every year from 1204 to 1209, and twice in 1210. In 1212, when
England was seething with discontent, he was back, granting the citizens the
privilege of holding the city at farm which they had briefly enjoyed under
Richard. In return, he exacted a down payment of £200 and three palfreys,
and an annual render of £160: 'the king had made a good bargain'.[49]

The king was in York again several times in the build-up to rebellion in
1214–15, a revolt initiated by a body of magnates dubbed by some chroniclers 'the Northerners', and with justice, even though not all were from the
north. In 1214–16 the county sheriff, assisted by the citizens, strengthened
the castle and city defences sufficiently to resist a siege by the rebel barons.
Nevertheless, when John was back in 1216, the citizens had to purchase his
'good will' for the huge sum of £1,000. Calm returned with the end of civil
war in 1217, but, as will be seen, the legacy of John's grants of civic autonomy were more long-lasting than the crisis.[50]

Crown, Church, and citizens

If York was by now irrevocably within a southern-based kingdom, it
remained the metropolitan see of the archdiocese of York and the hub of
royal administration for all Yorkshire, which until the twelfth century
included what are now Cumbria and north Lancashire. From the late
1060s the king's sheriff made the eastern castle his base, though it took
time for other functions to be centralized there. The county court, for
instance, was still held in early Norman times in 'the king's house' on Toft
Green (almost certainly that was where the county's Domesday inquest was
held), and in 1166 it met in the cathedral crypt.[51] From castle and king's
house the justice and administration of the shire were carried out; and
although the subject goes far beyond the city's history, it was of enormous
importance to it. Throughout the later Middle Ages, and indeed until the

49. Miller, 'Medieval York', 27, 33. The 1212 charter is enrolled in TNA, C 53/10, m. 6, and printed in *Rotuli Chartarum*, I, l. 187, and the key passage in A. Ballard, ed., *British Borough Charters 1042–1216* (Cambridge, 1913), 230–1.
50. J. C. Holt, *The Northerners* (Oxford, 2nd edn 1992); Miller, 'Medieval York', 27.
51. *EYC*, I, 405–7; *RCHMY* III, 106; D. M. Palliser, 'York's west bank', in P. V. Addyman and V. E. Black, eds, *Archaeological Papers from York* (York, 1984), 103, 108n.; Bartlett, *England under the Norman and Angevin Kings*, 152.

nineteenth century, a vast amount of business came to York, to the great advantage of the city's economy.

Royal justices held sessions in the city, sometimes in one of the castles, and at other times in private houses.[52] There were both royal and archiepiscopal mints, though the archbishop's right of coining was only intermittently exercised after 1100; otherwise, all coinage remained a royal monopoly except in the 1140s. Nor does this exhaust the list of royal powers. As lord of the city, the king enjoyed a wide range of tolls, charges, and fines, including an annual levy called *husgabel* on nearly all dwellings in his jurisdiction. Snarri the toll-gatherer (*theolenarius*), depicted with his money-bag on a seal of *c.*1150 found in York, could well have been a royal official. And because one of the 'forests' or royal hunting reserves was Galtres, just north of York, a mansion and prison were established for the royal larderer who administered it, named Davy Hall from the twelfth-century David le Lardener. He had extensive rights of tolls on bread, ale, grain, meat, and fish sold in the city.[53]

Yet, despite his extensive powers, the king was not the only great landholder in the city. Whereas many rural manors had a single lord, York was typical of county towns by having what Maitland called 'tenurial heterogeneity'. Many householders were tenants of other lords, of whom the greatest was the archbishop. As in most cathedral cities, the bishop had his own 'liberty' or exempt jurisdiction, which at York included far more than the cathedral close. Great Domesday and 'Rights and laws' between them make clear that Thomas of Bayeux, like his English predecessors, held one of the seven city wards and a third part of another.[54]

Once Thomas constituted a cathedral chapter, two parallel jurisdictions emerged: those of the archbishop himself, and of the dean and chapter, who controlled the Minster close and much else. The powers retained by the metropolitan himself were still extensive: in 1228 he was recorded as levying tolls on all merchants entering Micklegate Bar, while he also held an annual fair at Lammas (1 August). The Lammas fair, it is clear from later evidence, entailed the entire walled city being taken over for 48 hours by the archbishop's officers, who used all the city gates as toll points. This astonishing

---

52. Miller, 'Medieval York', 29, with references.
53. *EYC*, I, no. 142; Miller, 'Medieval York', 31; D. M. Palliser, 'York's earliest administrative record', *YAJ*, 50 (1978), 81–91. On Davy Hall: *VCHY*, 494–6. On the tolls: T. Widdrington, *Analecta Eboracensia*, ed. C. Caine (London, 1897), 251–2. Snarri's seal: G. Zarnecki et al., eds, *English Romanesque Art 1066–1200* (London, 1984), no. 373; Richard Hall, *English Heritage Book of York* (London, 1996), 65.
54. Maitland, *Domesday Book and Beyond*, 178.

privilege, still in force in the eighteenth century, can only have come about because it was enjoyed from at least the time of Archbishop Thurstan (1119–40), long before there was a city corporation.[55]

The wider role of the archbishop was undoubtedly diminished after the Conquest, because William I acted in conjunction with Archbishop Lanfranc to subordinate York to Canterbury, compelling Thomas of York in 1072 to accept Lanfranc's primacy. That story, and the sequel of friction between the two Church provinces which lasted nearly three centuries, cannot be pursued here; but it is worth noting Lanfranc's persuasive argument to the king, as reported by the York chronicler Hugh the Chanter. All Britain, he told William, should be subject to Canterbury's authority, and especially the province of York: otherwise 'some one of the Danes, Norwegians or Scots, who used to sail up to York in their attacks on the realm, might be made king by the archbishop of York and the fickle and treacherous natives of that province'.[56]

Hugh's *History*, a major source for the primacy dispute from a northern perspective, is unfortunately much briefer on other matters, and he has very little to say of the great achievements of Thomas of Bayeux, including his rebuilding of the cathedral, organization of its chapter, and rearrangement of the precinct. These achievements are now much clearer, thanks to the excavations of 1967–73, which demonstrated both the scale and quality of Thomas's cathedral, and to the researches of Christopher Norton, who judges that 'no other archbishop has had a greater or more lasting impact on York Minster except Paulinus'. It has been suggested that it was also probably Thomas who introduced to his province the Use of York, which liturgically was to mark out the archdiocese from most of the English Church which followed the prevailing Use of Sarum.[57]

King and archbishop were far the most powerful lords in the city—in the absence any longer of an earl—but they increasingly competed with other groups and individuals, especially the new monasteries and the leading merchants and craftsmen. The monastic foundations under the Norman kings have already been sketched, and they were not quite the final total, for

55. 1212 tolls: J. H. Harvey, 'Bishophill and the Church of York', *YAJ*, 41 (1965), 384n. Lammas Fair: F. Drake, *Eboracum* (London, 1736), 218; D. M. Palliser, *Tudor York* (Oxford, 1979), 182; B. English, ed., *Yorkshire Hundred and Quo Warranto Rolls*, YASRS 151 (Leeds, 1996), 258.
56. Johnson et al., eds, *Hugh the Chanter*, 4–5. I have preferred 'natives of that province' to the editors' 'Yorkshiremen'.
57. Norton, *Archbishop Thomas*, 33; M. C. Salisbury, *The Use of York*, BP 113 (York, 2008), 38.

around 1200 the church of St Andrew, Fishergate, was refounded as a Gilbertine priory, a double house of men and women. Far and away the richest was St Mary's Abbey, with its extensive royal and aristocratic gifts of lands. These included Alan the Red's grant to it of 'the borough in which the church is located, from Galmou [Bootham Bar] as far as Clifton and towards the water (of Ouse)', the basis of the abbey's control of the suburb of Bootham. And in its first fifty years St Mary's 'far outstripped the expansion of either Selby or Whitby' to become the richest monastery in Yorkshire.[58]

One other great ecclesiastical institution has not yet been considered, since its origins are obscure, and since it was not strictly a Norman monastic foundation, the Hospital of St Leonard between the Minster and the city defences. It had apparently begun as a pre-Conquest Hospital of St Peter, administered by the cathedral; an undated royal writ (of 1088?) confirmed to it a generous grant of a thrave (twenty sheaves) of corn from every working plough in the diocese of York. A late source, the *History of the Foundation of St Leonard's*, credits William II with a refoundation on a new site; it certainly attracted grants and privileges from Henry I and Stephen; and the *History* says that Stephen built it a new church dedicated to St Leonard. By the thirteenth century it had become a quasi-monastery, staffed by brothers and sisters following the Augustinian rule.[59]

It was especially the greater churches and monasteries which made jurisdiction in York so complex after 1066. 'The territory of the city', Miller reminds us, 'was not a single area of franchise. It was honeycombed with other franchises, some of them older than the liberty of the city', and especially the five great liberties (or franchises) of the archbishop, dean and chapter, St Mary's, St Leonard's, and Holy Trinity. The story of the thirteenth century was to be played out on a battlefield of competing jurisdictions.[60]

An inquest of 1106 found that the cathedral dean could hold a court for all offences committed on church lands inside and outside the city, and that the archbishop could levy tolls, *husgabel*, and profits of justice from his liberty

58. *EYC*, I, no. 350; *RRAN*, I, no. 313; Burton, *Monastic Order in Yorkshire*, 41–3, with the important reading of *usque Cliftonam* rather than Farrer's *versus Cliftonam*. For Galmou and Galmanho: J. H. Harvey, 'A Bootham mystery—Galmanho, Kenningdike, Werkdike', *YH*, I (1976), 13, 14, with map.
59. *VCH Yorks*. III, 336–45; *EYC*, I, nos 166–99; *RRAN*, I, no. 353. Fortunately, P. H. Cullum has now clarified the hospital's history in her *Cremetts and Corrodies*, BP 79 (York, 1991); 'St Leonard's Hospital, York', in R. Gilchrist and H. Mytum, eds, *Advances in Monastic Archaeology*, BAR British ser. 227 (Oxford, 1993), 11–18; 'St Leonard's Hospital, York, in 1287', in D. M. Smith, ed., *The Church in Medieval York*, BTC 24 (York, 1999), 17–28.
60. Miller, 'Medieval York', 38.

and properties in York. These extensive privileges became a model for others. Richard I granted St Mary's the same rights as St Peter's, explicitly including a court for the abbey's staff and tenants; St Leonard's built up a similar liberty from at least Henry I's reign; and both exercised jurisdiction not only over their walled precincts, but over their tenants living anywhere inside or outside York. Holy Trinity Priory was less privileged, but its claim to a court for its tenants, with power of capital punishment, was to be a flashpoint later. Consequently, the tenants of at least four of the exempt liberties were excluded from the citizens' courts once they were established; and when royal justices visited York, they held special sessions at the doors of the Minster, St Mary's, and St Leonard's.[61]

Clashes over jurisdiction were to be by no means the only sources of conflict as, from 1212–13, the city fathers flexed their muscles. The Crown, we have seen, had been the landlord of most householders, but increasingly many properties were given or sold to monasteries in York and throughout northern England. A royal inquest of 1228 uncovered evidence for the grant of at least 164 York houses and rents to thirty-two different ecclesiastical institutions, mostly before 1216; and the true total must have exceeded 250, since returns for nearly half the city parishes are missing. Given that by 1290 at least forty-six northern monasteries owned city property, and that many of the parish churches had been appropriated to monasteries, York was almost as important an ecclesiastical as a royal town.[62]

Despite this competition, the collective power of the citizens slowly made headway. They exercised some privileges by prescription—that is, they had no written authority for them—while others were granted by a succession of royal charters, starting with Henry II's of 1155–62. Kings had long found it convenient to delegate power to groups of leading townsmen (they were all males), reserving the right to withdraw those powers if order was not kept or taxes and dues not collected; and before the mid-twelfth century such delegation was often made by word of mouth. Henry II's charter confirmed to the citizens those rights they had enjoyed under Henry I, which has misled some commentators, even the great Stubbs, into

61. Miller, 'Medieval York', 38–9; AY 1, 220–5.
62. Rees Jones, 'Property, tenure and rents', ch. 4; TNA, E135/25/1; D. M. Palliser, ed., 'An early mortmain inquest', in Smith, ed., *The Church in Medieval York*, 1–15; Burton, *Monastic Order in Yorkshire*, 253.

assuming an earlier charter since lost; but as Miller put it, 'the substratum of the city's liberties... was laid down without warrant of a charter'.[63]

Furthermore, 'most of the towns that won liberties in the twelfth century... did so because they were already capable of acting collectively to negotiate for themselves'. That body at York was almost certainly the group of Domesday lawmen still active in 1106, when one of them, Ulviet son of Forno, was spokesman for the jury at the inquest on the cathedral chapter. In 1129–30 Ulviet's son Thomas bought from Henry I the right to be alderman of the York 'guild', i.e. a guild merchant of the type enjoyed in many towns, who had a monopoly of trade in their own city. Such bodies are not to be confused with the later merchant guilds, such as York had from 1357.[64]

Whether or not the *gildegard* of *c.*1080 mentioned in 'Rights and laws' was the hall of the guild merchant, York certainly had such a guild. Not only was Thomas its alderman, but there is also the evidence of a charter of Archbishop Thurstan granting the 'men' of Beverley all the liberties enjoyed by the men of York, including a *hanshus*. A hanse—an association of merchants for trading purposes—was sometimes synonymous with a guild merchant; and indeed Henry I's charter to Beverley, confirming Thurstan's grant, speaks of *gilde mercatorum* instead of *hanshus*.[65] It looks as though the lawmen had transformed themselves into a guild merchant: and that guild was one of the rights confirmed to York by Henry II. And that guild, in turn, must have transformed itself by unrecorded stages into the citizen body which could acquire rights of self-government from Richard I and John. But that is to anticipate.

63. Miller, 'Medieval York', 32. Cf. D. M. Palliser, 'Towns and the English state, 1066–1500', in J. R. Maddicott and D. M. Palliser, eds, *The Medieval State* (London, 2000), 127–45. For the assumption of a lost Henry I charter: W. Stubbs, *Select Charters*, ed. H. W. C. Davis (Oxford, 9th edn 1913), 131; W. Giles, *Catalogue of the Charters . . . and other . . . Documents belonging to the Corporation of York* (York, 1909), 11; C. W. Hollister, *Henry I* (New Haven and London, 2001), 2.

64. AY 1, 220–1; Pipe R. 31 Henry I (PRS, new edn 1929), 34; D. M. Palliser, 'The birth of York's civic liberties, c. 1200–1354', in S. Rees Jones, ed., *The Government of Medieval York: Essays in Commemoration of the 1396 Royal Charter*, Borthwick Studies in History 3 (York, 1997), 88–107, at 90–1. Cf. C. Gross, *The Gild Merchant*, 2 vols (Oxford, 1890); E. Coornaert, 'Les ghildes médiévales', *Revue Historique*, 199 (1948), 22–55, 208–43; Reynolds, *An Introduction to the History of English Medieval Towns* (Oxford, 1977), 82. The quotation is from Reynolds, 'English towns', in A. Haverkamp and H. Vollrath, *England and Germany in the High Middle Ages* (London, 1996), 273.

65. *EYC*, I, nos 95, 96; EEA V, no. 31. The term *hanse* has caused some confusion with the later imperial Hanse or Hanseatic League, but it first appears in an urban context in England and Flanders, not in Germany: H. Pirenne, *Les Villes et les Institutions Urbaines*, 2 vols (Paris and Brussels, 1939), II, 157 ff.; Coornaert, 'Les ghildes médiévales', 224–31; Reynolds, *English Medieval Towns*, 199; T. H. Lloyd, *England and the German Hanse 1157–1611* (Cambridge, 1991), 1. Henry II's York charter still survives in the city archives: YCA, MS A1; it is datable only by the attestation of Thomas Becket as royal chancellor.

In 1175–6 Henry II fined some leading citizens 'for having the king's benevolence', and Thomas of Beyond Ouse and his sons were fined specifically 'for the commune which they wished to make'. A commune was a sworn association, often urban, which had become a popular vehicle in Flanders and northern France to press for municipal autonomy: and it is surely no coincidence that Flemings had been in York in 1173–4 during the Young King's rebellion. It is not clear whether the illegal commune was set up in 1173–4, as Miller and I have suggested, or in 1175–6, a date which has the weighty authority of Tait and Reynolds: either way, it was quashed by Henry—as he had recently done with a similar commune at Gloucester. He was no more prepared to brook insubordinate townsmen than turbulent priests; and York remained firmly under the thumb of the royal sheriff.[66] The citizens did not have to wait long after Henry's death, however, for his sons to sell them privileges of real self-government, as we have seen: Richard's temporary grant of the fee farm in 1190, and John's regrant of the same privilege in 1212. Furthermore, two other signs of autonomy, elected officers and a corporate seal, were assumed by the citizens without a charter, though probably with tacit royal consent.

At some point between 1191 and 1207 the civic leaders were employing a common seal to authenticate their collective decisions, apparently inscribed 'The seal of the loyal citizens of York'. That was one of the key privileges being sought by the larger towns, and if it is as early as 1191 or so, York's would be the second earliest recorded municipal seal, after Oxford.[67] And from 1213 royal writs were being addressed to the mayor and reeves of York, evidence that the later pattern—an annually elected mayor assisted by three reeves or bailiffs—was already in place. No more is heard of the guild merchant after 1200, presumably because it had been subsumed into the new corporate body. Evidence that this was the case is that the main seat of civic government has been called the Guildhall or Common Hall (rather than the City or Town Hall) ever since its first mention in 1256. It probably already stood on its present site off Coney Street, a site previously occupied by the house of Hugh son of Lefwin, one of those fined for the 1173 civic

---

66. Pipe R. 1175 (PRS 22), 172, 179–80, 182–3; Tait, *Medieval English Borough*, 177; Miller, 'Medieval York', 26, 32; Reynolds, *English Medieval Towns*, 106; Palliser, 'Birth of York's civic liberties', 91.
67. British Museum, *Catalogue of Seals*, II, 218, no. 5542; R. B. Pugh in *VCHY*, 544; and further references in Palliser, 'Birth of York's civic liberties', 92n. The inscription is damaged; the second seal, probably 13th century, is clearly inscribed SIGILLUM CIVIUM EBORACI.

revolt—yet another possible link between the guild merchant and the later corporation.[68]

By 1215, seemingly, the increasing collective activity of the citizens was already being exercised at a level that affected daily life. Like all western Europeans, the townspeople lived in a world of multiple kinds of law and custom. Alongside the international systems of civil (Roman) and canon (Church) law was English royal law, and under that various forms of 'feudal', manorial, mercantile, and municipal law, much of it customary and unwritten. York developed its own body of customary law very early, covering important areas like trade, property ownership, inheritance, and family life: but we are severely hampered in understanding it because the city's medieval court records do not survive, and there is no known list of citizens' customs until the early sixteenth century. One or two surviving references to York customary law will be cited in Chapter 5, but it has to be accepted that a major source for urban life is lost to us.[69]

Society, economy, and culture

Between 1000 and 1300 there were major social and economic changes, including increases in population, commercial activity, and the quantity of money in circulation. Many of these developments, especially commercialization, were well under way by the twelfth century, and must presumably have underlain the aspirations of the more prosperous urban merchants and craftsmen towards self-government.[70] Furthermore, not only was population growing, but the urban share of that population was increasing. There are no reliable figures, but London's population may have doubled in the twelfth century, and indirect indicators (such as an increasingly crowded townscape) suggest that York's growth was also substantial. As for wealth, however much York may have been set back by the disasters of 1068–70, it seems to have

---

68. Palliser, 'Birth of York's civic liberties', 95–6.
69. Rees Jones, 'Property, tenure and rents', 2–8, for the lack of court records; *YCR*, IV, 184–8 for the nearest York has to a list of customs, though Widdrington, *Analecta Eboracensia*, 90–111, was able to draw on medieval court records since lost. For the importance of borough custom, see Reynolds, *English Medieval Towns*, 92–5, 126; and for the neglect of the subject, M. Kowaleski, 'The history of urban families in medieval England', *Journal of Medieval History*, 14 (1988), 50 ff.
70. Richard H. Britnell, *The Commercialisation of English Society 1000–1500* (Manchester, 2nd edn 1996); *Markets, Trade and Economic Developments in England and Europe, 1050–1550* (Farnham, 2009).

paid the Exchequer more in tax than any towns other than London, Winchester, or Lincoln. Under Henry II it ranked even higher, second only to London in its contributions to royal tallages, though by 1194–1206 it was overtaken by Bristol and Lincoln.[71]

An increasing population must have resulted from natural growth, immigration, or both. The current orthodoxy is that most pre-industrial towns had a surplus of deaths over births and required substantial immigration to grow, and there is no shortage of suggestions at York of immigration, both local and long-distance. Men named in twelfth-century deeds include many names from local villages, including Fulford, Cawood, Knapton, and Warthill; a few were named from smaller Yorkshire towns, such as Doncaster and Pontefract; while more distant arrivals came from Nottingham, Norfolk, and Cornwall. If we can believe a satirical sketch of English towns in the 1190s, York was also 'full of Scotsmen'. The great majority, however, must have been a mixed crowd of Yorkshiremen and Danes, who developed their own patois. For this we have the testimony of William of Malmesbury, who complained that 'the whole language of the Northumbrians, especially in York, is so grating and uncouth that we southerners cannot understand a word of it'. This, like a similar complaint from Ranulf Higden two centuries later, is evidence of a strong northern dialect shared by the city.[72]

It is hard to glimpse individuals from that period beyond their mere names, and more so to establish family relationships, or even—in some cases—to decide how many references are to the same person. Recent studies of two prominent churchmen well illustrate the problems. The father of Archbishop William has been recently shown to be a Herbert who had been granted Yorkshire estates by a previous archbishop, and not another Herbert identified by earlier scholars; and a much-cited study of Paulinus of Leeds, master of St Peter's Hospital, York, is shown to have conflated references to *four* different men, one of them confusingly called Paulinus of York.[73]

71. S. K. Mitchell, *Taxation in Medieval England* (New Haven, 1951), 313; M. Biddle, ed., *Winchester in the Early Middle Ages* (Oxford, 1976), 500–1; Bartlett, *England under the Norman and Angevin Kings*, 333.

72. *EYC*, I, 188, 191, 211, 218, 225, 242, 254, 258; J. T. Appleby, ed., *The Chronicle of Richard of Devizes* (London, 1963), 66; William of Malmesbury, *De Gestis Pontificum Anglorum*, ed. N. E. S. A. Hamilton, RS (London, 1870), 209; Bartlett, *England under the Norman and Angevin Kings*, 491.

73. Norton, *St William of York*, 10, 11, 203–38; D. X. Carpenter, 'The several lives of Paulinus', *NH*, 46 (2009), 9–29.

Nevertheless, leading families were starting to be recorded often enough for plausible links to be made between generations. One of the jurors of 1106, for instance, was Gamel son of Swartecol, possibly the Gamel holding York properties in Domesday. Given the rarity of the name Swartecol, his father was probably the moneyer Swartcol who struck coins at York between 1044 and 1071, and the same Swartcol who had held four Yorkshire manors in 1066—especially as one of those manors (Askham Richard) had the same Norman overlord in 1086 as Gamel's York housing.[74] We are on firmer ground with the family of Ulvet son of Forno, city lawman and foreman of the 1106 jury, and probably identical with the Ulf who struck York coins for both Henry I and Stephen. Thomas son of Ulvet was the man confirmed as alderman of York's guild in 1129–30; the same Thomas was around 1150 granted land in Holderness by Earl William, and was probably the same Thomas son of Ulf who struck coins for the earl. Confusingly, Thomas appears in charters between the 1140s and 1170s both as Thomas son of Ulvet and as Thomas of Beyond Ouse (*de Ultra Usam*). He was the man who with his sons tried to form a city commune in the 1170s, and those sons remained prominent until about 1200—one of them called Thomas son of Thomas of Beyond Ouse.[75]

Such families were, inevitably, among the rich and powerful: we cannot learn much about the far larger number of lesser townspeople, as they are seldom recorded at this period. Many poor craftsmen, day labourers, casual workers, paupers, and vagrants are beyond recall. We can only guess that like the non-freemen of later centuries, they had few or no economic or social rights, and a poorer diet and shorter life expectancy than the rich. Almost the only glimpses we have of them are the sparse details of sick and diseased individuals recorded as being miraculously cured, and the larger number whose burials have been studied, especially from the churchyard of the poor parish of St Helen-on-the-Walls. Among the former, thirty-three miraculous cures are recorded as taking place at the tomb of St William in Pentecost week 1177, six of them of inhabitants of York. Three had crippled limbs, one a humped back, and one was blind. Probably all were humble folk: the two

74. R. Fletcher, review of Palliser, *Domesday York*, in *YAJ*, 65 (1993), 198.
75. Most evidence for the family is assembled in C. T. Clay, 'A Holderness charter of William Count of Aumale', *YAJ*, 39 (1957), 339–42; Miller, 'Medieval York', 26, 32; English, *Lords of Holderness*, 158, 216; and Dalton, *Conquest, Anarchy and Lordship*, 154, 161, 183. The interval is rather long for the Thomas of 1130 to be also the commune leader of the 1170s: Clay and Miller accepted that, but D. E. Greenway (*Charters of the Honour of Mowbray*, RSEHNS 1, 1972, xxx, 83–4) identifies the commune leader as Thomas son of Thomas.

men were simply identified as 'Geoffrey' and 'Henry', and the three women
and a girl were not even named, though one—her cure attested by Archbishop Roger in person—was described as living in Walmgate. The skeletal
sample is much larger (nearly 1,050 individuals from St Helen's churchyard),
but it covers a wide time span and cannot be differentiated even by centuries. Dawes' study of 1980 found that most had apparently had an adequate
diet, but 36 per cent of adult men and 56 per cent of women died by their
mid-thirties.[76]

However, more recent work by Grauer and Mays has compared the
St Helen's burials to those from Wharram Percy, and the contrasts are interesting. More of the York group probably suffered from infectious disease for
longer periods than the rural group, perhaps because the townspeople lived
in a more 'pathogen-rich' environment exposing them to 'chronic gut infec-
tions': in compensation, the York group seem to have built up greater resistance to disease. More unexpectedly, both cemeteries display a shift between
about the eleventh and thirteenth centuries from long, narrow skulls to a
rounder shape (and then back again after 1300 or so). When this was observed
at St Helen's, it was attributed by some to the effect of ethnic changes after
1066, but that was always highly unlikely; and it is now clear that these
changes, still unexplained, were found in a remote village as well as a large
city, and indeed were widespread in western Europe.[77]

As for the work available in York—presumably the main attraction for
many of those drawn from villages and smaller towns by the hope of
better economic opportunities—evidence of crafts practised before the
thirteenth century is limited; but the few witnesses to early deeds identified by their trade included a merchant, a goldsmith, an innkeeper, a
tiler, and several saddlers.[78] The most prominent manufacturing sector
in early records, however, was textile working. York, like other towns,
seems to have shifted in the eleventh century from domestic weaving, often
by women, to male-dominated workshop production. Part of a horizontal
treadle-operated loom was discovered in Coppergate in a late eleventh-
century deposit, suggesting that the city was in the forefront of the new
technology. It was not long before the city's weavers were important enough
to form a guild, authorized by Henry II in 1163. The annual fee they paid

76. HCY, II, 531–7; Norton, St William of York, 153–7; AY 12/1, 28–9, 63.
77. AY 12/1, 75, 82–3, 113; S. Mays, 'The human remains', in S. Mays et al., The Churchyard: Whar-
    ram: A Study of Settlement on the Yorkshire Wolds, XI (York, 2007), esp. 111–13, 169–70.
78. EYC, I, 175, 178, 186, 230, 243, 252.

the Exchequer (£10) was second only to that of the London weavers, though by John's reign they struggled to meet the payments.[79]

It might be, however, that the weavers were recorded so early because of the value of their products and the royal interest (nearly all the urban craft guilds licensed by the king in the 1160s were of weavers). By the time that the records of new freemen survive (1272–3), leather craftsmen outnumbered textile workers, and judging from the predominance of cattle over sheep bones from excavations, the same may have been true in the twelfth century. Certainly three of the four York guilds next recorded after 1163 were leather crafts: glovers, saddlers, and skinners. There must, of course, have been large numbers of many other craftsmen—in the building, metalworking, victualling, and other sectors—but we can glimpse them only where their products survive archaeologically. Pottery, for instance, survives in large quantities, including 'beautifully produced York seal jugs', though it is not known whether any was made in the city itself rather than in rural potteries nearby.[80]

Local marketing must always have been widespread, and if Marketshire (Pavement) was one of the seven Domesday wards, the entire Pavement/Ousegate/Coppergate/Shambles area may already have formed a large series of markets, of which the meat market (Shambles) was only one part; fish markets were probably already located, as later, by Ouse and Foss Bridges. The markets—again judging from later records—will have attracted rural customers living up to half a day's journey away, and as elsewhere the main market day will have been Sunday, allowing time for both townsfolk and countryfolk away from their normal work. That is clear because Abbot Eustace of Flay, on a revivalist preaching tour in England in 1201, visited York, was honourably received by Archbishop Geoffrey, and persuaded at least some to give up Sunday trading.[81]

Since there was only one city bridge over the Ouse, and probably still only one on the Foss, water transport and ferries were crucial. The most vital traffic streets were those linking the bridges, the city gates (bars), and the cathedral, including Micklegate, Petergate, Stonegate, Fossgate, and Ousegate. Most important of all was already Coney Street ('King's Street'), which gave access between the castle, Ouse Bridge, and St Mary's Abbey,

79. AY 17/11, 1763–6, 1815, 1827; *EYC*, I, no. 349; H. Heaton, *The Yorkshire Woollen and Worsted Industries* (Oxford, 2nd edn 1965), 3; Miller, 'Medieval York', 44.
80. Miller, 'Medieval York', 44; A. Mainman and A. Jenner, *Medieval Pottery from York*, AY 16/9 (2013), 1315.
81. Bartlett, *England under the Norman and Angevin Kings*, 638.

and which had many quays and warehouses at its rear. It was Coney Street property which was bought by Durham Priory in the 1150s from Haco of Torksey, probably a merchant from that Lincolnshire river port. Domesday testifies to the importance of the water route between Torksey and York; Henry I ordered renewal of the Foss Dyke as a waterway; and when King John held a Christmas court in York, venison was shipped from Torksey. In the 1180s and 1190s Geoffrey Haget, a local lord and royal justice, had property in Coney Street, presumably as a base for his royal business. And certainly by the thirteenth century Coney Street was the location both of the Guildhall and of the main concentration of Jewish houses.[82]

Longer-distance trade is recorded sporadically. If we again admit miracle stories in evidence, one records a cargo vessel sailing from Bishop's (now King's) Lynn to York in 1069, and another some York merchants (*negotiatores*) sailing to Scotland with an unspecified cargo sometime in the twelfth century. William of Malmesbury wrote of German and Irish ships docking at York; a city merchant, William Selby, exported corn in 1166, probably to Flanders; and by 1183 wine, very likely from Gascony, was regularly shipped to York. Long-distance trade called for financiers to lubricate it by exchanging coins, and there are hints that in the 1160s and 1170s York moneyers like William Bretegate were chiefly engaged in exchange rather than minting.[83]

By John's reign, Exchequer records allow some measure of the importance of York's craft and trade sectors relative to other towns. In 1202, twenty-eight towns paid fines for exemption from royal regulations about standard cloth sizes, and—for what it is worth—York paid the second largest fine after Lincoln, with Newcastle third. That does not mean that York was the second largest clothmaking centre, but it clearly ranked high. As for overseas trade, returns survive of a short-lived tax on the exports and imports of east and south coast ports in 1203–5. London led with a payment of £837 (17 per cent of the total), Hull came sixth with £345 (7 per cent), York seventh with £175 (4 per cent), and Newcastle

82. G. V. Scammell, 'Four early charters relating to York', *YAJ*, 39 (1956), 87; Miller, 'Medieval York', 27; EEA 24, no. 29; Fletcher, *Bloodfeud*, 198; J. Bond, 'Canal construction in the early Middle Ages', in J. Blair, ed., *Waterways and Canal-Building in Medieval England* (Oxford, 2007), 167, 175–6.

83. *HCY*, I, 287–8; Burton, *Monastic Order in Yorkshire*, 26; Hass, *Medieval Selby*, 1, 78; William of Malmesbury, *De Gestis Pontificum*, 208–9; Miller, 'Medieval York', 41–2; I. Stewart, 'The English and Norman mints, *c.* 600–1158', in C. E. Challis, *A New History of the Royal Mint* (Cambridge, 1992), 88n., 93 and n.

eighth with £158 (3 per cent). Until the late twelfth century York had remained the leading Yorkshire port despite its location well inland, but once Hull was founded by Meaux Abbey as an outlet for its wool exports (1193), its rise was clearly rapid.[84]

Two groups who can in different ways be termed outsiders call for separate mention: ecclesiastics from outside York and those recent arrivals, the Jews. City life must have been strongly influenced by the many priests, monks, and nuns in the area, not only those resident in York. Within twelve miles (19 km) there were, for instance, six modest nunneries founded in the twelfth century, most of which had close relations with the city and looked there for supplies. The Cistercians sent to establish Rievaulx went via York, and it was there that Ailred—later its most famous abbot—heard of them; the second Yorkshire Cistercian house, Fountains, originated of course from St Mary's; and the first abbot of Hood (predecessor of Byland Abbey) was visiting York when he died in 1142.[85]

Many northern monasteries acquired York town houses through gifts and bequests, or bought them as bases for visits to the city. Fountains, for example, acquired several properties from the 1170s, mostly near the Ouse, while between 1180 and 1216 Rievaulx bought properties 'in the marsh of Hungate' close to the Foss. In both cases convenient warehousing for wool shipments was probably intended. Ecclesiastics were naturally not the only outsiders with town houses. Many northern knights and manorial lords possessed properties for their frequent visits. St Mary's Abbey granted a Bootham house to the constable of Richmond Castle 'for his lodging when he should come to York'; and a little later a Yorkshire knight let his house in Clementhorpe, requiring his tenant to provide him with 'fire, candle, salt and straw' when he came 'to town'.[86]

Outsiders in a different sense were the Jewish arrivals in the twelfth century. The earliest definite record is from 1176–7, when Josce of York lent money both to the king and to a Yorkshire baron. Their numbers before 1190 were fewer than is often said; and Ephraim of Bonn's estimate of 150

84. *Pipe Roll 6 John*, ed. D. M. Stenton, PRS NS 18 (1940), 218; N. S. B. Gras, *The Early English Customs System* (Cambridge, Mass., 1918), 222; E. Miller and J. Hatcher, *Medieval England: Towns, Commerce and Crafts 1086–1348* (Harlow, 1995), 100–3, 196.
85. Walter Daniel, *The Life of Ailred of Rievaulx*, ed. F. M. Powicke (London, 1950), 10; Burton, *Monastic Order in Yorkshire*, 99–107, 128–35; J. Burton, *The Foundation History of the Abbeys of Byland and Jervaulx*, BTS 35 (York, 2006), 10.
86. *EYC*, I, nos 216, 268, 304; G. Coppack, *English Heritage Book of Fountains Abbey* (London, 1993), 87; Palliser, 'An early mortmain inquest', 11.

men and women massacred that year is much more likely than Roger of Howden's 500 men (plus women and children). Persistent beliefs that the community reached its peak by 1190, and that Jews mostly shunned the city after the massacre, have been shown by Dobson to be almost the exact opposite of the truth: the community was to be the wealthiest, if not the largest, Jewry in England by 1221.[87]

It was 'a comparatively recent and fragile' Jewish community which suffered in 1190, and it may have suffered such an exceptional pogrom *because* it was so newly established that neither local society, nor the Crown, had yet come to terms with the problems it presented. Certainly the massacre had the opposite effect to that intended by the conspirators. Jewish financiers were back in York by 1201, and possibly even by 1195, presumably under royal protection. By 1205 King John had established an *archa* in York, one of 27 royal repositories for registering debts to Jews; and by 1208 the York Jews had formed their own 'commune' or self-regulating community under the king. The interest of the Jews in York can be best explained by demand for their financial services in a growing Yorkshire economy: the massacre was provoked not by townspeople but by indebted Yorkshire knights, a reminder of the paradox that English Jews lived in towns, but served 'the financial and economic needs of agrarian rather than urban society'.[88]

Nevertheless, that prospering agrarian society spent much of its wealth in York or at least through York merchants; and that wealth can be measured best today by the few survivals of York's great churches and their treasures. It might seem improbable to argue that twelfth-century York was an artistic and cultural centre of the first rank, given its distance from London, Canterbury, or Winchester—or even more from the Continental heartlands of Romanesque and Gothic. Yet Durham is even further north; but whereas its huge surviving Romanesque cathedral cannot be ignored, only foundations and fragments survive of the great contemporary churches of York.

Thomas's early Norman cathedral (*c.*1075–1100) survives only at foundation level, and Roger's new chancel (*c.*1155–75?) only in its crypt; similarly, the pre-1270 St Mary's is known mostly from excavations. Yet enough of their furnishings survive to show that both great churches housed work of

87. Dobson, *Jewish Communities*, 8, 10, 27, 34. For the belief that York Jews never recovered their pre-1190 importance, C. Roth, *A History of the Jews in England* (Oxford, 3rd edn 1964), 24; and for the persistent myth that Jews imposed a ban on living in York after 1190, Royle et al., *Clifford's Tower Commemoration*, 15.
88. Dobson, *Jewish Communities*, 26, 55, 59.

high quality, such as the Minster's exquisite Virgin and Child (*c*.1150), and some stained glass, probably of Roger's time, salvaged and reused when the cathedral was rebuilt. More monumental are thirteen life-size prophets and apostles of *c*.1170–1200 from St Mary's, which in Pevsner's judgement are 'magnificent by any standard', and which may have flanked the Romanesque west portal. More recently identified are twenty-four statues of about the same date which survive, badly weathered, high on the exterior of the Minster, and probably salvaged from the earlier building. They might have been part of a great scheme elaborating Thomas's west front, with prophets, apostles, and saints surrounding a lost Christ in Majesty. As often, lesser work survived when major churches were rebuilt: York still possesses four elaborately decorated Romanesque doorways to parish churches, part of a group of portals identified by Zarnecki as work of a 'Yorkshire school'. Their date, quality, and literary sources, together with the advowson of the churches, suggests that Archbishop Roger and his chapter were the main patrons. Altogether, Christopher Wilson is in no doubt that York was then 'the centre of a major regional school of English sculpture'.[89]

Nor was it only in art that York flourished after 1066: there is evidence for learning and scholarship also. Thomas I appointed a master of the schools— apparently a grammar school and song school attached to the Minster—and the dean and chapter certainly ran a school by the 1130s, under the chancellor but by 1194 with its own master. Since York's was a secular cathedral, a communal library was not essential, but there are a few twelfth-century volumes in the present Minster Library, which may or may not have been collected by Archbishop Roger. He was certainly a learned man, and he personally defended before the pope the chronicler and canon Roger of Howden. No major writers, seemingly, were active in the city, but Roger and William of Newburgh were chroniclers of national importance.[90]

89. *RCHMY* III, 25, plates 44, 46–9; IV, 16, 17, 23–4, plates 26, 30–7; L. A. S. Butler, 'The labours of the months and "the haunted tanglewood"', in R. L. Thomson, ed., *A Medieval Miscellany* (Leeds, 1982), 79–95; C. Wilson, 'The original setting of the . . . figures from St Mary's Abbey, York', in F. H. Thompson, ed., *Studies in Medieval Sculpture*, Society of Antiquaries. Occasional Papers, NS III (1983), 100–21; S. Oosterwijk and C. Norton, 'Figure sculpture from the twelfth century Minster', *FYMAR* 61 (1990), 11–30; Norton, 'The buildings of St Mary's Abbey', 275–8; N. Pevsner and D. Neave, *Yorkshire: York and the East Riding* (London, 2nd edn 1995), 36, 184. See also Zarnecki et al., eds, *English Romanesque Art*, illustrating much of the York glass and sculpture (nos 88–90, 140–1, 153, 166, 173–5) and including the judgements of Madeline Caviness on the glass (pp. 135–7) and Wilson on the sculpture (caption to no. 144).

90. *VCH Yorks.* I, 417–18; C. B. L. Barr, 'The Minster Library', in Aylmer & Cant, eds, 491; *EEA* V, no. 77; XX, xxxi.

Yet York was very much in touch with a wider world: the Conquest brought it into an orbit including that other Norman Conquest of southern Italy and Sicily. The Yorkshire lords crushing the Scottish invasion of 1138 were spurred on by the reminder that 'fierce England fell captive to you, rich Apulia flourished again in your possession'. 'Apulia' would here have included Sicily, and there were certainly links between Sicily and Yorkshire. Robert of Selby, apparently from the Ouse port, was chancellor to Roger II of Sicily from 1137 to c.1151, during which time (1146) he gave help to the exiled Archbishop William of York. It is surely not coincidental that York Minster possesses both the Virgin and Child of c.1150 already mentioned, with its close stylistic relationship to the Byzantine art of Sicily, and a Siculo-Arabic casket of the same time, possibly a gift from William. And some unusual coins of Stephen minted at York around the late 1140s were seemingly modelled on a ducalis of King Roger.[91]

A new townscape

Although the network of streets, lanes, and defences was largely in place by 1066, the impact of the conquerors was considerable. The two royal castles swept away much housing and even whole streets, and the eastern castle cut in two the Anglo-Scandinavian commercial heartland. The damming of the river Foss drowned much land by creating the King's Pool upstream, severing the old main route from Coney Street to Fishergate and diverting suburban development to Walmgate. Thomas of Bayeux's new cathedral was built not only on a vast scale but on a new and strict orientation, a 'majestic, crashing discord' across the layout of the Anglo-Scandinavian city, which had respected the Roman layout of nearly 45° to the points of the compass. And the new French lords reordered the townscape by adapting or creating what can be called urban manors: they were not a new phenomenon of the Conquest, but the wholesale transfer of landholding allowed major changes in the pattern.[92]

91. G. Zarnecki, *Later English Romanesque Sculpture 1140–1210* (London, 1953), 29–31; Blackburn, 'Coinage and currency', 186; Bartlett, *England under the Norman and Angevin Kings*, 107; D. S. H. Abulafia, 'Selby, Robert of', in *ODNB*; Norton, *St William of York*, 118–20.
92. Quotation: John Harvey, *York* (London, 1975), 10. Minster orientation (only 0.4° from true east): J. R. Ali and P. Cunich, 'The orientation of churches: some new evidence', *Antiq J*, 81 (2001), 165, 179. Urban manors: S. Rees Jones, 'Building domesticity in the city', in M. Kowaleski and P. J. P. Goldberg, eds, *Medieval Domesticity* (Cambridge, 2008), 72–84.

There was also beginning a more fundamental change which would have happened with or without a Conquest: the development of more durable buildings. Stone, already the building material of choice for major churches, became universal for even lesser churches, chapels, and hospitals. York participated fully in the national 'Great Rebuilding' of churches in stone between about 1050 and 1150, and the tower of St Mary, Bishophill Junior (*c.* 1050–75) is a striking surviving example (Plate 4). Defences were still mostly of earth and timber, but the city gates were being rebuilt in stone: the outer arch of Bootham Bar is of late eleventh-century date (Plate 5) and the lower stage of Micklegate Bar early twelfth. Both, as well as the lower levels of Thomas's Minster and some fabric of the parish churches, were built of reused Roman stone, still widely available in York until the early twelfth century.[93]

Nor was stone confined to churches and defences: by the later twelfth century it was also being used for domestic housing. The large numbers of stone houses recorded in property deeds suggest that they were becoming relatively common among prosperous merchants and craftsmen, who must have welcomed their durability and resistance to fire. As it happens, the two partly surviving examples are not mercantile but clerical: the mansion of the Minster treasurer and a house set back from Stonegate which was probably built for one of the cathedral canons. However, at least four other stone houses, demolished and replaced later in the Middle Ages, have now been excavated, one of them still surviving to a height of 5'6" (1.7m) beneath the fourteenth-century hall of the Merchant Adventurers.[94]

Yet the dominant building in the city was unquestionably the cathedral of Archbishops Thomas and Roger. Thomas's Minster was 366 feet (111m) long and 160 feet (49m) wide, with a nave roof perhaps 91 feet (28m) above the ground and a considerably higher tower. Roger rebuilt the eastern arm, adding a 'westwork' in front of the nave, erecting a college of chantry priests to the north, and probably building or enlarging the archiepiscopal palace in the close. His chancel must have been started in the 1150s and completed probably by 1175. After Roger, major building came to a halt until the 1220s.[95]

93. *RCHMY* II, 96, 117; *EYM*, II, entries indexed under 'Roman stone, reuse of'; R. K. Morris, 'Churches in York and its hinterland', in J. Blair, ed., *Minsters and Parish Churches* (Oxford, 1988), 191–9; J. Blair, *The Church in Anglo-Saxon Society* (Oxford, 2005), 407–17.

94. *RCHMY* III, p. lxi, V, 69, 75–6, 225; R. A. Hall, 'Secular buildings in medieval York', in *Lübecker Kolloquium zur Stadtarchäologie im Hanseraum*, III: *Der Hausbau* (Lübeck, 2001), 78–80; Rees Jones, 'Building domesticity', 83.

95. The series *EYM* has covered Thomas's cathedral, but not yet Roger's. However, current research is not only establishing the remarkable extent, grandeur, and innovation of Roger's Minster,

The second grandest Norman building must have been St Mary's Abbey. As built between 1088 and about 1130, it was little short of the Minster in size, at some 254 feet (77m) long and 152 feet (46m) wide, adjoined by a cloister 109 feet (33m) square, and by all the normal Benedictine monastic rooms. It was almost entirely replaced in the thirteenth century, though its foundations have been excavated. Of the other two greater monastic houses less is known. There are sufficient clues to show that Holy Trinity Priory was completely rebuilt between about the 1170s and the 1230s, but almost nothing is yet known of the layout of the wealthy St Leonard's before the thirteenth century.[96]

More important to most townspeople were the humbler parish churches, which proliferated as the city grew: twelve at least—perhaps up to twenty—existed by 1086, but forty or more by 1216. They are often poorly recorded: the early existence of two central ones, St Benedict's and St Sampson's, is known only because the king granted them in 1154 to Pontefract Priory, though their dedications suggest a much longer pedigree. Others were certainly new: All Saints, Peasholme, was built by a landholder for his tenants in the early twelfth century. His may well have been a new 'urban manor' of the kind that Rees Jones has identified for St Mary, Castlegate—a block of properties associated with a church for the tenants, and often other common facilities like ovens, mills, or marketplaces. Gradually, as throughout Western Europe, the Church imposed a parochial system with defined boundaries, the parishioners being required to attend and to pay tithes to their own church. An intermediate phase may be implied by a grant of land in Gillygate under Henry II: its occupants were required to attend St Olave's as their 'mother church' (*matrix ecclesia*) on its patronal day, though they lived near the newer church of St Giles which they presumably attended on other days. Their sheer number meant that parish churches were normally humble structures, with nave and chancel but no tower or aisles. That was certainly

but also demonstrating that the reconstruction of Thomas's building in *EYM* II needs considerable modification: S. Harrison and C. Norton, 'Reconstructing a lost cathedral', *Ecclesiology Today*, 40 (July 2008), 53–9. I have therefore not reproduced here the graphic but speculative three-dimensional reconstruction provided by Derek Phillips in *EYM*, II, 142.

96. St Mary's: C. Wilson, caption to no. 102 in Zarnecki et al., eds, *English Romanesque Art*; C. Norton, 'The design and construction of the Romanesque church of St Mary's Abbey, York', *YAJ*, 71 (1999), 73–88. Holy Trinity: D. A. Stocker, 'The priory of the Holy Trinity, York', in L. R. Hoey, ed., *Yorkshire Monasticism: Archaeology, Art and Architecture, from the 7th to 16th Centuries*, BAA Conference Transactions 16 (London, 1995), 79–96.

true of St Helen-on-the-Walls and of the still-surviving redundant church of St Andrew's, St Andrewgate.[97]

In comparison with the greater churches and the two castles, little would have been prominent in the urban landscape, even by 1215, apart from some of the greater houses of the clergy, the town mansions of rural magnates, and a few stone houses of leading citizens. One substantial house between Ousegate and Coppergate, seven bays wide to the street frontage, possessed a separate oven, probably in a detached kitchen at the rear. This lay clearly at the opposite end of the scale from that row of seven cottages mentioned in Domesday with a combined street frontage of only 50 feet.[98]

It is clear from documentary hints, as well as archaeology, that the city became steadily more crowded in the twelfth century, as house-plots were subdivided and new houses built, whether in new streets and lanes within the defences—such as, probably, Davygate—or in new extramural settlement. There is evidence for a planned suburb, perhaps built as the replacement of the Roman north-east fortress gate by Monk Bar led to a realignment of the street pattern. The new district, first recorded as Newbiggin ('new building(s)') in the late twelfth century, was built on open land owned by the archbishop and cathedral chapter, and regular property boundaries still existing in 1852 apparently equate to fifty houses held by the canon of Fridaythorpe in the 1280s.[99]

There is, so far, little excavated evidence for domestic buildings of the Norman, as opposed to the Anglo-Scandinavian period; but there are hints of a slow improvement in the durability of housing. At 16–22 Coppergate, the earliest post-Conquest new build was 'a simple, slight, post-and-wattle structure', replaced about 1150 by a sturdier building, but still with earth-fast upright timbers. The true box-framed timber house with good foundations does not seem to have arrived in York before the thirteenth century. However, there is at least evidence from Coppergate for roofing tile from the eleventh century onwards, which was of course more fire-proof than the usual thatch. The assumption that fires were an ever-present danger is reflected in an agreement between two neighbours,

97. *EYC*, I, nos 276, 298 (cf. no. 228 for a house identified by parish *c.*1200); *RCHMY* V, 10; AY 10.1, 37–9; Rees Jones, 'Building domesticity', 78–82.
98. *EYC*, I, no. 221; AY 1, 187; Palliser, *Domesday York*, 16.
99. H. G. Ramm, 'A case of twelfth-century town planning in York?', *YAJ*, 42 (1968), 132–5; Palliser, 'The medieval street-names of York', *YH*, 2 (1978), 13; Rees Jones, 'Property, tenure, and rents', I, 63–4.

datable to 1212–25, to maintain the fence and gutter between their houses 'until the first fire' (*ad primam combustionem*).[100]

The face York presented by about 1215 must have been one of an already crowded city huddled within its earthen ramparts and ditches, and with lengthy, straggling suburbs along the main roads outside the gates. The street pattern was much as it had been in 1066, with only one or two new roads but a good many more crowded side alleys, and new housing developments outside the walls. Within the defences, more land became available for housing and warehousing by building out into the river Ouse and by colonizing the appropriately named Marsh district inside the bend of the Foss, but at the same time more intramural and extramural land was being incorporated into ecclesiastical precincts. All of this can be glimpsed only in fragmentary form, but the same processes continued, better recorded, during the continued population growth of the thirteenth and early fourteenth centuries.

Appendix V: The rights and customs of the archbishop and chapter, *c.* 1080 and 1106

The earliest survey relevant to York, other than Domesday, is the undated inquest into 'the rights and laws which Archbishop T. has throughout York, within the town [*burh*] and without'. It was witnessed by twelve named men and 'all the inhabitants of the town [*burhware*] of York', as well as by the archbishop, the county sheriff, and others. From a generation later, there survives the verdict of an inquest of 1106 into the rights and privileges of the cathedral chapter. Since, unlike Domesday, both are later transcripts of lost originals, with some disputed or uncertain readings, their texts and reliability need to be considered.

'Rights and laws' is a fourteenth-century copy of a lost text, preserved in the Minster's 'Great White Register'. It is in Old English, with an accompanying Anglo-Norman translation; the form of the French suggests a translation made about 1200, when Old English was ceasing to be comprehensible. The fourteenth-century scribe transcribed both, but cannot have fully understood the English, and had difficulties even with the French version.[101]

100. *EYC*, I, no. 213; *AY* 10/6, 853; Hall, 'Secular buildings in medieval York', 91–2; Rees Jones, 'Building domesticity', 67.
101. York Minster Library, MS L 2 (Magnum Registrum Album), fo. 89r, v.

Both versions were first published by the great German scholar Liebermann in 1903, but relying on a transcript made by the York historian Robert Skaife. Fortunately, it has now been re-edited from the original both by David Rollason and by Brian Donaghey, the latter with valuable comments on the linguistic problems and with photographs. The original cannot at present be dated more closely than 1070 x 1088, though research on the witnesses might narrow it further. It might well have been based on a pre-Conquest list of archiepiscopal rights, updated for Thomas of Bayeux after 1070; but my earlier suggestion that it could have been compiled as a 'satellite' document for Domesday Book has been queried by David Roffe.[102]

The second text also survives only in a fourteenth-century transcript, this time preserved in the White Book of Southwell. In the 1330s the Southwell Minster chapter were ordered by the Crown to show their entitlement to their privileges and jurisdictions. The canons—who knew only that they shared the privileges of York—must have asked for help from the York chapter, whose reply helpfully quoted in full the findings of an inquest of the Yorkshire shire moot in 1106. The text was first edited by Leach in 1891, and has more recently been re-edited by Van Caenegem and by Rollason.[103]

Again, some readings are uncertain: but one crucial and disputed word is clear: the twelve jurors of 1106 are termed the 'wisest English of that county [*comitatus*]', whereas Leach and Van Caenegem read it as *civitatis* (city). Since the twelfth man named, Ulvet son of Forno, was described as hereditary lawman of the city, it raises a question whether *comitatus* was a slip of the transcriber's pen for *civitatis*. A. G. Dickens and I have both assumed that all twelve jurors were city lawmen, despite the singular *lagaman* against the final name.[104]

---

102. Palliser, *Domesday York*, 6–8, 25; AY 1, 210–13; B. Donaghey, 'The archbishop gets a new transcription', *Medieval Yorkshire*, 27 (1998), 26–40. For doubts on its status as a DB satellite: David Roffe, *Decoding Domesday*, 30n.

103. Southwell Minster, MS 1 (Liber Albus), 18–20; A. F. Leach, ed., *Visitations and Memorials of Southwell Minster*, Camden Society, n.s. 48 (London, 1891), 190–6; R. C. Van Caenegem, ed., *English Lawsuits from William I to Richard I*, Selden Soc. 106 (London, 1990), I, 138–43; AY 1, 220–5.

104. A. G. Dickens in *VCHY*, 21; Palliser, 'The birth of York's civic liberties', 90n.

5

Commune and capital

*c.*1215–1349[1]

The thirteenth century witnessed considerable growth in population, agricultural output, marketing, trade, manufactures, and urbanization throughout Western Europe. York played its part in that expansion, and the results are visible in the townscape even today: in the huge cathedral, its dimensions set by the transepts begun in the 1220s; in the eastern castle, rebuilt in stone from the 1240s; in the circuit of stone city walls begun in the 1250s; in the great second marketplace created by about 1250 from central clearances; and in the poignant surviving parts of St Mary's Abbey church, rebuilt from the 1270s, and before its destruction from the 1540s a close rival to the Minster in scale (see Map 5).

York's population, like that of other English towns, must have increased considerably until checked by the Great Famine (1315–22) and then the Black Death (1349). There are no direct measures of numbers before 1377, but if London reached a peak of 60–100,000 by 1350, and Norwich some 25,000, then York would have perhaps also had over 20,000 or even 30,000. Indirect indicators of size point in that direction. York's stock of parish churches was higher than that of any other city except London, Winchester, Norwich, and Lincoln, and it was still rising, from about forty in 1200 to forty-five by 1300. An even better index of urban importance, if not necessarily of size, is the foundation of friaries, those new and almost exclusively urban religious orders. York was one of only nine English towns to attract

---

1. For a preliminary sketch of this chapter to *c.*1300, see D. M. Palliser, 'York—Englands zweite Stadt?', in W. Hartmann, ed., *Europas Städte zwischen Zwang und Freiheit* (Regensburg, 1995), 155–67, trans. and revised as 'Thirteenth-century York—England's second city?', *YH*, 14 (1997), 2–9.

the four main orders; and furthermore all its four houses were among the twenty English friaries where provincial chapters were held. No other English town but Oxford (not even London) enjoyed such distinction.[2]

Certainly there is evidence for much more crowded conditions in York between 1200 and 1350 than in the previous 150 years. This may have been only in part because of increasing population, for two other forces influenced housing densities. One was the centripetal pull of new defences. William I had already divided the southern commercial districts by his two castles, and by damming the Foss to give extensive water defences upstream. This was followed by the extension, and then the replacing in stone, of the city walls, starting in the 1250s and completed in the 1340s with the Walmgate extension. The result was to create a corset of stone defences and to encourage some suburban townspeople to move inside, especially after 1314 when attacks by Scottish raiders came close. The second pressure was the result of establishment or enlargement of ecclesiastical precincts. The completed stone defences enclosed only 263 acres (106 ha), less than half the walled areas of either London or Norwich, and the Minster precinct, monasteries, and friaries occupied about a fifth of the walled city by the time of the Black Death.[3]

York was easily the largest and wealthiest English town north of the Trent, and one of two or three provincial capitals vying for second place to London. Its age-old advantage of access to navigable waterways was complemented by a network of main roads which by the thirteenth century was also second to London's. Its status as county town of the largest English shire, and of an ecclesiastical diocese and province which were even larger, brought much legal and administrative business to the city. As if this were not enough, it also became an alternative centre for national government under the first three Edwards when they intermittently moved north to fight the Scots.[4]

It should be no surprise, therefore, that York was marked on the contemporary Ebstorf world map, as well as on the Hereford *Mappa Mundi*; nor that

2. Population estimates: E. Rutledge, 'Immigration and population growth in early fourteenth-century England', *UHY 1988*, 15–30; *CUHB* I, 194–5; C. M. Barron, *London in the Later Middle Ages* (Oxford, 2004), 238; P. Nightingale, *Trade, Money and Power in Medieval England* (Aldershot, 2007), XIII, 95–8. Parish churches and friaries: *VCHY*, 365–404; Palliser, 'Thirteenth-century York', 3, but with correction of 10 towns to 9 by 1300.

3. *RCHMY* II, 3, gives 263 acres for the walled area. The ecclesiastical precincts, which I totalled at 21 ha ('Thirteenth-century York', 3), were calculated by the Ordnance Survey in 1852. The allowed for the extramural St Mary's, but not for all liberties within the walls.

4. Roads: as measured by frequency of royal journeys: B. P. Hindle, *Medieval Roads* (Princes Risborough, 1982), 14–17, 26, 40–2, 44, 51.

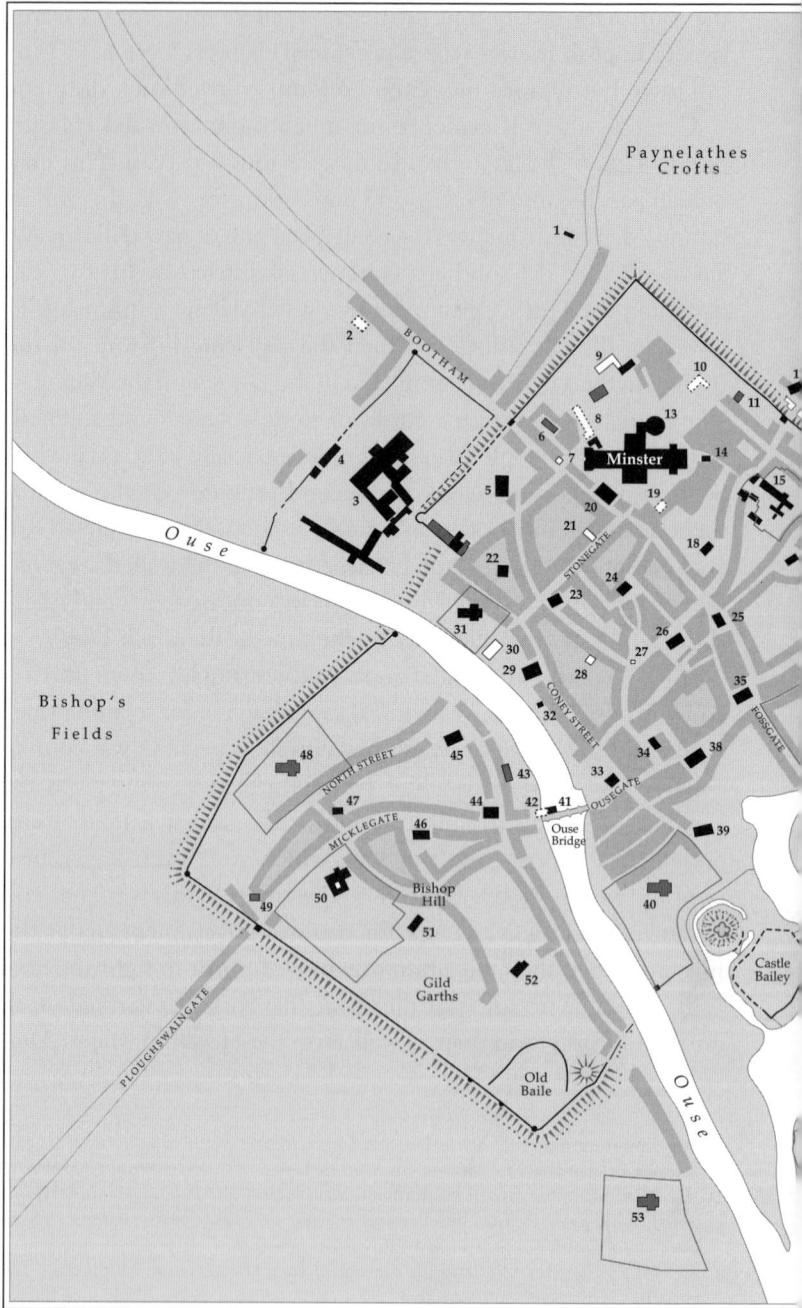

Map 5. York *c.*1300

Source: Adapted from a map in the forthcoming *British Historic Towns Atlas, Vol. V: York*, ed.
P. V. Addyman, by kind permission of the Historic Towns Trust.

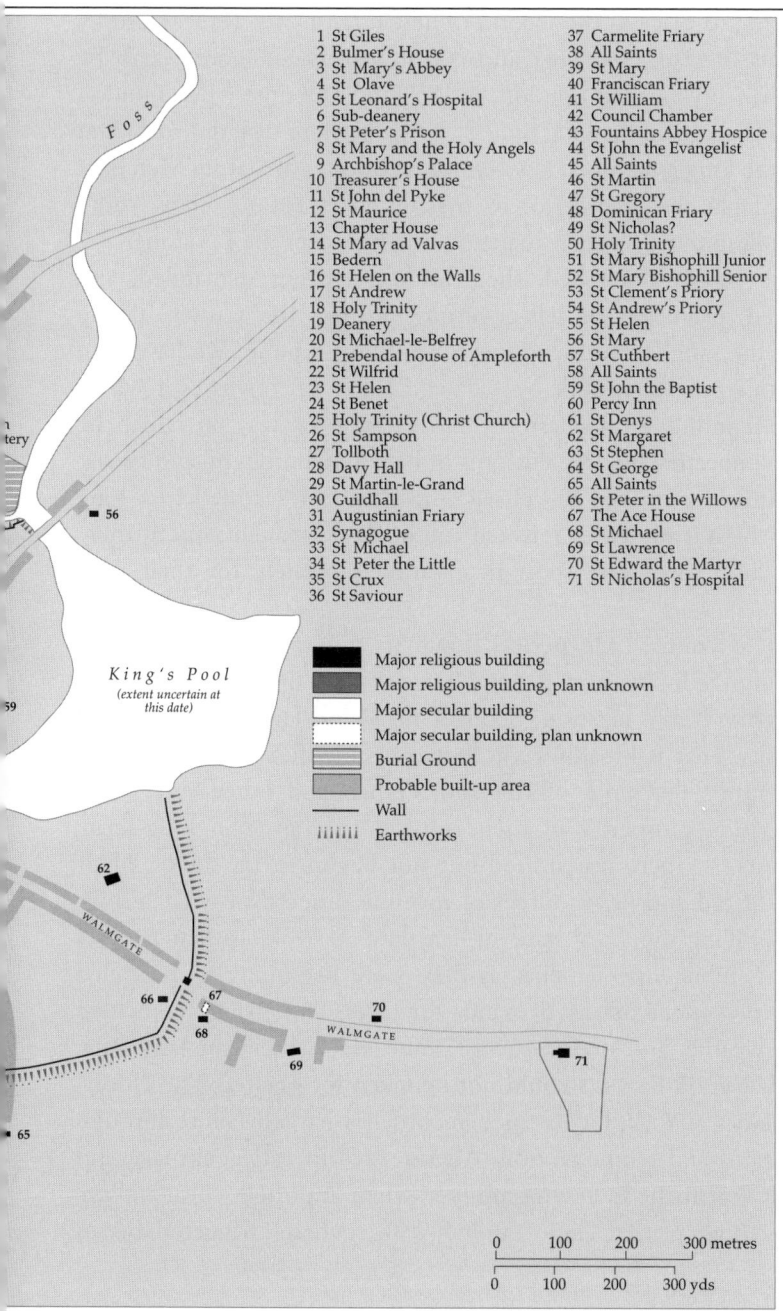

Foss

King's Pool
(extent uncertain at
this date)

WALMGATE

WALMGATE

1 St Giles	37 Carmelite Friary
2 Bulmer's House	38 All Saints
3 St Mary's Abbey	39 St Mary
4 St Olave	40 Franciscan Friary
5 St Leonard's Hospital	41 St William
6 Sub-deanery	42 Council Chamber
7 St Peter's Prison	43 Fountains Abbey Hospice
8 St Mary and the Holy Angels	44 St John the Evangelist
9 Archbishop's Palace	45 All Saints
10 Treasurer's House	46 St Martin
11 St John del Pyke	47 St Gregory
12 St Maurice	48 Dominican Friary
13 Chapter House	49 St Nicholas?
14 St Mary ad Valvas	50 Holy Trinity
15 Bedern	51 St Mary Bishophill Junior
16 St Helen on the Walls	52 St Mary Bishophill Senior
17 St Andrew	53 St Clement's Priory
18 Holy Trinity	54 St Andrew's Priory
19 Deanery	55 St Helen
20 St Michael-le-Belfrey	56 St Mary
21 Prebendal house of Ampleforth	57 St Cuthbert
22 St Wilfrid	58 All Saints
23 St Helen	59 St John the Baptist
24 St Benet	60 Percy Inn
25 Holy Trinity (Christ Church)	61 St Denys
26 St Sampson	62 St Margaret
27 Tollbooth	63 St Stephen
28 Davy Hall	64 St George
29 St Martin-le-Grand	65 All Saints
30 Guildhall	66 St Peter in the Willows
31 Augustinian Friary	67 The Ace House
32 Synagogue	68 St Michael
33 St Michael	69 St Lawrence
34 St Peter the Little	70 St Edward the Martyr
35 St Crux	71 St Nicholas's Hospital
36 St Saviour	

Major religious building

Major religious building, plan unknown

Major secular building

Major secular building, plan unknown

Burial Ground

Probable built-up area

Wall

Earthworks

0	100	200	300 metres
0	100	200	300 yds

it had recovered its place as the second richest English city as measured by tax assessments. In 1252, 1269, 1304, and 1312 it was tallaged more heavily by the Crown than any city but London; and in 1269, at a time when London was in difficulties, it paid the king only 43 per cent more than did York. And again, when the king established a system of certificates of Statute Merchant and Statute Staple, the records for its first decade (1285–94) show York's creditors handling more business than any others except the Londoners.[5]

As English towns flourished, their leading citizens demanded, and often acquired, privileges of self-government from the Crown, taking advantage of the king's need for money or political support. We have seen the start of this process at York by 1212–13; and royal towns as a whole benefited from John's 'great charter' (*Magna Carta*) of 1215, in which he confirmed the liberties and free customs of his cities, boroughs, and towns. Though he quickly revoked the charter, his death in 1216 led to a long minority in which it was twice reissued and made permanent; and further-more, towns like York were soon negotiating separately for their own privileges.

It is usual to contrast the period down to the 1290s—an economic boom, a benign climate, and general peace—and the following half-century of wars, heavy taxation, Scottish invasions, famine, disease, and heavy mortality. That is broadly right, but oversimplified. From the mid-thirteenth century the kings of England, France, and other states were tapping the rising prosperity of their subjects to engage in long-term, large-scale wars, a process intensified but not begun in the 1290s. Their exploitation of old and new sources of revenue ushered in what histor-ians are now calling the 'fiscal state' or 'tax state', provoking their peoples to demand assemblies (parliaments, as they were beginning to be called in England) to consent to any demands for taxes. The change coincided with terrible weather and a consequent famine, especially in the late 1250s, a reminder that good harvests could not be taken for granted. The chron-icler of St Mary's at York, for instance, recorded a harvest failure through 'continuous rains and tempests' from August 1259 to early February, and another 'great dearth' the following summer, when imported wheat and rye sold for very high prices. These famine years, perhaps triggered by an

---

5. Tallages: J. F. Hadwin, 'The last royal tallages', *EHR*, 96 (1981), 358; J. F. Hadwin, 'The medieval lay subsidies and economic history', *Econ HR*, 2nd ser., 36 (1983), 217. Certificates: P. Nightin-gale, 'The rise and decline of medieval York: A reassessment', *P&P*, 206 (2010), 6–9.

immense volcanic eruption with worldwide consequences, were made worse by the growing population in both town and countryside.[6]

This fraught period coincided with the political crisis of 1258–65, and the combination of political and economic uncertainty, coupled with the aspirations of townsmen, led to demands for wider representation of bodies negotiating with the Crown. Early parliaments always included peers, spiritual as well as temporal, and membership soon came to include county gentry also. Thus the archbishop of York and the abbot of St Mary's, as well as Yorkshire noblemen and leading gentry, took part; but demand was growing for urban representation also. As early as 1237 'citizens and burgesses' were present in one parliament, seemingly to press for marketing reforms in return for a tax grant. We do not know which towns elected representatives that year, but York was certainly among the towns summoned to Montfort's rebel parliament in January 1265, and thereafter frequently—certainly to all Edward I's parliaments for which full lists of burgesses survive. From 1290 'every subsidy on movable property was granted in a Parliament containing at least some elected representatives of the community', and always (where lists survive) including MPs from York.[7]

From around the 1290s, the English population levelled off, at about the same time as a climatic downturn, and then fell sharply during the Great Famine, thirty years before the Black Death caused even higher mortality. It was also an age of warfare and heavy taxation: indeed, the period 1294–1341 saw the heaviest levels of Crown exactions, both on towns and countryside, of the entire later Middle Ages. These were nationwide burdens, but the North suffered especially badly after Bannockburn (1314), when Scottish armies ravaged much of Yorkshire as well as the border shires, raids which coincided almost exactly with the Great Famine.

In compensation, the Scottish war also brought much of the government from Westminster to York for long periods, starting with Edward I from

6. Fiscal state: R. Bonney, ed., *The Rise of the Fiscal State in Europe, c.1200–1815* (Oxford, 1999), especially W. M. Ormrod's chapter, 19–52. Famines: E. Miller and J. Hatcher, *Medieval England: Rural Society and Economic Growth 1086–1348* (London, 1978), 57–9; H. H. E. Craster and M. E. Thornton, eds, *The Chronicle of St Mary's Abbey, York*, SS 148 (1934), 5; Derek Keene, 'Crisis management in London's food supply, 1250–1500', in B. Dodds and C. D. Liddy, eds, *Commercial Activity, Markets and Entrepreneurs in the Middle Ages* (Woodbridge, 2011), 54–5; Don Walker, 'London's volcanic winter', *Current Archaeology*, 270 (September 2012), 12–19.
7. M. McKisack, *The Parliamentary Representation of the English Boroughs During the Middle Ages* (Oxford, 1932), 19; J. R. Maddicott, *The Origins of the English Parliament 924–1327* (Oxford, 2010), 204, 224–5, 257, 291, 298. Quotation from W. M. Ormrod, 'The West European monarchies in the later Middle Ages', in R. Bonney, ed., *Economic Systems and State Finance* (Oxford, 1995), 129.

1298, continuing under the disastrous reign of his son, and not ending until in 1337 Edward III switched priority from Scotland to France. In all, some parts of the Crown's machinery of offices and courts were in York for 16¾ out of 40 years (some 42 per cent of the period), and that does not include several spells when the royal household was there without the other departments of state. It all gave the city 'a prominence in national affairs greater than at any time before or since'.[8]

Whether York fared better between the 1290s and the 1340s than England as a whole is difficult to know: there are no data on its population or (apart from Crown taxation) on its wealth. It is likely that the Great Famine caused mortality on a scale unequalled before the Black Death, amounting possibly to 5 or 10 per cent in towns and more in the countryside, and York may have suffered at least as much. The chronicler of St Mary's abbey, normally concerned with internal affairs of his house, gave detailed testimony for 1315 on terrible weather, scarcity, and high grain prices, and for 1316 'a huge mortality of men' through starvation, 'both rich and poor'.[9]

More particular to York, its reliance on wool exports for much of its prosperity was suffering after 1294: exports from Hull fell as much of the trade was diverted through London because of the damaging effects of war and piracy. In the latest survey of the city's fortunes, Pamela Nightingale is in no doubt that 'the decline of York's wealth began early in the fourteenth century', largely because of warfare, heavy taxation, and dislocation of the wool trade. In the decade 1300–9, certificates of unpaid debts show the city still second to London in commercial activity, but from 1327 Bristol ousted it from second place in the assessments to royal taxation. It is difficult to be sure, however, because York's relative wealth was undervalued for taxation.[10]

8. E. Miller, 'Medieval York', *VCHY*, 64; W. M. Ormrod, 'Competing capitals? York and London in the fourteenth century', in S. Rees Jones et al., eds, *Courts and Regions in Medieval Europe* (Woodbridge, 2000), 82.
9. I. Kershaw, 'The Great Famine and agrarian crisis in England 1315–1322', *P&P*, 59 (1973), 3–50 (with much Yorkshire evidence); W. C. Jordan, *The Great Famine* (Princeton, NJ, 1996), esp. 145–8; Craster and Thornton, eds, *Chronicle of St Mary's Abbey*, 67, 69.
10. W. M. Ormrod, 'York and the Crown under the first three Edwards', in S. Rees Jones, ed., *The Government of Medieval York* (York, 1997), 29; C. D. Liddy, *War, Politics and Finance in Late Medieval English Towns* (Woodbridge, 2005), 67; Nightingale, *Trade, Money and Power in Medieval England*, IX, 29; Nightingale, 'Rise and decline of medieval York', 5, 8–10. The statistics for York in 1300–9 (122 debtors and 653 creditors, against London's 124 and 374) I owe to Dr Nightingale.

Certainly Bristol and York were vying in the fourteenth century for the honour of being 'second city of the realm'. Given York's importance either way, it is regrettable that nearly all the early archives generated by its fledgling administration have been lost. It was not among the two dozen English towns which Geoffrey Martin identified as possessing surviving records from before 1300; and if York can now be added to the list, that is merely because of the recent identification of a fragmentary *husgabel* (house tax) roll of the 1280s. No continuous sequence of civic records, indeed, survives before the 1370s.[11]

Despite that, York is better documented than for any previous period, thanks to a combination of royal and ecclesiastical archives and to many hundreds of property deeds. Crown records from 1199 are informative on leading citizens; the archbishop's registers begin in 1225, the church court papers in 1303, and one series of registered wills in 1321, though the probate inventories meant to accompany wills do not survive before the Black Death. The church court's 'cause papers' are a mine of information, often including witness depositions, many from humble as well as prosperous townspeople. Furthermore, the surviving documents can be valuably used alongside the archaeological and architectural evidence, as a single example shows. Two medieval cemeteries were excavated, in Aldwark in the 1970s and off nearby Jewbury in the 1980s. Both had a similar orientation of burials and a lack of grave goods. Only the written records establish that one was the cemetery of a demolished church, and the other a Jewish burial ground. It is a sobering thought that if Jewbury's excavators had had no documentary help, 'it would have been regarded as just another medieval cemetery, with the church unaccountably missing'.[12]

The Crown and the city: 1213–98

York, after its brief privatization under Stephen, was to remain—like most large English towns—in royal hands, administered by the county sheriff and his assistants from the castle. They in turn were assisted by the bailiffs of the three Yorkshire ridings and their subdivisions, the wapentakes. Though the archbishop, the cathedral chapter, and the religious houses enjoyed 'liberties' or exempt jurisdictions, the majority of citizens answered to the king

---

11. G. H. Martin, 'The English borough in the thirteenth century', *TR Hist S*, 5th ser., 13 (1963), 129–31, 141; D. M. Palliser, 'York's earliest administrative record', *YAJ*, 50 (1978), 81–91. The earliest freemen's lists, starting in 1272–3, are later copies.
12. AY 10/1, 12/1, 12/3. Quotation from P. A. Rahtz's review of AY 12/3 in *Antiquity*, 69 (1995), 199.

through the sheriff. It was the Crown which granted them political and economic privileges, by a process aptly called by A. B. White 'self-government by the king's command'. Monarchs found it convenient to grant rights of municipal autonomy, while making it clear that they would revoke those rights if a city was not governed satisfactorily, or if law and order broke down. York was no exception.[13]

Between 1216 and 1290 royal visits to York were few, and were usually connected with Anglo-Scottish affairs. A generally friendly relationship between Henry III of England and Alexander II of Scots consolidated a long peace (1217–96), interrupted by only brief confrontations. In 1220 Henry was in York to negotiate his sister's marriage to Alexander, a wedding held in the Minster in 1221. The two kings met again in the city for Christmas 1229, and once more in 1237 to ratify the Treaty of York. By it, Alexander surrendered his claims to sovereignty over the Northern counties, in exchange for lands worth £200 a year.[14]

Henry hailed this as a 'firm peace', but a brief war scare soon caused him to think again. York's main (eastern) castle, still of timber, had been badly damaged by gales in 1228, and was called ruinous (*prostratum*) in 1237. Henry, passing north through the city with an army in 1244, decided to rebuild it in stone. The crisis soon blew over; the kings met at Newcastle, where Alexander confirmed the Treaty of York and agreed that his heir Alexander (III) should marry Henry's daughter. Nevertheless, Henry did not abandon his intention to rebuild York's castle. It is a measure of the importance he attached to it that in March 1245 he sent his master mason and master carpenter to view it; the former was no less a person than Henry de Reyns, who four months later was put in charge of the royal rebuilding of Westminster Abbey. York's castle was reconstructed in stone over the next quarter-century at a cost of nearly £2,000; its keep ('Clifford's Tower') was of a quadrilobe design which retained most of the strength of a round tower, while allowing flanking fire between the projecting lobes. From what survives, the new castle was clearly very impressive, and influenced by

13. A. B. White, *Self-Government by the King's Command* (Minneapolis, 1933); Barbara English, 'The government of thirteenth-century Yorkshire', in J. C. Appleby and P. Dalton, eds, *Government, Religion and Society in Northern England 1000–1700* (Stroud, 1997), 90–103; D. M. Palliser, 'Towns and the English state, 1066–1500', in J. R. Maddicott and D. M. Palliser, eds, *The Medieval State* (London, 2000), 127–45.
14. G. W. S. Barrow, 'The Anglo-Scottish border', *NH*, 1 (1966), 21–42; David Carpenter, *The Struggle for Mastery: Britain 1066–1284* (Oxford, 2003), 331; Maddicott, *Origins of the English Parliament*, 163, 457.

advanced French castle designs (Plate 6). As a result, there was no need to replace both baileys in stone, and Henry granted the northern one to the Franciscans as a more central site for their York friary.[15]

Henry's most lavish visit to York must have been that of 1251, to see his daughter married to the new Scots king Alexander III (1249–86). The festivities culminated on Christmas Day, when he knighted Alexander, and on the next day, when Archbishop Gray married the royal couple in the Minster. It must all have boosted the local economy: preparations went on for five months beforehand, including large-scale purchases of meat and fish from Yorkshire and further afield. The royal marshals came in advance to find accommodation for the guests, who included over 1,000 English and sixty Scottish knights.[16]

Henry may also have been spurred to look to the long-term interests of the city. Just as his 1244 visit had triggered rebuilding of the castle, that of 1251 saw the start of a series of annual grants of murage to the citizens, a tax they could levy towards rebuilding their defences; and that period of grants (1251–72) was just when most of the circuit of walls was rebuilt in stone. Furthermore, Henry issued a modest charter to York in 1252, followed by three more substantial charters in 1256 (two) and 1262. They will be considered later, but they are well summarized by Miller's judgement that they deprived the county sheriff of virtually all authority in the city. That does not mean that Henry's grants were irrevocable: he was then in a mood to cancel or suspend urban charters, and in 1255–7 he was initiating inquests into the rights claimed by many boroughs. York's 1256 charters were granted on 17 May, but less than five months later he suspended all the city's chartered rights and placed it under royal officials, because the mayor and bailiffs had failed to appear in person at the Exchequer. It was the only town he singled out for such harsh treatment that year, perhaps as a warning to the others.[17]

15. *HKW*, I, 104, 116; II, 839–90; *RCHMY* II, 60; John Harvey, *English Medieval Architects* (Gloucester, 2nd edn 1984), 251; Alan Young, 'The North and Anglo-Scottish relations in the thirteenth century', in Appleby and Dalton, eds, *Government, Religion and Society*, 79, 84–6. Given its long-term consequences for York, Henry's 1244 visit has been surprisingly neglected. Miller, 'Medieval York', 28, is explicit that Henry was not in York between 1237 and 1251. See also Christopher Wilson, 'Henry [de Reyns]', *ODNB*, 26, pp. 418–19; John Goodall, *The English Castle 1066–1650* (New Haven and London, 2011), 13–19.
16. M. Paris, *Chronica Majora*, ed. H. R. Luard, 7 vols, RS (London, 1872–83), V, 268; R. Vaughan, *Matthew Paris* (Cambridge, 1958), 4; Miller, 'Medieval York', 28.
17. Miller, 'Medieval York', 33; H. M. Turner, *Town Defences in England and Wales* (London, 1971), 115, 238; *RCHMY* II, 11; D. M. Palliser, 'The birth of York's civic liberties, *c.* 1200–1354', in Rees Jones, ed., *Government of Medieval York*, 95; D. A. Carpenter, *The Reign of Henry III* (London, 1996), 142–4.

Nor were Henry's high-handed actions confined to dealing with urban officers. It was also at that time that he milked the Jews to the point of ruining them. Between 1241 and 1255 he levied close to 100,000 marks (£67,000) in direct taxation on the English Jewish community, more than three times what he had assessed between 1221 and 1239. By 1255 Aaron of York, who had been the wealthiest, had paid over his entire fortune and was declared a pauper. The result was to cripple nearly all the wealthy Jews, though the York community was able to offer considerable credit to northern gentry and free tenants until the 1260s. Nevertheless, the stage was set for Henry's son to harry the English Jews before finally expelling them from the realm.[18]

It is not surprising that when the king clashed with his baronial opponents in 1258–65, the citizens' loyalties were doubtful. In 1263–4 there was conflict between rival claimants to the posts of county sheriff and keeper of York castle; at one point some rebel barons forced their way into York and compelled the citizens to pay them £100, while the St Mary's lands in Bootham and Marygate were 'wasted'. When de Montfort's faction were victorious over the royal forces, and held a parliament in January 1265, York was one of the towns summoned to send representatives; and it seems clear that they, like all the knights and burgesses present, were Montfort's supporters. Once the king was victorious and in firm control, York was among twenty-seven towns summoned before the royal council—probably those towns with rebel sympathies, now forced to appeal to keep or recover their chartered privileges. It may have been deliberate that when Henry summoned a parliament in September 1268 (in an abortive attempt to raise a tax) he held it in York to demonstrate his renewed authority.[19]

The reign of Henry's son Edward I (1272–1307) can be conveniently divided about 1294. Before then, he concentrated on domestic government, initiating a sweeping series of inquiries into royal rights, justice,

18. R. C. Stacey, '1240–60: A watershed in Anglo-Jewish relations?', *Historical Research*, 61 (1988), 136–8; R. B. Dobson, *The Jewish Communities of Medieval England*, BTS 39 (York, 2010), 56–61, 90–1.

19. The period is poorly recorded, and the September 1268 parliament or council is not listed in the standard reference work (*HBC*, 544). See McKisack, *Parliamentary Representation*, 3; Miller, 'Medieval York', 27–8; O. De Ville, 'John Deyville: A neglected rebel', *NH*, 34 (1998), 25–6; W. M. Ormrod, ed., *The Lord Lieutenants and High Sheriffs of Yorkshire, 1066–2000* (Barnsley, 2000), 59; Maddicott, *Origins of the English Parliament*, 257, 261, 267. Miller seems here to confuse the rebel seizure of York with an earlier attack on the abbey by the citizens in 1262 (*Chronicle of St Mary's*, 6).

and local government, the surviving returns to which cast light on the government of York as of many other communities. They confirm, for instance, that both the archbishop and the abbot of St Mary's were exercising their rights to their own courts, coroners, and gallows; and the city's jurors testified to the friction that separate jurisdictions produced. The abbot, they alleged, had refused to let their bailiffs arrest a monk who had killed a boy within his precinct. The jurors also criticized their own bailiffs for extortion over levying tolls and for letting thieves go free while pocketing the stolen goods. Worse still was one abuse alleged by the Ainsty jurors. The mayor and bailiffs, they said, had imprisoned a thief called Henry, son of Adam de Grimeston; when Henry 'began to indict some of the mayors of York... they quickly hanged him'.[20]

Such abuses of power (if true) could easily have persuaded Edward to suspend the city's liberties, as he did more than once to York and to other towns. In 1280 he did so on the ground that the civic officers had tampered with John's 1212 charter, and he kept control for three years. In 1290, briefly, York was one of eight leading towns taken into royal hands for non-payment or late payment of the annual fee farm; and in 1292 the king again revoked York's liberties, this time for five years. This last suspension, though perhaps oppressive to the citizens, proved a boon to historians, since preserved among the National Archives are the royal keepers' financial accounts for three-and-a-half years out of five—the more valuable as York's own financial accounts do not survive until a century later.[21]

Meanwhile, Edward had brought to a close the last, unhappy, phase in the history of England's medieval Jewry. For some time he had been harsher in hangings and confiscations of property: in 1279, for instance, he had seized the York synagogue and turned several Jewish houses into a royal wine cellar. The York community was effectively crippled, though Bonamy of York was so useful to Edward that when in 1290 all Jews were expelled from

20. Barbara English, ed., *Yorkshire Hundred and Quo Warranto Rolls*, YASRS 151 (Leeds, 1996), 73–6, 78–9, 88–95, 158–62, 254–9, very helpfully makes accessible the surviving returns for the city, Ainsty, archbishop, and abbey.
21. J. P. Bischoff and D. M. Palliser, eds, 'The Keepers' accounts for York, 1292–1297', in *RMY*, 9–46: n. 4 has references to all three suspensions. As noted there, that of 1280 was lifted in 1283, not 1282 as in Miller, 'Medieval York', 34. For Edward's suspensions of other towns' liberties, see E. Miller and J. Hatcher, *Medieval England: Towns, Commerce and Crafts 1086–1348* (Harlow, 1995), 319–20.

England by royal decree, Bonamy and his family were granted the rare privilege of a personal safe-conduct out of the realm. He moved to Paris to become 'the most famous example of an exiled English Jew in favour at the court of Philip the Fair'. Meanwhile, the remaining handful of Jewish tenements in York, including the Jewbury cemetery, were sold off in 1291, appropriately while Edward was in the city on his way to Berwick to adjudicate on the rival claimants to the Scottish throne.[22]

By the 1290s Edward had pressing financial needs which called for much more than the sale of Jewish property: and he was effectively creating 'a new tax-based parliamentary state', in which taxes were levied more heavily and more often, but in return for the consent of parliaments, assemblies which, as we have seen, regularly included burgesses from York and other towns when taxes were requested. By 1294, as John Maddicott puts it, 'the link between taxes and local representation... was now unbreakable'.[23] Taxation increased after the outbreak of war with France (1294) and Scotland (1296), and was especially heavy between 1294 and 1297. The credit given to York's merchants fell heavily in 1295, as did wool exports from Hull from 1296. Nor were taxes the only royal demands: York was, for instance, one of seven ports each of which built a galley in 1295 for naval service. By 1298 the city's economy was suffering badly.[24]

Help was at hand, however, when in that year Edward I moved his administration from Westminster to York. It is a move which has often been presented in strictly military terms: it was easier to direct a major Scottish war from a base halfway between London and Edinburgh. However, Ormrod has demonstrated that Edward, like his three successors, had mixed motives for moves between London and York. He may have wished to punish the Londoners, who had supported the political opposition in 1297; and he may also have had positive political as well as military reasons for choosing York. While he was campaigning in Flanders in January 1298, the leading opposition nobles, preparing for a Scottish campaign, met at York. They resolved to go no further north until royal concessions were guaranteed; and the bishop

22. Dobson, *Jewish Communities of Medieval England*, 68–73.
23. McKisack, *Parliamentary Representation*, 19; quotation: Carpenter, *The Struggle for Mastery*, 466; M. Prestwich, *Plantagenet England 1225–1360* (Oxford, 2005), 132; Maddicott, *Origins of the English Parliament*, 287–8.
24. M. Prestwich, *Edward I* (London, 1988), 384; Nightingale, 'Rise and decline of medieval York', 9–11.

of Carlisle pronounced excommunication from the Minster pulpit against anyone infringing Magna Carta. Edward wasted no time on his return in meeting many of the rebels' demands, and by April, when he held a royal council in York, the Scottish war was his main priority.[25]

A second capital? York and the Crown, 1298–1349

Hard on the heels of his great council, the king held a parliament in York in May (in the Minster's new chapter house), and installed in the castle the key royal courts of Exchequer and Bench (King's Bench and Common Pleas). The county sheriff had been forewarned to build a large but temporary structure (*hala*) in the castle for the Bench, and to adapt 'our hall of the same castle' for the Exchequer, together with a squared chequerboard, seating for the officials, and a bar 'for those pleading and those who ought to stand around'. He was also to prepare to accommodate the royal treasury in Henry III's keep. The Exchequer and Common Pleas remained in York continuously from May 1298 to December 1304, during which time Edward also held parliaments or other assemblies in the city in 1300 and 1303, one of them a body of burgesses from forty-two towns to discuss the national customs on wool exports.[26]

It is true that, after that exceptional six-and-a-half-year residence, later spells of government stays in York were shorter, but they remained frequent until the 1330s. It has become almost an orthodoxy today that London/Westminster was virtually becoming the capital of England under Edward I, but in the strict sense that is anachronistic, since government was where an itinerant king, his court, and his officials were. Tout long ago argued that it was only the outbreak of the Hundred Years' War that gradually turned Westminster into a capital in the modern sense; and Mark Ormrod has suggested that had Edward III from 1338 not given

---

25. Ormrod, 'York and the Crown under the first three Edwards', 16–22; Ormrod, 'Competing capitals?', 82–5. For the January 1298 troubles in York and the April Great Council there, see Prestwich, *Edward I*, 430 and n.107, 479.
26. For tables of the periods of residence in York 1298–1393: Ormrod, 'Competing capitals?', 80–3; A. Musson and W. M. Ormrod, *The Evolution of English Justice* (Basingstoke, 1993), 195–9. For the writ to the sheriff, *HKW* II 891; *PROME* 1.88; 2.30, 47–8; and for the 1303 assembly, Maddicott, *Origins of the English Parliament*, 319. Ormrod, 'Competing capitals?', 84n., gives the normal locations of courts and offices in York.

the French war priority over Scotland, 'York, rather than Westminster, might have been chosen as the heart of a new-style Plantagenet empire.'[27]

The frequent shuffling of Crown courts, offices, and household over a minimum of some 200 miles (320 km) was naturally costly in time and money. The documentation for a later move, of the Exchequer and Common Pleas in 1322, reveals that a caravan of twenty-three carts, each drawn by five horses, travelled overland from Westminster to Torksey, where it divided. Some officials rode on to York to make the castle ready, while the rest of the party accompanied the rolls and other records by boat. The whole move took thirteen days and cost nearly £92.[28]

With a periodic influx of courtiers, bureaucrats, servants, and soldiers, the injection of cash into the economy of city and region must have been substantial. To take one example of scale—again from a later period than Edward I—the royal household, when in York in 1327, spent nearly £59 on the single feast of Easter Day, and even more (£103) on Whit Sunday. It is no surprise that there was an increase in coins found in York from Edward I's reign.[29] Less desirable must have been local price inflation. In 1301 the royal council, in conjunction with the city council, issued regulations for trade and prices, the earliest detailed ordinances so far known for the control of trade in a provincial city. They were followed up in 1304 by presentments against those who had allegedly flouted them, naming no fewer than 384 men and women. Given that the lists are confined to offenders—and to members of only ten crafts—they are an impressive testimony to the size of York's service sector. Less reliable, perhaps, is the pretext that the price rises were caused by 'extortion' by the citizens: they must surely have been triggered by an excess of demand over supply, and have been as injurious to local consumers as to incomers.[30]

Certainly there must have been severe pressure on accommodation; hence the inclusion of a clause about checking rent rises, especially 'in the case of a newly-built hostelry or one repaired to enhance its value since the

27. T. F. Tout, 'The beginnings of a modern capital: London and Westminster in the fourteenth century', *Proceedings of the British Academy*, 11 (1921–3), 487–511; G. Rosser, *Medieval Westminster 1200–1540* (Oxford, 1989), 36; Ormrod, 'Competing capitals?', 76, 84–5, 90–1.

28. D. M. Broome, 'Exchequer migrations to York in the thirteenth and fourteenth centuries', in A. G. Little and F. M. Powicke, eds, *Essays in Medieval History Presented to T. F. Tout* (Manchester, 1925), 293–6.

29. D. A. Hinton, *Archaeology, Economy and Society* (London, 1990), 185–6; M. Vale, *The Princely Court* (Oxford, 2001), 310.

30. TNA, E13/26, mm. 75, 76; M. Prestwich, *York Civic Ordinances, 1301*, BP 49 (York, 1976), who gives a full translation on pp. 9–28.

arrival of the court'. It would not have been enough to reconcile some royal officials used to London: in vacation time in 1302 the Chancellor of the Exchequer complained that all his officials had gone home except one, who was left with him 'in this profane city'. The other side of the coin was the opportunities available to ambitious Yorkshire clergy. Hamilton Thompson drew attention long ago to York Minster as a 'training ground' for royal officials, and said that 'for a century after the reign of Edward I much of the executive work of government was in the hands of Yorkshire clerks'. Recent research has confirmed how right he was: in an extreme example, the key office of Keeper of the Rolls was held almost continuously by Yorkshiremen from 1295 to 1345, and in this and other departments 'the road to Westminster passed through York'.[31]

Even when Edward moved his administration back to Westminster, his officials continued to keep a close eye on York. In 1304–5 the Exchequer ordered the citizens to pay £73 allegedly concealed by a former mayor from the murage tax, and £110 for wines supplied to them by the king's butler. In both cases the citizens successfully petitioned the parliament of February 1305 for acquittance: the £73 had been lawfully spent in constructing the city walls, and the butler confessed he had been paid for the wine. Nevertheless, Edward had reason to be suspicious of financial chicanery at York. In the spring of 1305 his justices of trailbaston held court there, uncovering evidence of corruption and conspiracy among leading citizens. As a result, Andrew de Bullingbroke and fifty-three others were indicted at York before the justices of eyre in Hilary Term 1306, and then—as the charges were so serious—the case was deferred to Westminster. There they were convicted of setting up an illegal guild, using a charitable cover to subvert normal civic government. The action, clearly provoked by allegations from other townspeople, resulted in the dissolution of the guild and punishment of its members.[32]

The marks of royal and military links with York around the turn of the century are still visible in the cathedral. The present nave was begun in 1291, and most of the armorial shields represented there in stone and glass are of

---

31. A. H. Thompson, 'The medieval chapter', in Thompson, ed., *York Minster Historical Tracts* (York, 1927), no. 13 (unpaginated); J. L. Grassi, 'Royal clerks from the archdiocese of York in the fourteenth century', *NH*, 5 (1970), 12–33 (quotation from p. 16); Prestwich, *York Civic Ordinances*, 2, 3; Prestwich, *Plantagenet England*, 484.
32. *PROME* 2.78–9, 95; G. O. Sayles, 'The dissolution of a gild at York in 1306', *EHR*, 55 (1940), 83–98.

families active in Edward I's Scottish war. And the window given by Canon
Peter de Dene, probably *c*.1306–7, is dominated by heraldry proclaiming the
connections of Henry III and Edward I with other kingdoms, including
France, Castile, the Empire, and even the lost kingdom of Jerusalem. It can
be read as a metropolitan statement as well as an expression of pride in
Dene's royal service. It has been suggested recently that the chapter house,
completed as the nave was started, deliberately emulated that of Westminster, for both were used for parliaments as well as meetings of their clergy,
though that is not certain. Furthermore, a room was added over the chapter-house vestibule, probably in the 1290s, well equipped with a fireplace
and garderobe, possibly for visits by the royal household.[33]

Edward II also used York as a base, partly for the Scottish War, but also
to deal with threatened Northern rebellions (his cousin and leading
opponent, Thomas earl of Lancaster, had his main strongholds at Tut-
bury and Pontefract). Between 1309 and 1312 the royal household was
often in York, dealing with Crown business such as negotiations with
Flemish ambassadors. Indeed, the king's son and heir Edward (III) must
have been conceived in the city during one royal sojourn early in 1312.
After the English defeat at Bannockburn (1314), Edward II was in York
again, where he held a parliament, and submitted to the opposition's
demands. Thereafter, civil strife was temporarily eclipsed by the Great
Famine, and by increasingly destructive Scottish raids, which inflicted
damage on the North 'of a kind not seen since at least the eleventh
century'.[34]

Those raids, coupled with a lurch towards civil war, triggered a return to
York of the Exchequer, royal courts, and household for several lengthy spells
between 1318 and 1323, as well as seven parliaments or great councils.
Despite their presence, Scottish armies penetrated almost to Pontefract in
May 1318 and to York in September 1319. On the latter occasion the royal
chancellor, the archbishop, and the mayor of York, Nicholas Flemyng, raised

33. *FYMAR* 73 (2002), 18; Sarah Brown, *York Minster: An Architectural History c. 1220–1500* (Swindon,
    2003), 47, 56–8, 70–1, 123–5, 276–9; David Simpkin, *The English Aristocracy at War* (Woodbridge,
    2008), 147; W. Rodwell and R. Mortimer, eds., *Westminster Abbey Chapter House* (London, 2010),
    61–5, 90, 231. De Dene and his window: D. E. O'Connor and J. Haselock, 'The stained and
    painted glass', in Aylmer & Cant, eds, 348–51; Palliser, 'Thirteenth-century York', 7 and n. 51;
    F. D. Logan, 'Dene, Peter', in *ODNB*.
34. Miller, 'Medieval York', 54–5; Ormrod, 'York and the Crown', 25; Ormrod, 'Competing capitals?',
    82–5, 90 and n. 50; quotation: Prestwich, *Plantagenet England*, 261; Flemish embassy: *PROME*
    3.219–20. For maps of the Scottish raids, Campbell, 'Nature as historical protagonist', 290.

a scratch army which was defeated at Myton-on-Swale, the dead including the mayor and many fellow citizens. The king ordered the city walls to be strengthened and at a parliament in York (January 1320) concluded a two-year truce with Scotland. That interlude saw a brief civil war (1321–2), which was settled by a decisive royal victory at Boroughbridge, after which some rebels were tried at York. Several leading rebels killed at Borough-bridge were buried in York's Blackfriars, but none seems to have become the focus of a popular cult, as did Lancaster himself at Pontefract or as Arch-bishop Scrope was later to do in York itself.[35]

In April 1322 the king again held a parliament in the city, issuing the Statute of York which rejected the Ordinances issued by his enemies. He then invaded Scotland, disastrously: a counter-attack routed his forces somewhere on the North York Moors, and Edward was almost captured at Byland Abbey. The war was ended by a humiliating truce negotiated at Bishopthorpe (May 1323), after which the government left York for Westminster. It meant 'a blatant betrayal of the whole of the north of England, which was thereby abandoned to the mercy of the Scots'.[36]

After Edward was deposed in 1327, his young son Edward III, under the control of his mother Isabella and her lover Mortimer, came to York with an army against Scotland, staying there for over a month, while much of the Crown's administration remained longer. The campaign was a failure, and the army's presence brought bloodshed to the city's streets when Edward's ally John of Hainault brought over troops who clashed with the English soldiers. Furthermore, as often, the burden of war taxation was increased by purveyance, by which Crown officers could requisition transport and food. In July 1327 merchants bringing corn, meat, fish, and other foodstuffs to the city complained that their supplies had often been raided by purveyors, apparently without payment. Consequently, they said, they dared no longer come to York, and food prices had risen rapidly. Other merchants, however, including the de la Poles of Hull, found 'unprecedented scope for profiteer-ing' from the royal residence there.[37]

35. J. R. Maddicott, *Thomas of Lancaster 1307–1322* (Oxford, 1970), ch. VIII; Ormrod, 'Competing capitals?', 90. One charge against Lancaster was sending knights to York to try to secure civic support: Maddicott, *Thomas*, 312.

36. Quotation: Ormrod, 'Competing capitals?", 94; R. M. Haines, *King Edward II* (Montreal and London, 2003), 174, 273–4; Seymour Phillips, *Edward II* (New Haven and London, 2010), 435.

37. Miller, 'Medieval York', 56, 69; R. Horrox, *The De la Poles of Hull* (Beverley, 1983), 8; Ormrod, 'Competing capitals?', 80.

The presence of the young king and his administration produced two positive outcomes for the city. In June 1327 it was granted a royal charter, one of a series of generous urban grants made in the first three years of the reign, apparently to buy support for the new regime. In York's case the charter not only confirmed previous liberties, but added extra powers for the city's courts. And in January 1328 the king was back in York to marry Philippa of Hainault in the Minster; the location was chosen because the archbishop of Canterbury had just died and Melton of York officiated instead—but at least it must have boosted local trade.[38]

The Scottish war ended in 1328, but resumed in 1332, when the royal administration returned to York for six more years. Once again, northern wool merchants gained: the proportion of English wool exported from Hull rose from 12.4 to 17.2 per cent, and Hull's gains were at London's expense. Once more, innkeepers and retailers must have benefited from suitors to the royal courts and from three more parliaments held in York (1332, 1334, 1335). And once again, the Cathedral witnesses to the chivalric attitude of Yorkshire barons and knights, as well as their role as donors. The new nave's triforium incorporated a series of fifteen sculptures of knights and falconers of around 1330, while the great west door was flanked by figures of a Percy and a Vavasour holding blocks of stone and wood to commemorate their gifts of building material. On the debit side, the gains to York's economy were yet again offset by disruption to trade, high prices, and heavy taxation.[39]

After 1338, however, regional grievances were appeased. As Edward gave priority to France over Scotland, 'the taxation of the north was largely appropriated to its defence and was kept under special officers at York'. Nevertheless, links between Yorkshire and the royal administration remained close, and the court of King's Bench returned to York for seven terms in the 1340s, while many senior York clergy remained in the offices of state even when they were at Westminster. Edward also looked north for financial assistance in the French war: he had begun by relying on loans from Italian bankers, but from 1337 he turned increasingly to English creditors, from Yorkshire as well

38. The 1327 charter survives as YCA, A7. Miller, 'Medieval York', 69, dismisses the 1312, 1316, and 1327 charters as 'not of major importance' but 1327, like others of Isabella and Mortimer, went well beyond the usual confirmations of existing rights at a royal accession: W. M. Ormrod, *The Reign of Edward III* (Stroud, 2nd edn 2000), 163; and cf. C. D. Liddy, 'Bristol and the Crown, 1326–31', in W. M. Ormrod, ed., *Fourteenth Century England: III* (Woodbridge, 2004), 50–1.
39. Miller, 'Medieval York', 56; Ormrod, 'Competing capitals?', 80; Brown, *York Minster*, 120, 125–9.

as London. The most prominent was the Hull wool merchant William de la Pole, but one of Pole's associates was John Goldbeter, who headed a syndicate of York merchants lending to the Crown through London financiers under Walter Chiriton. In the two years 1347–8 alone, Goldbeter's syndicate loaned over £20,000 to Chiriton's company. It seemed a good time to lend, for the Scottish as well as French wars were going well for the king. 1346 was the year not only of Crécy but also of the crushing defeat of the Scots near Durham, when David II was taken prisoner.[40]

Church and culture

Before turning to York's development of self-government under the Crown, there is something to be said for considering the Church first. The archbishop and cathedral chapter were, after all, powers in the city long before mayors and bailiffs. Not only did they lead an organization which was all-encompassing in the sphere of religious belief and practice—for the citizens as for all others in the diocese and province—but they also had judicial power over many activities now wholly secular, including testamentary and matrimonial law. Moreover, not only did the Minster physically dominate the city, together with its neighbours of St Mary's and St Leonard's, but its archbishop and chapter were the wealthiest landholders in York after the king.

Starting with the archbishops, it is noteworthy that three of them before 1350 came to their post from service as royal chancellor and kept their political antennae tuned. Walter de Gray (1215–55), fourteen years after leaving the Chancery, still 'delight[ed] in gossip and news of the Court', and could still do friends of the current chancellor 'a favour'. Yet he became a committed and resident archbishop, and used his exceptionally long tenure to earn 'a place in the front rank of the "reforming bishops" of thirteenth-century England'. Indeed, he inaugurated a period of a century and a half when most archbishops 'enjoyed a close and personal relationship with their cathedral and their diocese', and it was not until after 1374 that their successors became grand, distant, and often non-resident figures.[41]

40. Quotation: J. Campbell, 'England, Scotland and the Hundred Years War', in J. R. Hale et al., eds, *Europe in the Late Middle Ages* (London, 1965), 192; E. B. Fryde, *Some Business Transactions of York Merchants . . . 1336–1349*, BP 29 (York, 1966); R. H. Britnell, 'Goldbeter, John', in *ODNB*.
41. C. A. F. Meekings, 'Six letters concerning the eyres of 1226–8', *EHR*, 65 (1950), 501 (mis-attributed in the journal and in Gross/Graves no. 504); R. B. Dobson, 'The later Middle Ages,

Gray spent as much time in the diocese as possible, though not in the main at his palace in the close. Instead, he bought a manor just outside York, and built there Bishopthorpe Palace, which became the normal residence for his successors when they were not touring their diocese and occupying their other manors such as Ripon, Cawood, Sherburn, and Beverley. The archbishops still used their York palace for great festivals, synods, and ordinations, but generally preferred what Hamilton Thompson called the 'freer atmosphere' of their other residences, where they would not tread on the toes of their cathedral chapter. Furthermore, as Gray still needed a London base for his increasingly reluctant visits to court and parliament, he also bought York Place in Westminster for himself and his successors, a mansion they retained until it was seized by Henry VIII and transformed into Whitehall Palace.[42]

Next to the king, the Church of St Peter was already the greatest power in Norman York; and its great estates inside and outside the city continued to expand throughout the twelfth and thirteenth centuries. However, a distinction should be made between the liberty of the archbishop himself and the liberty of St Peter, the privileged area of the dean and chapter, which by now was entirely separate. It was the chapter who ruled a 'scattered republic' of eighty-seven parishes (seven of them in York), and in addition a great many houses and manors which they held as landowners. As such, the chapter was involved in repeated clashes with the emerging city corporation, clashes which led to an 'inquest into the liberty of St Peter within York and its suburb[s]', held before royal justices in 1276. The jury found that by then the liberty included a formidable collection of 'lands' not only near the cathedral close, but in all parts of the city and outside the walls. Some can also be traced in the nearly contemporary *husgabel* roll of *c.*1284, which shows some properties paying the house-tax (*husgabel*) to the cathedral canons or vicars rather than to the king. It is clear from the researches of Sarah Rees Jones that the liberty cannot be closely equated with the old archbishop's shire. Much of the archbishop's land had passed to the chapter, largely to endow its prebends; but 'a significant "rump" of the archbishop's shire survived to be administered quite

1215–1500', in Aylmer & Cant, eds, 46–52, 75–86 (quotations from pp. 46–7, 98); R. M. Haines, 'Gray, Walter de', in *ODNB*.

42. A. Hamilton Thompson, *The English Clergy and their Organization in the Later Middle Ages* (Oxford, 1947), 74.

separately of the new St Peter's liberty until *c.*1300', while on the other hand the dean and chapter had been busily buying new properties.[43]

The heart of the Close and liberty was of course the Minster itself, the cathedral of Archbishops Thomas and Roger. Walter de Gray's arrival marked a turning point, for having revivified the chapter after the disastrous reign of Geoffrey Plantagenet, he turned to replacing the transepts on a vast scale. Canterbury Cathedral had been rebuilt from 1174 with a focus on its new cult of Becket, and in 1220 his remains were translated to a new shrine, a ceremony which Gray attended. He may well have been spurred on to emulate Canterbury, for he began the new south transept about 1225, and in 1226 secured the canonization of his predecessor William fitz Herbert. It is possible that the great York transepts and new central tower—all complete by 1255 and probably earlier—'were intended partly as a backdrop to St William's tomb at the east end of the nave, a relationship of tomb and transepts similar to old St Peter's in Rome'. The south transept was sufficiently complete by 1241 for him to establish there a chantry for his own soul and those of his predecessors, in which he was buried in 1255. The chantry was the richest ever endowed in the Minster and the tomb is perhaps the finest of its date in England.[44]

Gray's work inspired, after a pause, the continuation of rebuilding the minster on the same scale as the transepts, starting with the chapter house and vestibule (*c.*1280–95) and then the nave (*c.*1291–1350). The huge scale of the present cathedral, as completed after the Black Death, is therefore in a sense a memorial to the vision and ambition of Gray and his chapter. Measured by area of ground covered, John Harvey's calculations make York and Winchester jointly second in size after Lincoln among surviving medieval English cathedrals, though London's Old St Paul's vastly exceeded all three. It would not be right, however, to omit the role played by some of Gray's successors, notably William de Greenfield (1306–15) and William de Melton

43. Quotation: Thompson, *The English Clergy and their Organization*, 73; YML, MS L2(1), pt iv, fos 34v–45v, pr. (slightly inaccurately) in W. Dugdale, *Monasticon Anglicanum*, ed. J. Caley et al., VI, pt 3 (London, 1830), 1193–4; Palliser, 'York's earliest administrative record'; Rees Jones, 'Property, tenure and rents', 88–91.

44. Christopher Wilson, *The Shrines of St William of York* (York, 1977), 8, 24; Brown, *York Minster*, 10–45; Paul Binski, *Becket's Crown* (New Haven and London, 2004), 126. William's canonization was in 1226, not 1227 as usually dated: C. Norton, *St William of York* (Woodbridge, 2006), 199. Gray's tomb: H. G. Ramm et al., 'The tombs of Archbishops Walter de Gray (1216–55) and Godfrey de Ludham (1258–65)...', *Archaeologia*, 103 (1971), 101–47; M. J. Sillence, 'The two effigies of Walter de Gray...', *Church Monuments*, 20 (2005), 5–30. For other early chantries in the Minster, see J. E. Redford, 'The 1364 chantry survey at York Minster', in *RMY*, 47–87.

(1317–40), who were benefactors to the nave and its furnishings, though Melton has been reassessed as a patron of art linked to the court, rather than a generous giver.[45]

The Minster was, of course, the focus of a whole series of buildings. The courts of the archbishop and chapter were mostly held inside it, but other activities required separate buildings. North of the cathedral lay the archiepiscopal palace and treasurer's house and south of it the deanery; there were also separate houses for the other senior clergy and canons inside and outside the Close. Also within it were the archbishop's prison and mint, a courthouse and gaol for the liberty of St Peter, a masons' lodge, and three parish churches; and the Close was surrounded by a twelve-foot wall with four gates, under a royal licence of 1285.[46]

As the cathedral was not monastic, it needed no communal refectory, dormitory, or cloister, but instead the Close was crowded with 'a dense jungle of often small and transient urban tenements'. This meant that when, about 1250, the chapter decided to organize their deputies, the Vicars Choral, into a college, it had to be built outside the Close wall in what became known as the Bedern. York here set a precedent: it was the earliest English secular cathedral to organize its Vicars Choral into a college, a pattern followed by the other eight by about 1400.[47]

The Minster itself happily survived the Reformation more or less intact; the same is not true, of course, of the monastic foundations in York, and it is easy to forget how numerous, large, and imposing many of them were. St Mary's Abbey, the wealthiest, had lordship and jurisdiction over much of the city and wide estates across northern England; it was rich enough to afford a complete rebuilding of the abbey church between 1271 and 1294. Its precinct, enclosed by a wall from 1266, covered an area of some 12 acres (5 ha), and besides the usual monastic buildings it housed a court and prison within the main gatehouse on Marygate. The three other Benedictine houses— Holy Trinity Priory, St Clement's nunnery, and the cell of Whitby Abbey in Fishergate—were much less wealthy, as was the Gilbertine priory of

45. John Harvey, *Cathedrals of England and Wales* (London, 3rd edn 1974), 87; Brown, *York Minster*, 46–136; C. A. Stanford, 'Archbishop Melton's donations to York Minster', *YAJ*, 75 (2003), 77–89, drawing on Kraus's study of Melton's donations.
46. Katherine Edwards, *The English Secular Cathedrals in the Middle Ages* (Manchester, 2nd edn 1967), 276; Dobson, 'The later Middle Ages', 103–4; R. M. Butler, 'Notes on the Minster Close at York', *YH*, 14 (1997), 10–21.
47. Quotation: Dobson, 'The later Middle Ages', 103; R. Hall and D. Stocker, eds, *Vicars Choral at English Cathedrals* (Oxford, 2005), esp. chs 13–16.

St Andrew. Nevertheless, Holy Trinity was of some regional and civic importance, with its substantial walled precinct of about 7 acres (3 ha) off Micklegate, and sufficiently wealthy to afford a complete rebuilding of its church between about the 1170s and 1230s. It also claimed the right to hold a court for its tenants in the city.[48]

These were all enclosed houses, their monks, nuns, and canons having in theory only limited contact with townspeople except for the supply of goods and services, and exercise of their jurisdiction over their tenants. There must in some cases have been also family contacts, where urban families provided recruits to the houses: the sister and daughter of one York mercer, for instance, entered St Clement's nunnery.[49]

There were, however, other religious houses with pastoral and charitable purposes beyond their walls. The greatest was St Leonard's Hospital, part monastery, part almshouse, and with elements of a modern hospital for care of the sick. Its annual income of some £1,200 made it almost certainly the largest and wealthiest hospital in medieval England: in 1287 it housed 229 men and women in the infirmary and twenty-three orphans 'in the children's house'. That may have been untypical: St Leonard's apparently struggled financially if the total of adults went beyond a 'customary' 206, and it might reflect rural and urban poverty at the peak of the population boom. Relief was not confined to inmates: the hospital provided alms at the gate, and distributed meat and ale weekly to the city's leper houses and bread to the prisoners in the Castle. In 1293 it distributed weekly at the gate 261 loaves, 247 herrings, thirty-three dishes of meat, and thirteen gallons of ale. Clearly the hospital was helping as many or more outside its walls than within: there were 300 prisoners in York Castle alone.[50]

There were also numerous smaller 'hospitals' or *maisons dieu* in York—poorly recorded and hard to total—and four leper houses in the suburbs.

48. St Mary's: *VCHY*, 357–60; *RCHMY* II, 160–73, IV, 3–24; C. Norton, 'The buildings of St Mary's Abbey, York and their destruction', *Antiquaries Journal*, 74 (1994), 256–88. Holy Trinity: *VCH Yorks*. III, 389–90; D. A. Stocker, 'The priory of the Holy Trinity, York', in L. R. Hoey, ed., *Yorkshire Monasticism: Archaeology, Art and Architecture, from the 7th to 16th Centuries*, BAA Conference Transactions 16 (London, 1995), 79–96. St Clement's: AY 2/1. St Andrew's: AY 11/2.

49. *TE*, I, 34 (1390). Documented earlier cases are scarce, but in 1310 another citizen's daughter had sought to enter Hampole Priory. See Janet Burton, 'Yorkshire nunneries in the Middle Ages', in Appleby and Dalton, eds, *Government, Religion and Society*, 107, 113.

50. P. H. Cullum, *Cremetts and Corrodies: Care of the Poor and Sick at St Leonard's Hospital...*, BP 79 (York, 1991), 9–10, 29–30; Cullum, ed., 'St Leonard's Hospital, York, in 1287', in D. M. Smith, ed., *The Church in Medieval York*, BTC 24 (York, 1999), 17–28.

Among the largest and best endowed were St Nicholas, founded by St Mary's abbey partly for lepers, and St Mary's in Gillygate, founded in 1318 for six aged and infirm priests. Altogether at least six are firmly known before 1350, but the great age for their foundation was the century after the Black Death.

Finally, there were the new orders of friars, which rapidly became popular among laypeople, though it is not clear why: as Barrie Dobson notes, 'remarkably little is known...about the precise role played by the mendicant orders in English society'. The two largest orders, Dominicans (Blackfriars) and Franciscans (Greyfriars) apparently established York houses by 1230, followed by the Carmelites by 1253 and the Augustinians by 1272. Whatever their role, they clearly remained popular until their dissolution in the 1530s, attracting many more bequests from merchants and other citizens than the monasteries. They were also well staffed, with an estimated 157 friars in the four York houses before 1337, nearly a third of all friars in Yorkshire.[51]

Such was the range of religious houses in York other than parish churches and civic chapels. It is hard to assess their overall place in civic life, because the monasteries (though not the friaries) feature most in the archives when secular and ecclesiastical jurisdictions clashed. Such discord began almost as soon as the citizens acquired self-government: in 1226 the pope censured them from trying to tax the men of St Peter's and St Leonard's liberties. A royal writ of 1228 forbade Crown lands to be donated or sold to churchmen except with royal licence, and we have already seen from the York return, which survives in part, the scale of such gifts already made, probably totalling over 250 properties. The king, as chief landlord in the city, was clearly concerned, but Dr Rees Jones is surely right that so too were the city fathers: 'these church acquisitions may have represented a growing challenge to the powers of the newly established mayor and commonalty in their farm of the Crown's fee in York'. Furthermore, she suggests that the rebuilding of the city walls in stone from about 1250 was 'an expression of assertive self-confidence' by the citizens against rival jurisdictions, as much as a military necessity.[52]

51. R. B. Dobson, 'Mendicant ideal and practice in late medieval York', in P. V. Addyman and V. E. Black, eds, *Archaeological Papers from York* (York, 1984), 109–22; F. P. Mackie, 'The clerical population of the Northern Province...', *NH*, 43 (2006), 47. There were also two minor orders of friars in York, gone by 1312: D. Knowles and R. N. Hadcock, *Medieval Religious Houses: England and Wales* (London, 2nd edn 1971), 211, 249.
52. Miller, 'Medieval York', 39; Rees Jones, 'Property, tenure and rents', 138–42; D. M. Palliser, 'An early mortmain inquest', in Smith, ed., *The Church in Medieval York*, 1–15.

The bitterest clashes came in the century 1251 to 1354, when all five major ecclesiastical liberties were at odds with the city. Violence was used against St Mary's and Holy Trinity in the 1260s, some St Mary's men being killed and their houses burned; as a result, the archbishop placed the city under an interdict and St Mary's began a stone precinct wall. In 1275 the royal council adjudicated between the Minster, St Mary's, and the city, judging broadly in favour of the ecclesiastics; but the citizens were unreconciled. Parliaments more than once heard petitions about their infringement of the liberties of St Leonard's, but the worst violence came with more armed attacks by citizens on St Mary's in 1343 and 1350. These alarmed the Crown sufficiently for it to impose a settlement in 1354, which lasted more or less until the Reformation. This time its verdict was more favourable to the citizens, who regained control over the suburb of Bootham, though not Marygate.[53]

With or without these disputes, the townspeople's primary loyalties were to their parishes, neighbourhoods small enough in York to make them almost urban villages. This is clear from the increasing number of surviving wills, showing that citizens nearly always requested burial in their parish churches, which were also the focus of their bequests of furnishings and ornaments, and of requests for endowed prayers. The earliest layman's will apparently surviving complete, that of William de Dorem (1311) is fairly typical. He bequeathed his soul to God, the Blessed Virgin, and all the saints, asking for burial in St Michael's, Ouse Bridge, leaving the church his best 'cloth' as a mortuary fee. He allowed £3 6s. 8d. for his burial and for wax candles at his funeral, the candles to be distributed afterwards to St Michael's, another nearby parish church, and the Greyfriars and Blackfriars; 25 marks (£16 13s. 4d.) was to be paid to five chaplains to say masses for his soul for one year. Other, wealthier citizens were starting to endow chantries, where such prayers could be said for a longer term or in perpetuity. In 1305 John de Seleby petitioned parliament to be allowed to assign £4 worth of annual rents in York to found a chantry for the soul of his uncle, Master Adam de Norffolk.[54]

The number of parish churches had risen to about forty-five by 1300, but the tally proved unsustainable. At least one (St Benet's) was united to a

---

53. *PROME* 1.143; 2.36; 3.300; Craster and Thornton, eds, *Chronicle of St Mary's*, 6–9, 17–18, 68–9; Miller, 'Medieval York', 38–40, 68–9.

54. W. Brown, ed., *Yorkshire Deeds*, YASRS 39 (Leeds, 1909), I, 185–6; *PROME* 2.98. Brown printed Dorem's will from an original, current location unknown.

neighbouring church in 1263 and demolished before 1316, and two others are not recorded after 1294. The poverty of some city livings may well have been one cause of closures; only two York parishes—St Mary, Bishophill Junior, and St Olave—were wealthy livings in 1291, and both parishes included substantial rural lands which boosted their revenue from tithes.[55]

Yet money was still found readily for many of the surviving churches, as those that remain today show evidence of additional aisles and chapels and of new glass of the half-century 1300–50. And the newly popular perpetual chantries bear out the point. Almost forty are known to have been founded in the parish churches or in St William's Chapel between 1300 and 1350, mostly by aldermen and former mayors, whereas only one lay citizen (Richard Tunnoc) set one up in the Minster. Four of them were founded in St William's in a single decade (1321–31), two for laymen and two for clergy; and the mayor and his council seem to have deliberately 'equipped themselves and their city with a team of chaplains …directly at their service'.[56]

Chantry endowment by the wealthy, and the maintenance of over forty parish churches by the townspeople as a whole, are reminders of the importance of the Church in their lives. So much of the records inevitably concerns regulations, finance, and conflict that it is easy to overlook the shared religious world view that helped sustain the urban community. As in London, 'the emotion that was evoked by religious teaching and festivals and neighborhood loyalties, growing up around the parish churches, did much to keep friendships open between families that otherwise moved in different social spheres'.[57]

Most of the evidence for lay religious belief and practice in York postdates 1350, but there is sufficient to show widespread orthodoxy and piety. Until 1549 the Northern Province followed the liturgical Use of York, which differed in some respects from the prevailing English Sarum Use, though the distinction is not as clear-cut as used to be thought. The York calendar emphasized many northern saints, including William of York, whose cult was naturally fostered by the archbishops and Minster chapter. William's body was translated to a new tomb-shrine in 1284 in the presence

55. D. M. Palliser, 'The unions of parishes at York, 1547–86', *YAJ*, 46 (1974), 87, for five 13th–14th-century church closures, but of these St Mary-ad-Valvas was post-1376. 1291 tax on church livings: Miller and Hatcher, *Towns, Commerce and Crafts*, 377.
56. Chantries: R. B. Dobson, *Church and Society in the Medieval North of England* (London, 1996), 253–84 (quotation, p. 275); D. M. Smith, 'The foundation of chantries in the chapel of St William on Ouse Bridge, York', in Smith, ed., *The Church in Medieval York*, 51–68.
57. Sylvia Thrupp, *The Merchant Class of Medieval London* (Chicago, 1948), 38.

of the king and queen and many bishops and nobles, while the empty tomb was still revered, and was adorned with a lavishly decorated shrine—really a cenotaph—probably in the 1330s. William's cult has sometimes been depicted as an officially inspired cathedral campaign without widespread support, but the evidence of miraculous cures, of thank-offerings hung at the shrine, of pilgrim *ampullae*, containers for holy oil oozing from the tomb, and of alabaster carvings of St William intended for domestic use, all suggests that it was at least for a while a genuinely popular cult (Plate 7).[58]

A broader appeal still must have been that of ceremonies and processions, since public ceremony (both religious and secular) 'lay at the very heart of late medieval urban culture'. Again, the best evidence is post-1350, especially the Corpus Christi Plays, but they were to draw on a cult popular at York from the 1320s. The feast of Corpus Christi, the Thursday after Trinity Sunday, became an annual celebration in the thirteenth century and was observed in England from 1317; it was celebrated in the province of York by 1322, and proclaimed in the city in 1325. The observance included a procession in which clergy and laity followed a vessel containing the Sacred Host through the streets.[59]

Finally, the Church was still dominant in the fields of learning, literature, and the arts, as was to be expected. The cathedral maintained both a grammar school and a song school, and the chapter tried to forbid other clergy and laity from keeping schools (though their attempts are certainly evidence of a buoyant educational market), and were certainly unsuccessful in trying to suppress a rival grammar school at St Leonard's. The chancellor's teaching at the Minster grammar school would have been in Latin, as he is depicted doing in the Chancellor's window in the nave (*c.*1330); he is expounding St John's gospel from the Vulgate, while a student is taking notes in Latin. Elementary schools are not recorded in York before 1350, and we have no idea how many lay people there could read; but merchants, at least, would need a little numeracy and literacy. In the modest river port of Torksey, long in contact with York traders, the custom around 1345 was for an orphan son

58. P. S. Barnwell et al., eds, *Mass and Parish in Late Medieval England: The Use of York* (Reading, 2005); M. C. Salisbury, *The Use of York*, BP 113 (York, 2008). Cult of St William: Wilson, *Shrines of St William*; C. Davidson and D. E. O'Connor, *York Art* (Kalamazoo, 1978), 178–81; T. French, *York Minster: The St William Window*, CVMA (Oxford, 1999); Brown, *York Minster*, 88, 117, 123; Norton, *St William of York*, 149–202.
59. Quotation: C. Phythian-Adams, *Desolation of a City* (Cambridge, 1979), 179; R. Beadle and P. M. King, eds, *York Mystery Plays* (Oxford, 1984), p. x; Miri Rubin, *Corpus Christi* (Cambridge, 1991), *passim*.

of a burgess to be deemed of age at fourteen, or when he knew how to count 5s. 4d. (64d. or four of the old Danish *orae* of 16d.). John Goldbeter and his fellow merchants in the 1340s would have been unable to trade and lend on a large scale without adequate written records.[60]

There is little surviving evidence for the composition and copying of literary works which must have been widespread in York, though one or two manuscripts may reflect the presence of king and court there. One is a pictorial genealogy of British, English, and Scottish kings, probably compiled at St Mary's around 1301 to reinforce Edward I's claim to Scotland. Another is a continuation of a *Brut* chronicle, perhaps begun in London but completed in York, by an Exchequer clerk who moved there with his court in the 1330s; it shows a Northern interest, especially in entries for that decade.[61]

For surviving art and architecture (as opposed to vernacular building) we must turn above all to the cathedral. Its transepts and chapter house have been much praised (the huge 'Five Sisters' window is, in Pevsner's judgement, 'exquisitely beautiful'), the huge nave less so. There is usually respect for its individual design, which draws more on the French *rayonnant* style than most greater English churches, though the source of that design is still disputed. What is marvellous, however, is that the nave and chapter house, like the later chancel, still have most of their stained glass intact. The chapter house contains what has been judged the best-preserved ensemble of English narrative glass of that period, and the nave 'the most complete glazing ensemble of the first four decades of the fourteenth century'. Much of York's other medieval glass must have been destroyed (there survives a tantalizing fourteenth-century description of twenty-nine windows in St Mary's abbey church), but mercifully four parish churches preserve more or less intact windows of before 1350, and several more have extensive fragments. In short, York possesses—for this and the following period—'one of the finest collections of medieval stained glass to be seen anywhere'.[62]

60. Dobson, 'The later Middle Ages', in Aylmer & Cant, eds, 67, 70–2; J. A. H. Moran, *Education and Literacy in the City of York 1300–1560*, BP 55 (York, 1979). Torksey custumal: BL, Cotton Ch. II. 14; M. Bateson, ed., *Borough Customs*, Selden Soc. 21 (London, 1906), II, 159.
61. W. R. Childs and John Taylor, eds, *The Anonimalle Chronicle 1307 to 1334*, YASRS 147 (Leeds, 1991); John Taylor, 'The origins of the Anonimalle Chronicle', *NH*, 31 (1995), 61; R. R. Davies, *The First English Empire* (Oxford, 2000), 42–3.
62. Minster nave: Nicola Coldstream, 'York Minster and the Decorated style...', *YAJ*, 52 (1980), 89–110; Christopher Wilson, *The Gothic Cathedral* (London, 1990), 186–8; Nicola Coldstream, *The Decorated Style* (London, 1994), 35–7, 190; Brown, *York Minster*, 86–136. Stained glass:

Commune to corporation

Here, then, was the context in which the leading citizens had to make their way in negotiating with the Crown for more chartered rights, and equally importantly in extending as far as they could those 'prescriptive' rights which they already exercised 'without warrant of a charter'. They must have inherited from the lawmen and from the guild merchant a fledgling bureaucracy, some form of admission procedure for membership of the citizen body, and a *burghwarmot* or borough court to ratify property transfers and to adjudicate between citizens: the very name, though not recorded until the thirteenth century, is plainly the Old English *burhwaramot*. They must also have acquired some experience in diplomacy and litigation as a corporate body, whether in dealing with the king, with the archbishop and chapter, with the other ecclesiastical lords of liberties, or with local barons and knights. Almost all of this is, admittedly, unrecorded for nearly a century after the first elected mayor. Yet the fact that a civic seal was being employed by 1207, when it was used by 'the citizens of York' to notify Archbishop Geoffrey of the ownership of a parish church, implies that collective action was already becoming routine.[63]

The charter was presumably agreed in the borough court; but the city was still largely in the power of the royal sheriff, assisted by a reeve or reeves, of whom William Fairfax witnessed a deed before 1210, and Gerard the bell-founder (*campanarius*) another about 1206–11. In 1213 King John addressed one writ to the mayor and reeves (*prepositis*) of York, but another to the mayor and bailiffs (*ballivis*), and several other early writs use the two terms interchangeably. The reeves were presumably elected along with the mayor, and were soon found regularly addressed as bailiffs and treated as assistants to the mayor. In other words, their office appears to have evolved by 1213 from appointment by the king's sheriff to election by their fellow citizens.[64]

Pevsner and Neave, *Yorkshire: York and the East Riding*, 43, 50–4 (quotation from p. 50); Richard Marks, *Stained Glass in England During the Middle Ages* (London, 1993), 143–54; Chloe Morgan, 'A life of St Katherine of Alexandria in the chapter-house of York Minster', *JBAA*, 162 (2009), 146–78. St Mary's glass: G. Benson, *The Ancient Painted Glass Windows . . . of the City of York* (York, 1915), 182–4.

63. BL Add. Ch. 10636, pr. in *EYC*, I, no. 298; *VCHY*, 544; Palliser, 'Birth of York's civic liberties', 92 and n. 23.

64. *RLC*, I, 150–1; *EYC*, I, nos 245–6; A. G. Dickens, 'Norman and Angevin York: Some suggested revisions', *YAYAS AR* (1952–3), 37–8; Miller, 'Medieval York', 31. Miller dates the two deeds *c.*1200, but Dickens points out that Gerard's fellow witness was Robert Walensis, 'sheriff' (actually under-sheriff) 1206–11. For Walensis, see J. C. Holt, *The Northerners* (Oxford, 1961), 233; H. M. Thomas, *Vassals, Heiresses, Crusaders and Thugs* (Philadelphia, 1993), 69, 171, 204–6.

What, then, happened to York's guild merchant? We can make a shrewd guess that the leading townsmen who headed it as its alderman and assistants transformed themselves into the mayor and bailiffs from 1213. It cannot be proved for lack of evidence, and Gross showed long ago that in some towns guild merchant and borough corporation remained separate until the fourteenth or fifteenth centuries. However, two significant clues suggest that this was not so at York. Firstly, its guild merchant is never mentioned after 1200, and it must surely have gone by 1272–3, when freemen's admissions were entirely in the hands of the mayor (and by 1289–90 his financial assistants, the chamberlains). Secondly, the city's administrative headquarters, from 1256 at latest, was always called the Guildhall or Common Hall, never the City or Town Hall, probably because the mayor and corporation inherited it from the guild merchant. It is the more plausible because Sarah Rees Jones has shown that the present Guildhall probably stands on the site of the stone house of Hugh son of Lefwin, one of those fined for rebellion in 1173.[65]

Civic officials gradually multiplied. By the 1220s or 1230s three bailiffs were elected annually to assist the mayor; by 1229 there were also city coroners (known later to have been also three in number), and at a similar but unrecorded date there were bridgemasters, who collected and spent moneys for the upkeep of Ouse and Foss bridges. This modest list has two surprising omissions. The city's financial officers, the chamberlains (*camerarii*) are not firmly recorded before 1289–90, but must have existed earlier to deal with income and expenditure other than for the bridges. There must from the start have been also at least one clerk to deal with accounts, correspondence, and record-keeping, yet no post of 'common' (town) clerk is recorded until 1317. These gaps can be put down, probably, to simple absence of evidence, that lack of early civic archives already noted.[66]

The mayor and his officials must have engaged in a wide range of activities from the start, to judge from occasional hints. Clearly, the king expected efficient revenue raising to meet the high annual fee farm, as well as loans and taxes; and he must have assumed some system of keeping the peace, including the maintenance of a civic militia to aid him in time of war.

65. Charles Gross, *The Gild Merchant*, 2 vols (Oxford, 1890), I, 63, 83; Palliser, 'Birth of York's civic liberties', 95–6.
66. Bailiffs: the earliest firmly dated deed I know naming three is of 18 May 1236 (*YAJ*, 12 (1893), 97). Coroners and common clerk: Miller, 'Medieval York', 34, 74. Chamberlains: R. B. Dobson, ed., *York City Chamberlains' Account Rolls 1396–1500*, SS 192 (1980), p. xx. Bridgemasters: Palliser, 'Birth of York's civic liberties', 94.

For their part, citizens would want the upkeep of walls, bridges, Guildhall, and markets; the supervision of trade and crafts, especially victualling; and the recording and adjudication of property transfers and disputes. Much of this is obscure because the mayor exercised unrecorded customary rights and duties beyond those laid down by charter. We do know that the city fathers used the markets to enforce trade regulations by putting offenders in the pillory, as in many towns. In 1304 the royal council ordered them to pillory twelve city bakers, and to ensure that the bailiffs of St Leonard's pilloried four other bakers in their jurisdiction, all for overpriced bread. It is less clear how far the city could judge its citizens over disputes involving violence, though in 1301–2 the mayor and coroners heard a case of alleged assault and robbery in Stonegate, before it was called in to the King's Bench as beyond their powers.[67]

Geoffrey Martin has pointed out that the witnessing and registration of titles to property was 'one of the oldest functions...of the borough court', and that such registration was one of the chief distinctions between the law of privileged towns and the normal law of the land. Now we know that by mid-century the York Common Hall and Tollbooth were both used for the mayor's court, and that it heard cases involving city properties. The royal charter of 1256 accepted that all such cases should be heard there; and in 1270–1 it was said that a property deed enrolled there was as valid as a final concord in the royal courts. In fact such a system probably dates back to the start of civic autonomy, for the witness lists to dozens of surviving deeds from about 1217 onwards were headed by the current mayor and bailiffs.[68]

Widdrington, York's recorder from 1637 to 1661, preserved notes of 'customs, prescriptions and usages' from civic documents since lost, though often, unfortunately, without date or reference. Those scraps we can assemble from local sources, and those from central court records which have already been calendared, make clear that citizens could inherit property from their fathers without paying relief (effectively a Crown tax on inheritance); that widows had a right to part of their husbands' estates; and that some property, at least, could be freely transferred between citizens without

67. Thomas Widdrington, *Analecta Eboracensia*, ed. C. Caine (London, 1897), 100; Prestwich, ed., *York Civic Ordinances*, 20–1; J. Masschaele, 'The public space of the marketplace in medieval England', *Speculum*, 77 (2002), 402–3. Town militias: J. R. Maddicott, 'The oath of Marlborough, 1209', *EHR*, 126 (2011), 309 and n. 116.

68. G. H. Martin, 'The registration of deeds of title in the medieval borough', in D. A. Bullough and R. L. Storey, eds, *The Study of Medieval Records* (Oxford, 1971), 151, 155; Miller, 'Medieval York', 34–5; Palliser, 'Birth of York's civic liberties', 95, 100 n. 53.

need of permission from king or city. There was also a city custom that widows of freemen could 'be as free as thaire husbands was so long as they kepe thaym soole unmaryed', a custom recorded much later but probably preserving long-established practice.[69]

A legal judgement of 1226–7 upheld a York custom that a landholder need not answer a claim of wrongful possession unless it was made within a year; and in other cases of 1227–8 a widow was barred from 'her right' unless she claimed within a year, while a husband was judged able to transfer lands 'of his own possession' to his wife. This last case chimes with a common urban custom that lands purchased could be freely devised, but that lands inherited were subject to whatever laws of inheritance were in force. However, in a city claim of 1286–90 against St Mary's abbey, the citizens claimed that they held of the king by *husgabel* and that their tenements (not just those purchased) were all devisable by will.[70]

The mayor was elected annually, but re-election was common, and mayors were drawn from a 'narrow circle' of patricians (as Edward Miller calls them) in the sense of 'rich bourgeois playing a notable part in the government of a town'. Their names and dates are only patchily recorded before 1250, but enough references survive to show that the first known mayor, Hugh de Seleby (named in a royal writ of 1217) was mayor at least six times before 1236, his son John seven times or more (1251 x 1271), and John's son Nicholas four (1286–9). The Seleby family is admittedly untypical, but altogether the known mayors between 1217 and 1307 numbered only twenty-one individuals from seventeen families. Bailiffs were inevitably drawn more widely; the ninety-five bailiffs known over those ninety years came from about seventy families, though even so nearly half came from only twenty-one of those families.[71]

69. Widdrington, *Analecta Eboracensia*, 67–72; *YCR*, III, 126; Dobson, 'Admissions to the freedom of the city', 14 and n. 1; D. M. Palliser, *Domesday York*, BP 78 (York, 1990), 23.
70. Widdrington, *Analecta Eboracensia*, 67–8, 121; Bateson, ed., *Borough Customs*, II, 129; M. de W. Hemmeon, *Burgage Tenure in Medieval England* (Cambridge, Mass., 1914), 19, 131.
71. Miller, 'Medieval York', 34; E. Miller, 'Rulers of thirteenth century towns', in P. R. Coss and S. D. Lloyd, eds, *Thirteenth Century England* (Woodbridge, 1986), I, 130–1; E. Miller, 'English town patricians, c. 1200–1350', in A. Guarducci, ed., *Gerarchie Economiche e Gerarchie Sociali, secolo XII–XVIII* (Florence, 1990), 217–40; Miller and Hatcher, *Towns, Commerce and Crafts*, 344–5. I have a slightly larger database than was available to Prof. Miller, but with no additional mayors' names (though I make the total of mayoral families 17, not 18). The term 'patrician' is controversial: Susan Reynolds, *An Introduction to the History of English Medieval Towns* (Oxford, 1977), 67–8, 78–80.

It is clear enough, from property deeds and tax returns, that the mayors and bailiffs were drawn from the ranks of the richer citizens, and Edward Miller has found that most of them derived their wealth from trade, property holding, or a mixture of both. Hugh Seleby seems to have been at least a third-generation merchant, involved in shipping wool to Flanders and importing wine, some of which he supplied to the royal court. However, he also accumulated property, both urban and rural, and there is no evidence that his mayoral son or grandson were involved in trade. Other mayors and bailiffs were craftsmen, including goldsmiths; and one exceptional craftsman, the bellfounder and goldsmith Richard Tunnoc (bailiff in 1320 and MP in 1327) was the first known layman to endow a chantry in the Minster, where he was buried. He gave a window there, which still survives, depicting him donating the window to St William, flanked by scenes of bellfounding and bell-tuning (Plate 7).[72]

It may be that the greatest wealth of some early mayors came from trading in wool and cloth. We have seen that York ranked high among cloth-making towns in 1202; and a curiously neglected point about mayoral elections may relate to that. Their annual election date is not recorded before 1343, but from then on it was St Blaise's Day, 3 February, and there is no reason to think that it was new then: as the feast of the patron saint of wool-carders, celebrated even after the Reformation in the West Yorkshire clothing districts, it was a significant choice.[73]

It is not known how and by whom the mayor was chosen before 1343, or even whether he yet had a body of aldermen and councillors to assist him, though a mention in 1301 of a decision by 'the common council' does suggest a representative element. Yet whatever body advised or assisted the mayor, with a common seal and a common purse, must already have constituted in effect what later lawyers would call a corporation—a body capable of holding property in common, and of being able to sue and be sued at law like an individual. Earlier generations of historians were persuaded that urban corporations did not exist before the fifteenth century, but it has recently been

72. Miller, 'Rulers of thirteenth century towns', 133–6. Tunnoc: Dobson, 'The later Middle Ages', 96, and O'Connor and Haselock, 'The stained and painted glass', 350–3, both in Aylmer & Cant, eds; Brown, *York Minster*, 122, 131, 288; Redford, 'The 1364 chantry survey', in *RMY*, 71 and n. 226.
73. Palliser, 'Birth of York's civic liberties', 101; S. Rees Jones, 'York's civic administration, 1354–1464', in Rees Jones, ed., *The Government of Medieval York*, 137–8.

demonstrated convincingly that towns like York were effectively corporate long before that.[74]

Middling as well as richer citizens were clearly capable of collective action: the case of the suppressed guild of 1305–6, already touched on, is evidence of that. A mixed jury of twelve knights and twelve citizens accused fifty-four other citizens, led by Andrew de Bullingbroke (who had just stepped down as mayor) of conspiracy. They had, allegedly, instituted a convivial Guild of the Holy Trinity as a cover for manipulating civic government. In particular, they had used the guild to assist one another under oath, and to minimize their share of royal taxation by passing on the burden to others, a tactic successful because over half the city's tax assessors were guild members. The fifty-four were found guilty, imprisoned, and fined heavily; yet a boycott of them by fellow citizens was overturned in parliament in 1307 and Bullingbroke was re-elected mayor in 1309. Clearly the citizenry were divided—Bullingbroke had been attacked and severely wounded in his first mayoralty—but one clear demand by the accusers was that all decisions affecting the city should be taken openly before the mayor and bailiffs. It may well have been this dispute which provoked the creation of a formal body of city councillors to assist them in a more open and accountable government under the Crown.[75]

Citizens, townspeople, and visitors

Those who lived or stayed in York were a very varied population, and it is oversimplifying to call them all citizens. Firstly, of course, true 'citizens' (*cives*) or freemen—those who enjoyed political and economic privileges—were probably a minority of the adult male population, and included very few women. Most other residents—lesser craftsmen, petty traders and their families and apprentices; servants; paupers and beggars—were non-citizens (or, as they were later called, 'foreigners' as opposed to aliens). Distinct from

---

74. Miller, 'Medieval York', 77–8; Susan Reynolds, *Ideas and Solidarities of the Medieval Laity* (Aldershot, 1995), ch. VI, separately paginated.
75. *PROME*, 2.546, 562; Sayles, 'Dissolution of a gild at York'; Miller, 'Medieval York', 80; R. H. Hilton, *Class Conflict and the Crisis of Feudalism* (London, 2nd edn 1990), 16, 17; G. Rosser, 'Big brotherhood: Gilds in urban politics in late medieval England', in I. A. Gadd and P. Wallis, eds, *Guilds and Association in Europe, 900–1500* (London, 2006), 36. The court action began on 10 January 1306 (N.S.): Sayles implied (90 n. 4) that Bullingbroke was mayor all that year, but he was elected in 1305, and must have stepped down in January or February 1306.

both were the numerous priests, monks, canons, nuns, and friars, while
above all these in status were those residents serving Church and Crown,
including senior clergy and royal officials, and those northern nobles, gentry,
and abbots who chose to retain town houses for periodic visits. Finally, at its
peak of wealth and importance until the 1240s, there was the largest Jewish
community north of the Trent.

York's population may have reached a peak of some 20–30,000 around
the year 1300, if rough comparisons can be made with recent estimates for
London and Norwich. It is unlikely that fertility outpaced mortality in a
crowded and unhygienic environment, and if so a fair proportion of the
growing numbers of inhabitants must have been immigrants, whether 'betterment' migrants hoping to prosper in a large and fluid urban society, or
subsistence migrants desperate for work, or at least for food and shelter.
From the twelfth century it was a common urban custom that villeins or
serfs (nativi) reaching a town and remaining for a year without being
reclaimed by their lords could be free men, and although no York charter
spells out that right (as did, for instance, the royal charters of 1227 to Lincoln, Hereford, Gloucester, Shrewsbury, and Worcester), there is no reason
to doubt that the citizens exercised it by prescription, as did the burgesses of
Newcastle. Adam le Cerf, mayor of York in 1259, 1260, and 1270, was presumably a former villein himself, as was—it was said—a London alderman
a generation later.[76]

York's first register of freemen includes some 3,300 admissions
between 1272–3 and 1349–50, and is an invaluable database of (mostly
male) citizens. Many bore locative surnames derived from another town
or village; the very first man registered was Thomas de Fulford, and altogether twenty-eight of the thirty-six registered in 1272–3 had such
names, many from villages in the hinterland. Since hereditary surnames did
not become widespread until the fourteenth century or even later, many of
these men may have been named from their birthplace or at least their previous residence. McClure has analysed a sample of York freemen between
1272 and 1327 alongside early fourteenth-century samples for London and
three other towns, concluding that the larger the town, the higher the proportion of long-distance migration. Next to London, York has the smallest

76. Urban population estimates: refs in n. 2 above, and Prestwich, *Plantagenet England*, 20, 473.
    Freedom for serfs: Bateson, *Borough Customs*, II, 88–9; BBC, II, 136–7; Reynolds, *English Medi-
    eval Towns*, 71.

proportion of immigrants coming from less than 10 miles (16 km) away, and the highest proportion—over 27 per cent—from beyond a radius of 50 miles (80 km), higher even than that of Norwich.[77]

These men would mostly have been 'betterment' migrants, as would, presumably, the tiny but important group of alien immigrants, those born overseas. Over fifty men admitted to the franchise before 1350 were probably immigrants, in many cases with a surname derived from a Continental city. From the 1290s onwards there were many called 'le Flemyng', including James le Flemyng, mayor in 1298, and father of the mayor killed at Myton, some clearly with forenames suggesting Flemish birth 'rather than kinship with the landed family of that name long settled in Yorkshire'. The fifty or so included men specifically described as from five Flemish or Brabanter towns (Bruges, Dinant, Douai, Tournai, and Ypres), and others from Paris, Amiens, Cologne, and Florence. Nor can this be a full tally, for there are cases of immigrants not entered, such as Gaudin l'Orfevre (the goldsmith), whose son was enfranchised in 1315.[78]

More important than the origins of the townspeople was their wealth and social status, in a society that was clearly fluid in terms of social mobility, but with extremes of wealth. In the absence of lay probate inventories before 1350, wealth can best be measured from tax returns. The earliest two surviving for York are very incomplete, but sufficient to show huge variation in assessed wealth. Payments to the tallage of 1304 range from 5d. to 10 marks (£6 13s. 4d.), the last a composite payment by the widow and children of Laurence de Buthum (bailiff in 1288). The tallage returns of 1319 also reveal great disparities. Mayor Nicholas le Flemyng, just before he died at the battle of Myton, was assessed on goods worth over £33, greater than the value of all the other taxpayers in his parish (St Helen's, Stonegate) put together—more than thirty times the value of the goods of a nearby glasswright and sixteen times those of a plumber. More comprehensive is the recently discovered list of those paying the lay subsidy of 1334,

77. *YF*, I, 1–41, tabulated by Miller, 'Medieval York', 114–16; G. Redmonds, *Yorkshire: West Riding*, English Surnames Series I (London and Chichester, 1979), 31, 46, 125; P. McClure, 'Patterns of migration in the late Middle Ages', *Econ HR*, 32 (1979), 177–81. McClure's figures are helpfully reworked as histograms by J. A. Galloway, 'Urban hinterlands in later medieval England', in K. Giles and C. Dyer, eds, *Town and Country in the Middle Ages* (Leeds, 2005), 115.
78. *YF*, I, 1–40; quotation from Miller, 'Medieval York', 41; D. M. Smith, *A Guide to the Archives of the Company of Merchant Adventurers of the City of York*, BTC 16 (York, 1990), deeds indexed under 'Gaudin'.

covering nearly every parish. 851 heads of household are listed, paying between £5 and 2*d*. Those with moveable goods valued at less than six shillings were apparently exempt from paying, and in some York parishes there was not a single taxpayer.[79]

Poorer townspeople are almost invisible in the records before 1350, except when recipients of charity or when accused of crime and disorder. An ancestor of the Nevilles of Raby granted 'to all the paupers of York' the right to take firewood from his wood at Sutton 'to sustain their life'. Inevitably, some women were driven to prostitution: one of many attracted to ply her trade at the great St Ives fair in 1287 was Juliana of York. Like most cities, York alternated between tolerance and penalization: the 1301 civic ordinances 'deliberately juxtaposed pigs and prostitutes, and forbade both'.[80]

And for townspeople of all levels, the structure of households and the nature of family relationships are again areas almost impenetrable before 1350, apart from a few cases which may be untypical. We cannot even say whether most households were extended or nuclear, though some burgage plots were apparently subdivided into small houses for relatives of the principal householder, forming 'extended family networks'. We can infer, from the fragments of civic customs already noted, that widows of propertied citizens had the right to a generous dower, an aristocratic practice which by the thirteenth century was mirrored in many towns lower down the social scale. Widows and single women could clearly be householders in their own right, and were taxed as such to the tallage of 1304 and the subsidy of 1334. A few women traded in their own right: 32 women were enfranchised between 1275 and 1350, mostly after 1310. Interestingly, the terse entries suggest that the privilege could be inherited both through males and females. One female freeman was admitted as a widow, but before 1350 four men were enfranchised in right of their mothers. Furthermore, as was later the

79. 1304: W. Brown, ed., *Yorkshire Lay Subsidy, 30 Ed. I*, YASRS 31 (Leeds, 1897, misdated). 1319: TNA E 179/242/95: unpublished, but see Miller, 'Medieval York', 110 (for Flemyng) and P. Nightingale, *Trade, Money and Power in Medieval England* (Aldershot, 2007), IX, 6, 7. 1334: P. M. Stell and A. Hawkyard, eds, 'The lay subsidy of 1334 for York', *YH*, 13 (1996), 2–14, a return not known to R. E. Glasscock (*The Lay Subsidy of 1334*, RSEH, NS II, London, 1975).
80. Bodley, MS Dodsworth 9, fo. 60r (pre-1282, if Robert de Neville was the one who died that year): the manor must have been Sutton-on-the-Forest (*VCHNR*, II, 198). Prostitutes: E. W. Moore, *The Fairs of Medieval England* (Toronto, 1985), 255n.; quotation: Prestwich, *Plantagenet England*, 488.

case in some crafts, women may often have helped fathers or husbands in a family business.[81]

What we can begin to glimpse from this time is a little of the personal and family lives of women as well as men, thanks to the survival of 'cause papers' among the York church court files from 1303. Most survive from after the Black Death, but one earlier case is full of interest. It concerns the marriage in 1341 of Simon Munkton, a Stonegate goldsmith's son, to Agnes Huntington, orphaned daughter of a wealthy York merchant. The case came before the court in 1345–6, as Agnes petitioned for a separation or annulment. The final verdict is missing as often in such cases; but what is fascinating is the sheer level of detail reported by witnesses, including friends, neighbours, and servants. On the major issues—alleged violence by Simon and his pressure on Agnes to sell some inherited land—testimonies were divided and partisan; but there is also much preserving the flavour of neighbourhood life in Stonegate. For instance, Agnes had lived before the marriage in Mulberry Hall, and on one occasion the couple are said to have met at the back garden door facing Grape Lane, while at another time Agnes stood at a window while Simon threw her a ring over the garden fence.[82]

If women were largely outside the sphere of public life, and poorly recorded, the Jews were also excluded from most civic life but are much better documented. They were few in number—perhaps 200 on average in the thirteenth century—but numerous enough by about 1230 to need an extension to their cemetery. They seem to have reached a peak of wealth and influence in the 1220s and 1230s before being crippled by royal exactions from 1244 onwards. By 1219 their two leaders, Leo le Eveske ('the bishop') and his son-in-law Aaron of York were taxed among England's six richest Jews, and in 1241–2 as the two wealthiest of all. There is abundant material for a biography of Aaron, who had come to York from Lincoln in 1219 and married Leo's daughter Henna. In 1241–2 he personally paid £4,000 of the royal tallage on all English Jews (nearly one third of the national total), but in 1252 his property was seized by the king and restored

81. YF, I, 20, 22–3, 35, 42; S. Rees Jones, 'Building domesticity in the city', in M. Kowaleski and P. J. P. Goldberg, eds, Medieval Domesticity (Cambridge, 2008), 89, 90. Urban dower rights: Bateson, ed., Borough Customs, II, 120–9; Barbara Harvey, 'Conclusion', in Harvey, ed., The Twelfth and Thirteenth Centuries 1066–c.1280 (Oxford, 2001), 250.
82. F. Pedersen, Marriage Disputes in Medieval England (London, 2000), 25–58. Mulberry Hall: RCHMYV, 228.

only in part. In 1255 he was exempted from another tallage through poverty, but he must have retained some property when he died in 1268, as in 1270 Henna secured those lands and goods he had assigned to her, and she continued to hold some city property until 1280. Their nephew Josce le Jovene was prominent from the 1240s to the 1270s, while the last of his line in York, Bonamy *le Gendre*, whom we have encountered as favoured by Edward I, was so-called from being Josce's son-in-law.[83]

The fate of the English Jews as a whole mirrored that of Aaron himself: between 1241 and 1256 they paid over half their wealth to the king. York's Jews may have suffered more than most, for in 1255 they fell from second place to seventh among Jewish urban tax quotas. The expulsion of Jews from Newcastle (1234) and Derby (1261) left those of York geographically isolated; and like other Jews they were hard hit by laws first limiting, and then banning, all Jewish moneylending. A tally of seventy-six York Jews by 1276 (only nine of them women) implies a community of 150 at most; and that community never recovered from the coin-clipping accusations of 1276–9 and the subsequent hangings of leading York Jews, including Josce le Jovene. By 1290, when all Jews were expelled from England, only half a dozen Jewish householders seem to have been left in the city.[84]

Both the Jewish minority and the much larger Christian majority can be traced a little further through the evidence of their cemeteries. It is rarely that an individual burial can be identified and given a name and context: the richly detailed evidence from the Minster graves of Archbishops Gray (d. 1255) and Ludham (d. 1265) is exceptional. There are, however, the hundreds of anonymous burials from several cemeteries which have now been excavated and analysed. Evidence from nearly 1,050 burials from the churchyard of St Helen-on-the-Walls has been sampled above: unfortunately, though it is much the largest skeletal group scientifically excavated from York (or, indeed, from anywhere in England), it has not yet been possible to date them even to within a century: all we know is that they must range

---

83. Leo's *le Eveske* was apparently a title, possibly implying an office such as royal bailiff for the Jews: H. G. Richardson, *The English Jewry under Angevin Kings* (London, 1960), 124–9. On Aaron (unaccountably omitted from *ODNB*), see Michael Adler, *Jews of Medieval England* (London, 1939), 127–73; but this has been partly superseded and corrected by Dobson, *Jewish Communities*, entries indexed under 'York, Aaron of'. Wealth and tax: R. C. Stacey, 'Jewish lending and the medieval English economy', in R. H. Britnell and B. M. S. Campbell, eds, *A Commercialising Economy* (Manchester, 1998), 94–5; R. Mundill, *England's Jewish Solution* (Cambridge, 1998), 157–8.

84. Dobson, *Jewish Communities*, 56, 58, 66–7, 74; R. C. Stacey, '1240–60: A watershed in Anglo-Jewish relations?', *Historical Research*, 61 (1988), 135–50. Cf. Mundill, *England's Jewish Solution*, 157–8.

over the five or six centuries that the cemetery was in use before it was closed in the 1540s.[85]

More closely datable, however, are two smaller but still substantial sets: 271 individuals buried in the priory churchyard of St Andrew, Fishergate, between 1195 and 1538 (laypeople, women and children as well as canons), and over 500 Jewish burials from their extramural cemetery of Jewbury, datable to between about 1177 and 1290. Interestingly, the Jewbury population was in many respects similar to the Christian burials from other York sites, notably in the frequency of diseases traceable from skeletons, though Jewish women, at least, seem to have lived on average longer than the females from St Helen's. And Dr Simon Mays finds enough evidence from the St Helen's burials to suggest that female-led migration into York must already have been taking place before the Black Death, as it certainly was in the following century.[86]

To glimpse even a little of individual townspeople, however, is still hard at this period. What survive in the archives are mostly references to family relationships, piety, and business dealings, and those at the level of the prosperous and successful. Dodsworth in the seventeenth century saw the wills of four citizens between 1277 and 1349, all now lost, but the clauses he noted are concerned entirely with burial, property, inheritance, and pious bequests, though we do learn from the will of Katherine Gray, a widow of the parish of St Mary's, Castlegate (1349) that one of her children had become a nun at nearby Nun Monkton. William de Dorem (1311), whose will we have already noted for his pious bequests, also left robes to two servants; and hints of friendship or business may lie behind his gifts of 8s. 4d. to Robert Kyng 'which I promised for the repair of his houses', and of a mark (13s. 4d.) and a brass pot to Kyng's wife.[87]

Making a living

Even more than their predecessors, the people of York were much too numerous to be self-sufficient; and many must have been employed in

85. Ramm et al., 'The tombs of Archbishop Walter de Gray . . . and Godfrey de Ludham . . .', *passim* (a richly detailed report impossible even to summarize here); AY 12/1 (St Helen's burials).

86. AY 12/2 (St Andrew's) and 12/3 (Jewbury). For the distinctiveness of the Jewish population, AY 12/3, 523–6; and for important comparisons between St Helen's and Wharram Percy, but not always distinguishable by century, Simon Mays, 'The human remains', in Mays et al., *The Churchyard: Wharram* (York, 2007), 77–192 (female-led York migration, p. 191).

87. Dorem's will: n. 54 above. Dodsworth's will notes: Bodley, MS Dodsworth 91, fo. 169r, v.

making, selling, and distributing manufactured goods in return for food-stuffs and fuel, as well as importing other raw materials and manufactures which they could not provide themselves. However, though the city boasted a wide range of occupations and crafts, no one craft was dominant and what the city was best known for was trade rather than manufactures.

A traveller around 1250, listing the specialities of various towns—for example, different types of cloth for Lincoln and Beverley, Stamford and Colchester—was struck most by York's importance in trade (*regraterie*).[88] And more sober archival evidence points in the same direction. Between 1217 and 1350 the ruling elite became more dominated by merchants; it was to York and Hull merchants that the Crown looked for much credit by the 1330s and 1340s; and by the 1350s, growing overseas trade resulted in the forming of a mercers' or merchants' guild which was to dominate the econ-omy and government of late medieval and early modern York.

That, of course, does not mean that merchants and lesser traders formed a large proportion of the workforce. To measure numbers rather than domi-nance, we are fortunate to have one major exception to the absence of early civic archives: the huge first register of freemen admissions, which begins in 1272–3 and is uninterrupted from 1289 to 1671. It is, as Dobson says, 'the sin-gle most striking source in the corporation's archives', and the more valuable because from the decade 1301–10 onwards, it seems to have been a contem-porary record written up every year, listing the names of those who came before the mayor to swear the freemen's oath of loyalty to mayor and king.[89]

Any statistics drawn from the register cannot be pressed too far. Those for Edward I's reign are clearly incomplete and seem deliberately to have excluded some crafts (no weavers, for instance, were recorded before 1319). Those living in the liberties had no need to be enfranchised; and it is likely that, as Dobson shows, those claiming freedom by inheritance were not registered before 1397. There is no guarantee that totals fluctuated in line with the working population; it can be shown for later periods that peaks of admissions might reflect not increased population, but drives to boost civic revenue by compelling more craftsmen to register and pay.

88. C. Bonnier, 'List of English towns in the fourteenth century', *EHR*, 16 (1901), 501. Though Bonnier dated it 14th century, Carus-Wilson judged it 'almost certainly mid-thirteenth century': *EHD*, III, 881.
89. YCA, MS D1; R. B. Dobson, 'Admissions to the freedom of the city of York...', *Econ HR*, 2nd ser., 26 (1973), 1–22; D. Cannon, 'Catalogue of the contents of York, YCA, MS D1', in *RMY*, 135–54.

Table 5.1. Freemen admissions grouped by crafts 1272–1350

	1272/3–1306/7		1307/8–1349/50	
	Total	% of known occupations	Total	% of known occupations
Textiles	32	7	264	14
Provisions	130	29	448	23
Commerce and shipping	44	10	309	16
Leather	134	30	421	22
Building	9	2	59	3
Metal	79	17	263	13
Miscellaneous	24	5	183	9
Not recorded	315	–	593	–
TOTALS	767	–	2,540	–

Nevertheless, since between 1301 and 1350 over 80 per cent admitted gave a craft, the statistics assembled by Miller do give a valuable key to the occupational structure. His results, by craft groupings before 1350, are given in Table 5.1.[90]

It is clear, as Miller said, that 'the average freeman was not a merchant, but a craftsman'; and that, of those registered, 'about a third look like manufacturing craftsmen making up goods for direct sale to customers', especially leather- and metalworkers. Nearly one in four was employed in victualling, especially butchers, bakers, fishmongers, cooks, taverners, and innkeepers: the food trades formed a higher proportion than in similar samples for Winchester and Norwich, though even so the register probably understates their numbers. The lists of 384 victuallers and hostelers accused in 1304 of flouting the trade and price regulations—the most complete list of occupational names for any English town at this time—is revealing in two ways. Firstly, only a quarter of them can be traced in the freemen's register; and at no time before 1500 was the proportion of brewers, taverners, and hostelers among the freemen ever as great as in the 1304 lists. Secondly, it reminds us of the largely hidden world of female employment. Many brewers and hostelers in the 1304 lists and a majority of the regraters (dealers in foodstuffs) were women. Of the seventy brewers of 1304, forty-nine were

---

90. Miller, 'Medieval York', 43, 86, 114–16; Miller and Hatcher, *Towns, Commerce and Crafts*, 74–5, 81.

Plate 1. This view encompasses the two largest structures surviving from the later Middle Ages, the cathedral (Minster) and the city walls. Reproduced by kind permission of Prof. John Blair.

Plate 2a. William Lodge's 'prospect' of *c.*1678, taken from the south-west. It shows that even after the siege of 1644 and the severe damage, York still retained an essentially late medieval appearance, with its encircling walls, above which rose the cathedral, castle keep, and church towers. In front of the Minster's east end stands Micklegate Bar, the main gate to the road south to London. Reproduced by kind permission of York Museums Trust (York Art Gallery).

Plate 2b. Edmond [sic] Barker's 'South East Prospect of the Ancient City of York', published in 1718. As well as the cathedral and castle, Barker features 23 parish churches. Reproduced by kind permission of Ken Spelman Books.

Plate 3. The so-called Anglian Tower, which plugged a gap in the Roman fortress wall. Excavated in 1969–70, it bears a plaque attributing it to the Anglian period, and tentatively to the reign of King Edwin; but it is now thought likely to be of late Roman or sub-Roman date. Reproduced by kind permission of Prof. John Blair.

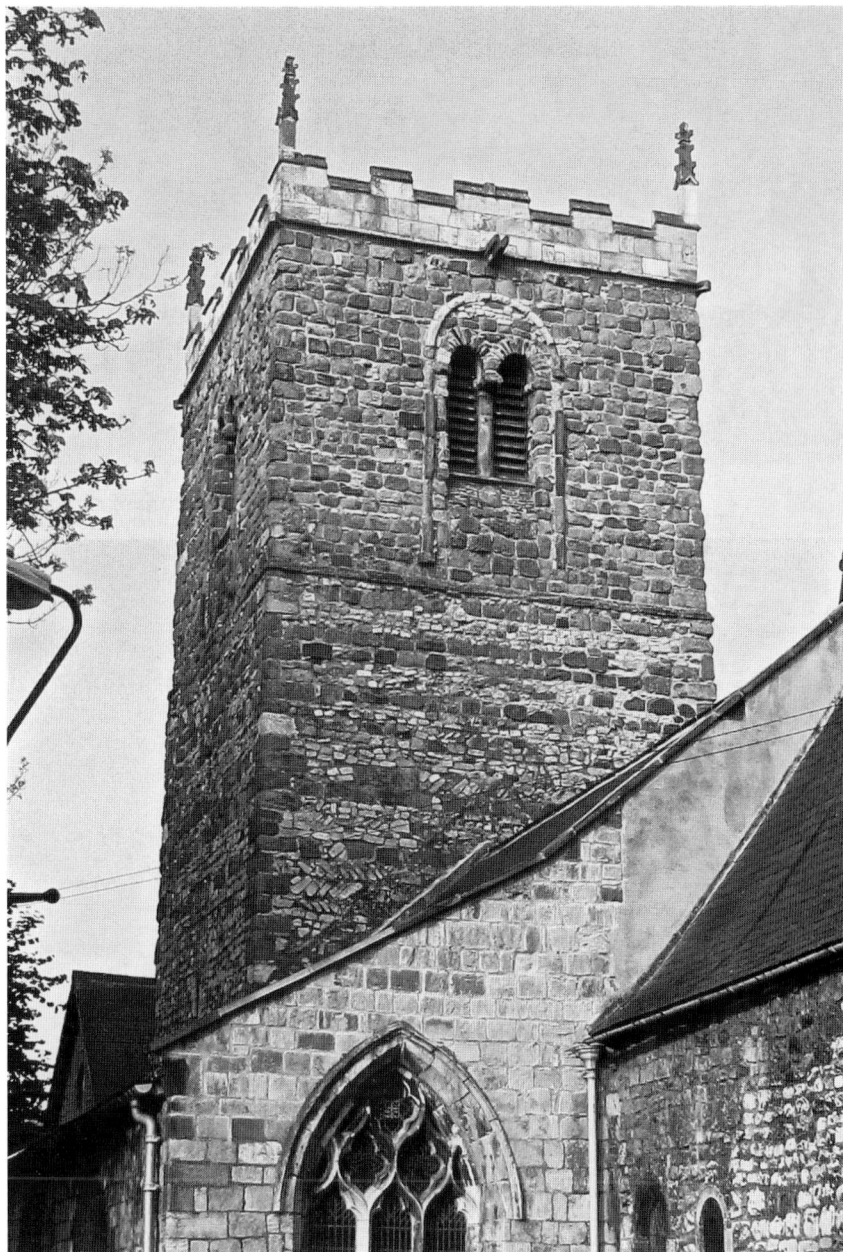

Plate 4. The tower of St Mary's church, Bishophill Junior. It is the oldest York building surviving above ground level, other than parts of the Roman defences. It was built mainly of reused Roman stone, probably *c.*1050–75. Reproduced by kind permission of Prof. John Blair.

Plate 5. Bootham Bar, the city gate straddling the main road north from York. Much of the present structure is of the twelfth to fourteenth centuries, but the outer arch is of the late eleventh century. Reproduced by kind permission of Prof. John Blair.

Plate 6. York castle from the south, sketched by Francis Place about 1685. In the centre is Henry III's great gatehouse, demolished in 1701 to make way for a new prison. Reproduced by kind permission of York Museums Trust (York Art Gallery).

Plate 7. Part of the Minster window commissioned by Richard Tunnoc, probably linked to a chantry which he founded near it in 1328. Tunnoc is shown offering a model of the window to St William of York, whose tomb was also nearby. Reproduced by kind permission of the Dean and Chapter of York.

Plate 8. A panel of early fourteenth-century stained glass in the Minster, apparently depicting wine selling. A customer, standing behind three barrels, proffers a coin, identifiable as a Henry III penny. Reproduced by kind permission of the Dean and Chapter of York.

Plate 9. 54–60 Stonegate. This range of three-storeyed houses is of the early to mid-fourteenth century; no. 60 (nearest the camera) has been dated to 1323. Reproduced by kind permission of Prof. John Blair.

Plate 10. Lady Row, built about 1316 along the street frontage of the churchyard of Holy Trinity, Goodramgate. It had originally nine or ten bays, each a separate dwelling of one room up and one down, and each with about 500 sq ft (45 m²) of floor space. Reproduced by kind permission of Prof. John Blair.

Plate 11. Trinity Hall, built for the Fraternity of Our Lord Jesus Christ and the Blessed Virgin Mary. From 1430 it was also the headquarters of the York mercers, and it is still owned by their successors, The Company of Merchant Adventurers. Reproduced by kind permission of the Company of Merchant Adventurers of the City of York.

Plate 12. Micklegate Bar, depicted by Moses Griffith in 1777, before its barbican was demolished. To its right is St Thomas's Hospital, demolished in 1863. Reproduced by kind permission of York Museums Trust (York Art Gallery).

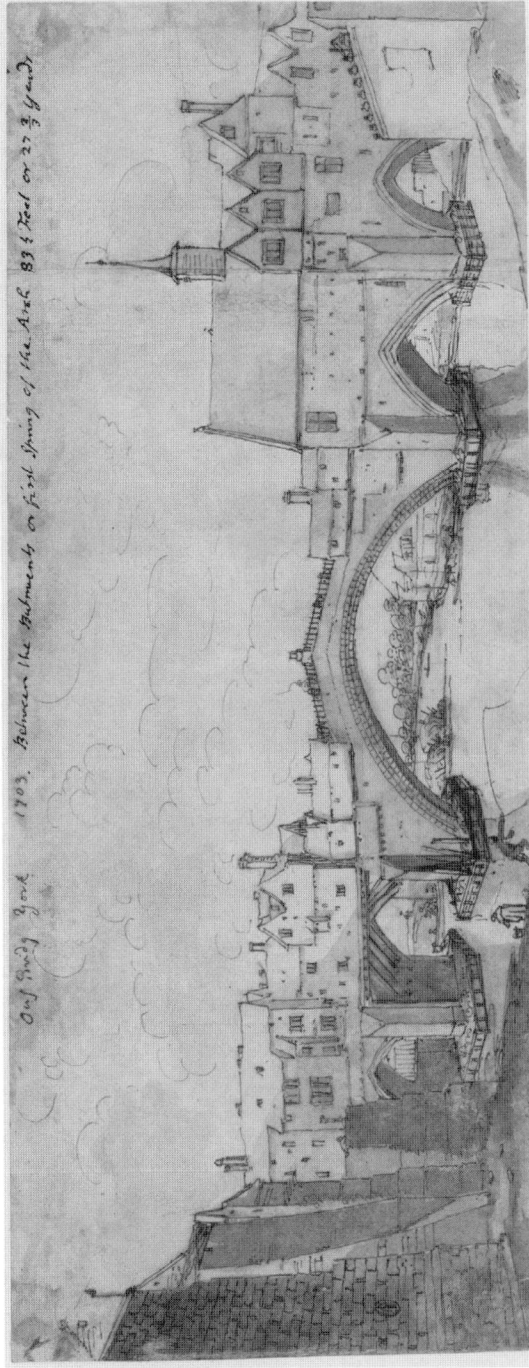

Within the text of the image (handwritten annotations):

Out Swing York   1703. Between the Abutments or first Spring of the Arch 83 ½ Feet or 27 ¾ yard.

Plate 13. Ouse Bridge from the north, sketched in 1703 by Francis Place, when the main structure was still medieval (apart from the central span, rebuilt after it collapsed in 1565). On the right are the civic chapel of St William, the council chamber, and beneath the chamber the two civic prisons. Reproduced by kind permission of the Department of Prints and Drawings, the British Museum.

Plate 14 and 15. Two panels from a set of six in a window in the church of All Saints, North Street. Each of the six depicts the same man (possibly Nicholas Blakburn Senior) performing one of the Corporal Acts of Mercy. Left: visiting the sick; right: feeding the hungry. Reproduced by kind permission of the Rev. Gordon Plumb.

Plate 16. The Red Tower, built to terminate an extension to the city wall as the King's Fishpond was drying out, and so leaving a gap in the defences. It was probably the 'newe towre' built in 1490 at the king's command. Reproduced by kind permission of Prof. John Blair.

Plate 17. The north-west side of Low Ousegate, sketched by Henry Cave. In publishing it as an engraving in 1813, he regretted that 'these houses . . . will be seen no more but in the plate . . . as they have been lately pulled down' to widen the approach to the new Ouse Bridge.

Plate 18. First Water Lane (now King Street), also published by Henry Cave in 1813. All the houses in this view were demolished in 1851.

men, ten women cited as wives, and eleven women recorded with no indication of marital status.[91]

Though the great majority of new freemen after 1300 were assigned to an occupation, it need not mean that each man or woman pursued only one craft. York merchants supplying Edward II's court included men who had been made free as a salter, two girdlers, a tailor, and a spicer. What is clear, however, is that the city's economy was complex enough to produce increasing specialization. Over a hundred different occupational designations occur in the register before 1350, including a gardener, a harper, a pottage-maker and a woodseller; and other specialists may be absent because they worked in the liberties. A clockmaker's seal matrix was recently discovered close to the Minster, datable to about 1300, and Hugh 'le Seler' of York occurs in 1333 as making a new seal for the bishop of Durham: yet neither appears in the freemen's register.[92]

Some craftsmen must have begun organizing themselves into guilds, run by the masters of each craft under rules approved by the civic authorities. Such we can deduce from the many later ordinances registered in the civic archives, though the only pre-1350 set to survive is that of the girdlers, who made buckles and horse harness as well as leather girdles. Leather, they agreed, could be bought only from York tanners; night work was forbidden; apprentices had to serve a minimum term of four years with a master; and buckle-makers paid by the day (journeymen) had to be common servants to all the master girdlers.[93]

In the absence of much pre-1350 documentation, the best evidence for crafts comes from their products and working tools. York Archaeological Trust have now published a huge number of finds, including some 6,000 objects of metal, stone, and textiles, illustrating crafts and industries between about 1066 and 1350, largely from Coppergate and Piccadilly. They include few surprises for those familiar with similar assemblages from Lincoln or Winchester, but they bring a sense of physical reality to daily life in York,

91. Miller, 'Medieval York', 43 (quotation); Miller and Hatcher, *Towns, Commerce and Crafts*, 81 (quotation), 326; Prestwich, *York Civic Ordinances*, esp. 8 n. 31, 22 n. 59; Prestwich, *Plantagenet England*, 474–5; J. M. Bennett, *Ale, Beer and Brewsters in England* (Oxford, 1996), 168, 235 n. 33.

92. Bartlett, 'Aspects of the economy of York', 321–7; Miller, 'Medieval York', 100; L. F. Salzman, *English Industries of the Middle Ages* (Oxford, 2nd edn 1923), 132; R. Hall, 'The earliest record of a clock at York Minster?', *FYMAR* 37 (2008), 69–73; R. Britnell, *Markets, Trade and Economic Development in England and Europe, 1050–1550* (Farnham, 2009), IX, 3.

93. *YMB*, I, 180–1.

especially the many cooking and eating implements, locks and keys, dress accessories, medical instruments, and horse and riding equipment. There are also many potsherds, apparently mostly from potteries in nearby villages which were exploiting suitable clay outcrops. Of industry in the strict sense, with fixed-place workshops, traces were found in 1957–8 of the working of animal horn off Petergate, but the best establishment now discovered is a foundry adjacent to the Vicars Choral college, in use from the late thirteenth century, which produced mainly cauldrons and other domestic vessels. And a fourteenth-century pottery kiln has at last been discovered on the southern edge of town, the first proof so far of what has long been suspected was another York industry.[94]

Working conditions are rarely recorded, but the cathedral's fabric accounts allow glimpses of the building trade. In 1344–5 the master of the works reported poor workmanship, quarrels among the masons, and misappropriation of materials. He also noted that W. the carpenter was old, and could no longer work at high levels (in altis): a younger man was to be employed for this and the old man to supervise defects. About eight years later the workforce was given strict rules about wages and hours. In summer the men were to work from sunrise until the evening ringing of St Mary's abbey's 'Langebell' and in winter from dawn to dusk. There were prescribed breaks for breakfast, dinner (prandia), a siesta in high summer, and an evening drink.[95]

Crafts and manufacturers were, of course, only part of the economic story: craftspeople had to buy their raw materials and sell their products, while an increasingly complex economy demanded more pure traders as well as a wide range of trading outlets. The city had its own markets and fairs, as well as—by this time—retail shops, if only in the sense that craftsmen could sell from their ground-floor 'shop' or workshop over a lowered board or window shutter into the street.[96] And beyond the city, travelling merchants could access a whole network of markets and fairs throughout Yorkshire and beyond, while until the early fourteenth century the most lucrative trade was often carried on in the great annual fairs of England and the near Continent.

94. AY 10/3, 17/15; AY 16/9, 1315. L. P. Wenham, 'Hornpot Lane and the horners of York', *Yorkshire Philosophical Society Annual Report* (1964), 25–56; B. G. Drummond, 'Pottery from Rievaulx Abbey', *YAJ*, 60 (1988), 33, 35; *Medieval Archaeology*, 47 (2003), 292–3.

95. J. Raine, ed., *The Fabric Rolls of York Minster*, SS 35 (1859), 161–4, 171–3; L. F. Salzman, *Building in England Down to 1540* (Oxford, 1952), 54–7; Barbara Harvey, *Living and Dying in England 1100–1540* (Oxford, 1993), 159–60.

96. See the 1301 ordinances for butchers and poulterers: Prestwich, ed., *York Civic Ordinances*, 13, 14.

Weekly markets proliferated all over England in the twelfth and thir-teenth centuries, and by 1300 there were about 150 in Yorkshire alone. This, of course, meant not only outlets for York's travelling merchants, but competition with the city's own markets. However, many other mar-kets were small and ephemeral, while York's were large, held probably (as later) three days a week, and with a long-distance pulling power. It is not-able that, when Yorkshire markets are mapped, there is a blank area close to the city in all directions.[97]

Some idea of the pulling power of York's markets, fairs and shops can be gained from the accounts of Bolton Priory in Wharfedale, which survive as a continuous run from 1286 to 1325. That wealthy Augustinian monastery lay over 50 miles (80 km) away, over roads often snowbound in winter, yet its canons were regular customers in York, paying carters to take back their bulkier purchases. These included cloth, furs, fish, wine, and spices, as well as barrels of tar for their sheep; and they sold there cattle and lead. In the fam-ine years 1317–21 they often sent to York to buy foodstuffs, especially wheat, barley, rye, and beans. The prior had his cope repaired there in 1306–7; in 1312–13 the canons spent 2s. 'for writing chronicles at York'; and in 1320–1 they bought there a painting of St Cuthbert. All this was much easier because they owned properties in at least three York streets, including a hospice with its own chapel where the prior and his agents could lodge. Moreover, Bol-ton was no isolated case: altogether at least fifty-one northern religious houses owned properties in York by 1290, presumably for commercial and social, as well as ecclesiastical, reasons.[98]

The city was not only a market for wealthy customers—whether monas-tic or aristocratic—but a well-placed entrepôt for wool, lead, and other goods from the hinterland to be shipped downriver to distant outlets. If wool was not sold there, its carriers would normally have to pay tolls at the city's quays: in the half-year Easter to Michaelmas 1292, half of the city's income handled by the royal keepers came from tolls on wool. Some of the richest Yorkshire monasteries sent wool to York to be sold to Italian mer-chants, and York appears as one of the English wool markets used by English

97. R. Britnell, 'Boroughs, markets and fairs', in *HANY*, 103–5; D. M. Palliser, 'Markets and towns in the Middle Ages', in *HAEY*, 74–5; Britnell, *Merchants, Trade and Economic Development*, esp. chs III, V, and new table, unpaginated, after V. 221.
98. I. Kershaw and D. M. Smith, eds, *The Bolton Priory Compotus, 1286–1325*, YASRS 154 (Leeds, 2000): York references are too numerous to list here, but the volume is well indexed; Palliser, 'Thirteenth-century York', 3 and n. 10.

monasteries in the list drawn up by Pegolotti around 1320. In one agreement with a Florentine company (1287), Rievaulx agreed to deliver eighteen sacks and 20 stone of wool annually at 'the house of the abbey at York'. Rievaulx, in fact, like Byland and Fountains, had its own woolhouses at Clifton, just upriver from York, whether to avoid tolls or simply to bypass its crowded streets.[99]

York craftsmen and merchants did not simply wait for other traders to come to York or through York, but ventured far afield themselves, fortified by the fact that their royal charters exempted them from paying tolls in other towns. York men are recorded buying wool round Richmond and Whitby; others as selling cloth and fish to the royal court in 1304; and others again in 1316–22 buying corn and other foodstuffs for the court from Lincolnshire, Nottinghamshire, and Norfolk. In a rare exception to the lack of systematic statistics, the certificates of Statute Staple and Statute Merchant survive from 1285, indicating that 'York's prosperity at the end of the thirteenth century was based mainly on its position as a collecting centre for the wool of north-west England.'[100]

York merchants and their agents were also prominent at the great international fairs held in the Midlands and South, which flourished between the 1180s and 1290s. The greatest were—in sequence from Lent to September—Stamford, St Ives, Boston, and St Giles (Winchester), to which Westminster (October) was added in 1248. Early evidence for northern patronage includes a riot at Boston Fair in 1241 which involved merchants from York and Beverley, while there must have been further friction in 1275, when the king ordered the bailiffs of Boston to let York citizens 'have their hanse and guild merchant in Boston fair' as in time past. Over the two decades 1240–59, York ranked fifth in value of goods supplied to the royal household at the major fairs. The York drapers alone must have been numerous, since they were renting twenty booths at St Ives in the 1280s and sixteen at Winchester in the 1290s. Nor was it only merchants and drapers who travelled to the fairs: Archbishop Giffard spent at least £20 at St Giles' Fair

99. B. Waites, 'Monasteries and the wool trade in north and east Yorkshire...', *YAJ*, 52 (1980), 114–16; J. Kaner, 'Clifton and medieval woolhouses', *YH*, 8 (1988), 2–10; Bischoff and Palliser, ed., 'Keepers' accounts for York', 13, 17, 18; E. Jamroziak, 'Rievaulx Abbey as a wool producer', *NH*, 40 (2003), 212–13; J. Bond, 'Canal construction in the early Middle Ages', in J. Blair, ed., *Waterways and Canal-Building in Medieval England* (Oxford, 2007), 189.

100. Miller, 'Medieval York', 100; Miller and Hatcher, *Towns, Commerce and Crafts*, 164; Nightingale, 'Rise and decline of medieval York', 8.

in 1270, and in the 1280s his successors spent at least £60 annually at St Ives and perhaps £30 at Boston. By the end of the century, however, both citizens and prelates gave up trading at the fairs and preferred to deal directly with London merchants and others.[101]

The city's most valuable export seems to have been wool destined for the Low Countries, much of it handled by 'alien' merchants. In 1260 Henry III granted exemption from murage payable in York by burgesses and merchants of Ghent, Ypres, Bruges, Douai, and St Omer. And in 1267 John Brilond, a wool exporter and a citizen of Lübeck and London, was established enough to advance the payment of York's fee farm to the king. Other Hanse merchants followed him to Yorkshire to buy wool, and a general arrest of alien shipping in 1294 trapped many more Hanse vessels in Yorkshire ports than anywhere else in England.[102]

From 1275 we can quantify the exports of English wool because it became subject to customs duties, under a system by which Hull was made a head port, with jurisdiction over all the ports of the Humber and the Yorkshire coast: between 1275 and 1350 Hull was usually the third busiest English wool port, behind only London and Boston. A customs account for Hull survives for the first year of the new system, 1275–6; it lists among many ships only one belonging to a York merchant, though three other York men paid customs on cargoes exported in other ships. Gradually, however, native Yorkshiremen began to eclipse the aliens in this trade. In 1303–4 about twenty York merchants appear in the Hull customs, trading to Stralsund, Hamburg, and Lübeck; and by 1310 Englishmen, many of them York merchants, handled half the wool exports through Hull. Bruges was a particular magnet: in 1332 the English wool merchants resident there included two from York, while John Goldbeter of York, who exported wool to Flanders on a large scale from the 1330s, was governor of the English merchants there in 1361.[103]

101. W. H. Dixon, *Fasti Eboracenses*, I, ed. J. Raine (London, 1863), 313–14; E. W. Moore, *The Fairs of Medieval England* (Toronto, 1988), entries indexed under 'York'; Derek Keene, *Survey of Medieval Winchester*, Winchester Studies 2 (Oxford, 1985), 1109; Miller and Hatcher, *Towns, Commerce and Crafts*, 170–6; P. Nightingale, *A Medieval Mercantile Community* (New Haven and London, 1995), 106–7.
102. A. E. Stamp, ed., *Close Rolls of the Reign of Henry III...AD 1259–1261* (London, 1934), 59; T. H. Lloyd, *England and the German Hanse 1157–1611* (Cambridge, 1991), 39, 44.
103. N. S. B. Gras, *The Early English Customs System* (Cambridge, Mass., 1918), 224–44; Miller, 'Medieval York', 100–1; W. R. Childs, *The Trade and Shipping of Hull 1300–1500* (Beverley, 1990), esp. 8, 10; A. F. Sutton, 'The Merchant Adventurers of England...', *NH*, 46 (2009), 222; Britnell, 'Goldbeter, John'.

It is difficult to know what York merchants imported in return for wool and cloth: wine, especially from Gascony, is the cargo most often mentioned, as for instance with Hugh de Seleby who imported wine from Anjou and on occasion sold some to Henry III, or Peter de Appelby, who was shipping wine to (or via) Newcastle around 1290 (Plate 8). Other mentions include cloth, wax, canvas, and oats from the Low Countries, and lead and bowstaves from Hanse merchants in 1351. There was no one dominant import comparable to the exported wool.[104]

Merchants and petty traders all needed coin and credit to operate. The Crown was mindful of the need for coin, its mint in York reopening in 1217, and striking as much as £21,000 in the recoinage of 1247–50. Martin Allen suggests a doubling of English silver coin in circulation between 1247 and 1290, and then another rise to a peak between 1310 and 1331: 'an enormous increase in the currency supported the commercialization of the English economy'. Not all benefited from this increase—the people in three York parishes possessed no taxable stores of coin in 1319—but there can be no doubt that a money economy emerged in England in the second half of the thirteenth century.[105]

Moneylending was also widespread, an activity far from confined to the Jews. Italian financiers were active in the North by the 1240s, when Aaron of York himself had to repay loans to merchants of Florence and Siena; and from 1277 York might even have been the location of a branch of the Riccardi of Lucca, 'living in York' (*Eboraco commorantes*). There was also extensive lending by the York Jews, at the peak of their prosperity, mostly to indebted northern landholders rather than citizens; and this continued almost to the end of that unhappy community's presence. A fascinating case before the Court of Common Pleas provides an example of the complexity such loans could entail. John Sampson of York had in 1288 agreed to pay Queen Eleanor 20 marks (£13 6s. 8d.), but while he was away in London the sheriff of Yorkshire had seized some of his property to enforce repayment. Thereupon John's nephew borrowed the sum from Laurence de Buthum, who without enough money to hand, borrowed from a merchant of Lucca, with

104. Miller, 'Medieval York', 42, 100–2; Miller and Hatcher, *Towns, Commerce and Crafts*, 186, 230; PROME 1.202.
105. M. Allen, 'Mint output in the English recoinage of 1247–1250', BNJ, 69 (1999), 207–10; J. L. Bolton, '... When did a money economy emerge in medieval England?', in Diana Wood, ed., *Medieval Money Matters* (Oxford, 2004), 9–12; M. Allen, 'The English currency and the commercialization of England...', in Wood, *Medieval Money Matters*, 38–9; Nightingale, *Trade, Money and Power*, IX, 6.

linen and silver cloths as pawn. When Laurence could not repay in time, the loan and pawned security were transferred to a York Jew or Jews. The further details need not concern us, but the court gave no judgement until 1304, long after the Jewish expulsion.[106]

Christian moneylending expanded as Jewish lending declined. Some York mayors became almost professional moneylenders, and two in the 1270s and 1280s, John le Espicer senior and Sir Gilbert Louth, lent extensively to Yorkshire gentry, while other York merchants lent to a range of northern knights in 1284–94 by providing credit for wool. Other notable moneylenders around the turn of the century included three successive deans of York Minster and one of its chancellors. The great period of lending, however, came from the 1330s and 1340s with the activities of large-scale merchants and moneylenders like John Goldbeter's syndicate.[107]

What can be concluded about the state of York's economy by the first half of the fourteenth century? There can be little doubt that its cloth industry declined, but John Munro sees York as more fortunate than many of the 'traditional drapery towns' of the thirteenth century. All suffered from an industrial crisis between about 1290 and 1330, followed by a revival from the 1340s, but a revival with a difference. Most of the 'vibrant urban cloth producers' after the Black Death were relative newcomers, and 'of the old traditional drapery towns, only York and Colchester revived successfully to retain their positions in the first or second rank of cloth exporters'. However, Nightingale's persuasive and well-documented analysis, as will be seen, suggests that the decline in York's wealth relative to other towns was not reversed after the 1340s and 1350s.[108]

A changing townscape

The urban landscape continued, between 1200 and 1350, to respond to the combined pressures of population growth, competing jurisdictions, the

106. Dobson, *Jewish Communities*, 62–4; Paul Brand, 'Aspects of the law of debt, 1189–1307', in P. R. Schofield and N. J. Mayhew, eds, *Credit and Debt in Medieval England c.1180–c.1350* (Oxford, 2002), 30: I am grateful to Professor Brand for more details of the case, which belongs to 1304, not 1306.
107. Dobson, *Jewish Communities*, 64–5; Nightingale, *Trade, Money and Power*, XI, 94–5; XII, 39, 40; Nightingale, 'Rise and decline', 9.
108. Quotation: J. H. Munro, 'The "industrial crisis" of the English textile towns, *c.* 1290–*c.* 1330', in M. Prestwich et al., eds, *Thirteenth Century England* VII (Woodbridge, 1999), 141; Nightingale, 'Rise and decline', 5; see Chapter 6 in this volume, pp. 182, 233.

development of defences, and the rebuilding of the cathedral and some of the greater churches. The main royal castle was rebuilt in stone between about 1245 and 1270, followed by the city walls in the central and Mickle-gate area (*c*.1250–70); the extramural St Mary's walls from 1266, heightened and strengthened *c*.1318–25; and finally the Walmgate and Fishergate section of city wall, which was begun in 1345. All of this put a tight cordon around the walled city, encouraging more crowded housing within the walls and leading, especially after about 1300, to a decline in the importance of some of the suburbs, especially those outside Fishergate and Walmgate Bars.[109]

Further pressure was put on space as the existing religious precincts expanded within the walls, and were joined by the new friaries. It is clear that their expansion and enclosure within stone walls 'involved the destruc-tion of housing and even entire streets': the Franciscans, for instance, absorbed before 1314 successively part of a street, an entire lane, part of the castle ditch, and finally all the houses in Castlegate and Hertergate adjoining their precinct. Nearer the Minster, there are clues in the maps and docu-ments suggesting that Blake Street originally continued north to Bootham Bar, before half the street was closed for the expansion of St Leonard's pre-cinct. Other pressures on space came from civic initiatives and the strength-ened city walls and gates entailed some clearance, such as the twenty-three houses demolished about 1240 around Micklegate Bar, while the creation of a large public marketplace by St Sampson's church, probably before 1250, must also have destroyed much housing.[110]

To compensate for the loss of housing, there was much new building both on existing plots—by subdivision, or by building upwards—and on former marginal land. In 1288 the citizens with properties abutting the Ouse claimed by ancient custom the right to extend their riverside properties 'on both sides of the water', and there is certainly evidence for this in the thir-teenth century from excavations in Coney Street, Coppergate, and Skelder-gate, while in 1303 Roger Mek was licensed by the Crown to enclose land from the riverbank adjoining Foss Bridge. Meanwhile, prosperous towns-people were making their houses more durable and fire-resistant and find-ing extra space by building upwards: these houses were either timbered over stone ground floors or were true timber-framed houses, either of which were stable enough for a second storey. By the early fourteenth century,

---

109. *RCHMY* II, *passim*; IV, 14–22; Rees Jones, 'Property, tenure and rents', 67–78.
110. Rees Jones, 'Property, tenure and rents', 60–2, 71.

even three-storeyed timbered houses were feasible: the earliest known is 60 Stonegate, recently dated by dendrochronology to 1323, making it one of the earliest datable three-storeyed town houses known outside London (Plate 9).[111]

These were substantial dwellings: but population pressure also produced ranges or rows of small houses, for rent, designed for poorer townsfolk, yet still true timber-framed structures rather than mere wattle and daub. Between 1304 and 1347 the Vicars Choral built nine new rows of small houses in the city centre, and in the same period at least five central parish churches constructed rows of such houses along the margins of their grave-yards. Nor were those all, for other such rows not on street frontages have been overlooked or misinterpreted. We can gauge their construction and durability because parts of these rows still survive, including most of Lady Row in the churchyard of Holy Trinity, Goodramgate. This, accurately dated by a documentary reference in 1316 and confirmed by dendrochronology, is probably the earliest datable row in England. Another, in Coney Street, is now only fragmentary, but its building contract of 1335 still exists. By build-ing such housing, the parishes were able to combine meeting housing needs with raising income for church purposes. In the case of Lady Row (Plate 10), the rents—apparently for ground-floor shops and first-floor living quar-ters—went to support a chantry of the Blessed Virgin Mary.[112]

With the increasing density of population, combined with frequent visits of the court, parliaments, and government offices, it is not surprising that the state of the streets and lanes often left much to be desired, not only by modern standards but by those of contemporaries. The earliest civic ordi-nances ordered human dung to be 'carried away', and gutters and drains kept clear, while pigs were not allowed in the streets. There were also to be four public latrines in the four city quarters or wards. Such orders must have

---

111. 1288 custom: *Yorkshire Inquisitions*, ed. W. Brown, YASRS 23 (Leeds, 1898), II, 55–6; AY 10/6, 686, 786–9; Rees Jones, 'Property, tenure and rents', 76–7; S. Rees Jones, 'Building domesticity in the city: English urban housing before the Black Death', in M. Kowaleski and P. J. P. Gold-berg, *Medieval Domesticity* (Cambridge, 2008), 67–8. 60 Stonegate: *RCHMY* V, 225–6; R. A. Hall, 'Secular buildings in medieval York', in *Lübecker Kolloquium zur Stadtarchäologie im Hanseraum* (Lübeck, 2001), III, 80–3; Sarah Pearson, 'Rural and urban houses 1100–1500', in Giles and Dyer, eds, *Town and Country in the Middle Ages*, 50.

112. Salzman, *Building in England*, 430–2; Philip Short, 'The fourteenth-century rows of York', *Archaeological Journal*, 137 (1979), 86–137; Rees Jones, 'Property, tenure and rents', 77, 209–10; Jane Grenville, *Medieval Housing* (London, 1997), 190–3; Hall, 'Secular buildings in medieval York', 81–3; Anthony Quiney, *Town Houses of Medieval Britain* (New Haven and London, 2003), 255–60; Rees Jones, 'Building domesticity', 71 and n. 23, 88.

been more honoured in the breach than the observance, for in 1318 the nobles, bishops, and others residing in York for the parliament complained apparently at the inadequate cleaning of the city. And in 1332 the young king expressed his disgust at 'the abominable smell abounding in the said city more than in any other city of the realm from dung and manure and other filth and dirt': the mayor and bailiffs were to have all the streets and lanes 'cleansed from such filth' and kept clean.[113]

Nevertheless, it would be anachronistic—despite the protests of king and parliament—to leave York on the eve of the Black Death as a city of filth and no more. Not only had resources been found for a magnificent cathedral and other churches, but for many substantial improvements in the housing stock, for the poorer as well as richer townspeople. The modest Lady Row and St Martin's Row would not have survived so long had they not been substantially built; and the contract for the latter shows that the upper floors could be heated, as each had a chimney and louvre. Furthermore, although York suffered severely in 1315–22—probably more than most towns further south, with the Scots war as well as the Great Famine—and was to suffer more in 1349–50, its citizens had the resilience to recover quickly.

113. *PROME*, 3.270; *CCR 1330–1333*, 610 (unfortunately both documents are incomplete); Prestwich, ed., *York Civic Ordinances*, 16, 17.

6

A golden age?

1349–*c*.1450

In 1349 the city was struck by one of the worst disasters in its history, when the epidemic known to contemporaries as 'the great pestilence' killed perhaps a third, or even half, of its population in under two years. This blow, coming only a generation or so after the Great Famine and the Scottish raids, might have been expected to ruin York. Yet it proved to be the prelude to a remarkable recovery in its size and wealth, making the city more populous than it would be again until the eighteenth century. It has even been suggested that the century following the Black Death (as the 'pestilence' is now known) was a golden age, when the citizens enjoyed greater prosperity—relatively and absolutely—than ever before.

That suggestion has become almost an orthodoxy since Neville Bartlett and Edward Miller wrote their classic accounts in the 1950s. Bartlett argued for an economic expansion during the second and third quarters of the fourteenth century, despite the Black Death, and then a continued boost to prosperity and population until about 1400. Miller similarly saw a rapid growth of York's economy throughout the century. Recent scholars have usually, with some qualifications, taken a similar line. To Sarah Rees Jones, the continued rise in rent levels, even after the plagues of 1349 and 1361–2, suggests a buoyant economy which attracted substantial migration, at least until about 1390. To Richard Britnell, cloth towns like York, Colchester, and Coventry were 'wonders of accumulating wealth in the later fourteenth century, only', he adds, 'to fall upon hard times in the fifteenth and early sixteenth.'[1]

---

1. Bartlett, 'Expansion and decline', *passim*; Miller, 'Medieval York', 84; Rees Jones, 'Property, tenure and rents', 248; R. Britnell, *Markets, Trade and Economic Development in England and Europe, 1050–1550* (Farnham, 2009), XX, 10, 14.

It should be added that, even for a relatively well-recorded century, the evidence is not conclusive, especially statistics of trade, taxable wealth, and population; and Britnell has warned that 'it is difficult to generalize about the performance of late medieval urban economies with any firm assurance'. Bartlett placed great emphasis on the role of clothmaking in York's post-1350 revival, but Pamela Nightingale has assembled a formidable body of data to conclude that 'the decline of York's wealth began early in the fourteenth century, and was not necessarily reversed by the later development of its cloth industry'. Textile manufacture could not make up for the decline of its wool trade, because 'the mediocre quality of its cloth exports' meant that its markets could not earn similar amounts of coin. The result is an interpretation of later medieval York that differs sharply from the standard one.[2] The debate is not yet resolved, but either way, the title of this chapter is not intended to endorse a rosy-tinted view of the period. The city was riven by bitter internal feuds, especially in the 1370s, 1380s, and 1400s; and Nightingale links these social tensions to the economic changes brought about in York and other large cities through the rise of the urban cloth industry.[3]

At that time York was widely considered second in status to London: on the Gough Map (c.1360) they alone are marked in gold leaf, and in 1354 both were granted the exclusive right to carry gilt or silver maces in civic processions. If the 1377 poll tax returns can be trusted, York was also the most populous town after London, and in 1378 its mayor and aldermen told the young king that they had spent more on ships for royal service than any other provincial city. And in an undated petition to the city council, probably in the 1390s, the lesser citizens or 'commons' asked for more rigorous entry standards for the city's franchise, to reflect the fact that York was 'a city of great reputation', 'always called the second city of the realm [la secounde Citee du Roialme]'.[4]

Perhaps there was a defensive ring to such rhetoric, for by then Bristol and Norwich were competing with York for that title. Bristol had overtaken York in taxable wealth in the early fourteenth century, and Norwich may

2. R. Britnell, 'The economy of British towns 1300–1540', in *CUHB* I, 313; P. Nightingale, 'The rise and decline of medieval York: A reassessment', *P&P*, 206 (2010), 5, 36, 39.
3. P. Nightingale, *Trade, Money and Power in Medieval England* (Aldershot, 2007), XIV, 35.
4. R. B. Dobson, 'The risings in York, Beverley and Scarborough, 1380–1381', in R. H. Hilton and T. H. Aston, eds, *The English Rising of 1381* (Cambridge, 1984), 118 and n.; W. M. Ormrod, 'Competing capitals? London and York in the fourteenth century', in S. Rees Jones et al., eds, *Courts and Regions in Medieval Europe* (Woodbridge, 2000), 87–8; C. D. Liddy, *War, Politics and Finance in Late Medieval English Towns: Bristol, York and the Crown, 1350–1400* (Woodbridge, 2005), 207–8; N. Millea, *The Gough Map: The Earliest Roadmap of Great Britain?* (Oxford, 2007). The petition (YCA, D 1, fo. 348r, v) must date to before 9 February 1400, when one clause was repealed.

have equalled or exceeded both in population. There was clearly some envy in York when Edward III made Bristol a county in its own right in 1373, the first city after London to acquire the privilege, a jealousy not assuaged until York acquired the same status in 1396. The city fathers were, however, perhaps unnecessarily touchy. Christian Liddy's fine comparative study of Bristol and York concludes that both were more or less equally placed 'at the apex of the provincial urban hierarchy', with Bristol possibly slightly the wealthier and York the more populous.[5]

The century after the Black Death is better documented for York than any earlier period. Church court depositions by witnesses, so valuable for daily life, survive in larger numbers, and the first of the archiepiscopal probate registers, including copies of many citizens' wills, begins in 1389. Furthermore, the richest early municipal records apart from the freemen's register, the two Memorandum Books, start in the 1370s, and the earliest surviving financial records in 1396–7. 'By the 1390s as never before', notes Barrie Dobson, 'one can write the history of the city…from its own records.' It is also a time which has left more surviving buildings than previous centuries. The archaeological evidence alone is a little thinner after 1350, if only because late medieval layers are more likely to have been removed by later cellars and foundations.[6]

Given the increasingly voluminous records and the large number of published studies based on them, it is impossible to do justice to them here. The economic evidence especially is both huge and hugely controversial, and the available statistics can be read in more than one way. Nor has it been possible to sample more than a fraction of the many unpublished records in the National Archives, since not all the relevant papers are filed where they might be expected. Michael Prestwich's discovery of the civic ordinances in an Exchequer plea roll was exploited in the previous chapter, and here it is possible to draw on a York alderman's inventory, which survives only because it was brought in evidence in a case before the Court of Common Pleas. Furthermore, two bodies of surviving evidence are so important that to explore them adequately would distort the balance of this book. By good

5. J. F. Hadwin, 'The medieval lay subsidies and economic history', *Econ HR*, 2nd ser., 36 (1983), 217; E. Rutledge, 'Immigration and population growth in early fourteenth-century Norwich', *UHY* 1988, 15–30; W. M. Ormrod, 'York and the Crown under the first three Edwards', in S. Rees Jones, ed., *The Government of Medieval York* (York, 1997), 29–33; Liddy, *War, Politics and Finance*, 11, 213.
6. R. B. Dobson, 'Craft guilds and city: The historical origins of the York mystery plays reassessed', in A. E. Knight, ed., *The Stage as Mirror: Civic Theatre in Late Medieval Europe* (Cambridge, 1997), 97.

fortune, the city preserves, both in the cathedral and in many of the parish churches, more later medieval stained glass than anywhere else in Britain, the subject of many scholarly studies, including so far three volumes published by the Corpus Vitrearum Medii Aevi (CVMA). Much material also survives on the York Corpus Christi Play (hereafter the York Plays), including an almost complete performance text. As the oldest and best preserved of the surviving English play cycles, it has an importance in the history of English drama which goes far beyond the scope of this book; it can be justifiably called York's most important contribution to later medieval culture.

The physical setting

Lord Esher, in his influential report of 1968 on York, summed up a widespread view of the medieval city. Even at its prosperous peak around 1350, he thought, it was congested, with 'noisome' alleys permanently at risk of fire and plague, while pigs and paupers 'infested its unpaved streets'. By the fifteenth century the citizens had built magnificent halls and churches, yet 'it was a city of exquisite architecture rising out of a midden'. It is a memorable phrase, but not quite fair to the citizens, even allowing for the anachronistic standard of judgement.[7]

The 'exquisite architecture' at least is not in question. The cathedral is not only much the largest medieval building in York to survive, but it has also sufficient left of its interior—especially its stained glass—to give some idea of how splendid it must have been before post-Reformation changes; and the greater part of it was constructed between 1361 and 1472. The Minster was, moreover, only the first among a cluster of greater churches. There is little evidence for major rebuilding at the others during that century, partly owing to destruction of the evidence at the monastic Dissolution, though the fact that the only two parish churches with spires (St Mary, Castlegate and All Saints, North Street) are the closest to the Greyfriars and Blackfriars might hint that both friary churches had spires, which the neighbouring churches copied on a smaller scale.[8]

There is abundant evidence that many parish churches were enlarged, enriched, or in some cases totally rebuilt. Two of the finest, St Crux and

---

7. Viscount Esher [Lionel Brett], *York: A Study in Conservation* (London, 1968), 1, 2.
8. As suggested by John Harvey, *York* (London, 1975), 79, 80, 84.

St Martin, Coney Street, have been virtually destroyed, but we know that the former was rebuilt between *c.*1400 and 1424 and the latter in the 1430s and 1440s. All Saints, Pavement, the grandest of the surviving churches, has less secure dates, but was clearly rebuilt in the fourteenth and fifteenth centuries. And, although it has long gone, the medieval Foss Bridge was rebuilt soon after 1400, when it acquired a lavish bridge chapel of St Anne, a pendant to the other civic chapel on Ouse Bridge.

Of civic building projects, the most important, the stone circuit of the city walls, was more or less complete—the Walmgate sector was added from 1345 and was probably still in progress until about 1380—but maintenance and repair were continuous, aided by the civic tax of murage. Royal licence to levy it was renewed regularly until 1449, when it was made permanent. There was also much work on the five main gates or bars in the fourteenth century, though exact dates are lacking. Militarily, they were strengthened by the addition of barbicans as defensive forebuildings: that at Walmgate Bar still survives, heavily renewed. However, the upper storeys of Micklegate and Bootham Bars, also added before 1400, were surely intended to impress visitors, facing as they did the main approach roads from London and the North. Micklegate Bar bears royal arms datable between 1350 and 1375; it is crowned by small statues of knights; and it was used from at least 1402 for the public display of traitors' heads (Plate 12).[9]

Other public buildings (in a broad sense) included a remarkable quartet of civic and mercantile 'guildhalls'. The earliest was the mercers' Trinity Hall off Fossgate, built between 1357 and 1368, with the addition of a rebuilt chapel in 1411 (Plate 11). This large two-storeyed structure of brick and timber—up to 87 ft (27 m) long and some 40 ft (12 m) wide—is a powerful testimony to the resilience of the mercantile community after the Black Death. Then followed St John the Baptist's Hall, erected by the tailors and drapers from about 1415, a suitable testimony to the wealth of the largest craft grouping and justly called 'the largest and least damaged craft guildhall in the medieval north of England'. Later came the civic Guildhall off Coney Street and the fraternity hall of St Anthony's, but though both are often

<hr/>

9. *RCHMY* II is comprehensive on the defences: see 13–15 (1345 building contract); 15–18 (1380 custody and murage grants); 95–101 (Micklegate Bar); 116–21 (Bootham Bar). See also H. M. Turner, *Town Defences in England and Wales* (London, 1970), 236, 238–41, for York's murage grants, and O. Creighton and R. Higham, *Medieval Town Walls* (Stroud, 2005), 141, for the northern context of the stone figures on three of the bars.

dated to the 1440s, the Guildhall was started only in 1449 and St Anthony's (apart from its chapel) in 1451.[10]

More abundant evidence survives for new domestic housing, which must have resumed quickly after 1349. Recruitment of building craftsmen to the franchise increased rapidly, doubling between the 1340s and 1350s, almost doubling again in the 1360s and 1370s, and reaching its medieval peak in 1411–20. Just as the mercers began their hall in 1357, so one of the best-surviving timbered domestic buildings—the main chamber block of Barley Hall, a monastic hospice of three storeys, has been dated dendrochronologically to 1359–60. Many other York examples are tentatively assigned to between 1350 and 1450, admittedly with few from tree-ring dates as yet. This can be attributed in part to more durable timber framing (more likely to survive than earlier housing), but there is a falling-off in datable houses after 1450–70, so it is probably a reflection of a real period of prosperity before that.[11]

The housing boom still followed the pre-1350 trends of, on the one hand, substantial houses of two and three storeys, and on the other, smaller houses, rows, and cottages for rent to poorer tenants. Both kinds are illustrated in one of the civic Memorandum Books, which includes copies of wills, property transfers, and leases, especially numerous between the 1390s and 1420s. In 1392, for instance, a chandler leased for twenty years what must have been a substantial Stonegate house, with a shop and more than one upper room (*solariis*). In contrast, Nicholas Warthill in 1413 owned not only a house of his own and other central properties, but also six messuages which he had built along the fringes of St Edward's churchyard, almost certainly for poor tenants in an urban fringe setting. Similarly, Alderman William Bowes had his own substantial house on Peasholm Green (the predecessor of the timbered Black Swan Inn), but in 1419 he also leased a plot of 'waste' land across the street, adjoining

10. The standard descriptions of all four, in *RCHMY* V, 76–93, now need some revision. All but the Guildhall are analysed in Katherine Giles, *An Archaeology of Social Identity: Guildhalls in York, c. 1350–1630*, BAR (BS) 315 (2000). For the tailors' hall, see also A. M. Mennim, *The Merchant Taylors Hall, York* (York, 2000), and R. B. Dobson and D. M. Smith, eds, *The Merchant Taylors of York*, BTS 33 (York, 2006), 3 (quotation), 183–98.
11. Heather Swanson, *Building Craftsmen in Late Medieval York*, BP 63 (York, 1983), 39–41; tree-ring dates: Charles Kightly, *Barley Hall York* (York, 1999), 4. For a national pattern, see Sarah Pearson, 'The chronological distribution of tree-ring dates, 1980–2001', *Vernacular Architecture*, 32 (2001), 69, with a peak in urban housing from the 1430s and a continuous decline after the 1460s.

St Cuthbert's churchyard, on which to build an unspecified number of new 'houses'.[12]

It is possible that York's aristocratic and gentry town houses—such as the Percy and Neville mansions in Walmgate—may have been courtyard mansions with generous frontages, though none has yet been encountered. However, the homes of urban merchants and craftsmen, even the wealthiest, seem to have had the characteristic long, narrow plots with the house gable-end on to the street. That does not mean that they could not display their status: No. 7 Shambles, a timbered shop and dwelling (admittedly post-1450), had the grander crown posts for the front gable, and queen posts for the rear, probably from 'a wish to be *seen* to be exclusive'. Nor were those tightly packed dwellings inflexible, or they would not have survived so long. No. 111 Walmgate (Bowes Morrell House), built around 1400, went through at least six phases of alterations for new uses and smaller rooms, demonstrating 'the flexibility of the timber-framed building'.[13]

The rows of dwellings for rent might be thought to have been intended for the relatively poor, but not all were. The three-storeyed 54–60 Stonegate comprised five or six dwellings of one bay each, but with prosperous tenants judging from the 1381 poll tax, including a tailor, a scrivener, and a possible goldsmith. Lady Row, Goodramgate, however, noted in the previous chapter, had minimal facilities for poorer tenants, including—so far as we can tell from the 1381 tax return—four 'labourers'. Each of its original ten units was of 'one up and one down' type, and there were no fireplaces or even hearths. The tenants 'could only warm themselves at winter braziers and take their food to York's bakeries to be cooked': they formed part of what Jane Grenville has called a 'bedsit' culture reliant on fast-food outlets, a culture previously identified in London by Martha Carlin.[14]

12. YCA, B/Y, fos 16–17, 31–2, 53, 56, 63–4; *YMB*, III, 25–6, 42–3, 70–1, 76–7, 88–9. The first entry has 'a messuage … with a shop and with solars [*solariis*]', the last word translated in *YMB*, III, 26 as 'upper storeys'.
13. Jane Grenville, 'Out of the shunting yards—one academic's approach to recording small buildings', in S. Pearson and B. Meeson, eds, *Vernacular Buildings in a Changing World*, CBA Res Rep 126 (York, 2001), 22–4.
14. Anthony Quiney, *Town Houses in Medieval Britain* (New Haven and London, 2003), 255–60; Jane Grenville, 'Urban and rural houses and households in the late Middle Ages', in M. Kowaleski and P. J. P. Goldberg, eds, *Medieval Domesticity* (Cambridge, 2008), 119–22. I follow Roger Leech (review of Quiney in *Medieval Archaeology*, 49 (2005), 486) in preferring the contemporary 'row' to the anachronistic 'terrace'.

Even these surviving buildings, as Grenville acknowledges, 'almost certainly represent the upper end of this market', and archaeology in Walmgate and elsewhere is beginning to find traces of much more ephemeral hovels of the very poor. If there were still 284 one-roomed houses in York in 1899, how many might there have been five centuries earlier? Nevertheless, though there was some zoning of poor housing, especially in the suburbs, many poor lived cheek-by-jowl with the more prosperous, whether in street frontages, churchyard fringes, or alleys off the main streets; and their richer neighbours had a real interest in preventing disease and accumulated rubbish. Thatched roofs were a problem in many towns, both as fire risks and as harbouring rats and fleas, but even rows for rent were being tiled by the fourteenth century, and not a single thatcher is recorded in the freemen's register.[15]

In the public space outside the home, the city council were from the 1370s clearly trying to create a more hygienic and orderly environment, whether in response to overcrowding, rising public expectations, or both. Their by-laws show them struggling to keep the streets clear of dung and obstructions; to prevent pigs and dogs roaming about; and to stop the disposal of butchers' offal and other waste in the Ouse. Horses were to be led to water, rather than ridden, to avoid danger to children playing in the streets. Furthermore, there was already some, if very limited, provision of public conveniences: Mayor Graa was proud of having had 'les Newpryvees' built beneath Ouse Bridge in 1367 (Plate 13). Some of the central streets were already being paved with cobbles and stone. No pavers were registered as freemen before 1380, but eleven were enfranchised in the following seventy years. The bridgemasters' accounts reveal regular payments for street paving from 1400, and between 1440 and 1456 John Bryg— clearly a man of experience—was paid for paving work both by the corporation and the cathedral chapter.[16]

15. B. S. Rowntree, *Poverty: A Study of Town Life* (London, 3rd edn 1902), 160; Swanson, *Building Craftsmen*, 20, 39–41. However, the very poor might have thatched their own hovels, and as late as the 1580s there were a few thatched roofs in York: YCA, E 31, pt. 1, pp. 53, 55, 57, 63, etc.

16. *YMB*, I, 15–18; YCA, D 1, fo. 6v (new privies); AY 2/2, entries indexed under 'paving'; Swanson, *Building Craftsmen*, 25–6, 40; Heather Swanson, *Medieval Artisans* (Oxford, 1989), 96; S. Rees Jones, 'York's civic administration, 1354–1464', in Rees Jones, ed., *The Government of Medieval York*, 110, 138–9.

Black Death to Peasants' Revolt: 1349–82

The pestilence or 'Black Death' was unwittingly brought into English ports about June 1348. It reached London by November and Yorkshire by the following March. There is the explicit evidence of a local chronicler that it struck York about Ascension Day (21 May) 'and raged until the feast of St James the Apostle' (25 July), though it clearly continued beyond that. There are no statistics for total mortality, but the archbishop's registers record that two parishes in every five in the archdeaconry of York (covering the city and the West Riding) were vacated in the year 1349–50 through the death of their clergy. In the deanery of the Christianity of York, which included most of the city parishes, at least twelve parishes out of thirty-seven lost their rector or vicar (in one parish, St Denys, twice within the year), while eleven city chantries lost their cantarist.[17]

Total mortality in England in 1348–50 is now thought to have been in the range 40–50 per cent, and there is no reason to think that York escaped more lightly. To make matters worse, the Black Death proved to be only the first of a series of nationwide epidemics, especially in 1361–2, 1369 (when York's mayor died in office), and 1375. The 'Anonimalle' Chronicle (connected with St Mary's Abbey) described that of 1375 as 'the fourth pestilence in the north country' and another in 1378, confusingly, as 'the fourth pestilence at York and particularly of children'. In addition, 1384 seemingly saw a further outbreak, judging by a surge of Yorkshire wills, while both chronicle and testamentary evidence indicate another in 1391, focused on the city. (Walsingham said that 11,000 died in York that year, an impossibly high figure.) Nevertheless, 1349 must have been far and away the worst, and it was long remembered. The only clearly contemporary event mentioned in the York Plays was the 'grete pestilence'; a witness recalled in a court case of 1365 that a girl had been born just after the '*magna pestilencia*'; and as late as the 1390s or thereabouts the pinners' craft were maintaining a candle which had been kept lit since '*la graunde pestilence . . . en l'an . . . mil cccxlix*'.[18]

17. *HCY*, II, 418, trans. in Rosemary Horrox, ed., *The Black Death* (Manchester, 1994), 95; A. H. Thompson, 'The pestilences of the fourteenth century in the diocese of York', *Archaeological Journal*, 71 (1914), 97–154, esp. pp. 105, 129 and n. 2, 152; Miller, 'Medieval York', 85. The nature of the pestilence goes beyond the present purpose, but recent DNA analysis seems to confirm its traditional identification as mainly bubonic plague: *Current Archaeology*, May 2011, 8.

18. BIA, MS C.P.E89/28; *YMB*, I, 87; Thompson, 'Pestilences', 114–17; V. H. Galbraith, ed., *The Anonimalle Chronicle 1333 to 1381* (Manchester, 1970), 50, 58, 79, 124; J. Taylor, W. R. Childs, and L. Watkiss, eds, *The St Albans Chronicle: The Chronica Maiora of Thomas Walsingham*, I: *1376–94*,

The immediate results of the plagues must have been appalling, both in mortality and in terms of the trauma suffered by survivors. The Crown responded to the shortage of manpower by the Ordinance (1349) and Statute (1351) of Labourers, both designed to prevent labour mobility and to peg wages to pre-1348 levels. The emergence of justices of the peace was one long-term result of the legislation, and they were given permanent responsibility for its enforcement from 1368. Another was resentment amongst labourers in a sellers' market, resentment which played a large part in the revolt of 1381. Nevertheless, 'towns do not seem to have had difficulty drawing in rural migrants', as is suggested by rises in urban rents and by high levels of freemen recruitment. Many towns, including York, were clearly 'able to offer sufficiently attractive employment prospects for artisans and labourers alike...to compete with rural labour markets'. The accounts of the Vicars Choral, the best source for York's rent levels at this period, show a broad reduction in rent values after 1349 and 1361–2, yet by 1364 rents were generally back to pre-plague levels, and thereafter they rose until about 1390 and did not decline until after 1401. As to freemen admissions, which had averaged fifty-eight in 1345–9, they rose to 212 in 1350, while the highest-ever medieval total, 219 in 1364, came two years after the 1361–2 plague. Other exceptional totals—in 1371–4, 1393, 1414, and 1439–41—also followed 'well authenticated outbreaks of plague in York or the north'. It is true, as Dobson observes in noting these correlations, that the freemen's register is often 'less an index of population growth than of mortality', but at the least it suggests no shortage of recruits to fill dead men's shoes.[19]

From this time, it becomes harder to disentangle the complex relationships between Crown and city, and—within the city—between corporation, 'commons', and guilds. There has been a tendency to view urban politics separately from town–Crown relations, but it is clear that royal pressures, the agenda of the city fathers, and the increasingly vocal demands of other citizens all impacted on one another. It may help, therefore, to consider the broad political narrative, national and local, before turning to the society,

---

OMT (Oxford, 2003), 912–13; Miller, 'Medieval York', 85; Horrox, ed., *The Black Death*, 234–5; J. Goldberg, 'Population and settlement in the later Middle Ages', in *HANY*, 97.

19. R. B. Dobson, 'Admissions to the freedom of the city of York in the later Middle Ages', *Econ HR*, 2nd ser., 26 (1973), 17, 18; Rees Jones, 'Property, tenure and rents', I, 238–53; P. J. P. Goldberg, 'Introduction', in M. Ormrod and P. Lindley, eds, *The Black Death in England* (Stamford, 1996), 8, 9.

economy, religion, and culture of the post-Black Death city. Fortunately, excellent recent surveys by Attreed and Liddy of provincial towns and the Crown include comparative studies of York and its leading competitors.[20]

There was considerable recovery from the ravages of the Black Death in the 1350s and 1360s, despite recurring epidemics. That recovery was assisted by an easing of financial and military demands from the Crown, especially with a temporary French peace (1360–9) and diminishing conflict with Scotland, as Edward III and David II came to appreciate that war was not to the advantage of either. Perhaps significantly, it was at this time, in 1357, that some leading citizens bought from the Crown their incorporation as a fraternity which became the Company of Mercers and Merchants, and had the confidence to start at once on their huge guildhall.

Even then, however, tensions among the city's elite were emerging which would disrupt civic politics. A complicated series of Crown actions over staples—the fixed markets through which all exported wool had to pass—included the creation of fifteen towns (including York) as domestic staples in 1353, but a return to an overseas staple at Calais ten years later. This impacted on civic politics as staple offices were used as a stepping stone to the mayoralty, and as early as 1357 led to a clash between Mayor de Langton and John de Gysburne, a clash foreshadowing that of 1380–1.[21] When the Anglo-French war resumed in 1369, it was less successful and more burdensome. Over the next six years, the Crown spent over £670,000 on it, much of it levied on townsmen, whether corporately or individually; and financial demands continued to be heavy after that, especially with the deeply unpopular poll taxes of 1377–81. To make matters worse, York's overall financial burden may have been proportionately rather heavier than those of the other major towns.

Taking taxes first, York's citizens had to find an average £92 a year towards the lay subsidies of Richard II, as against £54 for Norwich and £21 for Exeter; and the 1377 poll tax cost York more than any town but London. As for corporate demands, York was already paying its long-standing annual fee farm of £160 (more than Bristol's £140 or Norwich's £113) and in Richard's reign it had to meet an average £17 a year more than that in payments

20. L. Attreed, *The King's Towns: Identity and Survival in Late Medieval English Boroughs* (New York, 2001); Liddy, *War, Politics and Finance*.
21. C. D. Liddy, 'Urban conflict in late fourteenth-century England: The case of York in 1381', *EHR*, 118 (2003), 5, 7; Liddy, *War, Politics and Finance*, 110–31.

recorded on the Pipe Rolls. Corporate loans could also be substantial: when the Crown borrowed £9,200 from the English towns in the summer of 1370, London contributed £5,000, Norwich £667, and York £600.[22] Additionally, the Crown demanded direct contributions to the navy from port towns, both in lending merchant vessels and in building fighting ships at their own cost. Between 1375 and 1380 York had a record twenty-five ships in royal service: admittedly this was fewer than Bristol's forty, and furthermore the average tonnage of York's ships was only half those of the western port, but that is natural given York's situation well upriver and unsuitable for large seagoing vessels. In 1373 York built two barges for the king and in 1377 a third. The cost of three must have been huge, and it is not surprising that when the city requested the usual confirmation charter from the new king in 1378, they asked for it without further cash payments. In 1379, moreover, one of the city's barges—a 'fine' one according to the chronicler Walsingham—was lost with all hands in a naval battle.[23]

It was these pressures which led to disorder in York and then outright rebellion. The riots of November 1380 onwards, and the city's role in the national rising of June 1381, have often been treated separately, the first as the result of local issues and factions, the second as sharing in a rebellion over nationwide grievances. Yet, as in London, where there were serious internal conflicts in 1376–92, it was the interplay of local and national issues which proved toxic, as Liddy has shown: 'the major source of friction in late fourteenth-century York was the Crown'.[24] Both London and York saw divisions from the 1360s resulting from economic rivalries within their governing elites, coupled with demands from lesser citizens for more accountability from those elites as the pressures of Crown demands intensified. In each, one of the rival mercantile factions sought support from the lesser citizens—the draper John of Northampton in London, and the merchant Simon de Quixley in York. Quixley's target was Mayor John de Gysburne, who had been elected in November 1379 when John de Acastre died in office. There had been divisions within the elite, indeed, as far back as 1357, when Gysburne's attempt to become a bailiff had been blocked by Mayor John de Langton. Gysburne had nevertheless gone on to be three times

---

22. Attreed, *The King's Towns*, 153–4, 160–6; W. M. Ormrod, *The Reign of Edward III* (Stroud, 2000), 171 and n. 95. I have preferred Ormrod's £600 to Miller's £300.
23. Attreed, *The King's Towns*, 36, 61 n. 5; Liddy, 'Urban conflict', 1–32, at pp. 9–12; Liddy, *War, Politics and Finance*, 46–7; Taylor, Childs, and Watkiss, eds, *The St Albans Chronicle*, I, 294–5.
24. Liddy, 'Urban conflict', (quotation from p. 3); Liddy, *War, Politics and Finance*, 80–99.

mayor and also thrice one of the city's MPs, probably because he was of all his mercantile contemporaries 'the most experienced in royal service'. He also, almost certainly, 'exploited his privileged political position for personal financial gain'.[25]

There was, however, more to the unrest than corruption. Dobson long ago demonstrated that admissions of new freemen increased dramatically after 1350, as the city fathers generated more income by lowering admission fees. They did so, in part at least, to meet the Crown's financial demands, for more freemen meant more contributors to city taxes, in accordance with the 1312 charter. This, in turn, spurred the increasing body of lesser citizens to demand more accountability by the city council and a just sharing of tax burdens.[26]

It is perhaps no coincidence that the first clear evidence for formal consultation of the 'commons' by the city council dates from March 1380, during Gysburne's third mayoralty. It was then agreed by 'the whole commonalty' that there should be a sliding scale of fines for absence from council meetings: 12d. each from 'the twelve councillors' (later called aldermen), 8d. from 'the twenty-four', and 4d. from 'any of the craftsmen [artificers]'. The last must have corresponded to a wider body or outer council representing the craft guilds through their searchers, as we shall see. Later that year, the Twelve and Twenty-Four were apparently doing their best to share the burden of taxes more fairly. When they assessed the citizens for the third poll tax in November 1380, they levied it on only 4,015 taxpayers (as against 7,248 in 1377). Bartlett thought this represented widespread tax evasion, but Liddy shows that it represents a more equitable policy. In the richer parishes, the wealthy paid most and subsidized the others, while the very poor fringe parishes were exempted from the tax altogether.[27]

Despite such policies, tensions boiled over that same month. On 26 November 1380, as a horrified Parliament was informed, a crowd of York commons (*communes*) forcibly expelled Mayor Gysburne from the city, broke into the Guildhall, compelled Simon de Quixley to be 'their' mayor, and 'forced all the good men then in the said city' to swear loyalty to him. Their revolutionary intentions (if the report is correct) showed in their passing a

25. Liddy, 'Urban conflict', 6, 7, 15–31; Liddy, *War, Politics and Finance*, 87–93. For Gysburne and Quixley, see Bartlett, 'Economy of York', 417, 439; Jenny Kermode, *Medieval Merchants* (Cambridge, 1998), 338, 342.

26. Dobson, 'Admissions to the freedom', *passim*.

27. YMB, I, 39; Rees Jones, 'York's civic administration, 1354–1464', 122–3; Liddy, *War, Politics and Finance*, 40–1, 85, 93–6.

new ordinance that whenever 'the bells on the bridge' were rung backwards, it would be a signal for the city commons to meet to impose new
civic regulations. It did not last long, for the Crown's forces moved swiftly.
Twenty-two leading rebels (only one of whom had held high civic office)
were imprisoned in the Tower of London on 20 December and released a
fortnight later under bonds of good behaviour. Quixley was then elected
mayor on 3 February 1381, apparently peacefully and with no objection by
the Crown. On 1 May Gysburne and thirty-nine others were summoned
before the court of Chancery, where they were bound over under £40
penalties to keep the peace; and on the same day Quixley was ordered to
make all rich men not of any craft, and six representatives of each craft, also
to enter into £40 bonds to keep the peace.[28]

That peace was not kept for long. Details are sketchy, but on 17 June,
when rumours of rebels capturing London reached York, two things happened simultaneously: the 'rebellious commons' demolished the precinct
walls of the Blackfriars, and Quixley and the 'whole commonalty' met in
the Guildhall to try to stop any citizens taking cases to the royal courts. It
was almost certainly on the 17th also that the Greyfriars, St George's Chapel,
and St Leonard's Hospital were attacked. Then on 1 July a group led by
Gysburne allegedly stormed Bootham Bar and rode through York gathering
support: the Quixley–Gysburne feud then descended into what Dobson has
called 'something not too remote from gang warfare'.[29]

The Crown instituted a series of legal proceedings, and in February 1382
both factions were bound over to keep the peace. Nevertheless, violence
continued sporadically, and as late as November the mayor and council
were ordered to protect St Leonard's. By then, however, the turbulence was
over, and on 18 October the king in parliament issued a charter of pardon
for all offences committed by the citizens, on payment of a fine of 1,000
marks (£666 13s. 4d.). That does not reflect an exceptional punishment,
for it was less than fines imposed on some smaller towns: Beverley, which
had also rebelled, had to pay 1,100 marks. Nor was there any singling out

28. Miller, 'Medieval York', 81; R. B. Dobson, ed., *The Peasants' Revolt, 1381* (Basingstoke, 2nd edn 1983), 284–9; Dobson, 'The risings in York, Beverley and Scarborough', 120–1; Liddy, 'Urban conflict', *passim*; Liddy, *War, Politics and Finance*, 80–91. All had to rely on the text in *Rotuli Parliamentorum* (1783), but the new edition in *PROME*, VI.205–6 is almost identical. The lists of citizens bound over are in *CChR 1377–81*, 421, 486–7, 524–5.
29. Miller, 'Medieval York', 81–2; Dobson, ed., *Peasants' Revolt*, 287–9; Dobson, 'Risings in York, Beverley and Scarborough', 121–2.

of individuals for pardon, whereas Scarborough, fined 900 marks, had to find over half that sum from forty named burgesses. Finally, to show the Crown had drawn a line under the episode, Quixley was permitted re-election in 1382, and his leading supporter, William Selby, three times in the same decade, while Gysburne never again held high civic office.[30]

Apogee: 1382–1430

In contrast to the turbulence of 1380–2, the personal rule of Richard II was generally one of good town–Crown relations. Richard initiated a brief return of the offices of state from Westminster, and he granted two charters giving York the largest degree of urban self-government then permitted. These and other favours to the city and Minster led John Harvey to suggest a special bond between monarch and city: Richard, he argued, visited it often, showered it with privileges, and 'seriously contemplated' a permanent transfer of his capital to York. Nigel Saul and Mark Ormrod, however, have demonstrated that the king's attachment to York was less deep than Harvey believed. In particular, Richard did not spend long periods in the city—he was there only four or five times, never for more than a fortnight, and was much more often in Nottingham and Canterbury.[31]

Nevertheless, his actions had very positive results both in the short and long term. In June 1392 he brought there the key Crown departments, and although he stayed only ten days, his offices and courts remained there for some months, finding time (as in 1301) to impose ordinances on the city for maximum prices of food and drink. Richard's action was primarily, however, not a preference for York but an act of revenge against the City of London, which had refused him a loan; the choice of York, according to the well-informed Walsingham, was 'because of the good will of the people of York' and because his chancellor Thomas Arundel, who was also archbishop of York, 'wished these offices to belong to his own city'. As soon as the quarrel with London was patched up, Richard ordered his bureaucracy to

---

30. Miller, 'Medieval York', 82; Dobson, 'Risings', 122–3; *PROME*, VI.285–8.
31. J. H. Harvey, 'Richard II and York', in F. R. H. du Boulay and C. M. Barron, eds, *The Reign of Richard II* (London, 1971), 202–17; N. Saul, 'Richard II and the city of York', in Rees Jones, ed., *The Government of Medieval York*, 1–13; N. Saul, 'Richard II, York, and the evidence of the King's itinerary', in J. L. Gillespie, ed., *The Age of Richard II* (Stroud, 1997), 71–92; Ormrod, 'Competing capitals?', 97–8.

return to Westminster, though several courts were still in York after Christmas, and the last did not return until mid-January 1393.[32]

In that same January, York's MPs petitioned for a royal charter during a parliament in Winchester; their request almost certainly followed negotiations during and after Richard's visit the previous June. The petition emphasized York's close relationship with the Crown: London had styled itself 'the king's chamber' since at least 1328, and now York followed suit, the petitioners calling themselves citizens 'of your city *and chamber* of York'. The maximum autonomy then possible for a royal town involved the status of a 'county of itself' or county corporate, answerable directly to the king and not through a county sheriff, and coupled with the town's right to its own justices of the peace, a grant made to Bristol in 1373. Once York was allowed to follow suit in 1393 and 1396, it was quickly followed by Newcastle, Norwich, and others. Ormrod is surely right that York's two charters reflected the city's 'increasingly strident determination to keep up with its competitors'.[33]

This, however, is to anticipate. Richard's 1393 charter gave York only part of what Bristol had been granted; for any more, they relied on a further royal visit and more negotiations. For in 1396 the king returned for the whole of Holy Week and Easter Week during a royal progress through the Midlands and the North. He stayed in the archbishop's palace, held a royal Maundy in the Minster, and was well entertained by the corporation; a long bench was constructed for the mayor and aldermen for a meeting with him in the chapter house. Richard must have returned soon, as on Corpus Christi Day (1 June) he watched unspecified 'pageants' from a special enclosure, perhaps episodes from the Corpus Christi Cycle. The earliest surviving city chamberlains' account shows that the corporation spent £200 (nearly half the civic budget that year) on two silver dishes as a present for him.[34]

Saul has convincingly suggested that they had taken the opportunity of the previous royal visit to press for county status. Certainly, when Richard

32. Taylor et al., eds, *The St Albans Chronicle*, I, 938–9; Saul, 'Richard II, York and the evidence of the king's itinerary', 79; Ormrod, 'Competing capitals?', 97–8; C. D. Liddy, 'The rhetoric of the royal chamber in late medieval London, York and Coventry', *UH*, 29 (2002), 335–6. Price ordinances: Francis Drake, *Eboracum* (London, 1736), 243–4.

33. Saul, 'Richard II and the city of York', 2, 7; Attreed, *The King's Towns*, 37; Liddy, 'The rhetoric of the royal chamber', 327, 335–6; Liddy, *War, Politics and Finance*, 193–5, 200, 211–12; Ormrod, 'York and the Crown under the first three Edwards', 31–3; D. M. Palliser, *Towns and Local Communities in Medieval and Early Modern England* (Aldershot, 2006), 133–4.

34. Miller, 'Medieval York', 57 (dating the visit 1398); Harvey, 'Richard II and York', 209–11, 216–17; *REED: York* I: 9, 10; II: 695–6; R. B. Dobson, ed., *York City Chamberlains' Account Rolls 1396–1500*, SS 192 (1980), xxxii, 1–8; Saul, 'Richard II and the city of York', 5–8.

left York in April, a civic delegation under Mayor Frost accompanied him, spending five days with the court in Nottingham and then continuing to London for nearly six weeks; and Richard did—between his two York visits—issue a charter on 18 May, 'the most significant ever granted to the city'. The 1393 charter had made the aldermen *ex officio* justices of peace and of labourers; now York was elevated to the status of 'the county of the city of York', freed from all control by the sheriff of Yorkshire and the subordinate officials of the three ridings. The city's three bailiffs were replaced by two sheriffs, and mayor and sheriffs were to account for royal dues directly to the Exchequer. It was not cheap: the total cost of obtaining the charter was over £450—more than £1,000,000 in today's currency—but the mayor and aldermen must have thought it well worthwhile. Between them, 'these two charters set the seal on the city's medieval liberties'.[35]

York was now probably at its post-Conquest peak in terms of size, power, and prestige. There are no good comparative data for urban populations after 1377, when York was certainly second to London, but it was probably still in second place twenty years later. On Maundy Thursday 1396 King Richard distributed alms of 4*d.* each to 12,040 poor people there, a total which might provoke incredulity did we not have the audited total of £200 13*s.* 4*d.* The freemen's register tells a similar story: the peak single years for admissions had come earlier, following the worst epidemics (1350 and 1364), but if aggregated by decades, admissions increased almost continuously from 1301 to reach twin peaks in 1391–1401 and 1411–21. The prosperity which followed is reflected in the great building boom of the first half of the fifteenth century, as well as in the superb stained glass of the churches.[36]

Meanwhile, however, the city had to endure another bout of internal discord interacting with national politics. Richard II in his last years forfeited much goodwill by arbitrary financial demands from leading citizens, one of whom (Robert Savage) was so threatened that it may have hastened his death. That may explain why, when Henry Bolingbroke landed in Yorkshire in 1399, the corporation readily lent him 500 marks. At the same time, the commons were restive about civic taxes. In the petition of the late 1390s

35. W. Giles, *Catalogue of the Charters...belonging to the Corporation of York* (York, 1909), 12, 13; *CChR*, V, 336, 358; *BBC*, III, 132; Dobson, ed., *Chamberlains' Account Rolls*, 4–8; Rees Jones, ed., *The Government of Medieval York, passim,* esp. pp. 1 (quotations), 35–7, 114–15. The 1396 charter is printed in full in Thomas Madox, *Firma Burgi* (London, 1726), 246–7, and from the city's archives in *YMB*, I, 157–62.
36. Maundy total: Harvey, 'Richard II and York', 210 and n. 32. Freemen statistics: Bartlett, 'Expansion and decline', 22–3; Dobson, 'Admissions to the freedom', 17.

already cited, they asked the mayor and inner councils that no taxes be levied without prior consent of the wider body of citizens.[37]

By then, factions among the aldermen were crystallizing round William Frost and Adam del Banke, in almost a rerun of the earlier feud: Frost was son-in-law to Gysburne and inherited his great house in Micklegate, while Banke had been one of Quixley's supporters. More importantly, they had very contrasting careers. Banke, a dyer, followed the normal trajectory, working his way slowly up from enfranchisement (1371) through the junior civic offices. Frost was an outsider from a family of middling gentry, and was first chosen mayor (1396) only a year after becoming a freeman. He used that first mayoralty to negotiate the great charter in Nottingham and London, and was royally rewarded by Richard. Despite that, he supported Bolingbroke's usurpation as Henry IV in 1399 (he was a York MP in the parliament which ratified it) and was clearly much trusted by the new king. That was, perhaps, why his fellow aldermen re-elected him mayor for five successive years (1400–5), perhaps under pressure from Henry because Frost kept York quiet during the Percy rebellion of 1403.[38]

Not all citizens, however, liked what Walker called Frost's 'vice-regal conception of the mayoralty' or his acquiescence in Henry's policies, for by 1405 York was suffering both from economic recession and from heavy royal taxation. In that year's mayoral election, Frost was abruptly replaced by Banke; and then, as in 1381, civic feuds were overtaken by a major rebellion. An abortive rising by the earl of Northumberland triggered a more serious revolt in the York area under Archbishop Scrope and the earl marshal Thomas Mowbray. The so-called 'York articles of the rebels', posted up on the doors of city churches, listed very real grievances, and they drew support from the city itself, though Liddy's research suggests that the rising involved the clergy of York more than the laity. The rebels assembled on nearby Shipton Moor, but were tricked by the royal forces into disbanding, after which the leaders were hastily executed, their heads being displayed on Bootham and Micklegate Bars, except for the archbishop. He was

---

37. Carole Rawcliffe, in J. S. Roskell, ed., *HP 1386–1422*, I, 745; IV, 312; Saul, 'Richard II and the city of York', 13; Liddy, *War, Politics and Finance*, 98–9.
38. Rawcliffe, in *HP 1386–1422*, III, 138–41; Rees Jones, 'York's civic administration', 132–4; Simon Walker, 'The Yorkshire risings of 1405', in G. Dodd and D. Biggs, eds, *Henry IV: The Establishment of the Regime* (Woodbridge, 2003), 178–9; C. D. Liddy, 'William Frost, the city of York, and Scrope's rebellion of 1405', in P. J. P. Goldberg, ed., *Richard Scrope: Archbishop, Rebel, Martyr* (Donnington, 2007), 75–85.

beheaded separately at Clementhorpe, just outside the city wall, but allowed burial in the Minster.[39]

Scrope's execution deeply shocked many contemporaries, but on the citizens as a whole royal vengeance was limited. Henry humiliated and fined many leading citizens, dismissed Banke, and placed York under royal keepers. However, he made Frost one of those keepers; and when he restored the city's liberties in June 1406, Frost was duly elected mayor for an eighth term. After 1407, however, the city council reverted to the norm of electing resident mayors who had earned their spurs in junior offices; perhaps the Lancastrian regime had learned to be less heavy-handed. Certainly there is no mention of restiveness in the city in 1408, when the earl of Northumberland led a third revolt and died fighting at nearby Bramham Moor.

After that, town–Crown relations were peaceful for half a century. Henry V was in York once, with his new queen in 1421, when they were well received. It may have helped that he demanded much less in civic loans than had his father, especially if (as Gerald Harriss suggests) he was moved by his visit to contribute to the cost of the cathedral's new choir screen, with its effigies of kings since the Conquest facing the congregation and clearly designed to emphasize the legitimacy of the Lancastrian succession. His son, Henry VI, was also in York once before the civil wars (1448), when he visited St William's shrine, and celebrated the feast of St Edward's translation (13 October) in the Minster.[40]

More significant at an economic level were royal actions over currency and trade. The North had suffered from a shortage of coin as minting was almost wholly confined to London, so in the early 1420s York's royal mint was temporarily reopened during a national recoinage. Then in 1430 the York craft or 'mistery' of mercers, on the pretext of declining trade, obtained a royal charter incorporating them as a perpetual community, with a governor and two wardens, a common seal, and the right to acquire properties. It may have been an attempt to follow some London merchant companies,

39. Goldberg, ed., *Richard Scrope, passim*, and sources in n. 38. Quotation: Liddy, 'William Frost', 84. Heads displayed on bars: *RCHMY* II, 95, 116, and references there cited. Cf. also P. McNiven, 'The betrayal of Archbishop Scrope', *BJRL*, 54 (1971), 173–213, and his biography of Scrope in *ODNB*.
40. Civic loans: Attreed, *King's Towns*, 159–60. Choir screen: G. L. Harriss, ed., *Henry V: The Practice of Kingship* (Oxford, 1988), 25, 28–9, suggesting that the screen was begun before 1422, though it is usually dated later (e.g. Sarah Brown, *York Minster: An Architectural History c.1220–1500* (London, 2003), 232–3). Henry VI: *REED: York*, I: 73–4; II: 751.

who were obtaining royal incorporations at this time, and it set the seal on the dominance of the mercers and merchants in York's economic life.[41]

One reason for mutual support between the Crown and urban elites such as York's was the usefulness of merchants for their expertise as well as loans. Thomas Graa was much in demand for royal commissions from the 1370s to the 1390s, including an embassy to Prussia in 1388, and he served York as MP eleven times. William Frost also held many royal posts, as did Nicholas Blakburn senior, whose services included being Admiral of the Seas north of Thames (1406), as well as loans of nearly £150 to Henry V. There were also continuing close relations between the Crown and the Church of York. Protégés of John Thoresby (royal chancellor before becoming archbishop in 1373) staffed many royal offices, including keepership of the Rolls between 1371 and 1397, and some of that group remained in royal service into Henry IV's reign. And one reason the mercers acquired their 1430 charter was support from John Kempe, who in that year was both royal chancellor and archbishop of York.[42]

Civic government[43]

The machinery of civic government is obscure before the 1370s, but the broad outline is not in doubt. Its power was exercised mainly from two buildings, the civic complex on Ouse Bridge and the Guildhall off Coney Street. The former was a suite of rooms adjoining St William's Chapel, with the council chamber proper, for regular meetings of mayor, sheriffs, aldermen, and Twenty-Four, on the upper floor; elsewhere were a mayor's office, another for the Common Clerk, and space for the civic archives and current papers (Plate 13). The Guildhall was apparently much like its successor of 1449, with a large one-storey hall where the courts of mayor, bailiffs, and sheriffs were held, as well as the large gatherings necessitated

41. Maud Sellers, ed., *The York Mercers and Merchant Adventurers 1356–1917*, SS 129 (1918), xiii–xvii, 33–6; Miller, 'Medieval York', 106; Kermode, *Medieval Merchants*, 32 n. 42; Barrie Dobson, pers. comm.

42. Rawcliffe, in *HP 1386–1422*, III, 138–41, 218–20; Kermode, *Medieval Merchants*, 50–1, 335; Liddy, *War, Politics and Finance*, 131–8. Thoresby's patronage: J. L. Grassi, 'Royal clerks from the archdiocese of York in the fourteenth century', *NH*, 5 (1970), 25–7.

43. This section owes much to Sarah Rees Jones, 'York's civic administration, 1354–1464'.

by elections and by meetings of the larger council or the common citizens; there was also an adjoining inner chamber for meetings of the smaller, inner council.[44]

The corporation possessed a well-established structure and bureaucracy by 1350, and the mayor and his colleagues were already asserting their city's importance by better organized record-keeping. London had shown the way by producing a series of custumals (compilations of civic law, custom, and tradition designed for display as well as practical use), and York followed suit. The earliest is MS D.1, now known as the first freemen's register. It was apparently started around 1330 with lists of civic officials, and soon after that a separate compilation of freemen admissions now bound up with it: both were made more systematic by the 1350s. Other registers followed, including two Memorandum Books (A/Y and B/Y) begun in the 1370s, and a *Liber Miscellanea* (E 39). All seem to have been intended to emphasize the city's prestige, and to define its rights and powers in relation to the Crown and to rival jurisdictions.[45]

After the registers came systematic financial records: the chamberlains' account rolls by the 1390s and those of the subordinate bridgemasters in 1400. This may be just the accident of survival, but two energetic men between them held the key office of Common Clerk for over forty years, William de Chestre (1379–1403) and Roger Burton (1415–36), and we can be certain at least of Burton's contribution, since he did not shy from self-promotion.[46] Burton was an almost exact contemporary of the better-known John Carpenter, London's Common Clerk from 1417 to 1438. In his smaller sphere, Burton worked in a similar way, continuing and enlarging the scope of the civic records and distinguishing his additions clearly by a mark or signature. He gave prominence to his own achievements in the lists of officials, but he was also anxious to promote and praise his city. His additions to MS A/Y include not only the famous *Ordo Paginarum*, listing the

44. Guildhall: *RCHMY* V, 76–81. Bridge chambers: B. Wilson and F. Mee, '*The Fairest Arch in England': Old Ouse Bridge and its Buildings*, AY SS 1 (York, 2002), 49–52.
45. A/Y and B/Y are printed or calendared in *YMB*, and the freemen admission from D1 in *YF*. For the contents of D1 as a whole: Debbie Cannon, 'Catalogue of the contents of York, YCA, MS D1', in *RMY*, 135–54; and for the York registers as a whole: D. J. S. O'Brien, '"The veray registre of all trouthe": The content, function and character of the civic registers of London and York c.1274–c.1482', DPhil thesis, University of York (1999).
46. Dobson, ed., *Chamberlains' Account Rolls*; P. M. Stell, ed., *York Bridgemasters' Accounts*, AY 2/2 (2003). Burton and Chestre: Rees Jones, 'York's civic administration', 108–11; O'Brien, '"The veray registre of all trouthe"', 145–7, 155–7, 162–7, 242, 262–3.

Corpus Christi pageants, but also a copy of a chronicle of the York archbishops, suggesting that he saw the Church as an important part of civic history.
It was one of two pieces of non-archival material he added to the registers,
the other being an outburst of civic pride about York's state swords.[47]

The mayor was elected annually on 15 January and held office from 3
February. Like most other civic officials, he was expected to serve while
running his own business, though he was given an annual fee and could also
claim expenses. From the 1360s it was usual for the mayor to have served
previously as chamberlain and bailiff (and sometimes, before those, as bridgemaster), so that he was well experienced. The pattern of long-serving mayors was broken: John de Langton, mayor for twelve consecutive years
(1352–64) was almost the last, though Frost's eight terms ran him close.
Indeed, the council decided in 1372 that no mayor should be re-elected
who had served within the previous eight years, and in 1392 that none
should be re-elected until all his fellow aldermen had served.

The term 'election'—'choice' would be a better word—did not involve
a direct democratic vote. Until 1464 the outgoing mayor and the inner
council of twelve made two nominations in private, one of whom was then
chosen by the commonalty in the Guildhall. That does not mean that many
wished to seek the office, which could be burdensome and expensive. His
fee, £20 yearly in 1364, was raised to £40 (1385) and then £50 (1388), but
the expenses of obtaining the great charter were so great that when Frost
left office in 1397 he was allowed £100, and when he was re-elected in 1401
the commonalty agreed that he could keep 2.5 per cent of everything he
could recover from a royal debt of £1,000 in the city. The mayor could also
need protection for his dignity and even physical safety. More than one
junior officer had to be reprimanded or punished for insolence to him,
while in 1369 Roger de Selby claimed to have been assaulted in the course
of his mayoral duties.[48]

The mayor was assisted by three bailiffs until 1396, when they were
replaced by two sheriffs, elected annually to take office at Michaelmas, so as
to coincide with the Exchequer's financial year. Assisting both were the
chamberlains, usually three in number, and four bridgemasters, two each

---

47. YCA, A/Y, fos 219v–246v, 252v–255; B/Y, fo. 88v. Sellers did not print the chronicle or the
    Ordo in *YMB* II, but the *Ordo* has been printed in *REED:York*, I: 16–26; II: 702–11, and Percy
    prints the swords entry in *YMB*, III, 123–4.
48. *YMB*, I, 18–19, II, 110–11; Miller, 'Medieval York', 70–1, 80; Rees Jones, 'York's civic adminis-
    tration', 132–5.

for Ouse Bridge and Foss Bridge. All, like the mayor, were amateur admin-
istrators, chosen from the ranks of the freemen. A further important,
but occasional, office was that of the two members of parliament, almost
always chosen by the leading citizens from the ranks of aldermen and
councillors.[49]

There were also paid officials, of whom the most important were the
Common (town) Clerk and the recorder. The former, usually drawn from a
burgess or gentry family, and always a layman, was required to live within
the city and to work full time from an office adjoining the mayor's chamber
on Ouse Bridge. He was effectively 'the busy head of a busy writing office',
and was remunerated accordingly. The customary annual fee of John
Shirwood, Common Clerk from 1442 to 1471, was £7 17s. 4d., 'a substantial
salary by the contemporary standards of York and other towns'. In contrast,
the recorder—a legal expert used intermittently—had a 20s. retainer plus
26s. 8d. a year.[50]

Compared to the Common Clerk, the many lesser officials were much
more modestly paid. The mayor had two esquires—swordbearer and macebearer—and six sergeants, all paid under £3 a year. The sheriffs also needed
assistants—each had a serjeant-at-mace, responsible for summonses and
arrests, and there was also a sheriffs' clerk. Other officials included a bellman
for making public proclamations (paid 10s. a year in 1377), one or two
guards to hold the keys of the city gates, and by 1419 a keeper of weights
and measures. There were also market officials, keepers of the city staithes
(quays) and crane, prison guards, and collectors of tolls and taxes—a formidable bureaucracy.[51]

Finally, York needed a large number of paid or unpaid freemen to keep
order and enforce regulations at a local level. The city was divided into six
wards, and the thirteen aldermen (including the mayor) acted as wardens in
six groups, each group responsible for policing one ward and for holding
wardmote courts twice a year. Each ward comprised several parishes, with
their separate staff of constables and subconstables—sixty-two in total in

49. M. McKisack, *The Parliamentary Representation of the English Boroughs During the Middle Ages*
(Oxford, 1932), 158; Rawcliffe on the constituency and on individual MPs in *HP 1386–1422*, I,
742–50 and vols II–IV alphabetically; Liddy, *War, Politics and Finance*, 146–9.

50. R. B. Dobson, 'John Shirwood of York', in Margaret Aston and Rosemary Horrox, eds, *Much
Heaving and Shoving: Late-Medieval Gentry and Their Concerns* (privately pr., 2005), 109–20
(quotations from pp. 113, 115).

51. *YMB*, I, 26; II, 90, 260–1; Miller, 'Medieval York', 74; Rees Jones, 'York's civic administration',
140; Dobson, 'John Shirwood', 113.

1380, doubled to 124 by 1403. The senior constables were mainly from the mercantile elite, and their increase may have been because of a greater sense of insecurity after 1380–2. The constables were expected to pursue felons, guard the city walls and gates, and enforce street cleansing and road mending. In the fifteenth century, however, the wards and parishes lost some of their civil and criminal functions to the city courts, to the mayor and aldermen as JPs, and to the searchers of the craft guilds.[52]

The searchers' importance grew as they came to constitute part of the local government machine. It is clear from the 1380 ordinance that there was by then a concentric structure of councils assisting and advising the mayor. The innermost was the council of Twelve, beginning to be called aldermen by 1399. A second council was called the Twenty-Four, though they did not have a fixed number, since the retiring sheriffs seem to have joined it automatically on leaving office, whereas vacancies varied with the incidence of deaths, resignations, and promotion to aldermen. From around 1380 there was clearly a larger body to represent the wider body of freemen, which joined the other two councils for major decisions. It was often called the *communitas*, 'commonalty', and the implication of the 1380 ordinance is that it consisted of the searchers elected by their crafts. Modern literature often calls it the Forty-Eight, but there was no use of that term until much later, and—again—they do not seem to have had a fixed number.[53]

The reason for craft searchers being involved in civic government goes back to 1363, when a parliamentary statute required every urban craft to be policed by two searchers under the supervision of justices of the peace. The original intention was to treat the searchers as agents of Crown or city, but by the 1370s the craftsmen were coming to regard them as their representatives, and thus they came to form an outer council to be consulted by the mayor, Twelve, and Twenty-Four. It was that wider body which for instance in 1399 successfully petitioned the mayor and aldermen to limit the 'stations' of the York Plays route to twelve. By the early fifteenth century the corporation were able to take 'an increasingly managerial role' towards the Plays, as well as to craft activities in general.[54]

52. *VCHY*, 76–7, 314–15; P. M. Stell, 'Constables of York 1380–1500', *YH* 15 (1998), 16–25; Rees Jones, 'York's civic administration', 123.

53. *YMB*, I, 39; Miller, 'Medieval York', 78; Rees Jones, 'York's civic administration', 140.

54. *YMB*, I, 50–2; *REED: York*, I: 10–12; II: 697–8; Rees Jones, 'York's civic administration', 121–3. Quotation from Jeremy Goldberg, 'Craft guilds, the Corpus Christi Play and civic government', in Rees Jones, ed., *The Government of Medieval York*, 158.

Altogether, within the overall framework of national law, the civic authorities regulated and policed a wide range of activities—though, as so often with medieval sources, it is not easy to determine how successfully their regulations were enforced:

> From the perspective of the ordinary resident, the power of the civic government to regulate markets, control labour, police and cleanse the streets, deal with petty criminals, regulate building, monitor the local mint, register transactions of property, hear debt cases, to legislate on any matter of anti-social behaviour and exclude the officers of the king must have seemed pretty comprehensive.

These powers were considerably enlarged by the charters of 1393 and 1396. The parliamentary statute of 1363 had required every urban craft or trade to be policed by two of its members as searchers, who in turn were supervised by JPs; from 1393 that power devolved to the mayor and aldermen. Equally importantly, the new county status reduced the autonomy of York's ecclesiastical liberties. In 1354 the city had achieved a victory over St Mary's by restricting its powers to Marygate and the abbey precinct, excluding from its jurisdiction the street of Bootham and other abbey lands. The 1393 and 1396 charters made no mention at all of the ecclesiastical liberties: the cathedral dean and chapter protested and secured an amending royal charter, but it effectively clipped their powers. From 1393 they could no longer hold courts for all their lay tenants in the city, but only for those living in the Close and the Bedern or in houses outside the Close occupied by the chapter, their officers, or servants. Furthermore, the 1396 charter effectively allowed the city corporation to prevent interference in York by purveyors and other royal officials.[55]

Government was, as Miller put it, 'as much a matter of jurisdiction as of administration'. The mayor presided over a weekly court of 'common pleas' in the Guildhall for wills, dower, and many other matters, and over other courts for debts, for assaults, and for administration of escheated lands (properties reverting to the Crown), as well as, from 1393, the commission of the peace. The bailiffs (from 1396 the sheriffs) held a thrice-weekly 'Domesday' court for pleas of debt, trespass, and other matters, while from 1396 the sheriffs also held a county court for the Ainsty. The city was entitled to keep penalties imposed by the justices, and for breaches of the assizes of bread, ale, and wine; and the 1393 charter allowed the city to

55. Rees Jones, 'York's civic administration', 116–21, 127 (quotation from p. 127).

acquire lands to the value of £100, while a charter of 1407 granted another licence for a similar amount. These concessions mattered, for a large part of civic income came from property rents, and by 1442 the city's estate (including over 200 shops, houses, and plots) had a maximum value of nearly £200 a year.[56]

Finance was always a pressing problem for urban corporations, as their payments to the Crown included not only the annual fee farm but also taxes, loans, and corporate gifts. We can begin to measure York's civic income and expenditure from the 1390s, though not very satisfactorily. The first chamberlains' account roll surviving in the city's archives is that of 1396–7, covering only expenses and not receipts, and there are no complete account rolls before the 1440s. Fortunately, however, Hoyle has found in the National Archives an abstract of the accounts for 1391–2, which the city submitted to the Crown in 1533 to show how much their income had fallen (from £310 in 1391–2 to £141 in 1532–3). For 1396–7, admittedly an exceptional year with the royal visit and charter, total expenses were as high as £409.[57]

Financial pressures certainly underlay the complaints of the commons, and it was the need for additional income that apparently persuaded the corporation to sell the franchise to as many people as possible, and with some effect. The largest item among the revenues in 1391–2 was £125 for admissions to the freedom—40 per cent of the total—followed by £70 from bridgemasters' rents (23 per cent) and £58 from murage (19 per cent) and wharfage (7 per cent). However, the royal licence to acquire lands of up to £200 to support the bridges meant that property rents overtook freemen admissions. By 1433–4, net receipts from the bridgemasters totalled £118, as against £52 from new freemen.[58]

Skilled and experienced personnel were, of course, as important as financial resources. Nicholas de Langton, junior, and his son John, who between them held the mayoralty for twenty-eight years out of forty-two (1322–64), were (like the Selbys before them) wealthy from property more than trade. After them, however, not only did the office change hands much more

56. Miller, 'Medieval York', 69, 75–6; Rees Jones, 'York's civic administration', 128.
57. Dobson, ed., *Chamberlains' Account Rolls*, 1–8, 19–36; L. Attreed, 'Poverty, payments, and fiscal policies in English provincial towns', in S. K. Cohn and S. A. Epstein, eds, *Portraits of Medieval and Renaissance Living* (Ann Arbor, 1996), 330; Rees Jones, 'York's civic administration', 127–36; R. W. Hoyle, 'Urban decay and civic lobbying', *NH*, 34 (1998), 91; Attreed, *King's Towns*, 141.
58. Dobson, *Chamberlains' Account Rolls*, xxvii–xxix; Hoyle, 'Urban decay', 91.

often, but it was usually occupied by merchants. Of the twenty-one mayors between 1364 and 1396, at least fifteen were mercers or merchants: William Frost was exceptional in this respect as in much else, deriving his income apparently from land rather than commerce. Likewise, of the forty mayors serving between 1396 and 1450, with the exception of Frost, all but six were merchants. Thus, York's government was 'not so much an aldermanic as a mercantile oligarchy'.[59]

Most mayors, furthermore, were experienced not only in commerce, but also in civic business. What was *not* required was native birth, however. Some mayors originated from well beyond the city, though it is not possible to quantify the proportion, as birthplaces are often unrecorded. Frost apparently came from the Wolds, Thomas Esyngwald from Easingwold, and Nicholas Blakburn senior from Richmond, while Henry Wyman had arrived from Germany. It was far more important that new and ambitious arrivals gained acceptance by marrying into the established elite, as both Frost and Wyman did. 'The network of marriages which linked...merchant families was extensive and complex,' as Kermode points out. She illustrates this with genealogies linking a score of merchants, many of them mayors, through their own marriages and those of their children and grandchildren.[60]

Whatever their origins, mayors used their influence to stress the status and prestige both of their city and of themselves as embodying its power and dignity. A civic coat of arms was probably granted by Edward III: its earliest representations occur in the Minster's Lady Chapel and on the facade of Micklegate Bar. A cap of maintenance for the mayor's swordbearer is said to have been given by Richard II, who certainly presented a ceremonial sword, permitting the mayor to have it borne before him point upwards except in the royal presence. It does not survive, but the city still possesses a second sword, originally made for the Emperor Sigismund on his visit to Windsor in 1416. It was later acquired by a canon of St George's Chapel and presented to the city in 1439.[61]

59. Miller, 'Medieval York', 71, though I have taken mayoral statistics from various sources, as Miller gives only global figures for 1399–1509. For Frost's income, see Rawcliffe in *HP 1386–1422*, III, 139. Three men after 1396 were given craft designations when enfranchised (Thomas Esyngwald, sherman; Thomas Bracebrigg, weaver; John Carre, draper), but were called merchants by the time they were mayor.

60. Kermode, *Medieval Merchants*, 42–3, 80–5. For Wyman's birthplace, see n. 93.

61. Hugh Murray, *Heraldry and the Buildings of York* (York, 1988), 2–4; R. Marks and P. Williamson, eds, *Gothic: Art for England 1400–1547* (London, 2003), 216 (no. 82).

City, guilds, and plays

The city corporation was, as has been seen, becoming more assertive, both against rival cities and against rival jurisdictions in York, especially the ecclesiastical liberties. In particular, before turning to the Church itself and to religious life, it is worth exploring one of the most remarkable episodes in the city's history, the creation of a cycle of sacred drama which became a high point of the year, one moreover which was apparently the product of civic and not ecclesiastical initiative. There was clearly a close relationship between that cycle, the rise of the craft guilds which performed it, and the city council, though as Dobson points out, the main civic records begin 'just a little, but uncomfortably, late for the study of the mystery plays'. Fortunately, his own analysis allows for a convincing reconstruction.[62]

There are clear signs that the citizens reacted positively and surprisingly quickly to the appalling crisis of 1349–50. Firstly, there was the creation in 1356–7 of the precursor of the Company of Mercers or Merchants, a body which found the means to build its huge hall in only four years. Secondly, the creation and staging of an annual Corpus Christi Play, costly in time and money, was apparently undertaken within the quarter-century after 1350. Thirdly, this civic drama seems to have accelerated the organization of crafts and trades under civic supervision. This economic regulation, moreover, formed only part of a more systematic approach to civic bureaucracy and archival records from the 1370s. These and other developments may not only have followed the plague, but have been triggered by it, as Richard Beadle suggests:

> Survival from plagues and other disasters has traditionally moved communities to great acts of collective expression...Social and economic circumstances were, paradoxically, in some ways more favourable to an undertaking of the Corpus Christi play during the city's period of recovery from the Black Death than beforehand. The city prospered as never before, and, as...Dobson has recently pointed out, the first appearance in the 1380s to 1390s of abundant documentary evidence of formal organisation amongst the craft organisations...coincides with the earliest extended references to the Corpus Christi Play.[63]

62. Dobson, 'Craft guilds and city', 97.
63. Richard Beadle, 'The York Corpus Christi Play', in R. Beadle, ed., *The Cambridge Companion to Medieval English Theatre* (Cambridge, 2nd edn 2008), 100. Beadle is correctly following medieval usage, by which the whole cycle was called a play, and the individual scenes (or plays) were called pageants. However, I here call them the York Plays, a term now used by Beadle in his edition of the cycle. See Appendix VI in this chapter.

Yet it is not clear whether citizens and clergy spontaneously developed their own religious drama; whether the craft guilds organized themselves as social and economic bodies with a religious dimension, establishing the plays themselves; or whether the city corporation regulated both craft guilds and plays. To establish causation requires exact chronology, and that is just what is missing. The formation of the mercers' guild (who were to play the final spectacular Doomsday pageant in the plays) can be precisely dated from the records of the Crown and of the guild itself, but the marshalling of the city's crafts and trades into structured bodies with officers and regulations—and even the existence of some of them—is not well recorded until the 1380s and 1390s. The first possible record of any plays is in 1377, when rents paid to the city chamberlains included 2s. from a tenement on or in which 'three Corpus Christi pageants are stored'.[64]

The first unambiguous reference to a play cycle, and the participation of the crafts, is as late as Roger Burton's *Ordo Paginarum* of 1415, listing fifty-one episodes and, for each, the crafts assigned to perform them. It is not certain that the three 'pageants' of 1377, or even the 'play' (*ludum*) performed before King Richard in 1396, were parts of the cycle text we have, which was probably compiled in its surviving form in the 1470s. Nevertheless, Beadle has persuasively dated the composition of the original cycle to the generation after 1349. He is also sympathetic to Dobson's suggestions that the cycle was firmly controlled by a 'mercantile oligarchy' and that the project 'was actually first born in the York council chamber on Ouse Bridge'.[65]

The problem—if not its solution—may be clarified if we separate out the feast of Corpus Christi, the rise of the crafts, and the Play itself. The feast, celebrating the Real Presence of Christ's body in the host at Mass, was a movable one dependent on the date of Easter, and could fall on any day between 21 May and 24 June. It had been established in the Northern Province in the 1320s, and it became, in York as elsewhere, a day when the consecrated Host was carried ceremonially in procession. The rector of Rudby-in-Cleveland left £5 in 1366 'to the solemnity of Corpus Christi celebrated each year in the city of York', while in 1399 the corporation and Common Council ruled that all 'honourable' citizens should join the mayor

---

64. *YMB*, I, 10; *REED: York*, I: 3; II: 689. Both date the entry 1376; it was in fact 51 Edward III, i.e. January–June 1377 (N.S.)

65. Dobson, 'Craft guilds and city', 100–1; Beadle, 'York Corpus Christi play', 99, 100, 104.

in the procession. No surviving evidence establishes why the play cycle was also staged processionally or why it was attached to the feast. James plausibly saw the link as an attempt by York and other towns to use the image of Christ's Body to legitimate the social order, idealizing the need for cooperation between crafts and respect for rank.[66]

Pioneer scholars of medieval religious drama often assumed that the four major English play cycles surviving, wholly or partly—York, Chester, Towneley ('Wakefield'), and the so-called N-Town play—were the survivors of a widespread urban group of cycles, but recent scholars doubt whether such plays were ever the norm: Pamela King writes of a theatrical culture 'in which the familiar York and Chester cycles emerge as very ambitious but extraordinary oddities'. York may indeed have been not simply a surviving example of a widespread type, but the model which inspired the few other cycles. Not only is its text the earliest and best preserved, but the references to York and Beverley pageants in 1377 seem to be the earliest of all, followed closely by a 1386–7 agreement of the York tailors to keep up 'their pageant of Corpus Christi'.[67]

Whether or no the corporation commissioned the cycle, they certainly took early control over it. Even the initiation of a procession with the Host, as at Winchester, may have been 'civic rather than ecclesiastical'. By 1386/7 fines were levied on crafts negligent in maintaining their pageants, to be paid into the civic coffers; and from 1398 leading mercers were paying the corporation to 'hear the Play' before their doors. It prompts the suspicion that the usual route of the pageant wagons—from Micklegate via Stonegate and Petergate to Pavement—was determined by 'the desirability of passing as many York merchants' residences as practicable'.[68]

The York Plays constituted an enormous undertaking for the citizens, with some fifty separate 'pageants' or plays each produced by a different craft or group. The feast was within a period when warm and perhaps dry weather could be hoped for, and when days were long: at the summer solstice, which fell around 11 June at that time, there were about seventeen hours of daylight. Indeed, the Cycle's length demanded that: it comprised

66. *REED:York*, I: 1, 2, 12; II: 688, 699–700; M. E. James, 'Ritual, drama and social body in the late medieval town', *P&P*, 98 (1983), 3–29; R. H. Britnell, 'England: Towns, trade and industry', in S. H. Rigby, ed., *A Companion to Britain in the Later Middle Ages* (Oxford, 2003), 60.
67. *REED:York*, I: 3, 4; II: 689–91; Pamela King, in *Times Literary Supplement*, 10 October 2008, 26.
68. Meg Twycross, '"Places to hear the play": Pageant stations at York, 1398–1572', *REED Newsletter* 2 (1978), 10–33; Keene, *Survey of Medieval Winchester*, 129; Dobson, 'Craft guilds and city', 103–5.

well over 14,000 lines of verse, and although periodic attempts were made to shorten it, they can have had only a marginal effect. Furthermore, the Play was performed not at one but usually at twelve successive stations along a winding route from Micklegate to Pavement. The first pageant, the Creation, was staged before Holy Trinity gatehouse; the wagon was then wheeled downhill to the next station, while the second pageant was moved to the gatehouse, and so on. Until recently it was believed that the first performance started at 4.30 a.m., and that the cycle was played more or less in full, ending after midnight with the Last Judgement at its final station, though new research has revealed that the 4.30 time was an amending regulation of 1510, not in the original *ordo* of 1415; and the whole problem of understanding how, if at all, it could all have been staged in a single day has been reopened. Similarly, how it was staged, on or from wagons in the streets, is still controversial. Whatever the truth, the investment of the civic community in cost, time, and labour must have been immense. To take just one example, the script called for over 300 speaking parts—at least twenty-two actors were needed to play Christ—to say nothing of a large body of stagehands, musicians, and assistants.[69]

The York Plays span cosmic and human history from Creation to Last Judgement, drawn mainly from the Bible but with apocryphal additions. It has seemed obvious to most readers that it formed, as Roger Burton put it in 1426, a 'Play of the Old and New Testaments', though King has pointed out recently that the selection of episodes is biblically odd. She interprets the Plays' material in liturgical terms, seeing the services for Christmas, Easter, and Corpus Christi as central to the selection and interpretation of the text. Either way, scholars are generally agreed that the Plays exhibit a powerful consistency which contrasts with the other urban cycles: Beadle writes of its 'sense of grandeur and monumentality'. Part of this may be owing to its structure as well as literary quality: Rastall has demonstrated that its author(s) structured significant parts of the text according to numerological principles, making use of music as well as words. He has also argued that the few precious surviving pieces of its music are fine compositions of mainstream polyphony.[70]

69. Beadle, ed., *The Cambridge Companion to Medieval English Theatre*, esp. chapters by Beadle and by Meg Twycross; M. Twycross, 'Forget the 4.30 a.m. start', *Medieval English Theatre*, 25 (2003), 98–152.
70. YCA, A/Y, fo. 278; *REED: York*, I: 42; II: 728; Beadle, 'The York Corpus Christi Play', 104; Richard Rastall, *The Heaven Singing* (Cambridge, 1996); Pamela King, *The York Mystery Cycle and the Worship of the City* (Cambridge, 2006).

Yet it was performed and interpreted not by priests and theologians but by laypeople; and the intention must have been both entertainment and instruction, and underlying all an attempt to recreate the biblical story, especially Christ's Passion, as if it were happening in late medieval York. At the start of the Passion sequence, episodes acted out at street level must have encouraged the audience 'to imagine themselves as the first Palm Sunday crowds', and when Christ appealed from the cross to 'al men that walkis by waye or strete', the crowds were probably expected to feel implicated in His death. The identification of York and Jerusalem would have been strengthened by the apparent lack of attempt at historical costume, except perhaps for the Jewish priests, the Magi, and a few others: most actors would have looked like 'fifteenth-century Yorkshiremen of the same rank', using the tools of their trades. Such can be inferred both from textual references and from York's stained glass windows, which often depict the same scenes in similar ways; probably art and drama borrowed from each other. A local identification with the spectators would also have been strengthened by the Yorkshire dialect of the text. Yet paradoxically this deliberately localized drama became one of the most widespread legacies of medieval York, both in its own time, when it inspired at least one other play cycle, and also in modern times, when the periodic revivals since 1951 have been influential and popular both in Britain and North America.[71]

The Corpus Christi Play was not the only religious drama initiated in this astonishingly productive period. There was also a Creed Play in twelve pageants, each depicting one clause of the Apostles' Creed, and a Paternoster Play illustrating the Lord's Prayer. Both may have been inspired by the Austin friar John Waldeby, who preached public homilies in English on both the Creed and the Prayer. The first performance of the latter play had such an effect that a Paternoster Guild was formed by 1389 to stage it regularly for 'the consolation of citizens and neighbours', but in the fifteenth century both became the responsibility of the corporation, who sometimes substituted one or other for the Corpus Christi Play. The texts of both have, unfortunately, been lost, though the 1399 account roll of the Paternoster Guild has been recently found.[72]

71. Beadle, 'The York Corpus Christi Play', 101, 117; Beadle and King, eds, *York Mystery Plays: A Selection*, xxiv. Modern revivals: *The York Cycle Then and Now*, special issue of *Early Theatre*, 3 (2000); M. Rogerson, *Playing a Part in History: The York Mysteries, 1951–2006* (Toronto, 2009).
72. Toulmin Smith, ed., *English Gilds*, EETS, OS, 40 (London, 1870), 137–40; A. F. Johnston, 'The plays of the religious guilds of York', *Speculum*, 50 (1975), 55–90; J. Hughes, *Pastors and*

Religion and secular life

These Plays reminds us how much secular and ecclesiastical life interpenetrated one another, for the influence of the Church was immense. Every citizen or citizen's widow, for example, began a last will or testament by bequeathing his or her soul to God, usually coupled with the Virgin Mary and all saints. Most then continued with arrangements for the funeral and burial, to requests for prayers, and to pious bequests to churches and charities, before turning to division of their residual estate. A striking example is the mercer William Vescy (d. 1407), who requested burial in his parish church, All Saints, North Street; made lavish arrangements for his funeral there; paid for 400 masses for the ensuing four Fridays; and in a codicil left property worth five marks (£3 6s. 8d.) a year to endow a perpetual chantry there. He also left money and clothing to the poor, to road repairs, and to fourteen monasteries and nunneries to pray for him. And, exceptionally, he left sums to others to make vicarious pilgrimages on his behalf to twelve English shrines as well as Compostela.[73]

The Church was very visible and audible, not only through the physical dominance of cathedral and churches, or the constant presence of bells, music, masses, sermons, and processions, but also through the sheer numbers of clergy. The will of Alderman Bracebrigg (1436), who estimated that £5 would suffice to give 4d. to every parish priest and chaplain in the city, suggests a total of some 300; if we add 200 to 300 monks, canons, nuns, and friars, then perhaps 4 per cent of the population were in orders. It was still church courts that ruled on many issues later considered secular; it was ecclesiastical hospitals that provided most institutional care for the sick and elderly; and it was the Church which provided most formal education.[74]

The Minster dominated York even more as it was rebuilt. In 1361 Archbishop Thoresby began a new Lady Chapel on a scale matching the nave,

Visionaries: Religion and Secular Life in Late Medieval Yorkshire (Woodbridge, 1988),95–6, 156–7; Eamon Duffy, *The Stripping of the Altars* (New Haven and London, 1992), 66–7; D. J. F. Crouch, *Piety, Fraternity and Power: Religious Guilds in Late Medieval Yorkshire 1389–1542* (Woodbridge, 2000), 23–34; P. M. Hoskin, 'The accounts of the medieval Paternoster Guild of York', *NH*, 44 (2007), 7–33.

73. P. J. Shaw, *An Old York Church: All Hallows in North Street* (York, 1908), 87–8; Kermode, *Medieval Merchants*, 345; P. S. Barnwell et al., eds, *Mass and Parish in Late Medieval England: The Use of York* (Reading, 2005), entries indexed under 'Vescy'.
74. Bracebrigg's bequest: Dobson, *Church and Society*, 264–5. There are no statistics of the 1430s for all religious houses, but St Leonard's Hospital in 1423 included the Master, 16 chaplains, and 8 sisters as well as servants, choristers, orphans, and the sick poor: *PROME*, X, 178–9.

completed by his death in 1373 and funded by him personally. It was only
the first stage of an intended replacement of 'the ancient choir [*antiquus
chorus*]', which was completed between *c.*1394 and 1415. The collapse of the
old central tower in 1407 led to the final phase: the three great fifteenth-
century towers. Henry IV, anxious to repair relations after Scrope's execution, put his own master mason, William Colchester, in charge of rebuilding
the central tower; Colchester retained the York role until his death in 1420,
by which time the tower was well advanced. And in 1432–3 the two western
towers were begun, all three towers presumably complete when the Minster
was reconsecrated in 1472.[75]

The eastern arm has long lost most of its lavish medieval furnishings, as
well as the bright colours of stonework and carving, but it is still almost
filled, miraculously, with its original stained glass of *c.*1370–1440. The highlights are the great east window, painted and glazed by the workshop of
John Thornton of Coventry (1405–8), the St William window of *c.*1414
which can be attributed stylistically to the same team, and the later St Cuthbert window of *c.*1440. Until recently they have been viewed as a disparate
collection of images and narratives, but Christopher Norton, in an exhila-
rating reinterpretation, sees nearly all of them illustrating the Minster as the
northern mother-church, and 'the relationship of the Northumbrian church
to the Church universal'.[76]

What has been nearly obliterated is physical evidence for the unofficial
cult of Richard Scrope. Despite his execution for treason, he had been
allowed burial in a place of honour, in a part of the east end set aside by
Thoresby for archiepiscopal burials. His tomb at once became a focus of
popular devotion, and within a few months both Henry IV and his son John
were forbidding access to it by 'crowds [*concours*]'. They failed, for by 1409 it
had many visitors. When Richard's nephew, Archdeacon Stephen le Scrope,
died in 1418, he requested burial next to his uncle, and deliberately promoted Richard's cult by associating it with that of St William; and in or

75. J. Raine, ed., *The Fabric Rolls of York Minster*, SS 35 (1859), 174; T. W. French, 'The dating of
    York Minster choir', *YAJ*, 64 (1992), 123–33; C. Norton, 'Richard II and York Minster', in Rees
    Jones, ed., *The Government of Medieval York*, 56–87; T. French, 'Henry IV and York Minster',
    JBAA, 154 (2001), 84–91; Brown, *York Minster: An Architectural History*, 137–215, 232–5. I follow
    Brown's dates for the fabric and the glass.
76. Christopher Norton, 'Sacred space and sacred history: The glazing of the eastern arm of York
    Minster', in R. Becksmann, ed., *Glasmalerei im Kontext Bildprogramme und Raumfunktionen*
    (Nürnberg, 2005), 167–81.

about the same year, £150 was taken in offerings at the shrine, far more than for any English shrine except that of Becket.[77]

The cathedral remained, of course, the centre of church discipline and jurisdiction for city and diocese, as well as a focus of piety; it was especially important for those living within the liberty of the dean and chapter. Nevertheless, as citizens' wills reveal, their primary loyalties were to their parish churches, and not to the Minster or to the religious houses, even to St Leonard's, which we know housed 206 'sick poor' in 1423. The only significant exceptions were the four friaries, which attracted many gifts from citizens as well as local gentry and villagers; some citizens even requested burial in their churches.

It is hard to know what made the friaries so attractive, because both their buildings and most of their internal records were destroyed after 1538. They were clearly valued for their prayers, and perhaps for their scholarship and preaching. Among the York friars were some major figures, including Thomas Stubbs, author of a chronicle of the York Church, and the Augustinian John Erghome, who left a large private library to his house about 1372, making York, as K. W. Humphreys put it, 'potentially one of the great centres for scholarship late in the century': the library catalogue (of 646 volumes) survives (the only substantial catalogue from any English friary), though sadly few of the books it lists. Some friars were popular preachers, and one famous York sermon in 1426—admittedly by a visiting and not a resident friar—persuaded the city council to ban prostitution, enforce Sunday closing of shops and markets, and suppress disorderly behaviour during the feast of Corpus Christi.[78]

The parish churches, the most important communal buildings for most citizens, were the beneficiaries of many testamentary bequests for their fabric, ornaments, and furnishings (see Map 6). In addition, the wealthiest parishioners often left money for a chantry, a funerary monument, or a commemorative window. As it happens, the earliest surviving depiction of

---

77. Raine, ed., *Fabric Rolls*, 37, 193–6; *HCY*, III, 291–4; Ben Nilson, *Cathedral Shrines of Medieval England* (Woodbridge, 1998), 164; Brown, *York Minster: An Architectural History*, 229–31; Norton, 'Richard Scrope and York Minster', in Goldberg, ed., *Richard Scrope*, 138–214.

78. *YMB*, II, xlviii, xlix, 156–9; Miller, 'Medieval York', 96; R. B. Dobson, 'Mendicant ideal and practice in late medieval York', in P. V. Addyman and V. E. Black, eds, *Archaeological Papers from York* (York, 1984), 109–22; K. W. Humphreys, *The Friars' Libraries* (London, 1990), 11–154 (superseding M. R. James's edition of 1909); A. F. Johnston, 'The York Cycle and the libraries of York', in C. M. Barron and J. Stratford, eds, *The Church and Learning in Late Medieval Society* (Donington, 2002), 362–70. Quotation: Humphreys, *The Friars' Libraries*, xxviii.

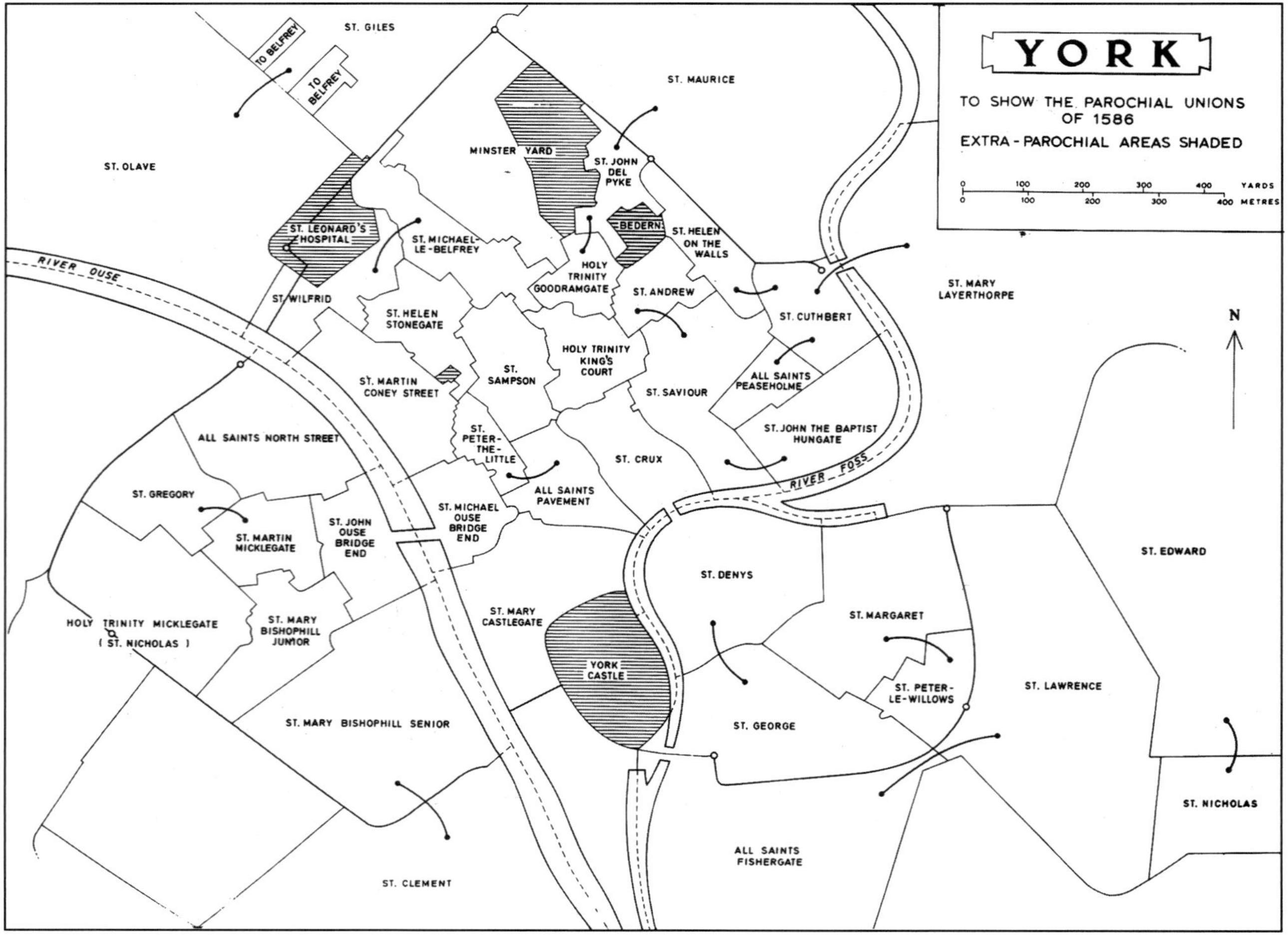

Map 6. York in the later Middle Ages, showing parishes and parish churches in existence after 1400

Source: D. M. Palliser, 'The unions of parishes at York, 1547–1586', Yorkshire Archaeological Journal, 46 (1974), 88

any English lay benefactor in glass is Richard Tunnoc (in the Minster in the 1320s) (Plate 7) and the second earliest Robert de Skelton, mercer and bailiff, kneeling as donor in a window in the parish church of St Denys (1354). As for chantries, at least thirty-five were established in York's parish churches between 1350 and 1450, and many more citizens were remembered in monuments and inscriptions, while those who could afford neither often left money for prayers for their souls.[79]

An exceptionally rich citizen could be commemorated in more than one place, as was Nicholas Blakburn senior. He chose burial in the Minster and founded at least three chantries, one in the civic chapel of St Anne and two in the Blackfriars, while he was also patron of four chantries in St William's Chapel and two parish churches. He may have hoped for prayers also from a wider constituency, for in his will he left forty marks ($£26$ 13s. 4d.) to provide a penny dole to the poor on the day of his burial, a dole which allowed for the enormous number of 6,400 recipients. Moreover, he, his son Nicholas junior, and their wives (both called Margaret) commissioned the fine east window of their parish church, All Saints, North Street, where they are depicted as kneeling donors. One Nicholas also commissioned another window there depicting the Corporal Acts of Mercy, in each panel of which a well-dressed merchant is performing the appropriate work of charity. Both windows are datable by heraldry and inscriptions to between 1412 and 1435 (Plates 14 and 15).[80]

The citizens, through their corporation, were anxious to keep the two civic bridge chapels under their own control. The Foss Bridge chapel of St Anne was completed only just before 1424, but by 1428 it contained three well-endowed chantries for four prominent York mercers: Nicholas Blakburn senior; Robert Holme senior and junior; and Alan de Hamerton. The bridge chaplains and cantarists were paid by and answerable to the city council: indeed, the corporation seems to have stretched the practice to cover all chantries founded by citizens. When the Church in 1388 demanded mortuary fees from the city's chantry priests, Mayor William de Selby declared that

79. Dobson, *Church and Society*, 261; C. M. Barnett, 'Commemoration in the parish church', *YAJ*, 72 (2000), 73–92. Skelton window: *RCHMY* V, 18; J. Alexander and P. Binski, eds, *Age of Chivalry* (London, 1987), 292–3 (no. 231); Richard Marks, *Stained Glass in England During the Middle Ages* (London, 1993), frontispiece and p. 12.
80. E. A. Gee, 'The painted glass of All Saints' Church, North Street, York', *Archaeologia*, 102 (1969), 153–7, 162–4; *RCHMY* III, 7, 8; Dobson, *Church and Society*, 258, 262n., 277, 279, 284; A. Rycraft, ed., *The Blakburns in York*, YLP (York, 2006), 2, 14–22, 75–6; Sally Badham, 'Commemoration in brass and glass of the Blakburn family of York', *Ecclesiology Today*, 43 (2010), 68–82.

all the chantries of this city and suburbs were and are founded by citizens and nobles of this city; and the priests of this city…having chantries, and the other stipendiary [priests] not having chantries, are the special *oratores* of the citizens, their patrons and masters.[81]

Perhaps the most important religious development in city and diocese after 1350 was a rise in what W. A. Pantin called 'affective piety', dwelling on Christ's humanity and suffering to deepen faith. Jonathan Hughes has argued for just such a spiritual flowering in the York diocese, partly through the influence of theologians and mystics, and partly through leadership by reforming archbishops John Thoresby (1352–73) and Thomas Arundel (1388–96). In 1357 Thoresby promulgated a programme to improve the religious instruction of the laity, accompanied by a widely circulated 'Lay Folks' catechism' put into English by a monk of St Mary's, John Gaytryge. It is probably no coincidence that their efforts were quickly followed by that growth of religious drama in the city already discussed, by an increasing use of devotional books by laypeople, and by growing numbers of religious recluses (anchorites) in York.[82]

The early fifteenth century saw, indeed, a 'great flowering of public devotions in the city', and there is evidence for that relating to one group of intermarrying mercantile and gentry families in the Micklegate area of the kind so often destroyed at the Reformation. Some, at least, of those families were directly implicated in the 1405 revolt, and the artefacts linked to them included the book which Archbishop Scrope had clutched at his execution, and a cup (mazer) which Scrope had blessed and which the wife of Mayor Henry Wyman bequeathed to the Corpus Christi Guild. Even more interestingly, the Wymans' only daughter married the son of Sir William Gascoigne, who lived in the same neighbourhood and was the royal judge who refused to condemn Scrope to death. Yet others linked to this circle by marriage were involved on the other side, including Mayor William Frost, and the Scrope cult may have been used to heal the divisions.[83]

---

81. *YMB*, II, lxiv, 19; Dobson, *Church and Society*, 265, 283. I have, like Sellers, left *oratores* untranslated: here it clearly means those praying for someone/something, not 'orators'.
82. Hughes, *Pastors and Visionaries*, esp. 95–6, 149–73, and his biography of Thoresby in *ODNB*.
83. Hughes, *Pastors and Visionaries*, 313–14; S. Rees Jones and F. Riddy, 'The Bolton Hours of York', in A. B. Mulder-Bakker and J. Wogan-Browne, eds, *Household, Women and Christianities* (Turnhout, 2008), 215–60 (quotation from p. 224); S. Rees Jones, 'Richard Scrope, the Bolton Hours and the church of St Martin in Micklegate', in Goldberg, ed., *Richard Scrope*, 214–36.

A striking survival from that circle is the Bolton Hours, apparently produced in York before 1420, one of the ubiquitous 'primers' or portable prayer
books of the laity. Such must have been 'my primer which I use daily'
bequeathed by one merchant's wife to her daughter, and the Bolton Hours
may have been commissioned by a merchant's wife, possibly Margaret,
wife of Nicholas Blakburn senior: the obits of Margaret's son-in-law John
Bolton, another merchant and mayor, and other relatives were added
later. Either way, Rees Jones and Riddy convincingly show links between
the book and the interlocking families connected to the Lords Scrope of
Masham, who owned a large town house off Micklegate. Archbishop Scrope
is depicted in two of the fifty larger miniatures in the book, 'the most
copiously illustrated surviving English Book of Hours of the fifteenth
century'.[84]

It would be wrong to suggest that the Micklegate/North Street district was exceptional in its lay piety. There are hints of equal zeal, for
instance, between Pavement and Hungate in the city centre. Between
1380 and 1440 York housed at least seven anchorites, devout recluses
who lived enclosed in cells, three of them near St Saviour's church.
Over half the mayoral wills in that period included bequests to them,
and a key influence seems to have been the Oxford-educated rector
Adam Wigan, who encouraged leading merchants in his parish and the
adjacent St John's, Hungate, to make bequests to them.[85] Large samples
of citizens' wills have demonstrated other ways in which lay piety
could find expression. The theme of the Corporal Works of Mercy
resonated with many others besides the Blakburns: Alderman Bracebrigg (1437) willed money for a thousand farthing loaves for the poor,
and his colleague John Russell (1443) gave double that amount in food
for poor relief. Some, like Alderman Thomas Holme, founded almshouses or *maisons dieu*, and many others made bequests to them. It is
possible that some such almshouses were intended for pious women

84. The Hours is YML MS Additional 2, described by Neil Ker and A. J. Piper, *Medieval Manuscripts in British Libraries* (Oxford, 1992), IV, 786–91, and K. L. Scott, *Later Gothic Manuscripts
1390–1490*, 2 vols (London, 1996), II, 119–21. For discussion, see Rees Jones and Riddy, 'The
Bolton Hours of York'; P. King, 'Corpus Christi plays and the "Bolton Hours"', *Medieval
English Theatre*, 18 (1996), 46–62; P. Cullum and J. Goldberg, 'How Margaret Blackburn taught
her daughters', in J. Wogan-Browne et al., eds, *Medieval Women* (Turnhout, 2000), 217–36;
A. Rycraft, ed., *The Blakburns in York*, YLP (York, 2006), 77–9; Eamon Duffy, *Marking the Hours*
(New Haven and London, 2006), 14, 15.
85. Hughes, *Pastors and Visionaries*, 70–1.

living together in the manner of Continental béguinages, like the 'poor widows' sharing a St Andrewgate house around 1400.[86]

Finally, citizens supported many social and religious fraternities, of which the best-recorded is the Corpus Christi Guild, founded by chaplains, merchants, and gentry. Its surviving register of admissions includes some 17,000 names from its foundation (1408) to its dissolution—admittedly mainly after 1450—and it became increasingly popular with citizens. The proportion of York testators leaving bequests to it rose from 25 per cent in 1411–20 to 35 per cent in 1441–50 and even higher later, making it more highly regarded than any other city fraternity.[87] Many other fraternities, less well recorded, attracted humbler citizens. David Crouch has assembled evidence for at least eleven parish guilds before 1450 and nine others after that date; they seem to have fulfilled varied pious and charitable functions at the neighbourhood level, as well as holding feasts and processions. At least fifteen groups of citizens maintained confraternities in the cathedral and the religious houses, mostly in the friaries. There were also two civic guilds other than Corpus Christi: that of St Christopher by 1394 and St Anthony's by 1418. St Christopher's Guild had a close relationship with the city council, and in 1445 was rich enough to be a partner with it in rebuilding the Guildhall in Coney Street.[88]

Such fraternities allowed lesser townspeople to participate in the benefits of prayers for the dead for modest subscriptions. Hughes has well evoked their social and religious world by looking at the wills of forty artisans in and around North Street between 1390 and 1450:

> The small world of these urban craftsmen was dominated by the parish church [of All Saints]... They were able to share the benefits of perpetual chantries by joining the gilds of St Christopher, St Francis and St Anthony: [in their testaments] they left the humble tools of their trade to their children... and they left small bequests to the fabric of the parish church, and made restitution to their community by paying forgotten tithes.[89]

86. P. Cullum and J. Goldberg, 'Charitable provision in later medieval York', *NH*, 29 (1993), 24–39; Roberta Gilchrist, *Gender and Material Culture* (London, 1994), 170–2; Henrietta Leyser, *Medieval Women* (London, 1995), 155–6.

87. R. H. Skaife, ed., *The Register of the Guild of Corpus Christi in the City of York*, SS 57 (1872); Crouch, *Piety, Fraternity and Power*, 170–84.

88. Eileen White, *The St Christopher and St George Guild of York*, BP 72 (York, 1987); Crouch, *Piety, Fraternity and Power*, 118–59.

89. Hughes, *Pastors and Visionaries*, 62.

Lay society

Those forty craftsmen lived in a teeming riverside district: the 1381 poll tax lists over 240 taxpayers in All Saints' parish, headed by the large household of the future mayor Adam del Banke, but—where occupations were recorded—numbering largely tanners and labourers. East of the Ouse, the city centre was even more crowded. The five acres of St Sampson's parish housed 207 taxpayers in 1381, giving it about four times the population density of, say, Kensington or Chelsea today.[90]

York is fortunate in the survival of most of its original tax returns for 1381. Unfortunately, only a handful of its parish returns are preserved for 1377, the most comprehensive of the three national poll taxes, but we do have the city totals, showing that 7,248 men and women over the age of fourteen paid that year. There is a consensus that population for 1377 can be estimated by adding 75–90 per cent to taxpayer figures, which would give York a total of some 13–14,000 inhabitants. Such multipliers, however, are inevitably shaky, given the known incompleteness of most poll tax returns. What is clear is that York's 7,248 taxpayers made it the largest town after London (23,314), closely followed by Bristol (6,345). Regionally, it was still unchallenged. No other Yorkshire town returned more than 1,000 except for Beverley (2,663), Hull (1,557), and Scarborough (1,393), though if the North is considered as a whole, York's nearest rival was Newcastle, whose 2,647 taxpayers did not include adjoining Gateshead.[91]

As we have seen, York's population probably continued to grow until about 1400–10, though it is impossible to quantify it. That growth occurred despite the epidemics of 1378, 1384, and 1391. To replace the losses by death, let alone to exceed them, immigrants from near and far were needed, and that is seemingly what happened. Surname evidence suggests that York's primary catchment area almost doubled between 1312–27 and 1360–81, with nearly as many incomers from 20 to 40 miles distant as from under 20. Most were from rural parishes, such as John from 'Wharrom' in 1359, possibly the

90. M. W. Beresford and J. K. St Joseph, *Medieval England: An Aerial Survey* (Cambridge, 2nd edn 1979), 176; Palliser, *Towns and Local Communities*, IX, 133; C. C. Fenwick, ed., *The Poll Taxes of 1377, 1379 and 1381, Part 3: Wiltshire–Yorkshire*, RSEH, NS 37 (Oxford, 2005), 133, 145, 154–5.
91. Published returns: J. I. Leggett, ed., 'The 1377 poll tax for the city of York', *YAJ*, 43 (1971), 128–46; Fenwick, ed., *Poll Taxes*, pt 3, 132–56. Commentary: P. J. P. Goldberg, 'Urban identity and the poll taxes of 1377, 1379 and 1381', *Econ HR*, 2nd ser., 43 (1990), 194–206. Rankings: Alan Dyer, 'Ranking of towns by taxpaying population: The 1377 poll tax', *CUHB* I, 758–60.

already shrinking village of Wharram Percy. Some were clearly abandoning farming life, like the ploughman accused in 1364 of fleeing his manor for York.[92]

And, as before, small but significant numbers were attracted from overseas. Between 1350 and 1450 about ninety-five 'Duchemen' and Germans became freemen, mainly from the Low Countries and the Rhineland. Before 1400 some were Flemish weavers, but after that metalworkers, especially goldsmiths, predominated. There was no bar to the ablest or most fortunate in becoming naturalized and rising to the top, especially if they married into the mercantile aristocracy. Henry Wyman, a Hanse merchant regularly trading with York by 1378, became a denizen in 1388 and was mayor three years running in 1407–10. His rise must have been assisted by his marriage to another mayor's daughter and co-heiress, and he lived to see his own daughter marry the eldest son of Judge Gascoigne. Similarly, the German merchant Henry Market, naturalized in 1430, was elected sheriff in 1442; probably only his death the following year prevented his rise to the mayoralty.[93]

A combination of population growth and the new policy of easier entry to the freedom boosted not only the numbers of freemen but also, probably, their proportion of the population. By the late fourteenth century perhaps one in three adult males was a freeman, as well as a very few women. The proportion may have been even higher: about half the taxpayers in 1377 can be identified in the freemen's register.[94]

Even so, many adults must have been barred from the benefits as well as the burdens of the franchise. The poll tax returns reveal an enormous disparity between wealth even among taxpayers, quite apart from the unknown numbers below the minimum threshold. In the wealthy parish of St Crux

92. *YF*, I, 53; G. Redmonds, *Yorkshire: West Riding*, English Surnames Series I (London, 1973), 125–8; P. McClure, 'Patterns of migration in the late Middle Ages', *Econ HR*, 2nd ser., 32 (1979), 180–1; C. Dyer, *Everyday Life in Medieval England* (London, 1994), 176–7.

93. Bartlett, 'Economy of York', 456; Kermode, *Medieval Merchants*, 341, 346; Meg Twycross, 'Some aliens in York and their overseas connections', *Leeds Studies in English*, n.s. 29 (1998), 359–80; R. B. Dobson, 'Aliens in the city of York during the fifteenth century', in J. Mitchell, ed., *England and the Continent in the Middle Ages* (Stamford, 2000), 249–66. Dobson suggests (264) that Wyman was from Hamburg, but Karl Kunze, ed., *Hanseakten aus England 1275 bis 1412* (Halle, 1891), 155n., says Prussia.

94. Leggett, 'The 1377 poll tax', 130; J. I. Kermode, 'The merchants of three northern English towns', in C. H. Clough, ed., *Profession, Vocation and Culture in Later Medieval England* (Liverpool, 1982), 8; Palliser, *Towns and Local Communities*, IX, 140. Kermode's figure is much higher than Bartlett's 22 per cent ('Expansion and decline', 22).

in 1381, two couples were assessed at 18s. and 17s. 4d. respectively, while 44 per cent of their fellow parishioners paid the minimum of 4d. Ingenious calculations by Bartlett and by Jeremy Goldberg have suggested that the corporation was trying to mitigate the burden on poorer taxpayers: the mean assessment in each parish in 1381 was 12d., but in some parishes richer inhabitants were apparently paying higher rates to allow others to pay less. Some impoverished outer parishes made no returns, perhaps because 'the political and social implications of burdening poor taxpayers, who could not be effectively subsidized, outweighed the fiscal benefits'. Well after 1381, nevertheless, the total tax borne by the city was seen as burdensome. When the wealthy Nicholas Blakburn senior made his will in 1432, he left £40 towards the city's tax 'for the help and relief of the whole community'.[95]

Missing from the tax returns are some of the wealthiest landholders, not through evasion but because they were gentry or nobles, based in their rural manors, who found a town house convenient. They included, for instance, the Percys and Nevilles in Walmgate and the Scropes and Gascoignes in the Micklegate area. Many parties to transfers of city houses included gentry owners, such as John Clervaux of Croft-on-Tees and Sir Thomas Marken-field of Markenfield Hall near Ripon. It is not surprising that the inquiry into the famous heraldic dispute between the Scropes and Grosvenors held three of its sessions in York (1386), with city examples of the Scrope arms called in evidence.[96]

For the resident citizens, another measure of the range of wealth is pro-vided by the inventories drawn up in proving wills, which survive in increas-ing numbers from about 1400. The mason Robert de Crakall (1395), for instance, left a net estate of nearly £60, whereas the weaver Geoffrey Couper and his wife (1402) left only £5 after deduction of debts. Remarkably, one lengthy inventory of an alderman John Louth (1435) survives because it was brought in evidence in a suit before the Court of Common Pleas. His estate was valued at £235, most of it accounted for by his stock of merchandise (£97) and the contents of his house (£94). Wills and inventories were nor-mally limited to movable goods and excluded real estate, though some alluded to those. Louth's fellow alderman Robert Holme junior left his wife one third

95. Goldberg, 'Urban identity and the poll taxes', 205–7; Rycraft, ed., *The Blakburns in York*, 18, 19.
96. N. H. Nicolas, ed., *The Scrope and Grosvenor Controversy*, 2 vols (London, 1832), I, 83–142; II, 270–347; *Yorkshire Deeds* I, ed. W. Brown, YASRS 39 (Leeds, 1909), 188; *Yorkshire Deeds* IV, ed. W. Brown, YASRS 65 (Leeds, 1924), 160.

of his lands and tenements 'for her dower, as her accustomed right'. Even without real estate, the sums listed in wills could be huge: the monetary bequests alone in the will of Nicholas Blakburn senior amounted to £644.[97]

Evidence is scarcer for humbler levels of society, but glimpses can be obtained from the so-called cause papers of the archbishop's Consistory Court, which survive in large numbers after 1350. In a series of remarkable studies, Goldberg has exploited them, in conjunction with the poll tax returns and other sources, to investigate family life, marriage, servanthood, population mobility, female employment, and related issues. His conclusions and methodology have been challenged, but he has defended himself convincingly.[98] His analysis of the 1381 poll tax suggests an overall adult sex ratio of 106 males to 100 females, whereas among servants it was 100 women to 75 men. For 1377, where evidence for servants is better (if only for a few parishes), over 30 per cent of the population aged over 14 were in service, and they were employed by 38 per cent of households. The discrepancy between sex ratios may have been because many servants were girls from the hinterland, often coming to town in their early teens, and staying in service often until their early twenties. It was a pattern especially common between about 1370 and 1420, when York's post-Black Death boom was at its peak. Servanthood was for many a stage in their life cycle and often a prelude to marriage: where age of marriage can be known, it was usually over twenty for women. Cash wages for female servants were generally lower than for males, and female servants often worked purely for food, clothes, and lodging. Goldberg's picture of female immigrants from the country receives support from the male-dominated sex ratio observed at Wharram Percy, where apparently 'female-led emigration left a rural population dominated by males'.[99]

Living-in servants were, however, not the poorest townspeople. There must have been many homeless, vagrants, beggars, prostitutes, and petty

---

97. Kermode, *Medieval Merchants*, 91, 335; AY 2/3, 493–5, 507–8; Susanne Jenks, ed., 'The inventory of John Louth, alderman of York', forthcoming.
98. P. J. P. Goldberg, 'Female labour, service and marriage in the late medieval urban north', *NH*, 22 (1986), 18–38; Goldberg, *Women, Work and Life Cycle*, and other studies. His debate with Pedersen is in *Continuity and Change*, 9 (1994), 349–54; 10 (1995), 405–36; 12 (1997), 425–55; and see Pedersen, *Marriage Disputes in Medieval England* (London, 2000), *passim*. I have consulted some of the same cases as Goldberg and I see no reason to doubt his findings.
99. Goldberg, 'Urban identity and the poll taxes', 200; Goldberg, *Women, Work and Life Cycle*, 158–202, 225–32 (figures from pp. 161, 164); Simon Mays, 'Part three: The human remains', in S. Mays et al., eds, *Wharram: A study of settlement on the Yorkshire Wolds*: XI, *The Churchyard* (York, 2007), 91–2.

criminals who scarcely surface in the surviving records. Prostitutes crop up most because of presentments for fornication, though they cannot all have been pursued rigorously, since some were called as witnesses before the church courts in tests of impotence over marriage annulments. The more fortunate poor might find themselves housed in St Leonard's or in one of the many small *maisons dieu*. In 1400 Archdeacon Dalby left 12*d*. 'to each bedridden [*languenti*] pauper in the city and suburbs': since he allowed the precise sum of £6 11*s*. for this, he presumably intended it to cover 131 poor, a knowable population for his executors.[100]

There is certainly enough evidence from the cause papers—which survive in greater quantities for York than for any other diocese—to show that women and servants were far from 'invisible' in the archives. The case of Marrays v. Roucliff (1368), for instance, which Goldberg mines impressively, has fascinating details of childbirth, godparents, wet-nursing, friendships, neighbourhood gossip, and so on. Space does not permit the discussion such evidence deserves, but Goldberg's broad conclusions are revealing nonetheless. His sample of marriage ages, for instance, suggests a norm for both husbands and wives of the early to mid-twenties. That would make York fit the early modern pattern of north-west Europe, rather than a supposed 'third world' model of teenage marriage. It would have limited the numbers of children, though it cannot therefore be assumed that small nuclear households were general. There are hints that city house-plots could contain a range of household types, including extended family groups.[101]

Evidence for York's society as a whole is patchy, but sufficient to confirm that it was one of great inequality. Freemen were privileged over 'foreigns'; masters over apprentices, journeymen, and servants; and most men over most women. Nevertheless, there is much to be said for stressing the unifying forces of communal solidarity and Christian teaching, which often (though by no means always) overcame the corrosive effects of inequality, conflict, and corruption. There was a powerful sense of civic unity in York, exemplified especially at the feast of Corpus Christi, and the inevitable tensions between rich, middling, and poor should not be confused with

100. Goldberg, *Women, Work and Life Cycle*, 151; Bronach Kane, *Impotence and Virginity in the Late Medieval Ecclesiastical Court of York*, BP 114 (York, 2008); A. Rycraft, ed., *The Testamentary Circle of Thomas de Dalby, Archdeacon of Richmond, d. 1400*, YLP (York, 2000) 28–9; AY 2/2, 503.

101. Goldberg, *Women, Work and Life Cycle*, 225–32; Rees Jones, 'Building domesticity in the city', 89, 90. Marrays v. Roucliff: BIA, CP E 89, partly pr. in translation in P. J. P. Goldberg, ed., *Women in England c. 1275–1525: Documentary Sources* (Manchester, 1995), 58–80.

deep-seated class antagonisms. As Susan Reynolds has put it, 'exclusive and unequal as was the cohesion of medieval urban society it was real and valuable to townsmen.'[102]

Behind the city's changing society lay a poorly recorded but important shift, as lay education and literacy rose. Grammar schools continued to be run by the cathedral and by St Leonard's Hospital (and unofficially by some of the Minster canons and vicars), catering for a minority of boys. There are, however, increasing hints of elementary schooling for a wider clientele, male and female. A York fuller, William de Ulskelf, left 40s. and two cows in 1391 to finance his son's schooling, and in the same year a merchant bequeathed £13 6s. 8d. for the education of two grandchildren. A few parish schools are occasionally mentioned, and some boys acquired basic literacy in song schools—the Minster precentor complained in 1367 that many chaplains, holy water carriers, and others held schools in churches and private houses 'for the instruction of boys in singing'.[103]

This must have underpinned the ability of many merchants and craftsmen to read and write—a few now left books in their wills—and the use of posters on church doors, as in the revolt of 1405, suggests widespread literacy. A tantalizing recent archaeological find is a set of eight wax tablets in a decorated pouch, datable to the late fourteenth century; the surviving text on them seems to be a poem in Middle English. There are hints in wills and from annotations in the Bolton Hours that some merchants' wives and daughters could read; and the iconography of the east window at All Saints, North Street, presumably chosen by the Blakburns as donors, is surely significant. The central image is of the young Virgin Mary being taught by her mother, St Anne, to read.[104]

Getting and spending

Increasing literacy must have lubricated trade and manufactures, especially as so many economic transactions were by then underpinned by written

102. Susan Reynolds, *Kingdoms and Communities in Western Europe 900–1300* (Oxford, 2nd edn 1997), 218.
103. J. A. H. Moran, *Education and Learning in the City of York 1300–1560*, BP 55 (York, 1979), 14, 15; J. A. H. Moran, *The Growth of English Schooling 1340–1548* (Princeton, NJ, 1985), 57.
104. *RCHMY* III, 7 and frontispiece; AY 17/12, p. 1975; *Medieval Archaeology*, 34 (1990), 22 and pl. XIII.

financial accounts and bills of credit. For a time, York gained considerably from increased clothmaking and overseas trade—the two being closely linked, since much of its export trade was in cloth. Together with Norwich, Salisbury, Coventry, and Colchester, it was one of those fortunate clothmaking centres benefiting from overseas demand in the later fourteenth century, and it was the decline in that demand between 1403 and 1421, and again after 1449, that was responsible, as much as anything, for its economic decline.[105]

Before considering merchants and overseas trade, however, York's crafts and trades as a whole should first be examined. Fortunately, the register of freemen's admissions is again available as our best guide to the occupational structure: indeed, more than ever, since between 1350 and 1450 almost 90 per cent of new freemen were given a craft designation. Miller's statistics can again be used to show the relative size of the craft groups (Table 6.1).

Naturally, these figures cannot provide a full and accurate picture. Quite apart from those with no recorded craft, there are the problems of freemen who changed occupation or practised dual occupations (John Richmond described himself as chapman, shipman, mariner, and merchant), of those exempt from the need for admission because they lived and worked within ecclesiastical liberties, of women often working in partnership with freemen husbands, and so on. To take just one striking example, the Minster treasurer John Newton (d. 1414), the wealthiest York canon of his generation, owned his own barge and also a furnace for smelting lead. Those limitations have been frankly faced by Dobson in his discussion of the register; nonetheless, as he also points out, 'there are few if any towns in late medieval England which lend themselves more readily to an analysis of the distribution of its crafts and trade.'[106]

105. R. H. Britnell, *The Commercialisation of English Society 1000–1500* (Manchester, 2nd edn 1996), 170; Britnell, 'The economy of British towns 1300–1540', 317–18, and Jennifer Kermode, 'The greater towns 1300–1540', 454, both in *CUHB* I.
106. Dobson, 'Admissions to the freedom'; R. B. Dobson, 'Yorkshire towns in the late fourteenth century', *Thoresby Society*, 18/1 (1985), 13. John Richmond: Kermode, *Medieval Merchants*, 5n. Newton's will: *TE*, I, 371; P. M. King, 'The treasurer's cadaver in York Minster reconsidered', in Barron and Stratford, eds, *The Church and Learning in Late Medieval Society*, 208. Confusion is also caused by the uncertain and variable dating in the register, but it seems fairly clear that most years began with the chamberlains' year of office on 15 January. Thus the peak entry year after the Black Death, given in Collins's printed edition as 1349, should be 1350 (or, strictly, 15 January 1350–15 January 1351).

Table 6.1. Freemen admissions grouped by crafts 1350–1450

Craft Group	1350/1–1399/1400		1400/1–1449/50	
	Total	% of known occupations	Total	% of known occupations
Textiles	1,190	28	901	21
Provisions	481	11	599	14
Commerce and shipping	688	16	673	15
Leather	650	15	536	12
Building	284	6	342	8
Metal	443	11	459	11
Miscellaneous	547	13	847	19
Not recorded	555	–	513	–
TOTALS	**4,838**	–	**4,870**	–

Source: Miller, 'Medieval York', 86, 114–16

That analysis is complicated after 1350 because, as we have seen, freemen were increasingly organized into craft and trade guilds under the control of the city council. Many of their regulations are enrolled in the city's records, including lists of the master craftsmen assenting to twenty-five such sets of rules, though only about 80 per cent of those men are recorded in the freemen's register. Heather Swanson's analysis of York's craftsmen and artisans is here especially valuable in drawing on the guild records, though not everyone has accepted her contention that the craft guilds were actually created by the city council as instruments of social and political control; some prefer to see them as voluntary associations of free craftsmen and women for mutual benefit and protection.[107]

Whatever the imperfections of the freemen's statistics, the broad picture is clear. Most strikingly, the textile sector had overtaken the victualling and leather crafts: indeed, it doubled in size from 14 to 28 per cent between the two halves of the fourteenth century, falling back a little after 1400. However, the vital food and drink trades are probably underrecorded, for reasons already given in connection with the 1304 civic ordinances. Most freemen were craftsmen, not traders; the proportion engaged in commerce

107. Bartlett, 'Expansion and decline of York', 20 n. 2; H. Swanson, 'The illusion of economic structure', *P&P*, 20 (1988), 29–48; H. Swanson, *Medieval Artisans: An Urban Class in Late Medieval England* (Oxford, 1989), largely on York, despite its title; Goldberg, *Women, Work and Life Cycle*, 34–5; Gerald Harriss, *Shaping the Nation: England 1360–1461* (Oxford, 2005), 289 and n.

and transport held steady at 15–16 per cent throughout the period from
1307 to 1450. Space does not allow discussion of most of the individual
crafts, but they were clearly catering for growing comfort as rising living
standards made consumer goods more affordable. Among the metalworkers, for instance, pewterers came to the fore as pewter tableware spread. No
pewterer appears among the new freemen before 1349, but six occur in the
following half-century, and twenty-six between 1401 and 1450.[108]

How does the occupational structure compare to those of other towns?
Caroline Barron has tabulated roughly comparable figures for late fourteenth-century London against those for York, Oxford, and Worcester; she
uses poll-tax data rather than freemen admissions, and separates textiles from
clothing, but the broad pattern is consistent. In 1381, for instance, one York
taxpayer in five was employed in textiles and clothing and one in four in
Oxford and Worcester. The most striking difference was in trading and
transport, where York's 18 per cent was far ahead of the other provincial
towns, though not of London.[109]

Textiles and overseas trade demand separate treatment, but it should be
noted that many of York's craftsmen other than weavers produced specialized
products in demand over a wide area. Robert de Patryngton, the Minster master mason from 1369, ran (or subcontracted) a workshop providing monumental brasses throughout Yorkshire. York's bellfounders were also in demand for
supplying church bells—those made by John Potter still hang in two Wolds
churches—and the city bowyers sold bows in bulk as far afield as Chester.[110]

Craft regulations from the 1370s onwards provide much information on
tools, products, working practices, and demarcation disputes. The crafts of
tanner and cordwainer (shoemaker), for instance, were kept apart to control
the quality of leather, while for similar reasons saddlers had to use leather
prepared by curriers. Other crafts were concerned about working hours,
monitoring of which was made easier by the introduction of a few public
clocks—one witness in a court case in 1394 testified to hearing ten struck
on 'the bell commonly called "Clokke" '. Other ordinances were concerned
with the workforce assisting the master craftsmen—including journeymen
(wage earners paid by the day) and apprentices. By the 1370s a seven-year

108. Swanson, *Medieval Artisans*, 76–7; Britnell, *Markets, Trade and Economic Development*, XX, 13.
109. C. M. Barron, *London in the Later Middle Ages* (Oxford, 2004), 66–7.
110. *YMB*, I, xlvi, 53; Bartlett, 'Expansion and decline of York', 19; *VCHER* VIII, 119, 147; Sally
    Badham, 'Monumental brasses', in C. Wilson, ed., *Medieval Art and Architecture in the East Rid-
    ing of Yorkshire*, BAA (London, 1989), 167–71.

apprenticeship was being insisted on by at least one craft, the bowyers, and around 1430 the cordwainers' journeymen were pushing for collective action to better their lot.[111]

Much discretion must have been left by the city council to individual crafts, as the example of female employment shows. In 1400 the weavers ruled that 'no woman . . . shall be put among us to weave' unless well trained. In some cases, however, women were well trusted. In 1430 one merchant was employing female servants to weigh and cost goods, to carry a large purchase to a customer's house, and to visit another customer to demand payment. And other women ran their own businesses, either in partnership with their husbands or as widows, quite apart from the sixty-five women recorded as admitted to the freedom between 1351 and 1450. Nichola Irby, for instance, though widowed in 1393, continued to trade as a merchant until her death two years later, while Alice Folston was a cloth trader in her own right, though married to another trader. At the same period, Agnes Hecche was trained by her father as an armourer.[112]

Many of York's crafts were of the kind that kept any provincial city viable; what made the city so prosperous after 1350 has been usually held to be, above all, clothworking and long-distance trade. The numbers of clothworkers becoming freemen rose sixteenfold between 1331 and 1371, while the drapers—intermediaries between cloth producers and merchants—also increased. The first surviving aulnage tax record for York, in 1394–5, shows that 3,256 broadcloths were sealed in York that year, in a wide range of dyes attractive to customers, although not all were necessarily made in the city.[113]

Special reasons have been sought by earlier historians for this boom in clothmaking, including the allegedly innovative role of immigrant textile workers. It is true that up to twenty clothworkers from Flanders and Brabant were admitted to the franchise between 1344 and 1380, but there is no evidence that they did more than swell the numbers in an already thriving industry. Rather, York was one of a number of leading towns with a reviving

111. *YMB*, I, 54–5,190–3; II, 162–6; III, 4, 5. Swanson, *Medieval Artisans*, 55, 58, 116. Clock 1394: BIA, CP E.159, trans. in Goldberg, ed., *Women in England*, 106.

112. *YMB*, I, 243; Swanson, *Medieval Artisans*, 71, 116; P. J. P. Goldberg, 'Women', in R. Horrox, ed., *Fifteenth-Century Attitudes* (Cambridge, 1994), 125; Goldberg, 'Women in trade and industry in York', *ODNB*, 60, pp. 52–3.

113. Bartlett, 'Expansion and decline of York', 23; H. Heaton, *The Yorkshire Woollen and Worsted Industries* (Oxford, 2nd edn 1965), 60; Miller, 'Medieval York', 88; Childs, *Trade and Shipping of Hull*, 11.

cloth sector at this time, along with Beverley, Bristol, Colchester, Coventry, and Salisbury, and the explanation has to be a wider one. The most convincing is that of John Munro, who stresses the concentration of those towns on luxury cloth exports, gaining their advantages from the taxes imposed on high-quality wool exports and the advantages of urban over rural locations for the industry; not until the later fifteenth century did most cloth production shift to the countryside.[114]

The cloths made in York were handled not only by drapers but also by mercers and merchants. A glimpse of one such man's business is the will of Alderman Robert Colynson (1450): he was a mercer and thus a dealer in luxury fabrics, but he employed his own workers, since he left 12d. each and 'a good breakfast' to the dyers, fullers, shearmen, and weavers working with him. Whether acting as middlemen between producers and customers, or, like Colynson, trading in goods made for them, mercers and merchants were the city's economic aristocracy. They had acquired their communal identity in 1357 when the king incorporated them as the Fraternity of Jesus and Mary, and they quickly followed up by building their large hall close to the bank of the Foss, and so conveniently located for shipping cargoes by water.[115]

The Fraternity was in origin a society for both men and women with devotional and charitable aims, but it quickly became subordinated to what was really a trading guild. Indeed, it may in reality have had economic aims from the start. Nightingale has suggested that the 1357 charter was sought because the York merchants, temporarily unable to export wool (because of a royal monopoly of wool exports granted to alien merchants), had begun to take a more serious interest in exporting cloth. By 1398 the mercers had searchers like the craft guilds; by 1420 they were calling themselves a 'community' of merchants (*mercatorum*), distinct from the fraternity, and in 1430 Henry VI incorporated them as the 'mistery of mercers [*misterie mercerie*]' of York.[116]

The mercers and merchants, judging from the Hull customs accounts, concentrated on exporting wool and cloth in return for wine, foodstuffs,

---

114. J. Munro, 'The symbiosis of towns and textiles', *Journal of Early Modern History*, 3 (1999), 1–74 (York's revival, pp. 33, 34).

115. Colynson's 1450 will was his second, but he did not die until 1458; BIA, Reg. 2, fo. 378; Shaw, *An Old York Church*, 97–8.

116. *YMB*, II, 8, 9 (misdated 1366); Sellers, ed., *The York Mercers and Merchant Adventurers 1356–1917* (SS 129, 198), x–xvii, 1–36; Nightingale, 'Rise and decline of medieval York', 18. The early accounts of the Fraternity have now been printed: A. Rycraft, ed., *Before the Merchant Adventurers*, YLP (York, 2007).

iron, and a variety of other raw materials and manufactures. The customs
statistics, backed up by other records (especially from the Hanse ports) suggest a peak of prosperity and trading activity around 1400. Not only were
levels of overseas trade higher than before 1350, but much more of it was
now in the hands of native merchants (including York men) than aliens.
What cannot be quantified—because it paid no national customs, and surviving toll records are scarce—is inland trade, but there are many indications
that trade with the rest of England also grew strongly as average incomes per
head rose and the home market expanded.

Some of that inland trade of York merchants involved buying raw wool
from many estates in Yorkshire and Lincolnshire, as well as leather from a
wide zone centring on the Vale of York, and lead from the Pennine lead-
mines. On the wool supplies, for example, Alderman Richard Russell
bequeathed in his will (1435) 'for distribution among the farmers of Yorks-
wold from whom I bought wool, £20, and in the same way among the
farmers of Lindsey, £10'. At a local level, much small-scale trade must have
been carried on in local markets and fairs, both York's own and the many
others in Yorkshire, though larger transactions were probably handled
directly by York's merchants and chapmen. Nicholas Blakburn senior must
have travelled extensively by road, since he funded the rebuilding of four
bridges over three Yorkshire rivers. Even craftsmen could travel considerable distances: the York potter Thomas de Bulmer must have been in the
capital in the 1360s, since he testified in a York case about what he had
'heard many in the city of London say'. In return, customers came some
distance to York to buy retail, like the obedientaries of Durham Priory and
Selby Abbey, or to buy in bulk for resale, such as the Northallerton chapman
who was supplied by a York merchant in the 1390s.[117]

Recent research in the files of the Court of Common Pleas has revealed a
network of credit and debt linking London with large towns like York, and
they in turn with their hinterlands. Around 1400, for instance, several York
traders were indebted to London mercers, drapers, and grocers, and at about
the same time one York merchant owed the huge sum of £54 to the London

117. TE, II, 56; Miller, 'Medieval York', 97–105; Bulmer's testimony: Goldberg, ed., Women in
      England, 79; Northallerton chapman: P. Nightingale, A Medieval Mercantile Community (New
      Haven and London, 1995), 369 n. 5. Yorkshire markets, with dates, are listed in Samantha
      Letters, Gazetteer of Markets and Fairs in England and Wales to 1516, 2 vols, List & Index Soc.,
      Special Ser. 32, 33 (London, 2003), 385–411. Blakburn's bridges: see Introduction to this
      volume, p. 8.

grocer John Colin. A more systematic picture has been drawn for Michael-mas Term 1424, tracing all debts owed to Londoners, Yorkers, and others. York provided more cases of debts to Londoners that autumn than any other place north of the Humber; in contrast, most of those indebted to York people came from the northern counties. London's commercial hinterland, in other words, already covered most of the south and Midlands and was extending north, whereas York's hinterland was much more regional.[118]

Customs accounts allow for some quantification of overseas trade, much of it in the hands of York merchants. The main export was wool, increas-ingly supplemented by finished or semi-finished cloth. Exports of cloth through Hull—of which York merchants normally exported at least half—rose from 8,000 cloths in 1357–67 to almost 38,000 in 1387–97, and their imports probably continued to increase in return. In 1383–4 and 1398–9, when wine imports can be attributed to individual importers, York mer-chants accounted for about a third of the 1,500 tuns of wine imported through Hull. The combined value of York merchants' foreign trade at Hull in the year 1398–9 has been estimated by Bartlett at a minimum of £10,400. That does not, however, necessarily mean a peak of commercial prosperity: Nightingale has pointed out the mediocre quality of York's cloth exports, and that on Bartlett's own figures 'when cloth exports through Hull were at their peak in the late fourteenth century they were worth only a quarter of its wool exports.'[119]

The wool after 1363 was mostly shipped to Calais, the staple port for English wool, and York merchants were prominent there. Most cloth, on the other hand, was destined for the southern Netherlands, to be sold at the four great seasonal fairs or marts of Flanders and Brabant, either for con-sumption locally or for resale to more distant markets. Beyond that region, however, York, Hull, and Newcastle merchants were beginning to trade more directly with the Baltic, despite intermittent opposition from the

118. Nightingale, *A Medieval Mercantile Community*, 356; D. Keene, 'Changes in London's economic hinterland as indicated by debt cases in the Court of Common Pleas', in J. A. Galloway, ed., *Trade, Urban Hinterlands and Market Integration c. 1300–1600* (London, 2000), 59–81; J. A. Gal-loway, 'Reconstructing London's distributive trade in the later Middle Ages', in M. Woollard, ed., *New Windows on London's Past* (Glasgow, 2000), 1–24; J. A. Galloway, 'Urban hinterlands in later medieval England', in K. Giles and C. Dyer, eds, *Town and Country in the Middle Ages* (Leeds, 2005), 122–5.

119. Bartlett, 'Expansion and decline of York', 25–7; Nightingale, 'Rise and decline of medieval York', 21.

Hanseatic League, a powerful federation of trading towns with diplomatic as well as economic muscle.

The part played by York men in the Baltic trade is not fully quantifiable, but judging from their goods seized during trading disputes, it was considerable. Henry Wyman, the immigrant who became a York resident and mayor, started as a merchant from Prussia regularly trading in the city. In the other direction, York merchants were equally active: when the goods of English merchants were seized in Prussia in 1385, the largest group was thirty-three York men, whose combined goods impounded were worth over £1,150. Appropriately, when the dispute was settled by the Treaty of Marienburg (1388), Thomas Graa of York was one of the three English ambassadors; and when renewed disputes led to more seizures of English goods in Prussia in 1403, five of the fifteen aggrieved individuals were York men, with cargoes including luxury cloths.[120]

Wool and cloth remained Hull's staple exports throughout the later Middle Ages, but imports were more varied. They included raw materials for the textile, metal, building, and shipbuilding trades; wine from Gascony; and luxury foods and spices from the Mediterranean and further east. Alderman Louth (1435) stocked ginger, cinnamon, pepper, cloves, and rice, while the chapman John Gryssop (1446) sold raisins, mace, cloves, ginger, pepper, and cinnamon. Herring and cod came from the North Sea and the Baltic: seven English ships returning from the Baltic in 1398–9, two from York, were loaded entirely with herring from Skania. High-quality furniture was also imported: Flemish and 'Pruce' (Prussian) chests and other items feature in many York wills and inventories. And craft expertise could also be imported. In 1373 a York bowyer was licensed to send four yeomen and two grooms to live in Prussia for four years to make bows and send them home.[121]

Nevertheless, however much York merchants traded long-distance, an increasing proportion had to be carried on through London after 1350, especially in wool to Calais and in many cases cloths to the Netherlands. The Statute Staple certificates show a rising proportion of English debts enrolled in London, from 33 per cent in the 1360s to 63 per cent in 1400–10, while those of York and Hull declined. Hull's wool exports increased in

---

120. Kunze, ed., *Hanseakten aus England 1275 bis 1412*, nos 222, 323; Miller, 'Medieval York', 102–3; T. H. Lloyd, *England and the German Hanse 1157–1611* (Cambridge, 1991), 65, 88–9.

121. Bartlett, 'Expansion and decline of York', 25–6; Childs, *Trade and Shipping of Hull*, 14–20; Lloyd, *England and the German Hanse*, 49, 89; AY 2/3, 570–1; Jenks, 'The inventory of John Louth', forthcoming.

proportion to those of London, but its denizen cloth exports, which had been over half those of London's in the 1360s and 1370s, slumped to a mere 13 per cent in 1405–9.[122]

A turning point: *c.*1430–50

Soon after 1400 York's prosperity seems to have peaked. Admissions to the franchise reached 196 in the year 1414—not far short of the record peaks of 1350 and 1364—and then fell steadily: the total for 1431–51 was 14 per cent lower than that for 1381–1401. Within that decline, the textile sector shrank proportionately as well as absolutely. Likewise, overseas trade through Hull and its outposts fell in every decade from 1407–17 to 1457–67, before a slight recovery. York's royal mint operated only intermittently (though the archbishop's mint was more active), hampering the levels of trade; and rents of city and chapter properties fell. Some of the details of this bleak picture, drawn by Bartlett and Miller half a century ago, have been modified, but the broad pattern is not in doubt.[123]

There has been a vigorous debate since the 1960s on urban 'decline' in later medieval England, one in which York is often cited as a prime example: it was one of a group of larger towns which flourished after the Black Death, only to fall back in the following century. It is a debate still unresolved, and perhaps irresoluble, since it turns on slippery definitions of decline, on muddled thinking about absolute and relative changes, and about the imperfect statistics for population and wealth. Nevertheless, it is a debate which has to be faced, vital as it is to place the story of York from about 1410/20 to 1550/60 into some regional and national context.[124]

York was certainly one of those large towns which had either developed or regained an important role as clothmaking centres after 1350, only to lose much of it again. That is often explained in terms of a national model, with clothmaking in the fifteenth century increasingly deserting large towns and

---

122. Nightingale, *Trade, Money and Power*, XIII, 101; Nightingale, 'Rise and decline of medieval York', 30, 31.
123. Bartlett, 'Expansion and decline', 27–9, summarizing Bartlett's own 'Economy of York'; Miller, 'Medieval York', 67, 89–91, 104–6; Rees Jones, 'Property, tenure and rents', 253–62.
124. Alan Dyer, *Decline and Growth in English Towns 1400–1640* (Basingstoke, 1991); Susan Reynolds, *Ideas and Solidarities of the Medieval Laity* (Aldershot, 1995), ch. XI; Alan Dyer, '"Urban decline" in England, 1377–1525', in T. R. Slater, ed., *Towns in Decline AD 100–1500* (Aldershot, 2000), 266–88; Palliser, *Towns and Local Communities*, chs XII, XIII.

cities for small towns (like Lavenham, Chipping Campden, or Halifax) or for rural production. However, Dyer would prefer us to think more in terms of regional systems. Between 1377 and 1525 towns with shrinking population and economies were especially concentrated in an eastern swathe from Suffolk to east Yorkshire, while a significant number of growing towns lay in southern and western counties. Thus 'the decline of York, or Boston, or Lincoln, should be seen as an aspect of the hardships of a regional system, in which failing key towns drag down their subordinates in the local hierarchy'. That was certainly true of at least some towns dependent on York. The decline of Hull's trade 'went hand-in-hand with that of York', while that of Scarborough's fishing industry from the 1430s was also linked to lowered demand from York, 'possibly the largest customer for Scarborough fish'.[125]

There was, however, more to the context of York's decline than a shift of clothmaking to other regions (including, be it said, the rising textile towns of the West Riding as well as southern and western England). A combination of adverse economic conditions, nationally and internationally, had been creating a recession even in London since the turn of the century, and although the capital was able to weather the worst of it, the effects were worse as they spread firstly to the countryside, then to the smaller provincial towns, and finally to the greater towns and cities. Wool and cloth exports declined, impelling the Londoners to take a greater share of them in compensation; English merchants were increasingly excluded from the Baltic by the Hanse after 1402; and there was a shortage of silver coin when the Calais mint closed in 1404. The total coin in circulation shrank to only about a fifth of what it had been around 1350, and although credit could be stretched to compensate, it could not expand indefinitely without enough coin to support it. And as the reduction of trade and shortage of coin affected provincial towns, their merchants could no longer afford the same credit to local customers who looked to them for supplies.[126]

As has been seen, Londoners were already sufficiently dominant by 1424 to be supplying credit on a large scale to York's merchants and chapmen, who in turn were offering credit to northern borrowers. At the same time, Londoners' wealth was enabling them to begin the process of dominating the society or company of English merchants involved in the lucrative trade

125. Dyer, '"Urban decline" in England', 283; *VCHER* I, 70 (for Hull quotation); Peter Heath, 'North Sea fishing in the fifteenth century: The Scarborough fleet', *NH*, 3 (1968), 66.
126. Nightingale, *Medieval Mercantile Community*, 353, 364–5; Nightingale, 'Rise and decline of medieval York', 31–2.

to the Low Countries—or, more strictly, Brabant, Flanders, Holland, and Zeeland. It was a body with no formal existence yet in England, but only in the Netherlands, with the merchants of London, York, and other towns forming branches of it. Theoretically, therefore, Londoners were not in charge, but in 1421 they orchestrated a takeover of its organization; and when the merchants of York, Norwich, Colchester, and other towns refused to cooperate, they were fined and overruled. From then on, the northern merchants increasingly complained about what was becoming effectively a London-dominated national body.[127]

Yet what made matters particularly bad for York (and Newcastle) more than merchant towns further south was an agrarian crisis, involving harvest failures and epidemics which severely affected the north-east in 1438–40. 1438 was the first of three unusually wet summers, leading to harvest failures and starvation; it also saw a 'grete pestylaunce' which was especially severe 'in the northe contraye', according to Gregory's Chronicle. Kermode's statistics for probate of York merchants' wills shows that eighteen died in the year 1438–9, almost as many as in an average decade. For all probate figures from the York Exchequer Court—not all, but perhaps half of them, testators from the city—then 1438 stands out as the worst year of the whole century, with over 200 deaths. The crisis was, it is true, widespread throughout England (and indeed north-west Europe), but it was particularly severe in the north-east.[128]

To make matters worse, the northern crisis was only the prelude to a 'great slump' in mid-century in both town and countryside, which affected agriculture, overseas trade, rents, and living standards. It struck London in the mid-1440s and rapidly spread through the provinces, reducing trade and employment in York, Colchester, and many other towns. As the fall in overseas trade struck the provincial ports, the wealth of the exporting markets fell, diminishing the amount of mercantile credit available, 'so that cities such as York and Durham suffered from the decline of Hull and Newcastle'.[129]

127. A. F. Sutton, 'The Merchant Adventurers of England', *NH*, 46 (2009), 219–29.
128. J. I. Kermode, 'Merchants, overseas trade and urban decline', *NH*, 23 (1987), 69 and n.; P. J. P. Goldberg, 'Mortality and economic change in the diocese of York, 1390–1514', *NH*, 24 (1988), 42, 45–6; A. J. Pollard, 'The north-eastern economy and the agrarian crisis of 1438–1440', *NH*, 25 (1989), 88–105. Pollard points out that the crisis may have been equally severe in the north-west, but that research on it is still needed.
129. Nightingale, *Medieval Mercantile Community*, 482–3; John Hatcher, 'The great slump of the mid-fifteenth century', in Richard Britnell and John Hatcher, eds, *Progress and Problems in Medieval England: Essays in Honour of Edward Miller* (Cambridge, 1996), 237–85.

It is therefore not surprising that the first signs of real economic distress appear at York in the late 1430s and the 1440s. London grocers were trying to break into northern markets, including York, and they often used provincial chapmen as their distributors: it is not surprising that, while many craft numbers declined, the numbers of York chapmen went on rising. One York chapman's inventory (1446) shows that though he was prosperous, he died owing nearly £18 to London merchants for goods supplied on credit, to be sold in his shop. Furthermore, civic income was falling, including house rents and revenue from the Common Crane for weighing goods. The Crown was persuaded by York's pleas of poverty to grant the first of many financial concessions: in 1442 the mercantile activities of non-citizens were restricted, while in 1449 the city was granted various concessions, including formal control over the Ainsty. That brought added revenue and also extra manpower for urban musters in time of war.[130]

Yet we should not exaggerate York's decline around 1450. It remained an attractive city for nobles, gentry, and monastic houses to base themselves in for business, shipping, or leisure. Fountains Abbey and Durham Priory, among others, were still purchasing staple items and luxuries there on a large scale. The corporation still had the resources to rebuild their impressive Guildhall; and even the textile sector was not yet finished—111 broadlooms were still operating in the 1450s, and in 1468–9 York still produced almost twice as many cloths as any other Yorkshire town.[131] Furthermore, the city was still impressive enough by contemporary standards to draw the admiration of two seasoned cosmopolitan visitors, admittedly before the crisis of the late 1430s. In 1431 the Burgundian ambassador, en route to Scotland, turned off the Great North Road to visit York, presumably simply because of its reputation: Philip the Good's biographer found the diversion 'unaccountable', but it is not clear why. Four or five years later there came another ambassador, Aeneas Sylvius (later pope as Pius II), also on a diplomatic mission to England and Scotland. His later notes from memory are regrettably brief, confined mostly to the Cathedral, but he did characterize York as 'a large and populous city' with no hint of its decline.[132]

130. Miller, 'Medieval York', 72–3; Nightingale, *Medieval Mercantile Community*, 366, 439–41, 448–9; Attreed, *The King's Towns*, 37, 62 n. 15, 71; Gryssop's inventory: AY 2/3, 572.
131. Heaton, *Yorkshire Woollen and Worsted Industries*, 75; Swanson, *Medieval Artisans*, 29, 36; Kermode, *Medieval Merchants*, 184.
132. Richard Vaughan, *Philip the Good* (London, 1962), 110; D. and M. Palliser, *York As They Saw It* (York, 1979), 7. Miller, 'Medieval York', 107, dates Aeneas Sylvius' visit to 1430.

Appendix VI: The York Plays

York's 'Corpus Christi Play', as it was then called, comprised a series of 'pageants' or individual episodes; in modern terms it was a cycle of plays, and I have followed Richard Beadle in his latest edition of them in calling them the York Plays. Since their first modern revival in 1951 they have acquired the misleading term 'Mystery Plays', a term which Beadle and King rightly call a 'late antiquarian invention'.[133]

The sole manuscript containing almost all the plays is a large volume, nearly all in the hand of a single scribe, known for some time to have been compiled between 1463 and 1477; Beadle has recently narrowed the likely date to *c*.1476–7. It is therefore difficult to be sure how much of it had been revised or rewritten by that time; it is, for instance, clear that the writer of the Nativity play drew on the *Revelations* of St Bridget, which were not available in England until *c*.1400.[134]

The manuscript, apparently compiled from prompt copies of the original pageant texts, had official status in York, where it was known as 'the Register'. After somehow leaving the corporation's possession, it passed through private hands before being bought in 1899 by the British Museum, and is now in the British Library (MS Additional 35290). It was edited in the original Middle English by Lucy Toulmin Smith as *York Plays* (Oxford, 1885), and more recently by Beadle as *The York Plays* (two volumes, EETS S.S. 23 (Oxford, 2009), and 24 (Oxford, 2013)). Beadle and Peter Meredith have published a facsimile as *The York Play* (Leeds Texts and Monographs: Medieval Drama Facsimiles, VII, 1983); and Beadle and Pamela King have edited *York Mystery Plays: A Selection in Modern Spelling* (Oxford, 1984; repr. with amendments, 1995).

The literature on the York Plays is vast, and cannot even be summarized here. For a recent survey with select bibliography, see Beadle's 'The York Cycle', in Beadle, ed., *The Cambridge Companion to Medieval English Theatre* (Cambridge, 2nd edition 2008), 99–124.

133. Beadle and King, eds, *York Mystery Plays*, p. x.
134. Beadle and King, eds, *York Mystery Plays*, p. 59; Richard Beadle, 'Nicholas Lancaster, Richard of Gloucester and the York Corpus Christi Play', in M. Rogerson, ed., *The York Mystery Plays: Performance in the City* (Woodbridge, 2011), 31–52.

7

'Great ruin and extreme decay'

c.1450–c.1540

Y ork, then, was suffering serious economic decline by mid-century, even
if it was still easily the largest town in the north; and the slump continued as cloth production and overseas trade both diminished (see Map 7).
Eloquent testimonies to the extent of decline are still visible in stone and
brick as well as in documents: one has only to contrast the handsome ashlar
facade of Walmgate Bar, for instance, with the humble brick Red Tower of
1490 nearby (Plate 16), to see the 'dispiriting' difference between what the
corporation could afford to build only a century or so apart.[1] However, as has
been seen, York's plight cannot be considered in isolation. In terms of population, for instance, its falling numbers were in one view typical of a 'swathe of
predominantly shrinking towns' stretching from York, Beverley, and Hull to
East Anglia, while in much of the West Midlands and the south, towns grew
as England's economic centre of gravity shifted. However, in the latest reassessment of urban populations, Steven Rigby finds little difference between
the Yorkshire trio and English towns as a whole. Taking the changes in the
ratio of urban to rural taxpayers between 1377 and 1524—a method which
avoids having to construct population multipliers from very different sources—
he suggests that York and four East Yorkshire towns held almost steady, containing 36 per cent of the Riding's population in 1377 and 35 per cent in 1524,
a smaller drop than for a larger sample of 100 towns throughout England.[2]

---

1. R. B. Dobson, 'Urban decline in late medieval England', *TR Hist S*, 5th ser., 27 (1977), 7.
2. Susan Reynolds, *Ideas and Solidarities of the Medieval Laity* (Aldershot, 1995), XI; Alan Dyer, '"Urban
decline" in England, 1377–1525', in T. R. Slater, ed., *Towns in Decline AD 100–1600* (Aldershot, 2000), 266–88; Palliser, *Towns and Local Communities*, XII, XIII; S. H. Rigby, 'Urban population
in late medieval England', *Econ HR*, 63 (2010), 405, 415–17. Rigby's East Riding total is made up
mostly of York, Beverley, and Hull: the other two are the much smaller Hedon and Skipsea.

Either way, there is little doubt that York was one of many towns which suffered in the fifteenth century as Londoners gained an increasing hold over English overseas trade; and there can be little doubt that York and other northern centres suffered more from the agrarian crisis of the 1430s than many towns in the Midlands and south. And it was the city's misfortune to be also at the centre of a political crisis as the two greatest northern families, the Percys and Nevilles, came to blows over control of the Vale of York in a period of Crown weakness. As Ralph Griffiths has shown, the real start of the so-called Wars of the Roses was not the first battle of St Albans (1455) but 'Heworth, Stamford Bridge, and the struggle for the city of York'.[3]

Nor is it a coincidence that civil war began in Yorkshire. The conventional view is that the Wars had little to do with the economy, but A. J. Pollard has pointed out that the agrarian crisis of 1438–40 led to a drop of 10 to 15 per cent in the income of northern landlords, giving both leading families a pressing incentive to enlarge their estates and to jockey for Court favour. Moreover, their Yorkshire estates lay close together. The Nevilles' main power bases were Middleham and Barnard Castle, but they also controlled the receivership of Sheriff Hutton, including many manors north and east of York. The Percy earls of Northumberland ringed the Vale with major estates centred on Leconfield, Wressle, Spofforth, and Topcliffe, as well as further north. When, in 1453, Sir Thomas Neville was awarded the former Percy manor of Wressle, matters came to a head.[4]

In August 1453 two of the earl's sons plotted with some York citizens to destroy much of the Neville family as they travelled north from Sir Thomas's wedding in Lincolnshire. They ambushed the wedding party at Heworth, just outside the city, in an inconclusive skirmish: of 710 men later indicted for the attack, over 100 were from York itself. In renewed fighting in 1454, the Percy brothers took control of York, savagely assaulting the mayor and recorder; but later that year the brothers were captured by the Nevilles in a second skirmish at Stamford Bridge. The warfare was small scale, but it triggered a general collapse of law and order in Yorkshire.[5] The citizens' own viewpoint on the violence around them is not clear—their

3. R. A. Griffiths, *King and Country: England and Wales in the Fifteenth Century* (London and Rio Grande, 1991), 364.

4. A. J. Pollard, *North-Eastern England During the Wars of the Roses* (Oxford, 1990), 91–6, 399.

5. Griffiths, *King and Country*, 321–64; Pollard, *North-Eastern England*, 245–65; Lorraine Attreed, *The King's Towns: Identity and Survival in Late Medieval English Boroughs* (New York, 2001), 294–6.

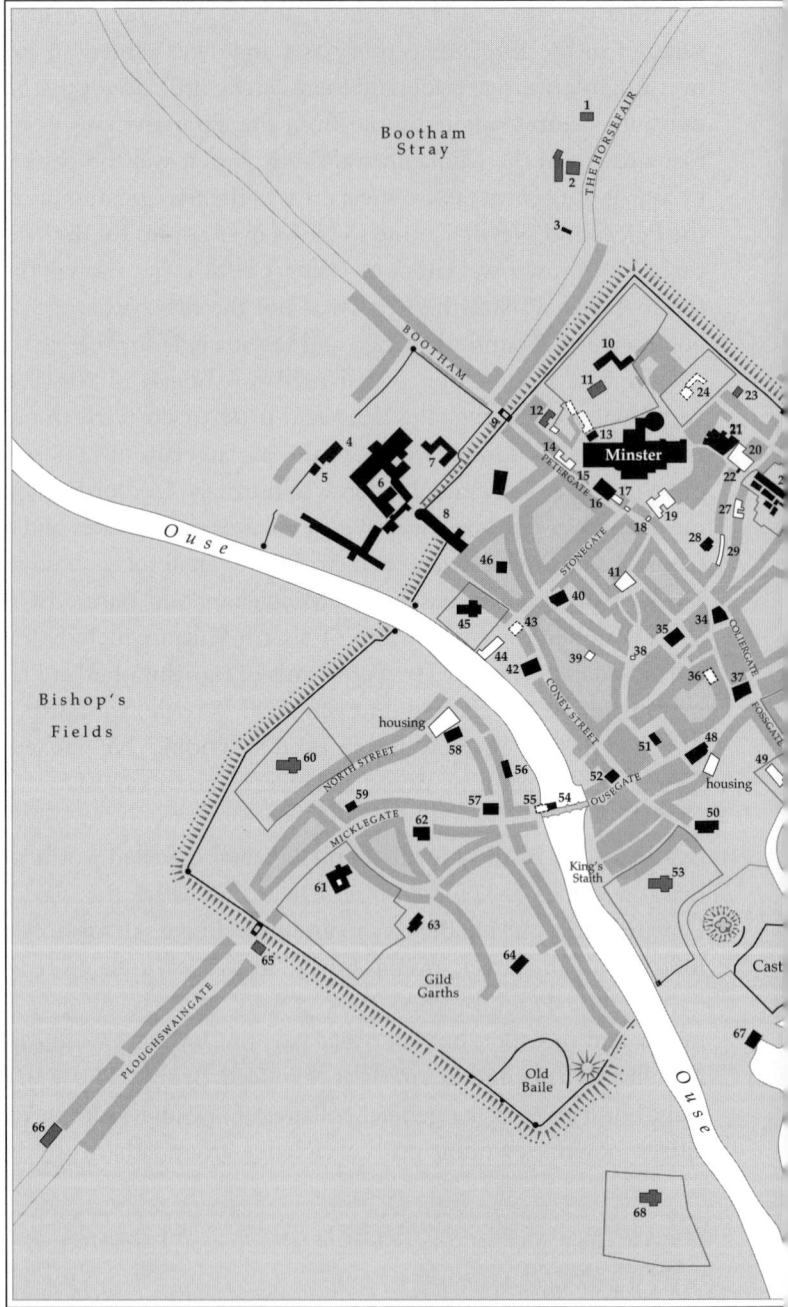

Map 7. York *c.*1500

Source: Adapted from a map in the forthcoming *British Historic Towns Atlas, Vol. V: York*, ed.
P. V. Addyman, by kind permission of the Historic Towns Trust.

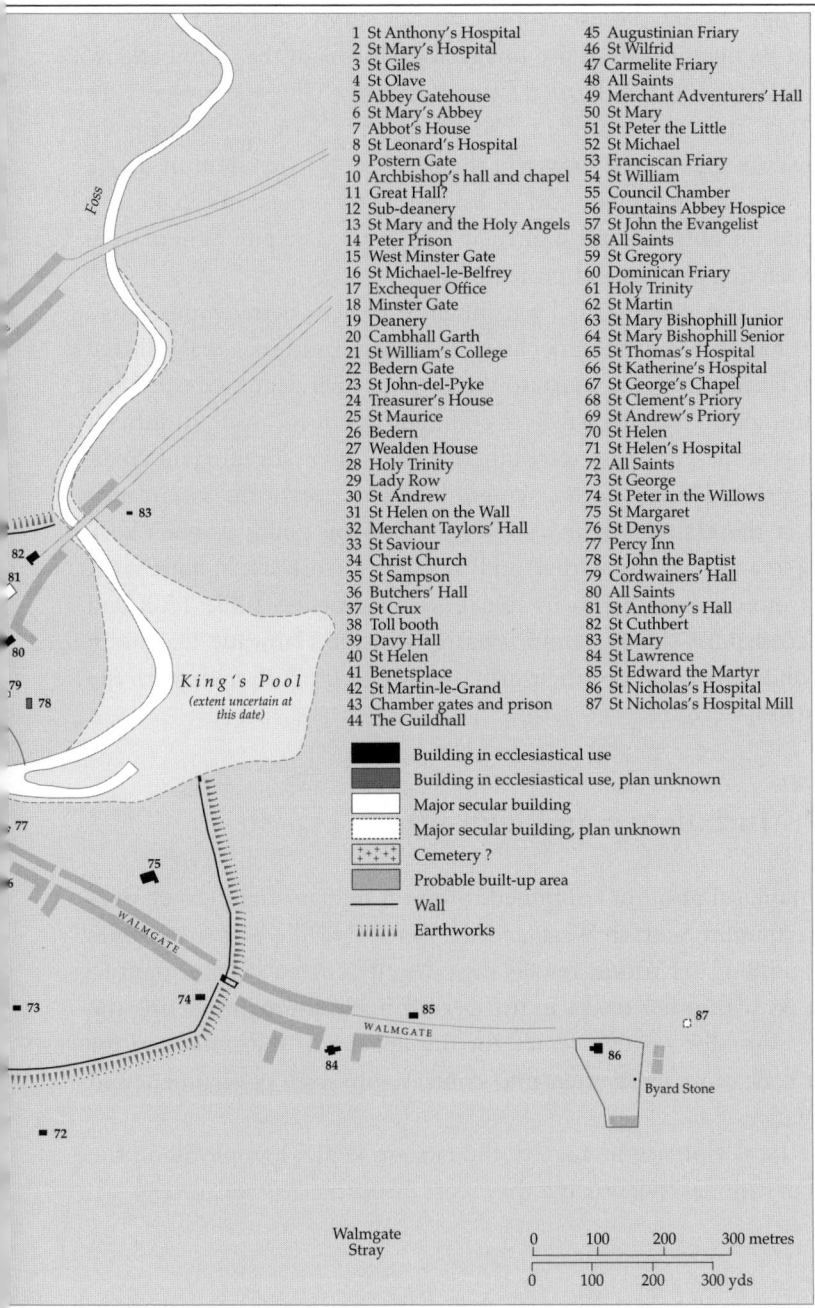

1 St Anthony's Hospital
2 St Mary's Hospital
3 St Giles
4 St Olave
5 Abbey Gatehouse
6 St Mary's Abbey
7 Abbot's House
8 St Leonard's Hospital
9 Postern Gate
10 Archbishop's hall and chapel
11 Great Hall?
12 Sub-deanery
13 St Mary and the Holy Angels
14 Peter Prison
15 West Minster Gate
16 St Michael-le-Belfrey
17 Exchequer Office
18 Minster Gate
19 Deanery
20 Cambhall Garth
21 St William's College
22 Bedern Gate
23 St John-del-Pyke
24 Treasurer's House
25 St Maurice
26 Bedern
27 Wealden House
28 Holy Trinity
29 Lady Row
30 St Andrew
31 St Helen on the Wall
32 Merchant Taylors' Hall
33 St Saviour
34 Christ Church
35 St Sampson
36 Butchers' Hall
37 St Crux
38 Toll booth
39 Davy Hall
40 St Helen
41 Benetsplace
42 St Martin-le-Grand
43 Chamber gates and prison
44 The Guildhall

45 Augustinian Friary
46 St Wilfrid
47 Carmelite Friary
48 All Saints
49 Merchant Adventurers' Hall
50 St Mary
51 St Peter the Little
52 St Michael
53 Franciscan Friary
54 St William
55 Council Chamber
56 Fountains Abbey Hospice
57 St John the Evangelist
58 All Saints
59 St Gregory
60 Dominican Friary
61 Holy Trinity
62 St Martin
63 St Mary Bishophill Junior
64 St Mary Bishophill Senior
65 St Thomas's Hospital
66 St Katherine's Hospital
67 St George's Chapel
68 St Clement's Priory
69 St Andrew's Priory
70 St Helen
71 St Helen's Hospital
72 All Saints
73 St George
74 St Peter in the Willows
75 St Margaret
76 St Denys
77 Percy Inn
78 St John the Baptist
79 Cordwainers' Hall
80 All Saints
81 St Anthony's Hall
82 St Cuthbert
83 St Mary
84 St Lawrence
85 St Edward the Martyr
86 St Nicholas's Hospital
87 St Nicholas's Hospital Mill

Building in ecclesiastical use
Building in ecclesiastical use, plan unknown
Major secular building
Major secular building, plan unknown
Cemetery ?
Probable built-up area
Wall
Earthworks

Foss

King's Pool
(extent uncertain at this date)

WALMGATE

WALMGATE

Byard Stone

Walmgate
Stray

0   100   200   300 metres
0   100   200   300 yds

council's minute books (House Books) do not survive before 1476—but glimpses can be obtained from the financial payments of the chamberlains, especially the annual section headed *Dona et Exennia*, 'Gifts and presents'. In the 1440s such sums were modest, usually under £2 or £3 annually. In 1453–4, however, gifts to the powerful totalled over £6, in addition to £4 spent on envoys to the Neville earl of Salisbury and others; and in 1454–5 the total spent in gifts was still higher, at nearly £8. The city fathers were desperately seeking patrons and protectors.[6]

Nevertheless, the looming civil wars might have been better endured had York and its region not been in decline. All of western Europe was affected by a bullion famine from the 1440s to the 1460s, which depressed trade and industry through the scarcity of silver coin; but its effects 'made it difficult for merchants at the periphery to compete with London. Insufficient credit was an important element, both a symptom and a cause of the ascendancy of London at the expense of the provinces.' London goods were in York shops by 1450 and probably earlier, and in 1449–50 York dyers, merchants, and spicers owed nearly £400 to two London grocers. While Hull and other east coast ports suffered from warfare with the Hanseatic League in 1468–74, Londoners tightened their grip on the crucial cloth trade with the Low Countries.[7]

Turbulence and civil wars: 1453–89

York's geographical position continued to give it military significance during the intermittent Scottish Wars; and the Percy–Neville power struggles until 1471 and the later Yorkist revolts kept the city's defences important to the Crown. As with other towns in this period, it was through meeting the demands of war—for military levies, for the upkeep of the walls, and for taxes—that York came most often into contact with royal government and its representatives.[8]

After the local violence in 1453–4, the citizens kept a low profile in the early stages of national civil war, but they were thrust centre stage in 1459–61.

6. Miller, 'Medieval York', 59; R. B. Dobson, ed., *York City Chamberlains' Account Rolls 1396–1500*, SS 192 (1980), 24, 33, 63, 74–5, 77, 94; Attreed, *The King's Towns*, 120–1.
7. J. I. Kermode, 'Money and credit in the fifteenth century: Some lessons from Yorkshire', *Business History Review*, 65 (1991), 475–501 (quotation from pp. 476–7).
8. David Grummitt, 'War and Society in the North of England, *c.* 1477–1559', *NH*, 45 (2008), 125.

Richard duke of York, who demanded recognition as heir to Henry VI, was supported by the Nevilles; they were again fighting the Percys, who supported Henry and his queen Margaret. In December 1460 Duke Richard was defeated and killed by a royal army at Wakefield Bridge; and the victorious Queen Margaret had his head displayed on Micklegate Bar at York. The county town was not a fortuitous choice. There is new evidence that in December some leading Lancastrians set up a temporary government there, in opposition to the Yorkists at Westminster, and that Margaret held a royal council in the city on 20 January 1461.[9] It did not last; her army marched south, but Duke Richard's heir—now proclaimed as Edward IV—marched north with the Lancastrians in retreat, and won a decisive victory at Towton, south-west of York, on 29 March. Henry and Margaret had barely escaped from the city before Edward entered, being received 'with great solempnyte and processyons'. He replaced his father's head with that of the executed Lancastrian earl of Devon, and celebrated Easter in York before marching south for his coronation.

The citizens took an active part in 1462 in campaigns against Lancastrian lords in Scotland and the Borders. In return Edward, who was back in York in 1463 and 1464, granted them £40 a year (later raised to £50) in recompense for the damage they had suffered in the war. Much later, the city council were to tell Henry VII that they had been loyal to Henry VI in sending many men to fight for him at Wakefield and Towton, paying for their loyalty by being 'robbid, spolid and rawnsomied' after Edward's victory, but there is no contemporary evidence for that, and it sounds like special pleading.[10]

If Edward IV did come to suspect the citizens' loyalty, it would have stemmed from the later events of 1471, when, having been forced into exile by resurgent Lancastrians, he landed on the Yorkshire coast, and moved on York along the Beverley road. The citizens were cautious, admitting him through Walmgate Bar only when he assured them he was returning to claim the duchy of York and not the crown. When, however, he did reclaim the throne and defeat the Lancastrians, he might well have had—as the city fathers put it to Henry VII—'your said orators in such disfavur that by his days they culd never be releved of ther said povertie'. It is doubtful, nevertheless, as a sufficient explanation for

9. Michael Hicks, 'A minute of the Lancastrian Council at York', *NH*, 35 (1999), 214–21.
10. Miller, 'Medieval York', 60; Dobson, ed., *Chamberlains' Account Rolls*, 113–15; *YHB*, I, 390.

York's economic plight; and in any case the king's younger brother was soon to prove a powerful advocate at court.[11]

The turning point came in 1471 when northern estates of the Neville earl of Warwick, who had died fighting for Henry VI, were granted to Edward's brother Richard duke of Gloucester, including the Yorkshire lordships of Middleham and Sheriff Hutton. Though Richard was never formally made the king's lieutenant in the north, that is what he effectively became; he resided much at his northern castles and was often in York. Indeed, he had come to know the city much earlier, having been present in 1465 for the enthronement of George Neville as archbishop, and from 1467–8 there are occasional records of municipal gifts to him. After the surviving council minutes begin, his many contacts with York are well documented.[12]

Richard's career from 1471 to 1483 was to make him, as Ross rightly says, 'unique among medieval English kings in the extent of his connections with the north of England'. It would be easy to give him too much prominence in a history of the city, given the abundant documentation and even more abundant discussions by modern historians, but neither can he be ignored. He undoubtedly cultivated northern connections both as duke and king; and it has even been suggested that the 13,000 badges of the white boar he distributed in the north in 1483 may have been a play on words, 'boar' for *Ebor*.[13]

The earliest relevant civic minutes are for 1476, when Richard appeared at Bootham Bar with an armed force to impose order in the city; there was clearly serious trouble, for some months later a grateful corporation granted him six swans and six pikes for intervening with his brother to dissuade him from revoking the city's liberties. In 1477 Richard and his duchess joined the city's Corpus Christi Guild; in the same year (1477) the city fathers appointed as their recorder Miles Metcalf, who was Richard's deputy chief steward for the duchy of Lancaster; and about the same time they called the duke 'our ful tendre and especial gude lorde'. It was doubtless Richard who smoothed the way for a lavish civic welcome to the king in 1478, on which the city

11. Miller, 'Medieval York', 60–1; *YHB*, I, 391; Attreed, *The King's Towns*, 80–1.
12. D. Palliser, 'Richard III and York', in Rosemary Horrox, ed., *Richard III and the North* (Hull, 1986), 55; A. J. Pollard, *Richard III and the Princes in the Tower* (Stroud, 1991), 45.
13. Charles Ross, *Richard III* (London, 1981), 44; Palliser, 'Richard III and York', 51–2, 55; Pollard, *Richard III and the Princes in the Tower*, 86; R. B. Dobson, *Church and Society in the Medieval North of England* (London, 1996), 229–30; D. A. Hinton, *Gold and Gilt, Pots and Pins* (Oxford, 2005), 253, 364 n. 47.

spent over £35, easily the largest sum among 'Gifts and presents' in the chamberlains' accounts for that period.[14]

The evidence for Richard's continuing links with York from 1478 to 1485—with the cathedral dean and chapter as well as the corporation—has been well documented and analysed many times. What remained of the Neville family were irreconcilably hostile to his power in the north, and when he had dealings with the citizens it was either alone or in company with the powerful but ambivalent Henry Percy, fourth earl of Northumberland. As lieutenant-general for the north, Richard three times summoned levies from the city and Ainsty in 1480–2 to fight the Scots, and in January 1482 he twice intervened with the king over a disputed mayoral election and a subsequent riot. Richard was also responsive to the citizens' economic troubles, which they attributed largely to the heavy burden of their annual fee farm, to economic competition from London, and to the obstruction of the Ouse and other rivers by fishgarths. The duke took up all three issues, 'lobbying the king to discriminate against London in York's favour (in which he failed) and backing the city's campaign to clear fishgarths (in which he was successful)', as well as trying to have the fee farm reduced. 'He was indeed', concludes Pollard, 'a benevolent lord to York', even if the city's economic problems were beyond government control. And he clearly developed close links with some of the York aldermen: tavern gossip in January 1483 suggested a party supporting Thomas Wrangwish for a second term as mayor, 'for he is the man that my lord of Gloucester will doo for', though it was not until 1484 that Wrangwish was re-elected.[15]

That year of 1483 proved crucial for both duke and city. When the king died unexpectedly on 9 April, Richard was at one of his northern castles. Having heard the news around the 15th, he went to York Minster to hold a memorial service for his brother, and to lead the northern nobles in pledging allegiance to his nephew, Edward V. He set off for London on 20 April, and on 10 May was made Protector of England. On 6 June York was asked to choose an unprecedented four MPs for a parliament in the name of the boy king, Wrangwish being named first; yet on 10 June Richard was asking its citizens for urgent military aid against the queen mother. The city council

14. R. H. Skaife, ed., *The Register of the Guild of Corpus Christi*, SS 57 (1872), 101; *YHB*, I, 8, 9, 78, 114–15, 128–9; Dobson, ed., *Chamberlains' Account Rolls*, 169–70. The crucial entry has Richard interceding for the 'conservacion' of the city's chartered liberties, not their 'confirmacion' as in *YCR*, I, 16.
15. Pollard, *Richard III and the Princes in the Tower*, 79; Palliser, 'Richard III and York', 56; *YHB*, II, 707.

responded rapidly, agreeing at once to send 200 horsemen under Wrangwish to London via Pontefract. They joined other northern troops in reaching London about 3 July, in time for Richard's coronation on the 6th—the
boy king having been deposed, and possibly already killed if one Yorkshire
source is correct.[16]

Only two weeks after Richard's coronation he set off on a lengthy progress
with his queen and their son, of which the climax was a stay of over three
weeks in York, where they resided at the archbishop's palace. The programme
was choreographed by Richard's secretary, John Kendall; even the feast day
of his arrival on 29 August was carefully chosen as 'what was, in York, tanta-
mount to a second Feast of Corpus Christi'. The highlights included a
performance of the Creed Play before the king and queen on 7 September;
the investiture of their son as Prince of Wales on the 8th, followed by a royal
progress through the streets; and a meeting with the leading citizens on the
17th, when Richard promised to reduce the city's annual fee farm from
£160 to £100.[17] Nor was this all, for it was probably while at York that
Richard summoned a mysterious 'council' and promised to found 'a colledge
at York of an hundreth priests', apparently a chantry college which would
have been 'the most ambitious chantry foundation ever contemplated by an
English king'. Furthermore, Richard might well have intended that college
as his own mausoleum, which would have followed his brother's choice of
Windsor. However, it was not to be: as with his hasty promises to the city
over the fee farm payments, his intentions for the new college were to prove
abortive.[18]

Nevertheless, a core of civic and clerical supporters remained loyal to the
usurper king for the rest of his short reign. In March 1485 the dean and resident canons summoned the mayor and aldermen to the Minster choir to
convey the pope's blessings on 'his subjects especially our soveraine
lord... King Richard'. And when Henry Tudor invaded the realm in August,
the corporation were prompt in offering the king help, sending eighty

16. *YHB*, I, 283–5, 713–14; Alison Hanham, *Richard III and his Early Historians 1483–1535* (Oxford,
    1975), 36–7; Palliser, 'Richard III and York', 57; C. F. Richmond, 'The death of Edward V', *NH*,
    25 (1989), 278–80.
17. *YHB*, I, 287–93; II, 729; *REED: York*, I, 152–3; II: 786–7; Ross, *Richard III*, 150–2; Palliser,
    'Richard III and York', 57–8; Pamela Tudor-Craig, 'Richard III's triumphant entry into York',
    in Horrox, ed., *Richard III and the North*, 108–16 (quotation from p. 113); Pollard, *Richard III and
    the Princes in the Tower*, 107–9; Neil Murphy, 'Receiving royals in later medieval York', *NH*, 43
    (2006), 243–54.
18. Dobson, *Church and Society*, 227–8, 246–50 (quotation from p. 228); Pollard, *Richard III and the
    Princes in the Tower*, 76.

soldiers to fight for him under the city's macebearer, John Sponer, though they did not reach Bosworth Field in time. Most strikingly of all, when Sponer returned to York the day after the battle, the council formally minuted his report in unequivocal terms: 'King Richard, late mercifully reigning upon us, was thrugh grete treason... pitiously slane and murdred, to the grete hevynesse of this citie.'[19] Clearly, Richard's desperate quest for support during his short reign had been successful with at least a core of city councillors and, perhaps, with many other citizens. When Henry Tudor sent an emissary to York two days after Bosworth, the mayor and aldermen went to meet him within the protection of the castle, because he 'durst not for fere of deth come thrugh the citie'. As late as 14 October 1485 the council—still avoiding dating their minutes by the new king's reign—could write openly of 'the moost famous prince of blissed memory, King Richard'.[20] It was to be many years before Henry VII could be satisfied of the city's loyalty.

The corporation's continued loyalty to Richard's memory is without parallel among towns caught up in the civil wars, though it should not blind us to other evidence suggesting a divided council and citizenry. The meetings of 23 August and 14 October were both attended by the mayor and four other aldermen who clearly endorsed them (explicitly signing the record of the October meeting) while there is good evidence that Thomas Wrangwish, unable to be present either time, was of their number. However, other aldermen were, perhaps deliberately, absent, including Richard York and William Todd, both of whom were to prove loyal supporters of the new king. And there are hints that the mass of the citizens were as divided as their leaders, including reported gossip against Richard and resistance in 1484 to an enclosure of pasture land which Richard had sanctioned. Yet it is hard to quarrel with Miller's judgement that Richard 'seems to have succeeded as no one else did—except perhaps Archbishop Scrope—in winning the hearts of the citizens'.[21]

Henry VII certainly strove hard, like Richard, to secure the city's loyalty, despite the fact that throughout the first year of the reign the council politely but firmly rejected his nominations for the offices of recorder and

19. Palliser, *Tudor York*, 42–3; Dobson, *Church and Society*, 250–1; *YHB*, I, 368–9. The key word is 'mercifully', which was misread as 'lawfully' by Drake, inexplicably copied by Raine in *YCR*, I, 119, and has been repeated in many standard works: Palliser, 'Richard III and York', 59, 77 n. 38.
20. Palliser, *Tudor York*, 43 and n. 1. The 24 August entry is missing from the MS, but was seen and printed by Francis Drake, *Eboracum* (London, 1736), 121. 14 October entry: *YHB*, I, 373.
21. Miller, 'Medieval York', 65; Palliser, 'Richard III and York', 62–9.

swordbearer. Henry was, however, happy to recommend that their Common Clerk John Haryngton continue in office, even though he had been clerk of Richard III's royal council. He included York in his first royal progress in April 1486, and was lavishly entertained. The corporation spent £66 on the visit, staging a series of carefully choreographed pageants which flattered the king and ignored their relationship with Richard. Soon afterwards, having been made aware of the unfinished business of Richard's promises, he remitted most of York's fee farm payments, 'we at our last being at our citie there seing the great ruyne and extreme decay that the same is fallen in'.[22] Henry was rewarded by the corporation's loyalty during the Yorkist rebellion of 1487. Just before the rising, Alderman Welles was murdered while taking personal charge of the guard at Bootham Bar, which was then attacked by the rebels; but the city was firmly defended by Mayor Todd and Alderman York. On a return visit to the city that summer, Henry knighted both men and later granted them annuities for life.[23]

The city fathers were less successful in holding out in 1489, when a Yorkshire tax revolt with Yorkist undertones erupted, triggered by the murder of the fourth Percy earl of Northumberland. They started firmly enough, taking defensive measures, and insisting to the royal sheriff that they themselves would guard the city for the king as 'his chaumbre'. Yet a week later, on 15 May, a group of rebels broke in through Walmgate and Fishergate Bars, aided by Wrangwish and other sympathetic citizens. It did not last, for the revolt collapsed before the king reached Yorkshire with an army, and on the 20th the mayor and aldermen were asking the archbishop to intercede for them with him. A judicial commission sat in York's Guildhall at the end of May and beginning of June, but many rebels were pardoned. In the event only one York man was executed; Wrangwish was sentenced to hang, but pardoned by the king, a pardon enforced by a bond of £500 by which he was banished from Yorkshire.[24]

22. Royal visit: *REED:York*, I, 146–52; *YHB*, II, 478–85; S. Anglo, *Spectacle, Pageantry, and Early Tudor Policy* (Oxford, 1969), 23–8; Attreed, *The King's Towns*, 86–8; Emma Cavell, 'HenryVII, the North of England, and the first provincial progress of 1486', *NH*, 39 (2002), 187–207. Henry and civic posts: *YHB*, I, 383–9, 392–4, 398; James Lee, 'Urban policy and urban political culture: HenryVII and his towns', *HR*, 82 (2009), 493, 495–6. Fee farm: *YHB*, II, 509–10; L. C. Attreed, 'The king's interest:York's fee farm and the central government, 1482–92', *NH*, 17 (1981), 37–9.
23. Palliser, *Tudor York*, 44; *YHB*, II, 550–88.
24. TNA, KB9/381; *YHB*, II, 646–52; M. A. Hicks, 'The Yorkshire rebellion of 1489 reconsidered', *NH*, 22 (1986), 38–62; M. J. Bennett, 'Henry VII and the northern rising of 1489', *EHR*, 105 (1990), 34–59; S. Cunningham, 'HenryVII and rebellion in north-eastern England, 1485–1492', *NH*, 32 (1996), 69.

Royal power revived: 1489–1529

Henry VII faced no more serious opposition in city or county after 1489, but he took no chances. Richard III had established a Council of the North in 1484, to control Yorkshire and possibly other counties on his behalf: its base was at Sandal Castle but its sessions were held at York. Henry did not immediately continue the policy, but after 1489 he made the earl of Surrey his lieutenant in Yorkshire, to operate from Sheriff Hutton castle near York; and from 1501 he made Archbishop Thomas Savage his lieutenant, to chair 'the council of the king at York'. Henry was also determined to continue a policy initiated by Edward IV and Richard III, by which ultimate royal control over towns was firmly asserted, although provided the urban elites kept order, they were given a wide measure of autonomy.[25]

That was starkly demonstrated in 1495. For a decade there had been an annual riot at Michaelmas as citizens battled with the Vicars Choral over common rights in the suburban pasture called Vicars' Leas. In the early 1490s, the abbot of St Mary's, acting for the earl of Surrey, tried in vain to 'appease' the quarrel, until King Henry lost patience. In February 1495 he summoned the mayor and leading citizens to Greenwich for an ultimatum face-to-face:

> I may not see the Citie go in utter ruyne and dekaye in defaute of you that shuld rewle, for rather of necessite I most and woll put in other rewlers that woll rewle and govern the Citie accordyng to my lawez.

The chastened mayor and his colleagues took the point, accepted mediation by Surrey, and kept quiet for some years. And when Henry's daughter Margaret stopped in York on her way to marry James IV of Scots, the corporation took care to entertain her with great ceremony.[26]

They must, nevertheless, have tested the royal patience once more the next year, when the mayoral election triggered riots over grievances against the council. Sixteen rioters were summoned before the king, who again warned the council to keep order, summoning if necessary the support of the archbishop and the Northern Council. Scarcely was order restored

---

25. Northern Council: Ross, *Richard III*, 182–3; Bennett, 'Henry VII and the northern rising', 48; R. W. Hoyle, 'The earl, the archbishop and the Council', in R. E. Archer and S. Walker, eds, *Rulers and Ruled in Late Medieval England* (London, 1995), 239–56; S. J. Gunn, biography of Savage in *ODNB*. Henry VII and towns: Palliser, *Towns and Local Communities*, VI, 144, and Lee, 'Henry VII and his towns', 493–510, for two different emphases.
26. *YCR*, II, 115–16, 186–9; Lee, 'Henry VII and his towns', 499.

before more serious trouble broke out in the area. Archbishop Savage and the Council were now at odds with the fifth earl of Northumberland, who had some local support: in May 1504 several York merchants were indicted for being his retainers, and three weeks later there was a brawl at Fulford, just outside York, when the earl came close to being murdered by the arch-bishop's servants. The citizens were only bit-players in this feud, but the mayor and aldermen had provided a wine reception for Savage on his way to Fulford, and one of the key participants in the fracas was the city's recorder, Brian Palmes, who claimed to have been successful in stopping the fight. It was, like the election riots, a reminder that the Crown could not yet reimpose effective law and order in the area. There was, however, no recorded trouble in York for the rest of Henry's reign; and perhaps he retained a memory that the city was impoverished enough without the further dis-ruption that direct royal rule would have caused. For when he came to make his will, he left money for his executors to complete his new founda-tion of the Savoy hospital in London and to set up similar hospitals in York and Coventry. Sadly, these two foundations, each of which was to have the princely sum of 20,000 marks (£13,333), are never heard of again: and it is unclear why Henry chose those above his other towns.[27]

York politics became violent again in the early years of Henry VIII's reign. Late in 1514 unspecified offences—probably the 'enormities' in the city which were condemned in a royal proclamation—caused the royal council to summon one of the aldermen to London; and in 1516–17 per-sistent riots and disputes over the elections of mayor and aldermen pro-voked royal intervention and a blistering message of Henry's 'dyspleasour'. Fortunately, the city fathers were successful in securing the support of the king's new chief minister, Cardinal Thomas Wolsey, the northern archbishop from 1514 and royal chancellor from 1515. Though he notori-ously never even visited his archdiocese until 1530, he took a close inter-est in the affairs of his cathedral city; when he interceded for the citizens with the king in 1517, he told them of his 'gret love and good mynd' towards them, 'all beyng our parysshon[er]s, and of the chief and prin-cypale place of our provynce and dyoces'. The corporation, in return, abandoned their usual policy of seeking the patronage of several powerful

27. YCR, II, 191–4; III, 1–7; Palliser, Tudor York, 45, 68; Hoyle, 'The earl, the archbishop and the Coun-cil', 245–56; Margaret Condon, 'The last will of Henry VII', in T. Tatton-Brown and R. Mortimer, eds, Westminster Abbey: The Lady Chapel of Henry VII (Woodbridge, 2003), 123 and n. 62.

men, and made Wolsey their sole patron, calling him in 1528 'our most especial and singular good and gracious lord'.[28]

These were not merely standard compliments, and it is clear that until his fall in 1529, the Cardinal was an effective supporter of the corporation's interests, so far as he could amid competing pressures and the many demands on his time. He was successful in defusing royal anger over the riots of 1516–17 and in securing royal letters patent to modify the civic constitution. He also secured York a statutory monopoly over the export of Yorkshire wools and fells (1523), and granted the citizens an indulgence giving them power to collect money nationwide for repairs to Ouse and Foss Bridges (1527), an act which Robert Swanson calls 'an extraordinary, perhaps unique, civic appropriation of indulgence administration'. He employed household officers to keep in touch with the corporation and keep him informed. In return, Wolsey was twice successful in having his nominee made the city's swordbearer, while on his part the cardinal made Alderman William Wright master of his York mint. Meanwhile, in 1525 the king had revived a Northern Council at Pontefract and Sheriff Hutton under the nominal leadership of his young son, the duke of Richmond; and significantly, Richard Page, recorder of York and in Wolsey's service, was vice-chamberlain of Richmond's household.[29]

The crucial area on which Wolsey could not help York was the worsening crisis in civic finance as a result of the fee farm payments. It will be remembered that in 1212 King John had granted the city self-government in return for an annual 'farm' of £160; but since 1322 the Crown had assigned much of it away, the largest portion of £100 to the Roos family. In 1513 Sir Thomas Lovell, guardian to the tenth Lord Roos, agreed to take 20 marks (£13 6s. 8d.) yearly in lieu of the £100, but in 1524 Roos demanded the £100 in full and payment of arrears, as he also did from Lincoln, which likewise owed him £100. This may have been the last straw which pushed the city into severe economic depression about 1525–6. Desperate threats from 1528 that the city would surrender their chartered liberties rather than pay were unavailing, and Wolsey's fall in 1529, quickly followed by annulment

28. *YCR*, III, 51–64 (quotation from p. 58); Nadine Lewycky, 'Cardinal Thomas Wolsey and the city of York, 1514–1529', *NH*, 46 (2009), 43–60 (quotation from p. 43).
29. Lewycky, 'Cardinal Thomas Wolsey', *passim*; R. N. Swanson, *Indulgences in the Pre-Reformation Diocese of York*, BP 119 (York, 2011), 15–17; B. A. Murphy, 'Fitzroy, Henry', in *ODNB*.

of the 1523 grant of a wool and fells monopoly, did not help; and it was to be left to Thomas Cromwell to negotiate a solution.[30]

Civic government in crisis? 1450–1530

The city's governors, then, had to cope with many challenges during eight decades which saw seven changes of monarch, five of them as a result of usurpation or civil war. That, of course, mattered hugely since the mayor and his colleagues were directly answerable to the king as lord of their city as well as monarch. Nevertheless, the basic structure of civic government remained largely unchanged, and much of what has been said of the period from 1396 to 1450 was equally true of the following eighty years. The mayor and sheriffs continued to run the city's administration, courts, and finances with the aid of the aldermen and Twenty-Four, the chamberlains and bridgemasters, the recorder and Common Clerk, and the many lesser officers already described, together with occasional wider meetings with the Common Council. They still administered the city from offices on Ouse Bridge, though they made increasing use of the larger Guildhall as rebuilt in 1449–59: it was not only the meeting hall for consulting the Common Council or the freemen as a whole, but also for special events like the performance of the Creed Play before Richard III and the trial of the rebels in 1489.

The mayor was still elected annually from the ranks of the aldermen, and the right choice was seen as crucial by many citizens, while perceived failure in office would long be remembered. Sixteen years after Mayor Kyrke had been forced to back down in the quarrel with the Vicars Choral, a miller was reported for saying in an alehouse that 'Maister Kyrke shulde never be maire [again] for he lost the Vicar Lees.' On the other hand, a successful mayor could be held in high regard. When John Stokdale left office in 1502, the council chose to minute fourteen achievements of his mayoralty, including securing the royal grant for two new fairs; the replacing of the pavements of Ouse Bridge and Pavement, and of 300 feet (91 m) of city wall; and gaining the king's support against encroachment on the street of Bootham.[31]

30. *YCR*, III, 106, 108, 110, 113, 116–17, 137; Palliser, *Tudor York*, 12–15, 48, 216; R. W. Hoyle, 'Urban decay and civic lobbying: The crisis in York's finances, 1525–1536', *NH*, 34 (1998), 85–92, 95–7; Lewycky, 'Wolsey and the city of York', 47–8.
31. *YCR*, II, 171; III, 36.

It was the importance of the office which led to clashes over the choice of mayor, frequently calling for royal mediation. In 1464 Edward IV ordered the crafts to nominate two aldermen, from whom the council were to choose one; in 1473 he ruled instead that the crafts could themselves elect one of the two, but it did not end the disputes, and in 1489 Henry VII restored the 1464 procedure. After further riots in 1516–17, Henry VIII imposed a different system under royal letters patent. The Forty-Eight were replaced by a Common Council of forty-one members, consisting of two representatives each of thirteen major crafts and one each from fifteen lesser crafts. It was to meet to assist the mayor, aldermen, and sheriffs, and (assisted by the twenty-eight senior searchers of the crafts) to choose candidates for mayors, aldermen, and sheriffs. It was in reality less 'democratic' than the previous system, for the city council chose the members suggested by the crafts, while commoners not on the new council were barred from mayoral elections.[32]

The importance of the mayoralty was also stressed by an increased insistence on status and respect. From the 1480s the term 'my lord [the] mair' came into use, and when Sir William Conyers threatened John Metcalfe, and called him a 'carle' (churl), the current mayor indignantly defended 'my brother John Metcalfe' who 'wurchipfully hath been... the Kyngs lieutenant [i.e. mayor] within this Citie'. Citizens were expected to doff their caps to the mayor and aldermen, to address them as 'Master', and on no account to call them by their first name or by the familiar pronoun 'thou'. All of this, however, may suggest insecurity in a status-conscious society, where urban rulers could fear pressure from local lords and gentry, resentment by colleagues, or rebellion by lesser citizens. In 1503, for instance, Alderman Neleson burst out, 'Master Maier... if ye do me wrang this yere I trust to be your felawe the next yere.'[33]

As for disorder from below, it rarely came to open rebellion as in 1380–1, but it was clearly discontent among the mass of citizens which lay behind mayoral election riots. The royal regulations of 1464 and 1473 for mayoral elections were intended to prevent 'dissensions' between the citizens, quarrels serious enough to prevent an election in 1471, on which Edward IV intervened and appointed the veteran William Holbek, who must have been

---

32. Miller, 'Medieval York', 71; Palliser, *Tudor York*, 68; J. I. Kermode, 'Obvious observations on the formation of oligarchies in late medieval English towns', in J. A. F. Thomson, ed., *Towns and Townspeople in the Fifteenth Century* (Gloucester, 1988), 89–90, 100–1.
33. Palliser, *Tudor York*, 63, 65, 94, 290, 298.

around seventy, and who had already held the office three times. Holbek was duly re-elected in 1472, yet in 1476 he took sanctuary in the Blackfriars, refusing to come to the Guildhall for fear of his life.[34]

In 1482 another disputed election provoked some rioters to ring the 'common bell' on Ouse Bridge, for which they were imprisoned on the orders of Edward and Duke Richard. And there were further election riots in 1504 and 1516–17, leading to Henry VIII's intervention and new election procedures. Edward Miller saw the whole period from 1464 to 1517 as one when the mercantile oligarchy was 'under heavy fire from a "democratic" movement which drew its strength from the crafts', claiming a greater say in civic affairs. 'Democratic' may indeed be a fair description for the freemen's attitudes: in 1475 the 'pore commonalte' petitioned the mayor, aldermen, and city council about civic debt, asserting that 'we ben all one bodye corporate...all inlike prevaliged of the commonalte, which has borne none office in the cite.'[35]

If it was a 'democratic' movement, it had strictly limited aims: to impose more economy and efficiency on civic government and financial management, not to change the type of men who held the key offices. The merchants, for instance, still dominated the mayoralty: of the seventy-two mayors between 1450 and 1540, forty-nine were merchants, three others specialized traders, while at least two others (a gentleman and a vintner) participated in overseas trade. Of the remaining eighteen, mostly craftsmen, six were goldsmiths and two others (the carver Thomas Drawswerde and the glazier John Petty) ran important workshops supplying church furnishings. Similarly, of the forty men representing York in parliament over those ninety years, thirty-one were merchants.[36]

The continued reliance on wealthy mayors and other senior officers (whether merchants or not) is not surprising. The constant refrain of both corporation and 'commons' from the 1450s to the 1550s was civic poverty, and the commons' petition of 1475 was a programme intended to alleviate 'the grete povertie of this cite' and 'to kepe the cite oute of dette'. It was well understood that mayors and sheriffs should be rich, as they were often

---

34. *CPR 1467–77*, 239; *YHB*, I, 60–1; Miller, 'Medieval York', 61, 82. Holbek had been enfranchised in 1425, and the mean age at which Tudor aldermen became freemen was 24: Palliser, *Tudor York*, 71.

35. *YHB*, I, 247–54; *YCR*, III, 1–7, 51–61; Miller, 'Medieval York', 82–4. 1475 petition: *YMB*, II, 246.

36. There is yet no full study of the MPs for the century, but see *HP 1509–1558* and E. L. Shields, 'The members of parliament for the city of York 1485–1515', *YH*, 11 (1994), 9–21.

called upon to make up civic deficits from their own money—several men
around 1500 were spared election as sheriffs for having less than £100 in
goods—and the commons were now urging similar wealth qualifications
for chamberlains and bridgemasters. Since they endorsed the norm that a
man should follow a *cursus honorum*—bridgemaster, chamberlain, and sheriff
before mayor—'a successful man could expect to bear the costs of repeated
officeholding, each bout of which would reduce his capital and force him
to begin a new cycle of accumulation'.[37]

From the 1440s on, the yield of nearly all the main sources of civic revenue tended to decline, and a deficit at the end of each financial year became
common. It is difficult to measure from the surviving chamberlains' accounts,
because they recorded all the income to which the city was entitled, but not
what was actually collected: but it seems clear that the position 'deteriorated
gravely from the 1460s onwards'. By 1486–7, the incoming chamberlains
inherited a deficit of over £506, which increased by £82 during the year, at
a time when they could not hope for a net annual income of more than
£200. Since chamberlains might have to meet deficits from their own pock-
ets and not be repaid for a year or more, the desperate council spread the
burden by raising their number—to four and then six between 1486 and
1501—before reverting to the traditional three.[38]

Why had matters become so bad? The largest income received by the
chamberlains was now payments from the bridgemasters for rents of
civic properties, after deductions for repairs, and for many payments to
chaplains and cantarists. That net income, £118 in 1433–4, fell to £39 by
1499–1500, 'perhaps the single most eloquent testimony' to civic decline in
the accounts. The next largest item, payments from new freemen, fared little
better: £52 in 1433–4 and £32 in 1499–1500, even though the corporation
tried to ease the burden from the 1440s by allowing payment in instalments.
Indeed, no significant item of revenue increased except for the farming-out
of tolls at the Common Crane; and matters continued to worsen until by
1532–3 total income was only £141, and ordinary expenditure exceeded
ordinary income by £24.[39]

37. *YMB*, II, 246; Palliser, *Tudor York*, 92–3; quotation: Hoyle, 'Urban decay', 106.
38. *YMB*, II, 246; Miller, 'Medieval York', 73–4; Dobson, ed., *Chamberlains' Account Rolls*, xxv, xxvi.
39. Dobson, ed., *Chamberlains' Account Rolls*, xxviii–xxx; J. Muggleston, 'Some aspects of the two late medieval chamberlains' account books of York', *YAJ*, 67 (1995), 133–46; Hoyle, 'Urban decay', 91.

The chamberlains could in fact manage, in good years, because of the sheriffs, who were responsible for paying the city's fee farm but who also paid £60 annually to the chamberlains, which was intended towards maintenance of the walls. They could continue to do so, however, only if the reductions in the city's fee farm promised by Richard III and Henry VII had been fulfilled or if the reduced settlement agreed in 1513 on behalf of Lord Roos had endured. It was the renewed demand for £100 a year by Roos (created earl of Rutland in 1525) which the sheriffs could not meet, and which led to the corporation's threats from 1528 to surrender their chartered liberties.[40]

Furthermore, one extra pressure was building up by the 1520s. There had long been complaints of well-to-do citizens refusing to accept civic office. As early as the 1440s, some men had purchased royal letters patent exempting them from civic office, a practice ended by statute in 1450 at York's request. Yet from the 1460s to the 1530s some merchants still managed to obtain exemption from office, or paid the city chamber fines to be allowed to do so. In the 1970s both Barrie Dobson and I saw this as a symptom, if not a cause, of York's decline. Jennifer Kermode has shown, however, that there was no shortage of men willing to serve, and that city demands for fines were often demanded of men who would anyway have been unwelcome in office, as a means of raising money. Having said that, the 1520s and 1530s did see a real change. In 1526 one of the two elected as sheriff refused to serve and moved house outside the city's jurisdiction, while the junior muremasters also refused to serve; and in 1529 and 1532 successive sheriffs tried to evade various payments required of them.[41]

Nevertheless, since the city even in those decades did not go bankrupt or surrender its liberties to the Crown, the normal routine of administration and justice somehow continued, and it would be wrong to forget that in the light of the council's increasing preoccupation with deficits and the fee farm. Fortunately, it is from this period that some of the routine can be better glimpsed. There are no surviving records for the mayors' courts, but those of the sheriffs' courts survive from 1471, and for 1491 and 1516–17 stray records of the humbler wardmote courts, while the council's minute books include many miscellaneous entries on arbitrations, fines, and petty

40. Hoyle, 'Urban decay', 86–92.
41. Palliser, *Tudor York*, 205; J. I. Kermode, 'Urban decline? The flight from office in late medieval York', *Econ HR*, 35 (1982), 179–98; Hoyle, 'Urban decay', 84, 89–90.

peacekeeping. Meanwhile at the parish level, largely unrecorded, the constables tried to keep the peace, arrest malefactors, and head the 'watches' manning the defences in time of war.[42]

The sheriffs' court of civil pleas handled huge numbers of cases between citizens (nearly 900 in the year 1478–9), mainly over debt and trespass. The mayor's court of common pleas presumably heard cases of property ownership, which are absent from the sheriffs' court records, as well as disputes over leases, wills, and dower rights. The wardmote courts dealt mainly with street cleansing, public sanitation, encroachments on public land, disorderly people, and uncontrolled dogs. In 1501 all six wards were ordered by the council to provide public stocks and fetters for the 'punyshment of begars, vacabunds and other mysdoers', an order which was promptly enforced.[43]

Economic recession

There can be no doubting the severe decline in the city's prosperity and importance, a decline probably exaggerated by the corporation, but accepted as genuine by successive monarchs and ministers of the Crown. There is, admittedly, an overquoted remark by a Venetian envoy in 1496–7 to the effect that York, with Bristol, was still one of the two most important English towns outside London, but that was certainly out of date. The lay subsidy of 1524–5—the first tax returns reliable for urban rankings since 1377—put York fourth or fifth by numbers of taxpayers and eleventh in terms of taxable wealth. Even if York was relatively underassessed that year, it had certainly fallen far since it rivalled or exceeded Bristol and Norwich.[44]

42. YCA, MSS E 25, 25A, F 1; P. M. Stell, ed., *Sheriffs' Court Books of the City of York 1471–1500* (York, 1999). Wardmote courts:YCA, CC 1a (1491); Bodley, MS Rawl. B 451, fos 2–5 (1516–17). Constables and watches: Miller, 'Medieval York', 77; *RCHMY* II, 36–8; P. M. Stell, 'Constables of York 1380–1500', *YH*, 15 (1998), 16–25.
43. Miller, 'Medieval York', 75–7; *YCR*, II, 165, 171; Richard Britnell, 'York under the Yorkists', in Britnell, ed., *Daily Life in the Late Middle Ages* (Stroud, 1998), 188–9.
44. C. A. Sneyd, ed., *A Relation . . . of the Island of England*, Camden Society, 1st ser. 37 (London, 1847), 41; Palliser, *Tudor York*, 22; *CUHB* I, 761, 765; Dyer, ' "Urban decline" in England', 275. Dyer's ranking of York as 11th by taxable wealth is more likely than the 15th place (calculated for all taxes 1523–7) suggested by W. G. Hoskins, which would put York below even tiny Lavenham: *Provincial England* (London, 1963), 70. Sneyd dated the Venetian description *c.*1500, but Ambassador Trevisan was in England in 1496–7, and the account was written in 1498.

Admissions to the city's freedom confirm the picture of declining population and economic attraction to immigrants, since over 70 per cent of new freemen are estimated to have been born outside York. Average recruitment was nearly 100 a year between 1350 and 1450, but it fell to sixty-nine in 1450–1500 and fifty-six in 1500–50: the lowest point was the year 1513–14, when only thirty-nine were admitted. True, averages conceal wide variations, with peaks often following epidemics as dead men's shoes were filled; and as for earlier periods, an unknown and perhaps varying proportion of craftsmen did not take up the freedom. There is, nevertheless, no reason to suppose that the downward trend was not a real one.[45]

The decline seems to have encouraged an easing of craft restrictions on labour, and there may even have been a little extra encouragement to women as well as men. The most conspicuous case of an active merchant widow, Marion Kent (d.1500) is from this period: after her husband's death in 1468 she traded on her own account and even sat on the council of the mercers' guild in 1474–5. A little later (1490), a female merchant was made a freeman by inheritance, having been trained by her father. These may have been highly untypical, but before long there was certainly a council policy of easing labour restrictions, if presumably mostly for men. From 1519 freemen were allowed to take as many apprentices, journeymen, and servants as they wished, overriding the restrictions in some craft ordinances, a policy which remained in force for forty years.[46]

Admittedly, despite this considerable decline in numbers of freemen, there was little change in the proportions entering different craft groups (Table 7.1).

Though textile manufacturing was in decline, the proportion of freemen involved in textile crafts (28 per cent at their peak in the later fourteenth century) held steady at around 20 per cent between 1400 and 1550. The decline of the other pillar of medieval prosperity, long-distance trade, admittedly, was reflected in the figures: the commercial sector did shrink from 15 per cent of all freemen in 1400–50 to 11 per cent between 1450 and 1550. Even so, merchants (including mercers and chapmen) remained the largest single occupation, with 310 admitted in 1450–1500 and 262 in 1500–50.

45. Averages from R. B. Dobson, 'Admissions to the freedom of the city of York in the later Middle Ages', *Econ HR*, 2nd ser., 26 (1973), 1–22; decadal totals are in Bartlett, 'Expansion and decline', 22. Proportion of non-native freemen: Palliser, *Towns and Local Communities*, XI, 113.
46. P. J. P. Goldberg, 'Women in trade and industry in York', *ODNB*, 60, p. 53; D. M. Palliser, 'The York freemen's register 1273–1540: Amendments and additions', *YH*, 12 (1995), 26; *YCR*, III, 68; Palliser, *Tudor York*, 212.

Table 7.1. Freemen admissions grouped by crafts 1450–1550[47]

Craft Group	1450/1–1509/10		1510/11–1549/50	
	Total	% of known occupations	Total	% of known occupations
Textiles	799	21	452	20
Provisions	621	17	467	21
Commerce and shipping	428	11	245	11
Leather	475	13	287	13
Building	243	7	190	8
Metal	380	10	252	12
Miscellaneous	787	21	330	15
Not recorded	353	–	31	–
TOTALS	4,086	–	2,254	–

The most striking change was a doubling of the proportion of freemen involved in providing foodstuffs, drink, and accommodation in inns over the later Middle Ages, from 11 per cent in 1350–1400 to 21 per cent in 1510–50, putting that group in first place, just ahead of textiles. Indeed, victuallers increased in numbers not only proportionately but absolutely, a sure sign that they must have had many customers in the hinterland and beyond, as well as in the city itself. Even so, the freemen's register may understate the numbers of victuallers more than those of other trades, given the ease of part-time employment in baking and brewing. Prosecutions for breaches of the assize of ale reveal at least 221 brewers and tapsters at work in 1450–1 and 247 in 1453–4, 'implying perhaps that ale was sold from about one household in every ten'. Most of those prosecuted were men, but wives of female servants must often have been doing the work. That was certainly what happened with baking by the 1530s, when many freemen's wives 'called tiplers' started baking white bread for sale. The freemen bakers protested, but the corporation allowed limited bread sales by the tiplers, whose products were clearly popular.[48]

A few manufacturing crafts continued to thrive even after 1450, suggesting a demand in city and region for increased domestic comforts. The tapiters

47. Miller, 'Medieval York', 86, 114–16, for figures from 1450–1510. I calculated decadal totals from 1500 in Palliser, *Tudor York*, 156–7, but using a different classification. For consistency, I have recalculated 1510–50 using Miller's classification. Chris Galley, *The Demography of Early Modern Towns: York in the Sixteenth and Seventeenth Centuries* (Liverpool, 1998), 34–5, 189–97, gives slightly different statistics to mine for 1500–49, but the discrepancies, as he says, result from 'a slightly different periodization and some grouping together of trades' (p. 36n.).

48. Heather Swanson, *Medieval Artisans* (Oxford, 1989), 21; Britnell, 'York under the Yorkists', 182; YCA, E22, fos 222–4.

(weavers of coverlets and domestic wall-hangings) accounted for fifty-five new freemen in 1450–1500 but 107 in 1500–50, and such hangings figure frequently in probate inventories. A rising demand for tableware caused a similar boom among pewterers, who by the early sixteenth century had almost a monopoly of northern pewter-making. Other specialized craftsmen with wide regional markets, at least until the Reformation, were church gla-ziers and carvers, as the careers of two non-merchant mayors illustrate. The glazier John Petty (d.1508) recorded in his will that he had done much work at Furness Abbey as well as York Minster and St Mary's, while the stone-carver Thomas Drawswerd (d.1529) undertook a major reredos at Newark (Notts.) and submitted an estimate for image work in Henry VII's chapel at Westmin-ster. Perhaps not surprisingly, he was York's richest taxpayer in 1524.[49]

   None of this, however, could compensate for the decline in cloth manu-facturing. Although the only statistical measures of that, the records of the aulnage (a tax on all cloth produced for sale), are not necessarily reliable, the broad trend for York was clearly downward. The best figures available suggest that 3,256 cloths were produced in the city in 1394–5, but only 2,288 by 1475–8. The decline was apparently brought about as clothmaking migrated from York to the smaller textile centres of the West Riding, where capital was more readily available, perhaps from prospering landowners and sheep farmers. In the 1460s and 1470s, for instance, Durham Priory shifted its large clothmaking orders from York to Halifax and Leeds.[50] It is not sur-prising, therefore, that the numbers of freemen enrolling in York's six main clothmaking crafts fell in nearly every decade from the 1440s to the 1520s. Admittedly, the numbers of tailors, who remained the second largest single occupation after the merchants, did not fall, but increasingly they had to source cloth made elsewhere. The stock of the tailor John Carter (1485) consisted almost wholly of 'southern' and 'western' cloth, the latter from Halifax, Craven, and Kendal; and soon 'Kendal men' were regularly bringing cloth to York for sale.[51]

49. Bartlett, 'Economy of York', 409, 438; Palliser, *Tudor York*, 162, 165, 172; J. H. Harvey, *English Medieval Architects* (Gloucester, 2nd edn 1984), 86–7; *HP 1509–58*, II, 54–5; C. Kightly, ' "The hangings about the hall": An overview of textile wall hangings in late medieval York', *Medieval Life*, no. 10 (York, 1998), 27–31.
50. Bartlett, 'Expansion and decline', 22; Palliser, *Tudor York*, 208–9; Swanson, *Medieval Artisans*, 29–30, 142–5; Jenny Kermode, *Medieval Merchants: York, Beverley and Hull in the Later Middle Ages* (Cambridge, 1998), 176, 317; John Munro, 'The symbiosis of towns and textiles', *Journal of Early Modern History*, 3 (1999), 68; M. Threlfall-Holmes, 'Newcastle trade and Durham Priory, 1460–1520', in C. D. Liddy and R. Britnell, eds, *North-East England in the Later Middle Ages* (Woodbridge, 2005), 141–52. The aulnage totals cited by Kermode are preferable to those which I cited in Palliser, *Tudor York*, 209.
51. *YCR*, II, 91; III, 32; AY 2/3, 648–52.

Much the same was true of York's overseas trade. Total trade through Hull, measured by customs accounts, fell in every decade from 1407–17 to 1457–67, stabilized and recovered for forty years, but then shrank again from 1507 to 1547. It is true that the share of York's merchants in the Hull totals cannot easily be separated out, but enough work has been done by Bartlett, Childs, and Kermode to show that York's share must have broadly reflected the Hull trend.[52] The city's trade with the rest of England, while not quantifiable like overseas commerce, must also have suffered. Clearly, it must always have had a minimum catchment area in its hinterland; in evidence on the Vicars' Leas in 1494–5, two men from satellite villages (Heworth and Huntington) testified to having come to York 'wekly' or 'every markid day' for over ten years. Further afield, however, competition from the West Riding towns was increasing. When the citizens acquired new chartered fairs in 1502, they were clearly hoping for men from Leeds, Bradford, Wakefield, and Halifax to bring cloth to them, but the fact that they had the fair grant proclaimed in twenty other Yorkshire market towns suggests a defensive attitude.[53]

The decline in York's share of overseas trade was, however, more serious: and a turning point, Pamela Nightingale has convincingly suggested, came in 1454, when the English garrison at Calais seized and sold all the wool in the town to recoup their unpaid wages. Yorkshire merchants were disproportionately hard hit because they had just exported much wool to Calais, 'whereas Londoners, possibly forewarned, had exported relatively little. So precarious had become the balance of cash and credit in the financing of York's trade that this loss undoubtedly explains why from 1455 wool exports from Hull plunged precipitately and never recovered.'[54] In any case, the balance of England's overseas trade was shifting in directions favourable to the Londoners rather than to ports further north, including Hull and Newcastle. For one thing, much east coast trade was with the Baltic, but the powerful Hanse towns—the so-called Hanseatic League—were restricting English trade with the Baltic, while there was open war between the Hanse and England between 1468 and 1474. Once the war was over, the Hanse merchants concentrated more and more Baltic trade through London; and London was also much better placed than the northern ports to dominate trade with the much more important overseas markets of Calais (for wool) and the Low Countries (for cloth).

52. Bartlett, 'Economy of York', 342–83; W. R. Childs, ed., *The Customs Accounts of Hull 1453–1490*, YASRS 144 (Leeds, 1986), *passim*; Kermode, *Medieval Merchants*, 263–75, 309–12.
53. YML, D & C Archives V, Box XII; *YCR*, II, 172, 175.
54. Pamela Nightingale, 'The rise and decline of medieval York: A reassessment', *P&P*, 206 (2010), 3–42 (quotation from p. 34).

York was also disadvantaged by the effects of the bullion famine of the 1440s, just when its merchants were trying to shift their export drive from wool to cloth. It was only when the Calais mint provided them with sufficient coin that they could invest more in cloth, although there was some relief in 1469–70 (the only year for which we have figures), when the revived York mint was able to strike 88 lb of gold and 1,312 lb of silver. Furthermore, when English coin production did increase substantially in the 1490s, London merchants, with more capital and credit than York's, were much better placed to increase their cloth exports.[55]

There was already a great and increasing concentration of English overseas cloth trade to the marts of Flanders and Brabant, a trade organized by the Company of Merchant Adventurers at the Netherlands end. That Company was gradually dominated by the London mercers, and in 1478 the merchants of York, Hull, Beverley, Scarborough, and other northern ports petitioned the royal council against the alleged abuse of that domination by the Company's governor, John Pykeryng. The complaint was at least partly disingenuous, since northern as well as London merchants benefited from the trade; and Edward IV merely ordered Pykeryng to treat the northerners more fairly. But the brute fact had become that cloth exports were increasingly channelled through London, in a trade dominated by Londoners.[56]

Increasingly marginalized in cloth exports, York's merchants turned instead between the 1470s and 1520s to trade in lead mined in the Pennines, much of which was shipped through York on its way to London or overseas. By 1505 merchants of London, Hull, Newcastle, Boston, and Lynn were having to pay charges at York's Common Crane on any cargoes of lead they bought; but increasingly York tried to take a cut in the actual sales by insisting that non-freemen could not sell directly to each other in York, but must deal through a freeman as intermediary. London merchants, however, obtained judgements in their favour in Star Chamber in 1519 and again in 1532, and York's brief attempt to use lead to compensate for declining cloth exports was over.[57]

55. Peter Spufford, *Money and its Use in Medieval Europe* (Cambridge, 1988), 356–62; Nightingale, 'Rise and decline of medieval York', 35–6.
56. Maud Sellers, ed., *The York Mercers and Merchant Adventurers 1356–1917*, SS 129 (1918), 75–80; A. F. Sutton, 'The Merchant Adventurers of England: The place of the Adventurers in York and the north in the late Middle Ages', *NH*, 46 (2009), 220–8.
57. W. Brown et al., eds, *Yorkshire Star Chamber Proceedings*, 4 vols, YASRS (Leeds, 1909–27), I, 151–5; III, 175–8; *YCR*, III, 17, 70–1, 75, 139; Palliser, *Tudor York*, 186–90; Kermode, *Medieval Merchants*, 273, 315, 318; Lewycky, 'Wolsey and the City of York', 48–9.

Altogether, York's overseas trade was now at a low ebb. Between 1350 and 1450 its merchants had handled at least half of Hull's trade, but by the early sixteenth century that proportion was down to one fifth. That is not incompatible with the continuing presence of a few very wealthy merchants, such as the three aldermen knighted by Henry VII—William Todd and Richard York in 1487 and John Gilliot junior in 1501. All held the offices of mayor and of governor of the mercers; all left wills revealing substantial wealth; and York and Gilliot were the last two citizens rich enough to found perpetual chantries. Nevertheless, these three, and a handful of others in York, were 'a tiny proportion of its inhabitants, and, compared with Londoners, were relatively poor'.[58]

Population and society

If the extent of economic decline is uncertain, so too is that of population shrinkage. There are simply no reliable yardsticks for English urban populations between the poll taxes of 1377–81 and the lay subsidies of the 1520s. The likelihood is, as we have seen, that York contained some 13–14,000 people in 1377, and even more by 1400, whereas by 1524–5 it was only some 7,000. When, therefore, the corporation told Henry VII that 'ther is not half the nombre of good men within your said citie as ther hath beene in tymes past,' they were probably right. They were also right to be alarmed: although the English population total continued to fall between 1377 and the late fifteenth century, it was seemingly nowhere near a halving.[59]

Nevertheless, none of this helps in assessing the chronology of shrinkage: if the city really had some 15,000 or more in 1400, what were the periods of rapid or gentle decline—and even temporary recovery—between then and the 1520s? Freemen's admissions, analysed by decades or by individual years, suggest a decline in most decades from about 1420, some recovery in the 1470s, and then renewed decline in every decade until the 1530s. Whether, however, these figures fairly reflect total population changes is questionable;

---

58. Bartlett, 'Economy of York', 148–95; Bartlett, 'Expansion and decline', 26, 31; W. R. Childs, 'Concentration, dependence and maritime activity...the case of Hull, Scarborough and their Yorkshire hinterlands', in D. J. Starkey and M. Hahn-Pedersen, eds, *Concentration and Dependency* (Esbjerg, 2002), 25; quotation: Nightingale, 'Rise and decline of medieval York', 36.

59. *YCR*, II, 9. 1524–5 estimate: Dyer, ' "Urban decline" in England', 275. National levels: Richard Smith, 'Plagues and peoples', in P. Slack and R. Ward, eds, *The Peopling of Britain* (Oxford, 2002), 181; M. Ormrod and P. Lindley, eds, *The Black Death in England* (Stamford, 1996), 28.

yet there is no alternative until parish registers begin.[60] Decadal averages smooth out what were often years of increasing numbers interspersed with heavy mortality, whether from famine or epidemic disease, which could more than wipe out the increase of many years. For the period before parish registration, the totals of wills proved in each year allow a rough index of the death rate. The population sample involved is confined to adults, mostly the more prosperous, and is heavily biased towards males. Nevertheless, any steep and sudden increase in wills proved is likely to represent, if anything, an even greater rise among the poor and vulnerable. Goldberg's figures from the York diocesan Exchequer Court, which are heavily weighted towards testators from the city of York, are therefore drawn upon here. I should add that I accept his assumption that the death of a testator (often unrecorded) was usually close in date to the probate of the will, rather than to the date of making it: most probate statistics therefore reflect actual deaths in the year concerned.[61]

1438 has already been noted as a year of harvest failure and 'pestylaunce' in York and the north. It produced the largest number of wills proved in the entire fifteenth century; and, significantly, it was followed by three years of high recruitment to the freedom of York. There followed two decades of relatively low totals before further bouts of high mortality in 1458–9 and 1466–8: the latter crisis may have been deeper and longer lasting than the figures suggest, as some years have incomplete probate records and 1470 is missing completely. There was certainly high mortality in 1471—the highest since 1438—followed by more in 1474, 1477, 1483, and 1484, accompanied or followed by higher numbers of freemen admitted. The 1470s will almost certainly have severely reduced the city's population. Epidemics continued to strike frequently, often in the same years as in London and other major towns, probably as the same disease (bubonic plague, judging from its seasonal pattern) spread through trading contacts. There was, for instance, high mortality in London, Norwich, and York in 1485–6, and at York alone in 1493, though neither produced record probate numbers at York. The first decade of the new century, however, brought several years with high numbers of wills proved, that of 1505 the worst in the city and diocese since 1438, with 1508 not far behind. At least twenty-four aldermen and city

60. Bartlett, 'Expansion and decline', 23; Dobson, 'Admissions to the freedom', 22; Palliser, *Tudor York*, 125–6.
61. P. J. P. Goldberg, 'Mortality and economic change in the diocese of York, 1390–1514', *NH*, 24 (1988), 38–55, supplemented by D. M. Palliser, 'Epidemics in Tudor York', *NH*, 8 (1973), 45–63.

councillors died between 1501 and 1510, more than in any other decade of the sixteenth century; and it was a disastrous period elsewhere, with epidemics in London, Chester, Exeter, Norwich, and Worcester.[62]

A decade of lower mortality was followed by a severe 'sickness' in 1520–2, when mayors died in office in two successive years, both in or after the peak plague month of July. It was probably widespread in the north; mortality at Durham Priory was the highest for a century, and it also coincided with outbreaks in London and Norwich. Then followed fifteen years of lower probate numbers before another severe summer epidemic in 1538, followed by above-average mortality in 1539–41; another respite, and then more epidemics in 1550–2 and 1558–9. Given this succession of blows, it is not surprising that the few early parish registers reveal no excess of baptisms over burials before the 1560s; and the corporation's claim in 1562 of York's 'evydent decaye and dymenishyng both of people and habitacions by the third part' may have been only too true.[63]

Nevertheless, immigrants continued to offset at least some of the 'natural deficit' between births and deaths. Some, doubtless, were escaping from bleak prospects in smaller towns or in the rural hinterland, and it was just this period—especially from about 1450 to 1520—which is now known to have been the worst for the so-called 'deserted medieval villages', central and eastern Yorkshire having one of the highest concentrations. Wharram Percy, for instance, still had sixteen households in 1458 but was virtually depopulated by 1517, and, nearer York, Steeton and Wilstrop disappeared around the 1480s as their lords evicted the few remaining tenants. It may be significant that deserted villages were also numerous in the hinterland of Coventry, another declining city anxious to bolster a dwindling population.[64]

There is no satisfactory source for the numbers and origins of York's immigrant population before the 1530s, but two types of evidence help. First, some citizens indicated their birthplaces in their enfranchisement or their wills. Of the aldermen, Sir Richard York, for instance, came (despite his name)

62. Goldberg, 'Mortality and economic change', 39, 42, 45–8; Paul Slack, *The Impact of Plague in Tudor and Stuart England* (Oxford, 1985), 60–1; Palliser, 'Epidemics in Tudor York', 46–7.

63. Palliser, 'Epidemics in Tudor York', 47–52; Palliser, *Tudor York*, 122–7; John Hatcher et al., 'Monastic mortality: Durham Priory, 1395–1529', *Econ HR*, 59 (2006), 676–7. 1562 complaint: *YCR*, VI, 33.

64. M. W. Beresford, 'The lost villages of Yorkshire', *YAJ*, 37 (1948–51), 474–91; 38 (1952–5), 44–70, 215–40, 280–309; M. Beresford and J. Hurst, *Wharram Percy Deserted Medieval Village* (London, 1990), 51, 101; Palliser, *Towns and Local Communities*, XIII, 18.

from Berwick-upon-Tweed, Robert Petty was from Urswick in Furness, as presumably was his brother John (who died in office as mayor in 1508); and John Besby hailed from Barrow-on-Humber (Lincs.). The cloth trade probably forged strong links across the Pennines: at least five Kendal men were enfranchised in the 1490s, all of them drapers, chapmen, or merchants. Secondly, as an unintended side effect of the intermittent Scottish wars, local hostility led to demands that Scots could not be made freemen, and those citizens from further north whose voices sounded Scottish could be targeted unless they proved English birth. Between 1477 and 1513 nearly thirty men had to do so by producing birth certificates from their home parishes, and most of them proved to have originated in the four border counties. One, Bertram Dawson from Bamburgh, must have found it especially humiliating, since when accused of alien birth he was already one of the Twenty-Four and about to be elected alderman. A late example of the same accusations occurred in 1530, when the tailor John Smyth had to prove that he was of Cumbrian birth. Strikingly, the four who gave sworn testimony to that—including the current master of the York tailors' guild—were all York residents but 'crystened all in oone font' at Abbey Holme like Smyth himself.[65]

A broader picture is possible at the very end of the period, with the survival of lists of the birthplaces of 361 freemen admitted between 1535 and 1566. The lists have already been published and analysed, and given their late date can be discussed very briefly. They show clearly that nearly three out of four were immigrants to York, and that of those one in three was from the immediate hinterland, within about 12 miles (20 km). Those from further afield fell into a clear pattern, coming much more from the north-west (the Yorkshire Dales and Cumbria) than from other directions. Four came from the continent, three of them French, though the most remarkable of the alien-born freemen of the period was admitted just a little earlier, in 1530. This was the Spanish-born goldsmith Martin Soza, who was naturalized in 1535 and prospered sufficiently to serve as sheriff in 1545–6 and to pay tax on £40 in goods that year, as much as five of the current aldermen. What brought him to York is nowhere recorded.[66]

The picture has so far been confined mostly to the freemen and the resident lay population; but, as before, York's society included more than traders,

65. James Raine, ed., *A Volume of Miscellanies* . . . , SS 85 (1888), 35–52; *YCR*, III, 130; Palliser, *Towns and Local Communities*, VIII, 185–6; XI, 111–12.
66. D. M. Palliser, 'Martin Soza—a Tudor Jewish convert?', in Edward Royle, ed., *Clifford's Tower Commemoration 1190–1990* (York, 1990), 56; Palliser, *Towns and Local Communities*, XI, 111–23.

craftspeople, and labourers. Quite apart from the ordinary clergy, whose living standards were often similar to their lay neighbours, there were groups of powerful and wealthy residents and regular visitors much less prominent in the city's records but nonetheless influential: rural gentry who kept up town houses; urban gentry who were resident; professional men who served Church and state in York as well as citizens—lawyers, notaries, clerks, surgeons, and others, now joined by printers and publishers; Crown agents in the castle; and the senior clergy of the cathedral and diocese, some of whom cut as grand a figure as any nobles or gentry.

The senior clergy, however humble their backgrounds, had sufficient wealth and status, down to the 1530s and beyond, to play a dominant part in city as well as diocese. When Archbishop Savage and the earl of Northumberland clashed at Fulford in 1504, Savage was en route to his palace at Cawood, accompanied by 140 horsemen; his behaviour towards the earl ('[I am] as good a gentleman as ye') sits uneasily with his lame excuses to the angry king: 'he was of litil substaunce but a poer gentylman and a yonger brother.' Brian Higden, dean of the cathedral from 1516 to 1539, was regularly escorted to the Minster on Christmas Day 'by 50 gentlemen before him in tawney coates garded with black velvet and 30 yemen behind him in like coates garded with taffata'.[67]

The earls of Northumberland were even grander figures, and their staff at Wressle Castle were frequent customers of York's traders. At the level of the greater county gentry, the Plumptons can be glimpsed in their links with York through their surviving correspondence. In 1477, for instance, (Sir) Robert Plumpton was in London, and sent home some broadcloth 'by Gretham of York', presumably a carrier; and for the peak period of the surviving letters, when Robert had inherited the estates (1480–1525), he probably maintained a house there: at least six letters from York were sent to him or his wife by family or servants. In 1490 the city corporation chose his illegitimate brother, another Robert, as their Common Clerk, while just before, when two aldermen were alleged to have slandered Sir Robert, Mayor Hancok was quick to investigate and apologize. With lesser gentry, however, the city fathers felt able to stand on their dignity, as we have seen with Sir William Conyers' insult to Alderman Metcalfe.[68]

67. Hoyle, 'The earl, the archbishop, and the Council', 246; Bodley, MS Dodsworth 125, fo. 104v.
68. Joan Kirby, ed., *The Plumpton Letters and Papers*, Camden Society 5th ser. 8 (London, 1996), p. 48 and nos 34, 65, 126–8, 150, 162, 173, 182, 207; *YHB*, II, 625; J. Taylor, 'The Plumpton letters, 1418–1552', *NH*, 10 (1975), 84.

Alongside the rural gentry were now men best described as urban gentry, especially younger sons and brothers of manorial lords. Citizens in the 1460s included Robert Crathorne, kinsman to a Cleveland family, who lived in the Pavement area and called himself variously gentleman and esquire, and Henry Salvan, esquire, brother of a knight and manorial lord. At the same period Brian Conyers, a younger son of Christopher Conyers of Hornby, combined lordship of the manor of Pinchinthorpe with a mercantile career in York and marriage to Alderman Neleson's daughter.[69]

Professional lawyers formed a pool of expertise for the city, archbishop, and diocese. The city's recorder and Common (town) Clerk were part of what Miller calls a new professional class, and both were often drawn from a group of interrelated gentry families. Recorders in the later fifteenth century included—apart from Miles Metcalfe, Gloucester's protégé—two members of the local Fairfax family, one of whom, William, became a Justice of the Common Pleas. Others were the long-serving Guy Roucliffe (1425–63), whose son was a baron of the Exchequer and whose grandson Brian Palmes was also recorder (1496–1509) as well as lord of the satellite manor of Naburn. Later, the office was long held by the Tankerds of Boroughbridge, Richard (1509–19) and William (1537–73), the latter brother-in-law to the equally long-serving Common Clerk Miles Newton (1519–50).[70]

By this period, too, there was more of a blurring of the traditional distinction between gentry and officeholders on the one hand, and civic merchants on the other. It was signalled at an honorific level from the 1490s, when the corporation minutes regularly referred to the mayor, aldermen, and recorder by the title of 'master', meaning gentleman, and from the 1530s when sheriffs and the Twenty-Four expected the same form of address. At a higher level, Henry VII created the first-ever civic knights, dubbing Mayor Todd and Alderman York in 1487 and Alderman Gilliot in 1501. Furthermore, although previous aldermen had held posts with Crown and Church, a handful now came to have positions more important than their civic duties. Nicholas Lancaster, merchant, Common Clerk, and then alderman, was one of Richard III's councillors, and the fact that he was mayor in 1485 may partly explain the corporation's strong support for the king that year. Richard York was a royal ambassador to the Hanse in 1491 and William

69. Miller, 'Medieval York', 109; R. E. Horrox, 'The urban gentry in the fifteenth century', in Thomson, ed., *Towns and Townspeople in the Fifteenth Century*, 27; Pollard, *North-Eastern England*, 104.
70. Miller, 'Medieval York', 74–5; Palliser, *Tudor York*, 74, 100. I owe the best list of pre-1500 recorders to the late P. M. Stell.

Wright master of Wolsey's archiepiscopal mint in the 1520s. More spectacular still were the careers of George Lawson and George Gayle, who both joined the aldermannic bench in the late 1520s. Though both served as mayor and MP, their real importance was elsewhere. Gayle (a goldsmith) was master of both York mints, royal and ecclesiastical, at various dates between 1526 and 1553, while Lawson held a string of Crown offices between 1514 and his death in 1543. Though he had a mansion in Lendal, he spent much time away from York, with military and financial responsibilities for Berwick-upon-Tweed and Tournai, and later helped to man the incipient Council of the North by 1526, and the revived Council by 1540; he was knighted at some time around 1531.[71]

Both men were, of course, far from typical even of the civic elite; surviving tax assessments for the city in 1524 and 1546 show just how untypical they were. In 1524 Lawson, not yet on the city council, was one of the three wealthiest taxpayers, worth £200 in goods, and that covered only his York home and not his others in Berwick and Wakefield; and when he died in 1543 he left an estate of over £7,500, £2,630 of it in York. Gayle came to wealth later than Lawson, but by 1546 he was taxed on 140 marks (£93 6s. 8d.) in lands and fees and in 1547 on 200 marks (£133 6s. 8d.). Both were at the apex of the 7,000 or so resident citizens and townspeople: but what of the rest of urban society? Here tax assessments are very helpful in providing nominal lists of so many, if only by assessed wealth and not by social status. That of 1524 was the most comprehensive, listing 874 individuals, and taking into its net all worth over £1 in goods or earning £1 or more in wages. The 1546 subsidy was more restricted, excluding wage-earners and those with goods of under £5, and it assessed only 355 taxpayers.[72]

In 1524 the three richest taxpayers owned one eighth of all goods assessed, while fifty-nine others were worth over £20 in goods; between them, these sixty-two accounted for half of the city's taxable wealth, excluding lands. At the other end of the scale, those worth under £10 accounted for 40 per cent of all taxpayers but only 26.5 per cent of the taxable goods, while wage-earners, with no taxable possessions, accounted for 38 per cent of those taxed. It is a picture of enormous inequality, but by no means exceptional. Wage-earners and those worth only £1 in goods formed an even higher proportion

71. Palliser, *Tudor York*, 44, 101 and n. 4; Gayle and Lawson: *HP 1509–1558*, II, 182–3, 500–2.
72. Palliser, *Tudor York*, 134–40; *HP 1509–1558*, II, 183, 502; TNA, E 179/217/92 [1524]; E 179/217/110 [1546].

of the taxed population in Exeter and Norwich. That may be, however, because prices and wages were generally lower in the north, so that more of York's wage-earners escaped the net by earning under £1 a year. The contrasts were less stark in 1546, because of the higher tax thresholds, but they show the same broad pattern. Those assessed on between £5 and £9 in goods were 36 per cent of all taxpayers but owned only 17 per cent of assessed goods, while those worth over £20 were 23 per cent of taxpayers but owned 55 per cent of the goods; and that does not include the thirty men assessed on lands and fees, not strictly comparable, whose richest member was George Gayle, who in 1553 could afford to spend £615 on a single purchase of ex-monastic property. With all this inequality, however, the city's taxpayers as a whole were clearly wealthier than those of the adjacent rural wapentake of the Ainsty, comparable figures for which have been calculated by Smith.[73]

Furthermore, there were great differences in the geographical as well as social distribution of wealth. The 1524 subsidy return shows a core of six parishes which paid on average over 40s. (£2) an acre, and adjoining them ten others paying over 10s.; between them, they covered most of the city centre. Flanking them, however, were parishes paying 10s. or less, which accounted for most of the parishes just inside and outside the walls. It was a long-term problem: in 1555 the corporation, pleading for a tax reduction from the Crown, claimed that seven outer parishes were so impoverished that an annual tax payment cost each taxpayer 'duble and treble more than theyr wholle yere rent'.[74]

The middling and poor of those parishes and elsewhere are inevitably less well recorded than the powerful and prosperous, though Goldberg's evidence from the ecclesiastical cause papers, drawn on in the previous chapter, continues to 1520. The York cases suggest to him a decline in the mid- to later fifteenth century in the immigration of unskilled and service labour, especially of women, and a shrinking of employment opportunities for single females as recession worsened. 'A woman's fulfilment came thus to be seen in terms of marriage and family', and he plausibly links such a changing norm to the surviving east window of Holy Trinity, Goodramgate, donated by its rector in the 1470s; unusually, the subjects include three biblical holy families with children. The reverse side of such a change would be the difficulty of providing for the dowries of poorer girls and the dangers of

73. Palliser, *Tudor York*, 136–8, 141.
74. D. M. Palliser, 'Some aspects of the social and economic history of York in the sixteenth century', DPhil thesis, University of Oxford (1968), 234–8 and map; *YCR*,V, 133.

poverty and prostitution. It may be significant that provision for such girls became more pronounced as works of charity. Alderman John Carre (1487) left £2 each to 'xv pore madyns well disposed to mariage', and the wealthy widow Joan Chamberlayn (1502) bequeathed funds from the sale of her home for 'pore maydens well dysposyd to mariages'.[75]

Prostitution remained an alternative for some women; but the corporation seems to have made more concerted efforts to ban or expel prostitutes after 1450, which would fit well with Goldberg's model. In 1482 they ordered 'common women' to move outside the walls, an order repeated in 1486. However ineffective, such orders were based on real complaints of nuisances: in 1483 large deputations from two adjoining Micklegate parishes came to the mayor to complain of Margery Gray, 'odirwys callyd Cherylipps', 'to whom ill dipossid men resortys, to the newsaunce of the neghbours'. Unfortunately, as so often in such cases, the result is not recorded.[76]

Goldberg suggests that as a result of economic contraction, women were increasingly forced to turn to service or marriage, that the age at marriage probably fell, and the marriage rate and birth rate probably increased. That may well be correct, though as he himself points out, it has to be 'an open debate' because of incomplete evidence before parish registration, that is, before December 1538, the start of the first surviving York register. There is, as we have seen, no clear evidence from those registers for a widespread excess of baptisms over burials until the 1560s. It may be that, unsurprisingly, richer families were enlarged in advance of the general population. Fifteenth-century mayors have been calculated to have had an average of only 1.09 sons alive when they made their wills, whereas a wider sample of alderman's wills between 1500 and 1550 produces 1.35 sons or 2.6 children.[77]

If York had any early surviving census, as does Coventry for 1523, household structure and size might be explored, together with the numbers of resident servants, as well as journeymen, apprentices, or others who might or might not live in. For it is clear enough that many children from poorer households served and boarded in the houses of the wealthy, a pattern evident in other towns and explicit at Coventry, where a 'householder' had a larger dwelling than a 'cottager':

75. Goldberg, *Women, Work and Life Cycle*, 155–6, 278, 299; P. E. S. Routh, 'A gift and its giver: John Walker and the east window of Holy Trinity, Goodramgate, York', *YAJ*, 58 (1986), 109–21.
76. *YHB*, I, 261; II, 466, 708, 723.
77. Goldberg, *Women, Work and Life Cycle*, 347, 350; Palliser, *Tudor York*, 97, 118; Henrietta Leyser, *Medieval Women* (London, 1995), 160.

> There was thus a fundamental division...between...those whose dwellings were deserted daily by the menfolk, and probably any others...who were old enough to go out to work; and...those homes where the inmates both lived and worked together with, in some cases, daily outside additions.

Thus in Coventry in 1523, a mean household size of 3.7 masks a range from 11.8 where the householder was worth over £100 in taxable goods to 2.8 for those too poor to be taxed. No such figures are possible for York, though a later survey (1574) found that labourers and their wives had on average only 1.1 children resident.[78]

The servant population shaded inevitably into the rootless, the footloose, the homeless, and the beggars, depending on the match between supply and demand, boom and recession. No early testimony survives as stark as that about Anne Godfray in 1576, but her type must have existed always: the wardens asked her 'dame' whether Anne had any goods, but were told that she had none but the clothes she wore. And she added that 'she is but my servant for a whyle, and I cannot tell when she will go away, for she will be here tonyght and away tomorowe.' It is not surprising that three testators between 1493 and 1511 left a farthing or a penny each to one thousand poor; and Alderman Neleson (1525) left a penny dole 'to every olde man and woman', which works out (if he calculated correctly) at 1,200 elderly poor alone.[79]

Some poor, like the last, would have been deemed too old to work, but others were able to but could not or would not find employment. This was an age, however, when national and local authorities were groping their way towards a policy over begging, distinguishing between what are often called the 'deserving' and 'undeserving' poor. In 1515 wardens were instructed to allow no one to beg 'that is myghty of body and not seke nor impotent [feeble]'. All beggars unable to work were to wear a token, and all others punished according to parliamentary statutes—though in fact that distinction was not made by statute until 1531. Yet the corporation continued to worry that beggars and the homeless were flocking in: in 1547 they ordered no new building for rent at under 6s. 8d. a year, 'for there is so many tenements within this citie of xx d and ii s farme by yere that vacabunds and beggars can not be avoyded'.[80]

---

78. Charles Phythian-Adams, *Desolation of a City: Coventry and the Urban Crisis of the Late Middle Ages* (Cambridge, 1979), 80–1, 241; Palliser, *Tudor York*, 118.
79. Palliser, *Tudor York*, 132, 144.
80. *YCR*, III, 46; IV, 149; Palliser, *Tudor York*, 81.

It is worth reflecting, nevertheless, that even in its darkest days, the city community never dissolved into chaos or anarchy, as the state and local authorities frequently feared might happen anywhere in England. Even in this relatively large city, with much mortality and population turnover, order was maintained. Something must be allowed to a strong corporate sense which bound incomers into a mutually supportive society, and something also, probably, to the Church's teachings and the message of the York Plays. The great inequality of status and income, moreover, was mitigated by the frequent failure of wealthy merchants' families in the male line, and by the downward mobility which pushed some into poverty and gave others a chance to rise. Such a rising man, for instance, was John Beane, the son of a capper, who became a freeman innholder in 1523–4 but that year was taxed only on wages of £1 a year. Yet he rose to be twice mayor and an alderman for a record forty years (1540–80), to acquire a rural manor, and to see his daughter Mary marry a landed gentleman from Westmorland, and thus to become an ancestor of the modern dukes of Northumberland.[81]

The urban context

The contrasts between mansions, 'houses', and 'cottages' are a reminder of a society with a huge range of wealth and poverty, of comfort and squalor, which was reflected in the whole urban environment and landscape. It was, for example, in 1472 that St William was translated to his new shrine and the whole cathedral reconsecrated to mark its completion, in the presence of five bishops, two dukes, and four earls: it therefore only achieved its present huge size fifty years before the Reformation, just when the city was in rapid decline. York's skyline was now dominated by the Minster's three towers, together with those of forty parish churches and of whatever large towers and spires crowned St Mary's, St Leonard's, Holy Trinity, and the other lost churches, along with Henry III's castle keep high on its Norman mound. Though two- and three-storeyed housing was more widespread than before, even their inhabitants must have felt dwarfed by the great buildings of Church and Crown. It was a point rubbed in when successive abbots of St Mary's from 1483 built a large new lodging for themselves just outside the city wall, or when a little later Archbishop

---

81. Robert Davies, *Walks Through the City of York* (London, 1880), 182–7; Palliser, *Tudor York*, 18, 94, 96, 107, 132; *HP 1509–1558*, I, 403–4. For a shrewd discussion of 'some factors limiting inequality' in York, see Bartlett, 'Economy of York', 258–63.

Rotherham doubled the size of his palace at Bishopthorpe, following the lead of the abbey and probably using the same craftsmen. Both were in the newly fashionable brick, with black vitrified patterns of the kind Wolsey was later to make fashionable in his Hampton Court.[82]

Brick, though it came early to Hull and Beverley from the Low Countries, took time in conservative York to become fashionable for citizens' houses. It was accepted for internal fireproof purposes—ovens, hearths, chimneys, and floors—but there is no record of a complete dwelling until about 1610, when a Micklegate house could be casually described as 'le read brick house'. Most substantial houses were still of timber, though the risk of fires had by 1450 ensured that most were roofed with brick tile rather than thatch; and 'wall tiles' or thin bricks were from about 1400 a common infill between timber uprights. True chimneys were still uncommon until the sixteenth century, with many upper rooms heated by braziers. A report of a riot in 1536 when gates on Knavesmire were burned mentions incidentally that the rioters had come 'for fyer' to a smith's house nearby: was it common for the poor to carry fire from house to house?[83]

There was, nevertheless, a huge range in the quality of domestic housing, with increasing space and comfort for wealthy merchants and urban gentry cheek-by-jowl with the poorly recorded hovels of the poor. Economic decay was compatible with the rebuilding of mansions on a larger scale, as a declining population allowed more space. Examples include the two adjacent houses rebuilt by Alderman Thornton in 1501 in North Street and Micklegate encroaching on to the street, with the showy feature of a projecting porch. In the next generation George Gayle must have built or rebuilt a grand house in the Bedern, judging from its fine Renaissance panels which are all that survive of it. None of this group of houses survives, but in Stonegate, of slightly earlier dates, there are still Mulberry Hall, a fine timbered mansion of about 1450, and nearby the reconstructed Barley Hall, which gives a good impression of what another mansion might have looked like in its heyday. Built as a monastic hospice around 1360, it may have been the house leased in 1466 to the goldsmith and future mayor William Snawsell.

82. Palliser, *Tudor York*, 32; John Hutchinson and D. M. Palliser, *York*, Bartholomew City Guides (Edinburgh, 1980), 149–50, 281.

83. Palliser, 'Some aspects of the social and economic history of York', 339, 363–5; Palliser, *Tudor York*, 32–3; *YCR*, IV, 3; *RCHMY* V, p. lxxiii. Cf. Sue Margeson, *Norwich Households*, East Anglian Archaeology 58 (Norwich, 1993), 87–8, 236.

If so, it was probably he who rebuilt its great hall and flanking residential wings, and it has been refurnished to look as it might have done in 1483, when Snawsell was one of the civic party welcoming Richard III. The facsimile textiles and other furnishings, many brightly coloured, give a vivid impression of the opulence expected by the civic elite. Even this richly furnished house does not seem to have had all its windows glazed, though by c.1510–20 domestic glass windows were becoming commoner.[84]

Some of the other mansions of the prosperous can be recaptured from their wills and inventories. John Colan, a goldsmith, certainly lived in Barley Hall, and in his inventory it was described as having a hall, parlour, kitchen, two chambers, and a workshop, furnished with woven and painted hangings, and a garden (1490). Later, a city councillor in the same parish, John Litster (1541), had a three-storey house of eight or nine rooms, while the Stonegate house of stationer Neville Mores (1538) was still larger, with at least ten rooms and a stable. There was a fireplace in one of his two parlours, and a chimney above it. A servant or servants lived in, for one chamber contained 'the madyns bedd'. Also among the larger properties must have been the numerous inns for travellers. When a royal visit was expected in 1537, the city council enumerated 1,035 beds in them and stabling for 1,711 horses, excluding the Minster Close and other ecclesiastical liberties, and also excluding lodgings available for their friends in the houses of the aldermen and merchants.[85]

The houses of the poor have left no trace either in surviving fabrics or in inventories, but it would not be surprising if many were of one, or at most two, small rooms. Even of those leaving a will and inventory, some were as modest: the carpenter Thomas Cok (1510) had only a hall and a 'bowtyng house': in the latter he slept and stored his tools. The smallest houses recorded in inventories were usually those of the poorer clergy. A chantry priest at St Saviour's (1547) and the last rector of St Helen-on-the-Walls (1551) each had only two rooms, hall and parlour. In both, the parlour served as a bedroom, while the cantarist at least used his hall as a kitchen.[86]

84. YCA, B 8, fos 113r, 121–3; *RCHMY* V, pp. lxxiii, 189, and plate 197; Britnell, ed., *Daily Life in the Late Middle Ages*, 177 and colour plate between pp. 90, 91; Charles Kightly, *Barley Hall, York* (York, 1999), 4; Jane Grenville, 'The urban landscape', in R. Marks and P. Williamson, eds., *Gothic: Art for England 1400–1547* (London, 2003), 255.
85. Palliser, *Tudor York*, 33–4. Colan: *TE*, IV, 56–60; *AY* 2/3, 664–7 (where '1440' should read '1490'). Mores: D. M. Palliser and D. G. Selwyn, 'The stock of a York stationer, 1538', *The Library*, 5th ser., 27 (1972), 210. Census of inns: Palliser, *Tudor York*, 166.
86. Palliser, *Tudor York*, 33.

As for the context of housing—the streets, lanes, quaysides, and public open spaces—they were beginning to be improved despite the economic decline. The city Staith (quay) and many streets were paved, and by the 1460s some pavement repairs were being paid for by the chamberlains. Admittedly, the paving seems to have consisted of cobbles or stones set in sand, and easily broken up by the ironbound wheels of carts; when the main streets were 'newe pavyd' in 1523–4 at the 'great costs and charges' of the householders, such carts were banned. There were also attempts to control the disposal of rubbish; to keep the streets cleaned, and even to require minimal street lighting: from November 1527 each alderman and councillor was supposed to have a lantern lit over his door from 5 to 9 p.m.[87]

The picture of York at this time is therefore a mixed one, and not perhaps as dire as the corporation regularly asserted in their pleas of poverty. Nevertheless, and especially after 1500, the wealth of some citizens and clergy coexisted with what can only be called dereliction in much of the city's housing stock. The corporation's repeated proclamations against immigrant vagabonds put it beyond doubt that a city in decline still attracted the desperate, hoping for shelter, work, charity, or theft. There was no shortage of decayed housing to rent cheaply or simply abandoned as the population declined; and the presence of wealthy churchmen, officials, and aristocrats assured some likelihood of alms.

Income from the properties of the Vicars Choral stabilized around 1500, but corporation rents continued to fall, as, probably, did those of many private landlords. The temptation must often have been to demolish empty houses to save the cost of repairs, since in 1524 the council ordered citizens to 'take downe no houses that stands towards the comon strete' without the mayor's permission. And in 1532 and 1533 they instructed their MPs to seek a private act of parliament allowing York to seize the sites of demolished houses if their owners refused to rebuild. They did not succeed at once, but it was clearly a problem in many towns, for in 1540 a public statute authorized such a policy in thirty-six named towns, including York, though it cannot be taken as evidence that all thirty-six were suffering decline.[88]

87. *VCH York*, 119; Palliser, *Tudor York*, 24, 27; Dobson, ed., *Chamberlains' Account Rolls*, 112–13, 128, 133, 164; Britnell, 'York under the Yorkists', 178.
88. Bartlett, 'Economy of York', 187; Palliser, *Tudor York*, 214–15; Palliser, *Towns and Local Communities*, XII, 118; Alan Dyer, *Decline and Growth in English Towns 1400–1640* (Basingstoke, 1991), 43–5; Robert Tittler, 'For the "re-edification of townes": The rebuilding statutes of Henry VIII', *Albion*, 22 (1990), 591–605.

Church and culture

Meanwhile the Church continued to be central to most aspects of civic life, private and public. It is all too easy to let the events and processes, usually grouped together as the English Reformation, cast a long shadow backwards, and to see the English Church as in need of radical reform. That view was still an orthodoxy when A. G. Dickens described the process of Reformation in the 1950s and 1960s, firstly at the level of the diocese of York and then for England as a whole; but it is now much questioned. For the Church in the city and diocese of York remained active and virtually unchallenged down to the 1520s and 1530s. It continued to command allegiance from the citizens—in some cases fervent allegiance—and to be active in charity, poor relief, education, and culture. In some areas deliberate destruction has obliterated much of the evidence, most notably for the religious houses and their libraries, and even for the cathedral itself. Only sixteen books are known to survive from its large library, where Leland lamented that 'now almost no good books are left'. Also destroyed was almost all the choral music from pre-Reformation York, though fragments of the so-called 'York Masses', composed between about 1490 and the 1520s, have been recently recovered: they confirm that 'York had a rich musical tradition, closely connected with developments elsewhere'.[89]

The Minster liberty was also an early centre of printing and publishing. A breviary for the Use of York, printed at Venice in 1493, was probably published at York, and between 1507 and 1535 at least ten other books printed elsewhere were published there. At some time before 1510 a York stationer, Gerard Wanseford, imported a large consignment of books from France, mostly service books but also 'alphabeta', sheets of paper or parchment with the alphabet and often the Lord's Prayer, suitable for elementary teaching. The consignment is known from evidence given in a court case after Wanseford's death by Ursyn Mylner; Mylner was, with Hugo Goes, one of two immigrants who actually printed books in the city during the brief period around 1509–16. Admittedly, there is little evidence for book printing in York for over a century after 1516; and equally, what evidence we have for book ownership does not suggest a city in the forefront of Renaissance

89. D. M. Palliser, *The Reformation in York 1534–1553*, BP 40 (York, 1979 reprint), 16; Eamon Duffy, *The Stripping of the Altars: Traditional Religion in England 1400–1580* (New Haven and London, 1992), 6; Lisa Colton, 'Choral music in York, 1400–1540', in P. S. Barnwell et al., eds, *Mass and Parish in Late Medieval England: The Use of York* (Reading, 2005), 47–56.

learning. The shop of the Stonegate stationer Neville Mores, appraised at his death in 1538, included 126 books, mostly theological, liturgical, and legal, and with seemingly none by contemporary scholars and humanists. On the other hand, the locally born Richard Oliver, rector of All Saints', North Street, who died in 1535, seems to have been moving into a different intellectual world, that of Christian humanism. He owned a copy of a recent bilingual Latin and Greek dictionary as well as Erasmus's *Adages* and the *Epistles* and *Offices* of the newly fashionable Cicero.[90]

Oliver's will suggests that he may have been educated at the Minster school of St Peter, and since there is no evidence that he attended Oxford or Cambridge, he may have learned his Latin there and perhaps some Greek. Both St Peter's and St Leonard's grammar schools seem to have functioned until 1539 for advanced schooling, with elementary and song schools in at least some of the parish churches. It is clear, at least, that a considerable (if unquantifiable) proportion of the laity could read, judging from frequent references to public notices; and there is explicit evidence in 1509 that the mayor and nine of the eleven aldermen present at a crucial council meeting could write. No doubt much education was at a basic level in English, though by 1556 there is startling evidence of some lay literacy in Latin, when a church court case reveals the ability of at least two laymen in one central parish, a baker and a scrivener, to correct their priest's Latin.[91]

Before the 1530s, there is almost no evidence for anticlerical feeling among the York laity, other than periodic disputes over the boundaries between civic and ecclesiastical jurisdictions—and even those were mild after the violence of the thirteenth and fourteenth centuries. The more than 800 citizens' wills which I have examined for the period 1501–46 suggest a laity conventionally pious, while church court records reveal almost no charges of heresy in York before 1528, in sharp contrast to London, Coventry, or even nearby Hull. As late as 1540, an unlucky Northumbrian visitor passed through a city churchyard

90. Elizabeth Brunskill, 'Missals, portifers and pyes: Early printing in York', in B. P. Johnson, ed., *The Ben Johnson Papers* (York, privately pr. 1975), II, 1–35; Palliser, *Tudor York*, 170; Palliser and Selwyn, 'The stock of a York stationer', 207–19; Claire Cross, 'York clerical piety and St. Peter's School on the eve of the Reformation', *YH*, 2 (1978), 17–20. Cf. Cross, 'York clergy and their books in the early sixteenth century', in C. Barron and J. Stratford, eds, *The Church and Learning in Late Medieval Society* (Donington, 2002), 344–54. Lisa Liddy has kindly drawn my attention to the inventory of John Warwycke, stationer, who in 1542 had a 'printing chamber' with a printing press.

91. Palliser, *Reformation in York*, 16; Palliser, *Tudor York*, 173–6; Palliser, *Towns and Local Communities*, III, 20; X, 101–3; Claire Cross, 'Lay literacy and clerical misconduct in a York parish during the reign of Mary Tudor', *YH*, 3 (1980), 10–15.

on St Mary Magdalen's eve: heard to call out that the saint was 'Mary hoore', he was promptly denounced to the archbishop's vicar general.[92]

That does not mean that there was not the occasional accusation against citizens over popular religious scepticism. Nor does it mean that alternative belief systems such as astrology or white witchcraft could not coexist with Christianity. The most startling case of that to come to light, in 1509–10, involved a York merchant, Thomas Jameson, consulting a wizard about recovering a runaway servant. He was diverted into conjuring a spirit to help him and others, including two priests, to track down a hidden chest of gold. When word got out, the group were sentenced to public penance in the church courts. It would not be fair, however, to assume that such practices were common: Jameson had hesitated to take part because 'there was grate rumor upon it as well at York as in the countrey'.[93]

Relations between city and cathedral were ambivalent. On the one hand, the corporation were keen to defend their jurisdictional rights along the boundary of the Minster liberty: when the sheriffs' sergeants drew blood at one of the Minster gates, and were ordered by the Minster treasurer to do public penance, the city council forbade them to comply; and when later the civic priests of St William's were summoned before the Vicar General, the mayor pointedly told them to attend 'bycause it were the kyng's cause and for non other cause'. That did not prevent the corporation from collectively attending special services in the Minster, or indeed from holding occasional council meetings inside it, 'behind St Christopher'. Yet it was not central to everyday piety, and though many citizens left a bequest to its fabric fund, it was usually a traditional 4*d*., far less than was often given to parish churches and friaries. It was, indeed, the friaries which remained popular until their dissolution in 1538. It was common for the corporation to arrange for annual prayers and for craft guilds to attend masses 'within one of the frears', and the city council turned to local friars to preach before them in 1535 and 1538, while as late as 1535 one alderman, John Besby, chose burial in the Greyfriars rather than in his parish church. Most telling of all, the proportion of city testators

92. A. G. Dickens, *Lollards and Protestants in the Diocese of York 1509–1558* (Oxford, 1959), 17, 18, 21, 30–7, 50, 247; J. A. F. Thomson, *The Later Lollards 1414–1520* (Oxford, 1965), 195–200; Palliser, *Reformation in York*, 32; Palliser, *Tudor York*, 233, 249–52.
93. James Raine, ed., 'Proceedings connected with a remarkable charge of sorcery', *Archaeological Journal*, 16 (1859), 79–81; Palliser, *Tudor York*, 233.

leaving bequests to the four friaries between 1531 and 1538 (41 per cent) was higher than ever before.[94]

Most lay testators, unlike Besby, asked for burial in their own parish church or churchyard, and it was that church which had first claim on their loyalty and affection. In a poverty-stricken city, some churches were falling into disrepair—St John's, Hungate, was effectively disused by 1534—but those in rich parishes continued to be refurbished or even enlarged: the tower of All Saints, Pavement, was crowned by an octagonal lantern which looks like a modest copy of that on the Cloth Hall at Bruges of 1482. And one church notoriously in decay, St Michael-le-Belfrey, was handsomely rebuilt by the Minster dean and chapter between 1525 and 1537, and sets of new windows were donated by wealthy parishioners, including the Spanish-born Martin Soza. There is no sign, from the payments to the active team of craftsmen involved, that this was to be the end of a tradition—indeed, one of the very last parish churches to be rebuilt in England for over a century.[95]

The number of endowed prayers and requests for masses meant that there was a constant round of services in most churches. If some chantries were amalgamated from the 1470s, and the endowment of new chantries by citizens ceased after 1509, this reflects a diminution in prosperity rather than piety; certainly obits and funeral masses continued in demand. Each parish priest was expected to read out regularly a bede roll, reminding the congregation of benefactors to be prayed for, a practice which must have impressed itself on the hearers. Agnes Maners left nine houses to St Margaret's parish around 1500; and witnesses as late as 1585 remembered her name from the bede roll still being recited under Henry VIII and Mary I. And there was much use of the churches for private prayer as well as services and parochial meetings. A complaint about the leaking roof of the old Belfrey church in 1510 had noted its deterrent effect on parishioners who 'daily abydes longe in the church and loves to say thar devocions'.[96]

The best picture of parish life comes from the recently rediscovered churchwardens' accounts for the riverside parish of St Michael, Spurriergate,

94. *YCR*, II, 61; III, 40; Palliser, *Reformation in York*, 2, 3; Palliser, *Tudor York*, 227–8; Michael Robson, 'Benefactors of the Greyfriars in York...', *NH*, 38 (2001), 221–39; Robson, 'The Grey Friars in York, *c.* 1450–1530', in J. G. Clark, ed., *The Religious Orders in Pre-Reformation England* (Woodbridge, 2002), 109–21.
95. Angelo Raine, *Mediaeval York* (London, 1955), 37–40, 84; D. M. Palliser, 'The unions of parishes at York', *YAJ*, 46 (1974), 87, 97; *RCHMY* V, lii, 36–9.
96. TNA, E 178/2661; Raine, ed., *Fabric Rolls of York Minster*, 262; Palliser, *Tudor York*, 206, 228.

almost the only such consecutive accounts to survive from the north of England before the Reformation. Beginning in 1518, they furnish a mass of factual detail on parishioners, workmen, and parish properties as well as the church itself. Among other unexpected records is the continuing acquisition of houses for rent by this prosperous parish; its estate reached its greatest extent after 1508, with a portfolio of over thirty houses, accounting for most of the church's yearly income. The accounts are, however, an even more important source for the functioning of the church before the 1540s, and the changes made necessary by the first phase of the Reformation, though this has to be teased out of the dry financial entries. The account books have none of the committed statements which accompanied the documented changes in nearby Adwick-le-Street or in distant Morebath.[97]

St Michael's was crowded with the apparatus of parochial devotion: it possessed at least nine altars, ten images or statues, and a full complement of stained-glass windows. It is clear that the rector and wardens of St Michael's continued with the traditional liturgy, furnishings, and ornaments as long as they could. New wall paintings were added—St Christopher in 1527 and the devil in 1533—and a window with the Tree of Jesse was repaired in 1533 also. New organs were installed in 1536 and 1542; and obits continued to be observed until the last year of the surviving accounts, 1548. There is no mention of substantial changes to worship until Edward VI acceded in 1547, when 'the seyntes was takyn down' and locked away, the roods and altars also; the 'tabylles and images' were also removed, as was the mechanism for moving the Lenten veil. It all smacks of minimal compliance, ready for restoration if official policy were to change.[98]

The devotional life of the laity, therefore, still centred round their parish churches, except on some major festivals. The feast and morrow of Corpus Christi, with their play cycle and civic procession, continued as before, as did the other civic plays of the Creed and the Paternoster. It is clear that the York Plays continued to be amended and revised, becoming so central to the citizens that from 1476, remarkably, they regularly took precedence over

97. C. C. Webb, ed., *Churchwardens' Accounts of St Michael, Spurriergate, York, 1518–1548*, 2 vols, with continuous pagination, BTC 20 (York, 1997). For two very different ways of 'fleshing out' the dry accounts, see E. Brunskill, 'Two hundred years of parish life in York', *YAYAS AR* (1950–1), 17–58; C. Cross, 'A priest and his parish', in Barnwell et al., eds, *Mass and Parish in Late Medieval England*, 89–107. Adwick: A. G. Dickens, 'Robert Parkyn's narrative of the Reformation', *EHR*, 62 (1947), 58–83. Morebath: Eamon Duffy, *The Voices of Morebath* (New Haven and London, 2001).

98. Webb, ed., *Churchwardens' Accounts*, 7, 123, 154–5, 316–17, 331.

the Church's liturgical procession, which was deferred until the next day. Beadle has now provided evidence that the consolidated Register of the Play text was compiled in about 1476–7, probably by the newly appointed Common Clerk Nicholas Lancaster, and perhaps at the request of Lancaster's patron Richard of Gloucester.[99] The Plays must have successfully entertained or instructed enough citizens to continue for so long through good and bad times in financial terms. From at least 1485 changes were made to the roster of crafts assigned to perform particular pageants, as some became too small or poor to continue, but there was no suggestion made, even in the depths of the civic financial crisis, that the cycle should be abandoned.

The mid-century crisis

Before that, however, this conservative city had to endure four decades of radical change, economic and political as well as religious. It is impossible to date precisely the 'end' of medieval York, but the 1530s and 1540s have a better claim than most. They were the decades which saw what Charles Phythian-Adams, in his fine study of an equally hard-hit city, has called 'medieval mirrors shattered'.[100]

It had been in 1528–9 that the desperate city had threatened to surrender its charters to the Crown if its financial plight, especially its inability to meet the earl of Rutland's demands for £100 a year, could not be alleviated. Yet in October and November 1529 matters became worse under a combination of local and national crises. Thomas Wolsey, the city's powerful patron, was dismissed as lord chancellor in October just as parliament was about to meet, and one of that parliament's first acts was to repeal the citizens' monopoly of wool and fells exports which Wolsey had secured for them. At the same time five junior city councillors stirred up a revolt of 400 York commoners against the mayor over financial burdens; the duke of Richmond's council had to intervene to support the mayor's authority. In 1531 the city again threatened to surrender their liberties if their fee farm and other charges were not reduced, and in 1532 they mounted a serious campaign for government support, aided by the new chief minister, Thomas Cromwell, who apparently promised to be a 'good maister' to 'the power city'. Although Rutland's claim was not yet settled, Cromwell did help

99. Richard Beadle, 'Nicholas Lancaster, Richard of Gloucester and the York Corpus Christi Play', in M. Rogerson, ed., *The York Mystery Plays: Performance in the City* (Woodbridge, 2011), 31–52.
100. Phythian-Adams, *Desolation of a City*, 275–8; cf. Palliser, *Towns and Local Communities*, X, 115.

between 1532 and 1534 over legislation and litigation to improve navigation of the Ouse and Humber for the benefit of Hull and York.[101]

Meanwhile matters of concern well beyond York were coming to a head. In May 1534 the Convocation of the Province of York, meeting in the Minster chapter house, renounced the authority of the pope and accepted royal supremacy over the Church. The change was starkly underlined less than a month later, when the king's antiquary, John Leland, visited York. He was accompanied by Sir George Lawson, who in his double role as city alderman and Crown official seems to have been instrumental in getting Cromwell's support for the city. Leland noticed on display in the Minster the 'tables' of the Vicars Choral with their short histories of England and the Minster, and when he found a record of King John's submission to the pope, Lawson cut out the offending line and sent it to Cromwell: the tables survive and the mutilation is still visible.[102]

For the moment, the citizens were less concerned with such matters—the apparatus of the Church as it affected them remained intact—than with civic disorder and finances. A complex feud between aldermen over the Guild of SS Christopher and George, involving allegations of corruption, led to intervention by Chancery, Star Chamber, and the Council in the North in 1533–4, and was probably at bottom connected with the city's financial burdens. Fortunately for York, its MPs were able at last to secure a comprehensive settlement of the fee farm and other financial issues with the aid of Cromwell and Lord Chancellor Audley. For in the final session of the Reformation Parliament (February to April 1536) an act was passed which reduced the annual payment to Rutland to £40—still much more than the £13 6s. 8d. they had paid Lovell, but far short of the £100 Rutland had been demanding. The complicated settlement did reduce the expenditure of the city chamber, and though it did not effectively cut the sheriffs' financial burdens, it put a limit on them. The city was also discharged of its payments to seven chantries and three obits, which were thereby effectively dissolved, saving a further £32 a year. The statute ended a long period of uncertainty in York's affairs, and the corporation warmly thanked Cromwell on 1 June for his 'grete paynes', so much so that 'bothe wee and the chylde that is ungottyn shall have cause to pray for you for ever.'[103]

101. YCR, III, 120–8; Palliser, Tudor York, 48; Hoyle, 'Urban decay and civic lobbying', 97–101.
102. Letters & Papers of Henry VIII, VII, App. no. 23; YCR, III, 139; Palliser, Reformation in York, 4, 5.
103. Statutes of the Realm, III, 582–4; A. G. Dickens, 'A municipal dissolution of chantries at York, 1536', YAJ, 36 (1944–7), 164–73; Palliser, Reformation in York, 4; Palliser, Tudor York, 48–9; Hoyle, 'Urban decay', 85, 101–3, 108.

The relief came just in time before city, minister, and king had other urgent priorities. For that parliamentary session which passed York's act also decided that monastic houses worth less than £200 a year might be suppressed by the Crown, an action which proved very unpopular in some regions, including much of the north. Initially, however, it passed off peacefully. Of the three York priories affected, St Andrew's was spared; but Holy Trinity and St Clement's were leased to two friends of Lawson's, Leonard Beckwith and William Maunsell, who were, like him, northern officials of the Crown, and the monks and nuns were ejected.[104]

York was already restive that summer for reasons financial rather than religious, despite the parliamentary concessions: there were serious riots in May when the corporation tried to enclose the common 'stray' or pasture of Knavesmire to help the city's finances. Nevertheless, there are signs that religious discontent was also present. In August a play of St Thomas put on by certain 'papists' provoked a 'seditious rising', and in September words were exchanged in the Merchants' Hall hinting at aldermen hostile to the Crown's religious policy. Then a widespread series of northern rebellions—the self-styled Pilgrimage of Grace—broke out in early October; the York 'commons' rose in sympathy with them, and the rebel forces were admitted within the walls between the 16th and the 20th. Thus was York again thrust centre stage into a national crisis, the most serious revolt faced by the Crown in the sixteenth century.[105]

The Pilgrimage has been much studied and its causes endlessly debated. The traditional view that it was primarily a religious revolt, almost a crusade—as its leaders said—was attacked by Dickens, who used York and Yorkshire evidence to stress social and economic grievances; but it seems likely that the Pilgrimage was indeed primarily, as George Bernard puts it, 'a critique of the Henrician Reformation', especially in its hostility to monastic suppressions. The Pilgrims' 'Grand Captain', Robert Aske of Aughton near York, was received at the Minster by 'the whole quire of the cathedral church'. He then ordered the dispossessed religious to be allowed back into their houses, an order clearly obeyed with both Holy Trinity and

104. Palliser, *Reformation in York*, 6.
105. *YCR*, IV, 1–3; Palliser, *Reformation in York*, 7–11; Palliser, *Tudor York*, 49, 50. Much new research has been done on the Pilgrimage since the accounts just mentioned: see esp. C. S. L. Davies, 'Popular religion and the Pilgrimage of Grace', in A. Fletcher and J. Stevenson, eds, *Order and Disorder in Early Modern England* (Cambridge, 1985), 58–91; M. L. Bush, *The Pilgrimage of Grace* (Manchester, 1996); R. W. Hoyle, *The Pilgrimage of Grace and the Politics of the 1530s* (Oxford, 2001); G. W. Bernard, *The King's Reformation* (London, 2005), 293–404.

St Clement's, and indeed with at least fourteen of the other fifty-one northern monastic houses which had been suppressed.[106]

Since rebellions entailed great risks, it is not surprising that the city council tried to leave no evidence of their involvement. Their minute book 13 has no entries at all for October 1536; the next entry refers obliquely to 'discencion' in York and an entry for 8 November breaks off abruptly, while on 23 November an entry about a deputation to join the Pilgrim army at Doncaster to negotiate with the Duke of Norfolk is even more curious. The start of the minute is in regular form, but the crucial entry about the deputation is written in a large, semi-literate scrawl, the same hand adding the sheriffs' names to the attendance list. It is as if the mayor vacated the chair to one of the sheriffs, who took over the meeting.[107]

The rebel army did indeed meet Norfolk's royal army at Doncaster, where they were tricked into surrender; and it was largely statements and confessions after the revolts were over that show something of what had happened in York between October and December. A great rebel council was held somewhere in the city between 21 and 25 November, when the clergy were asked for their advice before the negotiations with Norfolk; and there was clearly a group of leading sympathizers on the city council, probably including Lawson himself. Robert Aske lodged at Lawson's house in Lendal, adjacent to the Austin friary, whose prior John Aske (possibly a relative) was also sympathetic. John Pickering, prior of the York Dominicans, was even more active and was regarded by Henry VIII as one of the worst offenders: he wrote a ballad to encourage the Pilgrims, which was 'almost in every man's mouth'. Not all the city, however, supported the revolt: a poem written in 1537 by Wilfrid Holme, a loyalist gentleman of Huntington near York, identified the mayor as one who would have resisted the rebels had he been sure of support from the city's 'commons'.[108]

Once the rebellions were over, those implicated were concerned to show loyalty during the smaller revolts of early 1537, and there is no evidence that York was involved in those. Nevertheless, the king made them an excuse to punish leaders of the first risings, and to cancel the promise he had made to the rebels to hold a parliament in York. Pickering was hanged at Tyburn and

---

106. Palliser, *Reformation in York*, 9–11; Palliser, *Tudor York*, 50; Bernard, *The King's Reformation*, 327, 334, 345–6, 404.

107. YCA, B 13, fos 79v, 80r, only partly pr. in *YCR*, IV, 15, 16.

108. Dickens, *Lollards and Protestants*, 118; Palliser, *Reformation in York*, 8–11; Bernard, *The King's Reformation*, 334.

several northern monks and laymen in York: Aske himself was hanged at the castle on 12 July, a market day, Henry having fixed on York as the place where Aske had been 'in his greatest and most frantic glory'. The only oddity was that the monks of Holy Trinity remained in possession and unmolested until December 1538, even though the Crown chose to call it 'lately suppressed' and to grant away some of its lands.[109]

Henry considered visiting the north in the summer of 1537, to demonstrate his power and his clemency, but in the event he postponed it until 1541. He did, however, persist with further monastic dissolutions, perhaps all the more determinedly after his fury over the rebels' demands. Only St Clement's had gone in 1536, but in November 1538 St Andrew's and the four friaries were persuaded to surrender their houses to the Crown, followed by Holy Trinity in December 1538, St Mary's in November 1539, and St Leonard's on 1 December: in a little over a year all York's medieval religious houses were gone. The consequences included the dispossession of sixty-one monks, four canons, at least sixty-one friars, and the staff of St Leonard's Hospital, as well as the nine nuns of St Clement's: some 150 men and women in all, excluding servants. All but the friars were given pensions, and a considerable number of the monks and friars found other posts within the Church in York or elsewhere. That, however, takes no account of the effect on the citizens as the dissolved churches were sold off and demolished, the endowed prayers for the dead ended, and the furnishings removed or destroyed, even recent tombs; there is no record that Alderman Besby's Greyfriars tomb of 1535, or any others, were spared.[110]

More positively, the shock of the rebellions had at last persuaded the king and his ministers of the urgent need for more effective government of the north to replace the duke of Richmond's council. In 1537 a more powerful King's Council in the North was established, and from 1538 to 1549 its president was Bishop Robert Holgate, who became archbishop of York in January 1545 and who provided firm government. One initial problem was to find a suitable residence for him and his officials, a problem solved when St Mary's was suppressed, and the abbot's house transformed and extended from 1539–40 into the Council's headquarters under the name of the King's

---

109. Palliser, *Reformation in York*, 11.
110. Palliser, *Reformation in York*, 12 and n.; Palliser, *Tudor York*, 236. Since I listed examples of dispossessed religious in *Reformation in York*, 12–14, a thorough survey of the evidence has been published: Claire Cross and Noreen Vickers, *Monks, Friars and Nuns in Sixteenth-Century Yorkshire*, YASRS 150 (Leeds, 1998).

Manor. The Council seems to have succeeded in keeping the north peaceful, largely because of Holgate's firm leadership.[111]

The city fathers must have been preoccupied in the late 1530s by more local matters than the King's Council. There was continued friction over civic finance for some time after the 1536 settlement, five of the ex-chamberlains being imprisoned in 1537 for not settling their end-of-year debt. Then followed an outbreak of 'pestyllence' in the summer of 1538, which—probate figures suggest—was the worst epidemic for thirty years. Then there were the enormous repercussions of the monastic dissolutions of 1538–9, though those were not discussed on record by the city council, still cowed after the crushing of rebellion. As with the Pilgrimage, the city fathers felt it prudent to turn a blind eye, and there is not even a mention in their minute books until December 1541. By then they had apparently retained as an adviser Leonard Beckwith—receiver of the augmentations (suppressed monastic houses) in Yorkshire.[112]

Just before that, in September 1541, Henry VIII made his one and only northern progress, to seal the pacification of the north after the Pilgrimage, and this may also be taken as a seal on the end of medieval, Church-dominated York: the king underlined the point by staying at the former house of the abbot of St Mary's. It proved to be a satisfactory visit for him in political terms, with a grovelling submission by the recorder on behalf of the mayor, aldermen, and commons for their part in a 'traterous rebellyon'. £140 was presented to the king and queen (in two gold cups worth £10 each), a sum successfully raised in part by a local tax and in part through donations from 'substanyall' citizens. More money was found for pageants and ceremonies, and the mayor, recorder, aldermen, and Twenty-Four all paid individually for violet gowns for the occasion. Somehow, the considerable costs were all met.[113]

Nevertheless, the city continued to lose some of its assets as a result of royal policies. The shrines of St William and 'St' Richard had apparently been dismantled already and their jewels and precious metals confiscated: now,

111. A. G. Dickens, *Robert Holgate*, BP 8 (York, 1955); Palliser, *Tudor York*, 50–1; Norton, 'The King's Manor', in Pevsner and Neave, *Yorkshire: York and the East Riding*, 186.

112. YCA, B 15, fo. 65r; *YCR*, IV, 18–24, 30; Palliser, 'Epidemics in Tudor York', 48–9; Palliser, *Tudor York*, 235–6.

113. *YCR*, IV, 54–70; J. J. Scarisbrick, *Henry VIII* (London, 1968), 427–8; Palliser, *Tudor York*, 50; R. W. Hoyle and J. B. Ramsdale, 'The royal progress of 1541, the North of England, and Anglo-Scottish relations, 1534–1542', *NH*, 41 (2004), 240–65; C. J. Sansom, 'The Wakefield conspiracy of 1541 and Henry VIII's progress to the north reconsidered', *NH*, 45 (2008), 217–38; T. Thornton, 'Henry VIII's progress through Yorkshire in 1541 . . .', *NH*, 46 (2009), 231–44.

during the royal visit, the Privy Council ordered the same treatment for the reliquary containing St William's head. This of course entailed an end to pilgrimages to both shrines and to the valuable offerings there. An inventory of 1509–10 gives some idea of the wealth of the ornaments confiscated. That confiscation could be and was justified as an attack on superstition; the same could not be said of the fate of York's two grammar schools, one or both of which seem to have been closed—if not deliberately—as part of the monastic dissolutions. In 1535 one had been housed in St Leonard's Hospital, and that certainly vanished; that of the Minster seems to have relied on its poor scholars boarding at St Mary's, and though documentation is lacking, it may have had to close too. Fortunately, Archbishop Holgate founded a new grammar school in 1546, while the cathedral school of St Peter was officially refounded in 1557, though not effectively until after 1565.[114]

Furthermore, a second dissolution of ecclesiastical institutions was planned in 1545 and implemented under Edward VI in 1548. This time, the target was 'all chauntries, hospitalls, colleges, free chappells, fraternyties, brotherhedds, guyldes, and sallaries of stipendarie priests' in England and Wales. The confiscations had a particularly severe impact in a city with so many such institutions as York. Not only did the hundred or more chantries vanish, with all the cycle of prayers for the dead they had commemorated, but also the great civic guilds of Corpus Christi and SS Christopher and George, despite protests by the corporation. So too did the smaller and poorer parish guilds, which can have brought the Crown little money, but which probably made a grievous rent in the fabric of their parochial communities. There were also threats to the very existence of craft and trading bodies with an overt religious aspect. The Merchants' hospital was listed as to be dissolved under the statute of 1545, and though it continued to function, the company had difficulties over a Crown claim to ownership of their Hall until 1587. The tailors saw their fraternity of St John the Baptist dissolved, though their hall was not threatened.[115]

In the midst of these dissolutions, the City Council staged one of their own. They had already used the parliamentary statute endorsing their fee

114. D. M. Palliser, *The Reformation in York 1534–1553*, BP 40 (York, 1971), 16–18; Christopher Wilson, *The Shrines of St William of York* (York, 1977), 10. R. N. Swanson, ed., *Catholic England* (Manchester, 1993), re-edits the 1509–10 inventory.

115. William Page, ed., *The Certificates of the Commissioners appointed to Survey the Chantries . . . in the County of York*, SS 91, 92 (1894–5), 76; Palliser, *Tudor York*, 239–40; D. M. Palliser, *A Brief History of the Company of Merchant Adventurers* (York, 2008), 7, 8; R. B. Dobson and D. M. Smith, eds, *The Merchant Taylors of York*, BTS 33 (York, 2006), 44–5.

farm settlement of 1536 to dissolve some city chantries; now, in 1548, they obtained a local act allowing them to close some of their poorer parish churches, subject to the archbishop's consent (see Map 6 in Chapter 6). Though the closures were not finally ratified until 1586, it is clear that one in three of York's churches were actually closed—and in most cases demolished—in 1548–9. Here was one area where a doctrinally conservative corporation had hard economic motives for a local dissolution, and one benefiting citizens rather than the Crown. It should be added, however, that six of the churches, originally to be sold for good prices, were instead sold at knock-down prices to the mayor personally, to four fellow aldermen, and to the Common Clerk. One of them, Alderman Richard Goldthorpe, had already bought or leased the sites of two of York's suppressed priories, St Andrew's and St Clement's.[116]

More important still, at least in financial terms, was the massive change of property ownership entailed. There were probably fewer than 2,000 houses in York, of which before the 1530s over half belonged to the cathedral, the religious houses, the parish churches and the chantries. Those seized by the king were quickly sold. The London mercer and financier Sir Richard Gresham, for instance, who had already invested tens of thousands of pounds buying monastic properties to resell at a profit (including Fountains Abbey) bought 464 ex-monastic houses in York in 1545. In 1549 about 150 more houses, formerly funding chantries, were sold to two government officials, Matthew White and Edward Bury, both of them murdered within two months by rebels furious at the chantry dissolutions. Much city money must have drained away in rents to non-resident landlords, at least for a time, though the city corporation succeeded in buying en bloc the lands of the guild of SS Christopher and George in 1549, and in 1552 acquiring a lease of those of the Corpus Christi Guild.[117]

Such massive institutional and economic changes were clearly unpopular among many citizens. To follow their shifting beliefs would go beyond the scope of this book, and I have attempted it elsewhere. Suffice it to say that Dickens, who traced the early progress of Yorkshire Protestantism in masterly fashion, was in no doubt that York was well behind the tide. Of the five largest provincial cities, he notes, Protestantism appeared strong by 1558 in Norwich, Bristol, and Coventry, but not in York or Newcastle. At York, 'with

116. Palliser, *The Reformation in York*, 15, 21, 22; Palliser, 'Unions of parishes', 89–102.
117. Palliser, *The Reformation in York*, 17, 24–5; Palliser, *Tudor York*, 221; Ian Blanchard's biography of Gresham in *ODNB*.

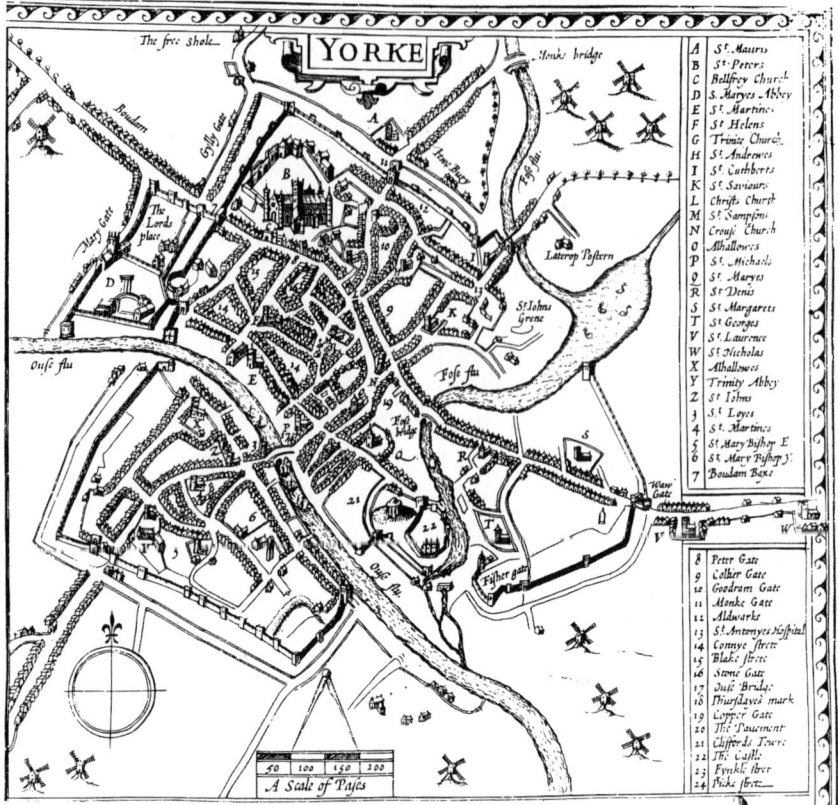

Map 8. John Speed's plan of York, 1610
The first properly surveyed plan of the city, though its combination of an accurate
ground plan with a bird's eye perspective of buildings disguises it. See R. A.
Skelton, 'Tudor town plans in John Speed's *Theatre*', *Archaeological Journal*, 108
(1952), 109–20.

Source: An inset plan in Speed's *The West Ridinge of Yorkeshyre with The most famous and fayre Citie Yorke
described* (London, 1610), reprinted with his other county maps in his *Theatre of the Empire of Great
Britaine* (London, 1611).

its relatively large and influential clerical population, the movement remained
weak compared with its success in neighbouring Hull'. Many examples
could be adduced of the conservatism of York's laity, but perhaps, from a
medieval perspective, an especially striking one was their stubborn clinging
to their Catholic street theatre. The Corpus Christi Play was performed
almost every year until 1569, with the full support of the corporation, and
the then mayor staged the Paternoster Play for the last time in 1572.[118]

118. A. G. Dickens, 'The early expansion of Protestantism in England 1520–1588', *Archiv für
    Reformationsgeschichte*, 78 (1987), 197–8; Palliser, *Tudor York*, 239, 242, 246–7.

It is not possible here to trace the economic fortunes of the city after the 1540s. Its population may have begun to recover by then, for the lay subsidy of 1524–5 implies a total of perhaps only 7,000, whereas the chantry certificates of 1548 imply over 8,000. Nevertheless, there were further severe epidemics in 1549–52 and 1558–9, and Queen Mary I granted the citizens tax relief in 1553, 1555, and 1558, each time citing their poverty: it did not help that Lord Shrewsbury, president of the Northern Council, was based in Sheffield. However, a turning point came when Sir Thomas Gargrave, vice-president of the Council, persuaded Elizabeth I's chief minister, Cecil, that York should become the sole headquarters of the Council: without it, the city would 'in shorte tyme moche decay'. The Council was duly settled in the King's Manor in 1561, and at the same time a new Northern Ecclesiastical Commission was set up in York. Both brought much business to the city in the following eight decades, and the North benefited from firmer government and more security, helped also by a peace treaty in 1560 which more or less ended endemic Anglo-Scottish warfare. Elizabethan and early Stuart York became moderately prosperous, and by 1662 it was almost level with Norwich and above Bristol as the highest-ranked English provincial town for the hearth tax.[119] It was this reviving city which was depicted by John Speed in his fine plan of 1610, on which the King's Manor is marked as 'The Lords place' (Map 8).

119. *YCR*, V, 97–8, 135–6, 179; Palliser, *Tudor York*, 53, 219, 260–87, 296–7; W. G. Hoskins, *Local History in England* (Harlow, 3rd edn 1984), 278; *CUHB* II, 122–3, 473. This is an English ranking: in British terms Norwich and York came fourth and fifth after London, Edinburgh, and Glasgow.

Conclusion

York is one of those cities which still preserves much of its medieval past: its Minster, parish churches, city walls, guildhalls, and surviving streets and houses are justly famous. Since 1945 it has profited from new directions which have enhanced its attractions for the medievalist, including the foundation of academic institutes, culminating in the establishment of two universities and a Centre for Medieval Studies, the creation of the York Archaeological Trust, and the revival and serious study of the York Plays. No apology is therefore necessary in retelling the city's medieval story in the light of recent research.

That story is inevitably a provisional one, as new discoveries and reinterpretations of existing evidence constantly modify the picture. It is also a partial one, because the past can never be wholly recovered even for a city with abundant written and physical remains: historians have always to remember the difference between absence of evidence and evidence of absence. The story is also partial for another reason. When documents start to become as abundant as archaeological evidence, as they do by the thirteenth century, there is a real danger of emphasizing those events and processes which were recorded in writing. In particular, social and economic historians often rely on records which are quantifiable, such as rentals, financial accounts, and customs records, which can tell only part of the story. 'Only limited aspects of the past', we are reminded, 'can be understood in this way, and the precision offered by figures is often spurious'.[1]

Making all allowances for partial or absent information, certain broad themes have, I believe, emerged from the thousand years of York's history surveyed above. The first two are surely the city's location and the Romans' genius in fixing on it. Though the Romans did not arrive in an unpopulated

---

1. Sir Keith Thomas, 'New ways revisited', *Times Literary Supplement*, 13 October 2006.

district—it was already 'a managed landscape'[2]—it was they who chose it for a legionary fortress and then for a true urban settlement. They were prepared to accept the drawbacks of a floodable site in a marshy vale in return for the compensating advantages. The site is on a ridge, a glacial moraine, crossing the Vale of York and meeting the river Ouse at the lowest point at which it could be bridged. The Roman policy was quickly justified, as the fortress developed suburbs and then a major civilian town, one which attained the rank of a *colonia* and of a provincial capital.

In its Roman origins, York typified many major medieval towns, and for good reasons. As A. L. F. Rivet put it:

> Colchester, Gloucester, Lincoln and York, Canterbury, Winchester, Chichester, Dorchester and Leicester, Cambridge and Worcester, all revived after the Dark Ages and are still county towns today. The implication of this must surely be that these places, both as administrative centres and as markets, were as well sited as they could be in relation to the agricultural exploitation of Britain not only in Roman conditions but in the conditions that prevailed in the Middle Ages and later...The pattern is strikingly modern.[3]

By no means all of England's largest medieval towns had Roman origins, but Rivet's essential point is correct. The leading Romano-British towns had sites suiting the needs of a pre-industrial economy, and not until the eighteenth century were most of them displaced at the head of the urban rankings by the new industrial cities.

That is sufficient justification to begin any study of a medieval city like London or York with its Roman predecessor, even though all Romano-British towns, without exception, seem to show a period of virtual desertion in the fifth and sixth centuries. The natural advantages of their sites were still in place once the post-Roman English kingdoms had developed sufficiently to need towns, especially those of defence combined with accessibility. Indeed, the Romans had improved on those attractions with their network of straight metalled roads linking town to town. So it was that the new English masters of York and the north kept up *Eburacum*'s fortress defences, some at least of its intramural streets, and most of the roads which

---

2. Patrick Ottaway, 'Roman York', in Patrick Nuttgens, ed., *The History of York from Earliest Times to the Year 2000* (Pickering, 2001), 2.

3. A. L. F. Rivet, *Town and Country in Roman Britain* (London, 2nd edn 1964), 76. (Canterbury and Colchester are not county towns today, but both were important administrative centres in the Middle Ages.)

radiated out in all directions. Furthermore, Pope Gregory's decision in 601 to locate one of the two projected English archbishoprics there was decisive for the city's future; it added a permanent ecclesiastical dimension, of national importance, to the city's functions.

If the legacy of *Eburacum* is familiar, the same could not be said, until a generation ago, of *Eoforwic*, 'Anglian' York. Before 1985–6, scholars were bemused by the lack of archaeological evidence to justify Alcuin's picture of a flourishing church and city. However, it is now clear that *Eoforwic* (as its very name suggests) included a trading *wic* or *emporium*, but situated outside the fortified Roman core. Alcuin's 'general seat of commerce [*emporium*] by land and sea' was no mirage, and York takes its place alongside *Lundenwic*, *Hamwic*, and Ipswich in the pattern of major trading ports around the North Sea between the seventh and ninth centuries. Here is a classic demonstration that previous absence of evidence did not prove evidence of absence. What remains a problem is the near-absence of identified patterns of settlement in York's hinterland. That might be because too little excavation has yet taken place there, or it might be, as Julian Richards suggests, that *Eoforwic* was a trading settlement tightly controlled by the king and the archbishop, with as yet little relationship to a developing rural economy.[4] Either way, it seems likely that York played a similar role in Northumbria to that played by London in Mercia, Ipswich in East Anglia, and *Hamwic* in Wessex.

The sprawling kingdom of Northumbria was dismembered in the 860s, the southern part, based on York, falling under Viking control. Their conquest was brutal and destructive in the short run, but before long the city was flourishing again. Its polyfocal settlements coalesced into a major port handling long-distance trade and housing a thriving manufacturing sector. By about 900 it had spread south of the fortress into a new zone of houses, workshops, and warehouses. The inhabitants traded with Ireland, Scandinavia, and the Baltic, and exotic imports came from as far as Samarkand and the Red Sea: no other Scandinavian settlement in Britain or Ireland has been so productive of finds except Dublin. It may be no surprise that, according to Richard Hall, *Jorvik* became the largest city in England apart from London, with an estimated population of 10–15,000.[5]

4. J. D. Richards, 'Defining settlements: York and its hinterland AD 700–1000', in S. Rees Jones et al., eds, *Courts and Regions in Medieval Europe* (Woodbridge, 2000), 49, 50. Cf., however, Chapter 2, n. 30.
5. R. A. Hall, 'York', in H. Beck and H. Steuer, eds, *Reallexikon der Germanischen Altertumskunde*, Band 34 (Berlin and New York, 2nd edn 2007), 387.

How many of that population were of Scandinavian descent is unknown, but whether small or large they certainly created an Anglo-Scandinavian society which proved resistant to the growing power of the new English kingdom to the south. Their most positive achievement may have been to stimulate not only an international trading city but one with close ties to its developing countryside. Richards has suggested that 'it is only with the Viking takeover that it is proper to speak of a true hinterland for York, comparable with that of the Roman period, and as continued into the later medieval period.'[6]

When the West Saxon king Athelstan seized York in 927 he effectively created a new English kingdom, with York as its second city. It did not change the essential character of its government and society, for the new kings appointed Anglo-Scandinavian earls and bishops to rule the north on their behalf. Even after the defeat of Eric Bloodaxe and the final English reconquest of York, it continued to look east for its trade and prosperity. The city, together with Lincoln and Norwich, was one of a series of towns in former Viking-controlled eastern England which boomed more than the old urban centres further south and west. Between 973 and 1066 the most productive royal mints after London were York and Lincoln, even exceeding Winchester.[7]

The two Anglo-Scandinavian centuries (866–1066) were thus crucial to York. It became a true regional capital in the economic sense, a role it retained throughout the Middle Ages. It was also true politically: when the English kings extended the old West Saxon shire system into Mercia and Northumbria, York was made the only shire town north of the Humber, as well as the usual seat of the Northumbrian earls.

The Norman Conquest, inadvertently triggered by the Northumbrian revolt of 1065, has usually been thought catastrophic for York and the north, as Northumbrian rebellions provoked the Norman king William to respond with a scorched-earth policy. Two chroniclers in particular have been repeatedly quoted to the effect that over 100,000 Northumbrians starved to death, and that 'between York and Durham no village was inhabited'. The so-called Harrying of the North was certainly exceptionally brutal, but I have given reasons to suspect that the level of death and destruction

6. Richards, 'Defining settlements', 50.
7. *CUHB* I, 750–11; see Chapter 3, n. 54. For 'English' history starting in 927: Patrick Wormald, 'Sir Geoffrey Elton's English: A view from the early Middle Ages', *TR Hist Soc*, 6th ser., 7 (1997), 318.

has been much exaggerated.[8] Numerous city-centre excavations since the
1970s have found no trace of any widespread destruction layer; and there are
many indicators that, as after 866–7, the city recovered quickly. The first
reliable yardstick after Domesday Book, the royal pipe roll of 1129–30, ranks
York as the fourth wealthiest town in England (after London, Winchester,
and Lincoln), while by the 1160s it was back in second place.[9]

Between 1100 and 1300 York shared in a general western European
growth in the number, size, and wealth of towns. English towns benefited especially from the closer trading links fostered with the Continental possessions of the Norman and Angevin kings, as well as from the
arrival of Jewish settlers; it is no accident that the first royal charter to
York (1155–62) protects its trade in England and Normandy, while the second and third (1189, 1200) added Aquitaine, Anjou, and Poitou. English urban
economies grew not only absolutely but proportionately: that is, the increase
in commercial activity outstripped population growth.[10] That encouraged
merchants and craftsmen in royal towns to demand firstly more self-government and then representation in the national assemblies (or parliaments)
which kings increasingly called to negotiate with their leading subjects.
York was successful in both, justified by the fact that it was still by the 1330s
second only to London in taxable wealth. Indeed, one recent survey concludes that in the fourteenth century, other than London, 'York alone
achieved a size or status comparable to large European towns such as Antwerp,
Bremen or Lyon.'[11]

Between 1300 and 1500 commercialization continued, in the sense that
wealth per head increased even while total population stagnated, fell sharply
from 1348–9, and then stabilized at a lower level.[12] In York's case, there was
clearly some economic recession after 1300 as its wool and cloth trade con-
tracted, though it is hard to know how far that decline was compounded by
the devastation of raids during the Scottish War of Independence, or mitigated by the presence of the royal court which that war brought to the city.

8. D. M. Palliser, 'Domesday Book and the "Harrying of the North" ', *NH*, 29 (1993), 1–23; see
   Chapter 4. The point is worth stressing because the traditional view is still widely held: see e.g.
   the colourful image of King William 'enthroned in the burnt out shell of York Minster, with
   snow gently falling through the charred embers of the roof': George Garnett, *The Norman
   Conquest: A Very Short Introduction* (Oxford, 2009), 120.
9. Martin Biddle, ed., *Winchester in the Early Middle Ages* (Oxford, 1976), 500.
10. R. H. Britnell, *The Commercialisation of English Society 1000–1500* (Manchester, 2nd edn 1996), 228.
11. Jennifer Kermode, 'The greater towns 1300–1540', in *CUHB* I, 441.
12. Britnell, *Commercialisation of English Society*, 228.

Certainly, however, York recovered remarkably quickly after the catastrophic Black Death, despite frequent returns of the plague. It was between 1272 and 1485, and especially between 1300 and 1450, 'that the majority of the most powerful and attractive visual memorials York now has to offer its innumerable visitors were...brought to completion'.[13]

The best recent estimates give late medieval England a larger minority of town-dwellers than used to be believed—perhaps 15 per cent or more by 1300, 20 per cent in 1377, and, after perhaps a fall in the fifteenth century, a return to 20 per cent by 1524.[14] Those broad figures, however, even if of the right order of magnitude, average the differing fortunes of growing and shrinking towns. York was one of several leading towns which boomed between about 1380 and 1420 before declining slightly, and then after about 1450 increasingly fast: Beverley, Boston, Colchester, Coventry, and (later) Salisbury are other examples. The growth is explicable in most cases by a revival of wool trade, cloth industry, and overseas trade in general; and the mid-fifteenth-century slump by an economic crisis in which Londoners were best placed to take a higher share of a shrinking economic cake, at the expense of many provincial towns.

Nevertheless, there are features particular to York which may have increased the rates of growth, and then of decline, more than the urban average. In the later fourteenth century it was well placed geographically to benefit from growing Anglo-Hanseatic trade, and from an increasing market for Yorkshire wool and textiles. Its broader craft and service economy prospered as it enjoyed a large influx of labour from its hinterland. By the 1420s, however, overseas trade through Hull was in decline; in the 1430s the city suffered from severe epidemics and from the widespread north-eastern economic crisis; and after 1450 the cloth industry increasingly migrated from old-established centres— York, Beverley, Ripon—to newer West Riding competitors like Leeds and Halifax. York's decline was masked for some time as the city lived on the accumulated capital of its earlier prosperity: the Guildhall was rebuilt on a handsome scale between 1449 and 1459, and major expenditure on church enlargements and new housing did not come to an end until about the 1470s.

From the 1520s there is evidence of a slow recovery of national and urban population, including York's, but the city did not recover its old

13. Barrie Dobson, 'Later medieval York', in Nuttgens, ed., *The History of York*, 101.
14. C. Dyer, 'How urbanized was medieval England?', in J.-M. Duvosquel and E. Thoen, eds, *Peasants and Townsmen in Medieval Europe* (Ghent, 1995), 169–83; *CUHB* I, 4, 741–2.

regional dominance as much as Norwich and Bristol, for instance, did. Changing economic patterns meant that the West Riding textile towns and Hull took much of the wealth that had formerly been generated by York. It was also the city's bad luck that just as Thomas Cromwell helped to solve its financial problems, in 1536, he also initiated those ecclesiastical confiscations which were so shattering in urban communities which depended heavily on ecclesiastical foundations and traumatic for those resistant to the new doctrines. York was here in company with Canterbury, Coventry, Lincoln, and Winchester rather than with, say, Ipswich, Norwich, or Southampton.

Nevertheless, there was also a positive side to the Crown's policies from the 1530s which ensured York at least a partial recovery of its position as northern capital. The settling of the King's Council in the Northern Parts at York from 1539 was followed in 1561 by its permanent establishment there, joined by a new Ecclesiastical Commission for the Northern Province. Both sat for the next eighty years in the city, attracting huge numbers of offenders, suitors, and witnesses, and turning York into a miniature Westminster. There is plentiful evidence for the city's renewed prosperity, which was boosted by a generous royal charter to the Company of Merchants in 1581. Overseas trade grew again, and the city increased its attraction as a social capital for the northern gentry. New and substantial timber-framed houses were constructed in large numbers: unlike their predecessors of a century earlier, most were equipped from the start with the comforts of window glass, wainscot panelling, and fireproof chimneys, and the inventories of leading merchants display wealthy furnishings.

Yet all of this failed to measure up to the peak prosperity of 1350–1450; and the city's fortunes were now based almost entirely on administrative and social functions and on revived trade: there was no substantial manufacturing to match the late medieval cloth industry. Once the Northern Council and Ecclesiastical Commission were abolished in 1641 (despite protests by the city corporation), York had to rely more and more on its status and its social functions. As the mayor and council put it around 1660, 'Leeds is nearer the manufactures, and Hull more commodious for the vending of them; so York is, in each respect, furthest from the profit.' They exaggerated, for in 1662, as has been seen, the city was still ranked third for the national Hearth Tax, behind London and Norwich but ahead of Newcastle. By 1700, however, York had been overtaken by Newcastle (with Gateshead) as the largest town in the north, and by 1801 it had also been overtaken, within Yorkshire, by Leeds, Sheffield, and Hull. 'York was no longer the undisputed capital of the North.'[15]

It is that decline which inadvertently preserved so much of pre-1540 York until the coming of industry and railways, and in part even today. For medieval York had never been unique, but had been, rather, one of a number of major towns of the second division, after London. It was very important in the age of the *emporia*, but not more so than Ipswich or Southampton; equally important between the tenth and thirteenth centuries, but no more than Winchester or Lincoln; and still competing as second city in the fourteenth and fifteenth centuries, but alongside Bristol and Norwich. What makes it special today is its survival, when other great medieval provincial cities have been largely rebuilt because of their post-medieval success, or because of the destruction wrought by city replanning and by aerial bombardment. It is the scenario of Lavenham or Sandwich on a larger scale: a town with so much medieval and sixteenth-century fabric because it had no later age of economic greatness (Plates 2a, 2b).

Even at York, the replacement of medieval and early modern buildings has been much greater than modern tourist publicity allows, as a glance at Henry Cave's drawings of 1813 makes clear (Plate 17). Micklegate, for instance, was 'near full' of timbered mansions until the late seventeenth century, before it became a street of Georgian brick. King Street, depicted by Cave as also full of picturesque if dilapidated timber-framing, was entirely rebuilt in 1851 (Plate 18), and Little Shambles almost obliterated as recently as 1955. Nevertheless, more than enough remains to justify York's reputation as a medieval city, a city which 'still tends to rule its modern successor from the grave', both by its walls, street-plan, and surviving buildings, and by the emotions it still evokes among residents and visitors.[16]

---

15. See Chapter 7, n. 119; quotation: D. M. Palliser, *Tudor York* (Oxford, 1979), 288; quotation: David Hey, *A History of Yorkshire* (Lancaster, 2005), 284.
16. Francis Drake, *Eboracum* (London, 1736), 280; Henry Cave, *Picturesque Buildings in York* (London, 1813): King Street is illustrated as First Water Lane in plate 37; *RCHMYV*, 149, 156. Quotation: Dobson, 'Later medieval York', 100.

Bibliography

MANUSCRIPT SOURCES

London, British Library:
Add. Ch. 10636 (charter and seal *c.*1200)

London, The National Archives:
Great Domesday Book (Alecto Facsimile, 1988)
C 53/10, m. 6 (1212 city charter)
E 13/26 (1301 civic ordinances)
E 135/25/1 (*c.*1228 mortmain inquest)
E 179 (lay subsidy returns)
KB 9/381 (1489 trial of rebels)

Oxford, Bodleian Library:
Dodsworth MSS
MS Rawl. B 451 (wardmote court book)

Southwell Minster:
MS 1 (Liber Albus)

York, Borthwick Institute for Archives:
CP ('Cause Papers')
Probate Registers

York, City Archives:
Manuscripts from the following classes, mostly calendared in William Giles's
    Catalogue of 1909 (see below) except for C 60 (husgabel roll *c.*1284)
Class A (city charters)
Class B (House Books)
Class C (chamberlains' and bridgemasters' accounts)
Class D (registers of freemen admissions)
Class E (registers and memorandum books, including A/Y and B/Y)

York, Merchant Adventurers' Company:
Various manuscripts, all calendared in D. M. Smith's *Guide* of 1990 (see below)

York, Minster Library:
L 2 (Magnum Registrum Album)
Class M (probate records)
MS Additional 2 (Bolton Hours)

PRIMARY PRINTED SOURCES

Alcuin: The Bishops, Kings, and Saints of York, ed. Peter Godman, OMT (Oxford, 1982)
The Anglo-Saxon Chronicle: A Revised Translation, eds Dorothy Whitelock et al. (Cambridge, 1961)
The Anglo-Saxon Chronicles, ed. Michael Swanton (London, 2000)
The Anglo-Saxon Chronicle: A Collaborative Edition, vol. 6: *MS D*, ed. G. P. Cubbin (Cambridge, 1996); vol. 7: *MS E*, ed. Susan Irvine (Cambridge, 2004)
The Anonimalle Chronicle 1307 to 1334, ed. W. R. Childs and John Taylor, YASRS 147 (Leeds, 1991)
Baedae Opera Historica, ed. Charles Plummer, 2 vols (Oxford, 1896)
Bede's Ecclesiastical History of the English People, ed. Bertram Colgrave and R. A. B. Mynors, OMT (Oxford, 1969)
Before the Merchant Adventurers: The Accounts of the Fraternity of Jesus and Mary, ed. Ann Rycraft, YLP (York, 2007)
The Blakburns in York: Testaments of a Merchant Family in the Later Middle Ages, ed. Ann Rycraft, YLP (York, 2006)
The Bolton Priory Compotus 1286–1325, ed. Ian Kershaw and D. M. Smith, YASRS 154 (Leeds, 2000)
Calendars of Charter Rolls, 1226–1516, 6 vols, HMSO (London, 1903–27)
Calendars of Close Rolls, 1272–1485, 45 vols, HMSO (London, 1892–1954)
Calendars of Patent Rolls, 1226–1509, 52 vols, HMSO (London, 1891–1916)
The Certificates of the Commissioners appointed to Survey the Chantries, Guilds, Hospitals, etc., in the County of York, ed. William Page, 2 vols, SS 91, 92 (1894–5)
Charters of the Vicars Choral of York Minster, ed. N. J. Tringham, 2 vols, YASRS 148, 156 (Leeds, 1993, 2002)
The Chronicle of St Mary's Abbey, York, ed. H. H. E. Craster and M. E. Thornton, SS 148 (1934)
The Church in Medieval York: Records Edited in Honour of Professor Barrie Dobson, ed. D. M. Smith, BTC 24 (York, 1999)
Churchwardens' Accounts of St Michael, Spurriergate, York, 1518–1548, ed. C. C. Webb, 2 vols, BTC 20 (York, 1997)
The Customs Accounts of Hull 1453–1490, ed. W. R. Childs, YASRS 144 (Leeds, 1986)
Early Yorkshire Charters, ed. William Farrer and C. T. Clay, 12 vols (various publishers, 1914–65)
English Episcopal Acta, 5: York 1070–1154, ed. J. E. Burton (Oxford, 1988); 20: *York 1154–1181*, ed. Marie Lovatt (Oxford, 2000); 27: *York 1189–1212*, ed. Marie Lovatt (Oxford, 2004)

English Historical Documents, I: *c.550–1042*, ed. Dorothy Whitelock, 2nd edn (London, 1979); II: *1042–1189*, ed. D. C. Douglas (London, 1953)

The Fabric Rolls of York Minster, ed. James Raine, SS 35 (1859) [much amended by John Browne, *Fabric Rolls and Documents of York Minster*, 2nd edn (York, 1863)]

The Friars' Libraries, ed. K. W. Humphreys (London, 1990), 11–154 [the catalogue of the York Augustinian friars' library]

The Historians of the Church of York and its Archbishops, ed. James Raine, 3 vols, RS (London, 1879–94)

Hugh the Chanter: The History of the Church of York 1066–1127, ed. C. Johnson; 2nd edn rev. M. Brett et al., OMT (Oxford, 1990)

'The inventory of John Louth, alderman of York (17 July 1435)', ed. Susanne Jenks (forthcoming)

'The lay subsidy of 1334 for York', eds P. M. Stell and A. Hawkyard, *YH*, 13 (1996), 2–14

The Ordinal and Customary of the Abbey of St Mary York, ed. L. McLachlan and J. B. L. Tolhurst, 3 vols, Henry Bradshaw Society, vols 73, 75, 84 (London, 1936–51)

Parliament Rolls of Medieval England, ed. Christopher Given-Wilson et al., 16 vols (Woodbridge, 2005)

The Poll Taxes of 1377, 1379 and 1381, Part 3: Wiltshire—Yorkshire, ed. C. C. Fenwick, RSEH, NS 37 (Oxford, 2005), 132–56

Probate Inventories of the York Diocese, 1350–1500, ed. P. M. Stell, AY 2/3 (2006)

Records of Early English Drama: York, ed. A. F. Johnston and Margaret Rogerson, 2 vols (Toronto and Manchester, 1979)

Records of Medieval York: City, Church and Crown, ed. Debbie Cannon, BTS (York, forthcoming)

Register of the Freemen of the City of York, ed. Francis Collins, 2 vols, SS 96, 102 (1897, 1902)

The Register of the Guild of Corpus Christi in the City of York, ed. R. H. Skaife, SS 57 (1872)

Sheriffs' Court Books of the City of York 1471–1500, ed. P. M. Stell, York City Archives (York, 1999)

Sources for York History to AD 1100, ed. D. W. Rollason, AY 1 (York, 1998)

Testamenta Eboracensia, ed. James Raine Sr, James Raine Jr, and J. W. Clay, 6 vols, SS 4, 30, 45, 53, 75, 106 (1836–1902)

The Testamentary Circle of Thomas de Dalby, Archdeacon of Richmond, d. 1400, ed. Ann Rycraft, YLP (York, 2000)

York Bridgemasters' Accounts, ed. P. M. Stell, AY 2/2 (York, 2003)

York City Chamberlains' Account Rolls 1396–1500, ed. R. B. Dobson, SS 192 (1980)

York Civic Ordinances, 1301, ed. Michael Prestwich, BP 49 (York, 1976)

York Civic Records, ed. Angelo Raine, 8 vols, YASRS 98, 103, 106, 108, 110, 112, 115, 119 (Leeds, 1939–53)

York Clergy Wills 1520–1600, ed. Claire Cross, 2 vols, BTC 10, 15 (York, 1984–9)

'The York Freemen's Register 1273–1540: Amendments and additions', ed. D. M. Palliser, *YH*, 12 (1995), 21–7

The York Gospels, ed. Nicolas Barker, Roxburghe Club (London, 1986)

York House Books 1461–1490, ed. L. C. Attreed, 2 vols, continuously paginated (Stroud, 1991)

York Memorandum Book, vols I, II [= A/Y], ed. Maud Sellers, SS 120, 125 (1912–15); vol. III [= B/Y], ed. J. W. Percy, SS 186 (1973)

The York Mercers and Merchant Adventurers 1356–1917, ed. Maud Sellers, SS 129 (1918)

York Plays, ed. L. T. Smith (Oxford, 1885)

The York Plays, ed. Richard Beadle, two volumes, EETS S.S. 23 (Oxford, 2009) and 24 (Oxford, 2013)

'York's earliest administrative record: The husgabel roll of *c.*1284', ed. D. M. Palliser, *YAJ*, 50 (1978), 81–91

The Yorkshire Domesday, ed. Ann Williams and G. H. Martin, Alecto Historical Editions, 2 vols (London, 1992)

Yorkshire Hundred and Quo Warranto Rolls, ed. Barbara English, YASRS 151 (Leeds, 1996)

SECONDARY SOURCES

[Articles are not listed separately where they have been printed or reprinted in any collective volume listed here]

Addyman, P. V., ed., *The British Historic Towns Atlas, Vol. V: York* (Oxford, forthcoming)

Addyman, P. V. and Black, V. E., eds, *Archaeological Papers from York presented to Maurice Barley* (York, 1984)

Addyman, P. V., Hall, R. A., et al., eds, *The Archaeology of York*, in progress (London and York, 1980–): selected fascicules and volumes are listed below by author

Allott, Stephen, *Alcuin of York c. A.D. 732 to 804* (York, 1974)

Attreed, L. C., *The King's Towns: Identity and Survival in Late Medieval English Boroughs* (New York, Oxford, etc., 2001)

Aylmer, G. E. and Cant, Reginald, eds, *A History of York Minster* (Oxford, 1977)

Badham, Sally, 'Commemoration in brass and glass of the Blackburn family of York', *Ecclesiology Today*, 43 (2010), 68–82

Ballard, Adolphus, ed., *British Borough Charters 1042–1216* (Cambridge, 1913)

Ballard, Adolphus and Tait, James, eds, *British Borough Charters 1216–1307* (Cambridge, 1923)

Barnwell, P. S. et al., eds, *Mass and Parish in Late Medieval England: The Use of York* (Reading, 2005)

Bartlett, J. N., 'The expansion and decline of York in the later Middle Ages', *Econ HR*, 2nd ser., 12 (1959), 17–33

Beadle, Richard, ed., *The Cambridge Companion to Medieval English Theatre*, 2nd edn (Cambridge, 2008)

Beadle, Richard, 'Nicholas Lancaster, Richard of Gloucester and the York Corpus Christi Play', in Margaret Rogerson, ed., *The York Mystery Plays: Performance in the City* (Woodbridge, 2011), 31–52

Bindoff, S. T., ed., *The History of Parliament: The House of Commons 1509–1558*, 3 vols (London, 1982) [York MPs' biographies by D. M. Palliser]

Blackburn, Mark, *Viking Coinage and Currency in the British Isles* (London, 2011)

Blair, John, ed., *Waterways and Canal-Building in Medieval England* (Oxford, 2007)

Blunt, C. E. et al., *Coinage in Tenth-Century England* (Oxford, 1989)

Britnell, R. H., *The Commercialisation of English Society 1000–1500*, 2nd edn (Manchester, 1996)

Britnell, R. H., 'York under the Yorkists', in R. H. Britnell, ed., *Daily Life in the Late Middle Ages* (Stroud, 1998), 175–94

Britnell, R. H., *Markets, Trade and Economic Development in England and Europe, 1050–1550* (Farnham, 2009)

Brown, Sarah, *'Our Magnificent Fabrick': York Minster: An Architectural History c. 1220–1500* (Swindon, 2003)

Bullough, Donald, *Alcuin: Achievement and Reputation* (Leiden, 2004)

Burton, Janet, *The Monastic Order in Yorkshire 1069–1215* (Cambridge, 1999)

Challis, C. E., ed., *A New History of the Royal Mint* (Cambridge, 1992)

Childs, W. R., *The Trade and Shipping of Hull 1300–1500*, East Yorkshire Local History Society (Hull, 1990)

Cramp, Rosemary, *Anglian and Viking York*, BP 33 (York, 1967)

Crouch, D. J. F., *Piety, Fraternity and Power: Religious Gilds in Late Medieval Yorkshire 1389–1547* (Woodbridge, 2000)

Cullum, P. H., *Cremetts and Corrodies: Care of the Poor and Sick at St Leonard's Hospital, York, in the Middle Ages*, BP 79 (York, 1991)

Cullum, P. H. and Goldberg, P. J. P., 'Charitable provision in late medieval York', *NH*, 29 (1993), 24–39

Dalton, Paul, *Conquest, Anarchy and Lordship: Yorkshire, 1066–1154* (Cambridge, 1994)

Darby, H. C. and Maxwell, I. S., *The Domesday Geography of Northern England* (Cambridge, 1977)

Davidson, Clifford and O'Connor, D. E., *York Art: A Subject List of Extant and Lost Art…*(Kalamazoo, 1978)

Dawes, J. D. and Magilton, J. R., *The Cemetery of St Helen-on-the-Walls, Aldwark*, AY 12/1 (York, 1980)

Dean, Gareth, *Medieval York* (Stroud, 2008)

Dickens, A. G., 'The "shire" and privileges of the archbishop of York in eleventh-century York', *YAJ*, 38 (1952–5), 131–47

Dickens, A. G., 'York before the Norman Conquest' and 'Tudor York', in *VCHY*, 2–24, 117–59

Dobson, R. B., 'Admissions to the freedom of the city of York in the later Middle Ages', *Econ HR*, 2nd ser., 26 (1973), 1–22

Dobson, R. B., 'Urban decline in late medieval England', *TR Hist S*, 5th ser., 27 (1977), 1–22

Dobson, R. B., 'The risings in York, Beverley and Scarborough, 1380–81', in R. H. Hilton and T. H. Aston, eds, *The English Rising of 1381* (Cambridge, 1984), 112–42

Dobson, R. B., 'Yorkshire towns in the late fourteenth century', *Publications of the Thoresby Society*, 59 (1985), 1–21

Dobson, R. B., *Church and Society in the Medieval North of England* (London, 1996)

Dobson, R. B., 'Craft guilds and city: The historical origins of the York mystery plays reassessed', in A. E. Knight, ed., *The Stage as Mirror: Civic Theatre in Late Medieval Europe* (Cambridge, 1997), 91–106

Dobson, R. B., 'Aliens in the city of York during the fifteenth century', in J. Mitchell, ed., *England and the Continent in the Late Middle Ages* (Stamford, 2000), 249–66

Dobson, R. B., 'John Shirwood of York: A Common Clerk's will of 1473', in M. Aston and R. Horrox, eds., *Much Heaving and Shoving: Late-Medieval Gentry and their Concerns*, (pr., 2005), 109–20

Dobson, R. B., *The Jewish Communities of Medieval England: The Collected Essays of R. B. Dobson*, ed. Helen Birkett (York, 2010)

Dobson, R. B., and D. M. Smith, eds, *The Merchant Taylors of York*, BTS 33 (York, 2006)

Donaghey, Brian, 'The archbishop gets a new transcription', *Medieval Yorkshire*, 27 (1998), 24–40

Drake, Francis, *Eboracum: or the History and Antiquities of the City of York* (London, 1736)

Duckham, B. F., *The Yorkshire Ouse: The History of a River Navigation* (Newton Abbot, 1967)

Dyer, A. D., *Decline and Growth in English Towns 1400–1640* (Basingstoke, 1991)

Dyer, A. D., '"Urban decline" in England, 1377–1525', in T. R. Slater, ed., *Towns in Decline AD 100–1600*, (Aldershot, 2000), 266–88

Fellows Jensen, Gillian, *Scandinavian Personal Names in Lincolnshire and Yorkshire* (Copenhagen, 1968)

Fellows Jensen, *Scandinavian Settlement Names in Yorkshire* (Copenhagen, 1972)

Fellows Jensen, 'The origin and development of the name York', in AY 1, 226–37

Fellows Jensen, 'The Anglo-Scandinavian street names of York', in AY 8/4 (2004), 357–71

Fleming, Robin, *Kings and Lords in Conquest England* (Cambridge, 1991)

Fletcher, Richard, *Bloodfeud: Murder and Revenge in Anglo-Saxon England* (London, 2002)

French, T. W., *York Minster: The Great East Window*, CVMA Summary Catalogue 2 (Oxford, 1995)

French, T. W., *York Minster: The St William Window*, CVMA Summary Catalogue 5 (1999)

French, T. W. and O'Connor, David, *York Minster: A Catalogue of Medieval Stained Glass: Fasciule 1: The West Windows of the Nave*, CVMA, vol. III (Oxford and New York, 1987)

Fryde, E. B., *Studies in Medieval Trade and Finance* (London, 1983)

Garrison, Mary, 'The library of Alcuin's York', in Richard Gameson, ed., *The Cambridge History of the Book in Britain*, vol. I: *c.400–1100* (Cambridge, 2011), 633–64

Gee, Eric, 'The painted glass of All Saints' church, North Street, York', *Archaeologia*, 102 (1969), 151–202

Gilchrist, Roberta and Mytum, Harold, eds, *Advances in Monastic Archaeology*, BAR British ser. 227 (Oxford, 1993)

Giles, Katherine, *An Archaeology of Social Identity: Guildhalls in York c. 1350–1630*, BAR British ser. 315 (Oxford, 2000)

Giles, Katherine, and Dyer, Christopher, eds, *Town and Country in the Middle Ages*, Society for Medieval Archaeology Monograph 22 (Leeds, 2005)

Giles, William, *Catalogue of the Charters… and Other Books, Deeds and Old Documents belonging to the Corporation of York* (York, 1909)

Goldberg, P. J. P., 'Mortality and economic change in the diocese of York, 1390–1514', *NH*, 24 (1988), 38–55

Goldberg, P. J. P., 'Urban identity and the poll taxes of 1377, 1379 and 1381', *Econ HR*, 2nd ser., 43 (1990), 194–216

Goldberg, P. J. P., *Women, Work and Life Cycle in a Medieval Economy: Women in York and Yorkshire c. 1300–1520* (Oxford, 1992)

Goldberg, P. J. P., 'Women in trade and industry in York', *ODNB*, 60 (2004), 52–3

Goldberg, P. J. P., ed., *Richard Scrope: Archbishop, Rebel, Martyr* (Donington, 2007)

Graham-Campbell, James et al., eds, *Vikings and the Danelaw* (Oxford, 2001)

Grierson, Philip and Blackburn, M. A. S., *Medieval European Coinage…*, vol. I: *The Early Middle Ages (5th–10th Centuries)* (Cambridge, 1986)

Griffiths, R. A., 'Local rivalries and national politics', *Speculum*, 43 (1968), 589–632, repr. in his *King and Country: England and Wales in the Fifteenth Century* (London, 1991), 321–64

Hadley, D. M., *The Northern Danelaw* (London, 2000)

Hadley, D. M. and Richards, J. D., eds, *Cultures in Contact: Scandinavian Settlement in England in the Ninth and Tenth Centuries* (Turnhout, 2000)

Hall, R. A., 'York', in H. Beck and H. Steuer, eds, *Reallexikon der Germanischen Altertumskunde*, Band 34 (Berlin and New York, 2007)

Hall, R. A. et al., *Aspects of Anglo-Scandinavian York*, AY 8/4 (2004)

Hall, R. A. and Hunter-Mann, K., *Medieval Urbanism in Coppergate: Refining a Landscape*, AY 10/6 (2002)

Hall, Richard, *The Viking Dig: The Excavations at York* (London, 1984)

Hall, Richard, *English Heritage Book of Viking Age York* (London, 1994)

Hall, Richard, *English Heritage Book of York* (London, 1996)

Hall, Richard, 'Secular buildings in medieval York', in *Lübecker Kolloquium zur Stadtarchäologie im Hanseraum*, III: *Der Hausbau* (Lübeck, 2001), 77–99

Hall, Richard and Stocker, David, eds, *Vicars Choral at English Cathedrals: Cantate Domino* (Oxford, 2005)

Hart, C. R., 'William Malet and his family', *ANS*, 19 (1997), 123–65

Hartley, Elizabeth, ed., *Alcuin & Charlemagne: The Golden Age of York* (York, 2001)

Hartley, Elizabeth et al., eds, *Constantine the Great: York's Roman Emperor* (York, 2006)

Hartshorne, Pamela, ed., *The York Merchant Adventurers and their Hall* (London, 2011)

Harvey, J. H., 'Bishophill and the Church of York', *YAJ*, 41 (1963–6), 377–93

Heaton, Herbert, *The Yorkshire Woollen and Worsted Industries: From the Earliest Times up to the Industrial Revolution* (Oxford, 1920)

Higham, N. J., *The Kingdom of Northumbria AD 350–1100* (Stroud, 1993)

Hill, David and Metcalf, D. M., eds, *Sceattas in England and on the Continent*, BAR British ser. 128 (Oxford, 1984)

Hodges, Richard and Hobley, Brian, eds, *The Rebirth of Towns in the West AD 700–1050*, CBA Research Report 68 (London, 1988)

Horrox, Rosemary, ed., *Richard III and the North* (Hull, 1986)

Horrox, Rosemary, ed., *Fifteenth-Century Attitudes: Perceptions of Society in Late Medieval England* (Cambridge, 1994)

Hoyle, R. W., 'The earl, the archbishop and the Council', in R. E. Archer and S. Walker, eds, *Rulers and Ruled in Late Medieval England* (London, 1995), 239–56

Hoyle, R. W., 'Urban decay and civic lobbying: The crisis in York's finances, 1525–1536', *NH*, 34 (1998), 83–108

Hoyle, R. W., *The Pilgrimage of Grace and the Politics of the 1530s* (Oxford, 2001)

Hughes, Jonathan, *Pastors and Visionaries: Religion and Secular Life in Late Medieval Yorkshire* (Woodbridge, 1988)

Johnston, A. F., 'William Revetour, chaplain and clerk of York, testator', *Leeds Studies in English*, n.s. 29 (1998), 153–71

Johnston, A. F. and Ostovich, Helen, eds, *The York Cycle Then and Now*, Early Theatre, special vol. 3 (Hamilton, Ont., 2000)

Kaner, Jennifer, 'Clifton and medieval woolhouses', *YH*, 8 (1988), 2–10

Kapelle, W. E., *The Norman Conquest of the North* (London, 1979)

Keene, D. J. and Corfield, P. J., eds, *Work in Towns 850–1850* (Leicester, 1990)

Kemp, R. L., *Anglian Settlement at 46–54 Fishergate*, AY 7/1 (York, 1996)

Kemp, R. L. and Graves, C., *The Church and Gilbertine Priory of St Andrew, Fishergate*, AY 11/2 (York, 1996)

Kermode, J. I., 'Urban decline? The flight from office in late medieval York', *Econ HR*, 2nd ser., 35 (1982), 179–98

Kermode, J. I., *Medieval Merchants: York, Beverley and Hull in the Later Middle Ages* (Cambridge, 1998)

Kightly, Charles and Semlyen, Rachel, *Lords of the City: The Lord Mayors of York and their Mansion House* (York, 1980)

King, Edmund, ed., *The Anarchy of King Stephen's Reign* (Oxford, 1994)

King, Pamela M., *The York Mystery Cycle and the Worship of the City* (Cambridge, 2006)

Kowaleski, Maryanne and Goldberg, P. J. P., eds, *Medieval Domesticity: Home, Housing and Household in Medieval England* (Cambridge, 2008)

Lang, J. T., *Corpus of Anglo-Saxon Stone Sculpture*, vol. III: *York and Eastern Yorkshire* (Oxford, 1991)

Lewycky, Nadine, 'Cardinal Thomas Wolsey and the city of York, 1514–1529', *NH*, 46 (2009), 43–60

Liddy, C. D., 'Urban conflict in late fourteenth-century England: The case of York in 1380–1', *EHR*, 118 (2003), 1–32

Liddy, C. D. *War, Politics and Finance in Late Medieval English Towns: Bristol, York and the Crown, 1350–1400* (Woodbridge, 2005)

Lilley, J. M. et al., *The Jewish Burial Ground at Jewbury*, AY 12/3 (York, 1994)

Lindkvist, H., 'A study on early medieval York', *Anglia*, 50 (1926), 345–94

McClure, Peter, 'Patterns of migration in the late Middle Ages', *Econ HR*, 2nd ser., 32 (1979), 167–82

McKisack, May, *The Parliamentary Representation of the English Boroughs During the Middle Ages* (London, 1932)

Maddicott, J. R., *The Origins of the English Parliament 924–1327* (Oxford, 2010)

Magilton, J. A., *The Church of St Helen-on-the-Walls, Aldwark*, AY 10/1 (York, 1980)

Mainman, Ailsa and Jenner, Anne, *Medieval Pottery from York*, AY 16/9 (York, 2013)

Marks, Richard, *Stained Glass in England During the Middle Ages* (London, 1993)

Metcalf, D. M., ed., *Coinage in Ninth-Century Northumbria*, BAR British ser. 180 (Oxford, 1987)

Metcalf, D. M., *Thrymsas and Sceattas in the Ashmolean Museum, Oxford*, 3 vols (Oxford, 1993–4)

Metcalf, D. M., *An Atlas of Anglo-Saxon and Norman Coin Finds 973 1086* (London and Oxford, 1998)

Metcalf, D. M., 'The coinage of King Aldfrith of Northumbria (685–704) and some contemporary imitations', *BNJ*, 76 (2006), 147–58

Miller, Edward, 'Medieval York', in *VCHY*, 25–116

Miller, Edward, 'Rulers of thirteenth-century towns: The cases of York and Newcastle upon Tyne', in P. R. Coss and S. D. Lloyd, eds., *Thirteenth Century England, I: Proceedings of the Newcastle-upon-Tyne Conference* (Woodbridge, 1986), 128–41

Miller, Edward and Hatcher, John, *Medieval England: Towns, Commerce and Crafts 1086–1348* (London, 1995)

Moran, J. A. H., *Education and Learning in the City of York, 1300–1560*, BP 55 (York, 1979)

Moran, J. A. H., *The Growth of English Schooling 1340–1548: Learning, Literacy and Laicization in Pre-Reformation York Diocese* (Princeton, NJ, 1985)

Morris, R. K., 'Alcuin, York and the *alma sophia*', in L. A. S. Butler and R. K. Morris, eds, *The Anglo-Saxon Church*, CBA Research Report 60 (London, 1986), 80–9

Morris, R. K., 'Churches in York and its hinterland: Building patterns and stone sources in the 11th and 12th centuries', in John Blair, ed., *Minsters and Parish Churches: The Local Church in Transition 950–1200* (Oxford, 1988), 191–9

Moulden, Joan and Tweddle, Dominic, *Anglo-Scandinavian Settlement South-West of the Ouse*, AY 8/1 (York, 1986)

Murphy, Neil, 'Receiving royals in later medieval York: Civic ceremony and the municipal elite, 1478–1503', *NH*, 43 (2006), 241–55

Newman, P. R., 'The Yorkshire Domesday *clamores* and the "lost fee" of William Malet', *ANS*, 22 (2000), 261–77

Nightingale, Pamela, *A Medieval Mercantile Community: The Grocers' Company and the Politics and Trade of London 1000–1485* (New Haven and London, 1995)

Nightingale, Pamela, *Trade, Money, and Power in Medieval England* (Aldershot, 2007)

Nightingale, Pamela, 'The rise and decline of medieval York: A reassessment', *P&P*, 206 (2010), 3–42

Norton, Christopher, 'The buildings of St Mary's Abbey, York, and their destruction', *Antiquaries Journal*, 74 (1994), 256–88

Norton, Christopher, 'The Anglo-Saxon cathedral at York and the topography of the Anglian city', *JBAA*, 151 (1998), 1–42

Norton, Christopher, 'The York fire of 1137: Conflagration or consecration?', *NH*, 34 (1998), 194–204

Norton, Christopher, 'The design and construction of the Romanesque church of St Mary's Abbey, York', *YAJ*, 71 (1999), 73–88

Norton, Christopher, *Archbishop Thomas of Bayeux and the Norman Cathedral at York*, BP 100 (York, 2001)

Norton, Christopher, 'Sacred space and sacred history: The glazing of the eastern arm of York Minster', in Rüdiger Becksmann, ed., *Glasmalerei im Kontext: Bildprogramme und Raumfunktionen* (Nürnberg, 2005), 167–81

Norton, Christopher, *St William of York* (Woodbridge, 2006)

Ormrod, W. M., 'Competing capitals? York and London in the fourteenth century', in Sarah Rees Jones et al, eds, *Courts and Regions in Medieval Europe* (Woodbridge, 2000), 75–98

Ormrod, W. M., ed., *The Lord Lieutenants and High Sheriffs of Yorkshire, 1066–2000* (Barnsley, 2000)

Ottaway, Patrick, *Roman York* (Stroud, 2nd edn 2004)

Palliser, D. M., 'The unions of parishes at York, 1547–1586', *YAJ*, 46 (1974), 87–102

Palliser, D. M., 'The medieval street-names of York', *YH*, 2 (1978), 2–16

Palliser, D. M., *Tudor York* (Oxford, 1979)

Palliser, D. M., *Domesday York*, BP 78 (York, 1990)

Palliser, D. M., 'Domesday Book and the Harrying of the North', *NH*, 29 (1993), 1–23

Palliser, D. M., 'Thirteenth-century York—England's second city?', *YH*, 14 (1997), 2–9

Palliser, D. M., *Towns and Local Communities in Medieval and Early Modern England* (Aldershot, 2006)

Palliser, D. M., ed., *The Cambridge Urban History of Britain*, vol. I: *600–1540* (Cambridge, 2000)

Pedersen, Frederik, *Marriage Disputes in Medieval England* (London, 2000)

Phillips, Derek, *Excavations at York Minster*, vol. II: *The Cathedral of Archbishop Thomas of Bayeux* (London, 1985)

Phillips, Derek and Heywood, Brenda, *Excavations at York Minster*, vol. I: *From Roman Fortress to Norman Cathedral* (London, 1995)

Pirie, E. J. E., *Coins of the Kingdom of Northumbria c. 700–867* (Llanfyllin, 1996)

Pirie, E. J. E., *Thrymsas, Sceattas and Stycas of Northumbria: An Inventory of Finds Recorded to 1997* (Llanfyllin, 2000)

Pollard, A. J., 'The north-eastern economy and the agrarian crisis of 1438–1440', *NH*, 25 (1989), 88–105

Pollard, A. J., *North-Eastern England during the Wars of the Roses: Lay Society, War and Politics 1450–1500* (Oxford, 1990)

Radley, Jeffrey, 'Economic aspects of Anglo-Danish York', *Medieval Archaeology*, 15 (1971), 37–57

Raine, Angelo, *Mediaeval York: A Topographical Survey Based on Original Sources* (London, 1955)

Ramm, H. G., 'A case of twelfth-century town planning in York?', *YAJ*, 42 (1968), 132–5

Ramm, H. G. et al., 'The tombs of Archbishops Walter de Gray (1216–55) and Godfrey de Ludham (1258–65) in York Minster, and their contents', *Archaeologia*, 103 (1971), 101–47

Rees Jones, Sarah, ed., *The Government of Medieval York: Essays in Commemoration of the 1396 Royal Charter*, Borthwick Studies in History 3 (York, 1997)

Rees Jones, Sarah and Riddy, Felicity, 'The Bolton Hours of York: Female domestic piety and the public sphere', in A. Mulder-Bakke and J. Wogan-Browne, eds, *Household, Women and Christianities* (Turnhout, 2005), 215–60

Reynolds, Susan, *Ideas and Solidarities of the Medieval Laity: England and Western Europe* (Aldershot, 1995)

Richards, J. D., ed., *The Vicars Choral of York Minster: The College at Bedern*, AY 10/5 (York, 2001)

Rigby, S. H., 'Urban population in late medieval England: The evidence of the lay subsidies', *Econ HR*, 63 (2010), 393–417

Roberts, Brian K., *Landscapes, Documents and Maps: Villages in Northern England and Beyond AD 900–1250* (Oxford, 2008)

Roffe, D. R., 'Domesday Book and Northern society: A reassessment', *EHR*, 105 (1990), 310–36

Rollason, D. W., *Northumbria, 500–1100: Creation and Destruction of a Kingdom* (Cambridge, 2003)

Roskell, J. S., ed., *The History of Parliament: The House of Commons 1386–1422*, 4 vols (London, 1993) [York MPs' biographies by Carole Rawcliffe]

Royal Commission on Historical Monuments (England), *An Inventory of the Historical Monuments in the City of York*, 5 vols (London, 1962–81)

Salisbury, M. C., *The Use of York: Characteristics of the Medieval Liturgical Office in York*, BP 113 (York, 2008)

Saul, Nigel, 'Richard II, York, and the evidence of the king's itinerary', in J. L. Gillespie, ed., *The Age of Richard II* (Stroud, 1997), 71–92

Sayles, G. O., 'The dissolution of a gild at York in 1306', *EHR*, 55 (1940), 83–98

Shields, E. L., 'The members of parliament for the city of York 1485–1515', *YH*, 11 (1994), 9–22

Short, P., 'The fourteenth-century rows of York', *Archaeological Journal*, 137 (1979), 86–137

Sillence, M. J., 'The two effigies of Archbishop Walter de Gray (d. 1255) at York Minster', *Church Monuments*, 20 (2005), 5–30

Smith, A. H., *The Place-Names of the East Riding of Yorkshire and York*, English Place Name Society 5 (Cambridge, 1937)

Smith, D. M., ed., *A Guide to the Archives of the Company of Merchant Adventurers of York*, BTC 16 (York, 1990)

Smyth, A. P., *Scandinavian York and Dublin: The History and Archaeology of Two Related Viking Kingdoms*, 2 vols (Dublin, 1975–9)

Smyth, A. P., *Scandinavian Kings in the British Isles 850–880* (Oxford, 1977)

Spall, C. A. and Toop, N. J., 'Before *Eoforwic*: New light on York in the 6th–7th centuries', *Medieval Archaeology*, 52 (2008), 1–25

Stacey, R. C., 'Crusades, Martyrdoms and the Jews of Norman England, 1096–1190', in Alfred Haverkamp, ed., *Juden und Christen zur Zeit der Kreuzzüge* (Sigmaringen, 1999), 233–51

Stocker, D. A., 'The priory of the Holy Trinity, York: Antiquarians and architectural history', in L. R. Hoey, ed., *Yorkshire Monasticism: Archaeology, Art and Architecture, from the 7th to 16th Centuries*, BAA Conference Transactions 16 (London, 1995), 79–96

Story, Joanna, *Carolingian Connections: Anglo-Saxon England and Carolingian Francia, c. 750–870* (Aldershot, 2003)

Story, Joanna, 'Bede, Willibrord and the letters of Pope Honorius I on the genesis of the archbishopric of York', *EHR*, 127 (2012), 783–818

Sutton, A. F., 'The Merchant Adventurers of England: The place of the Adventurers of York and the north in the late Middle Ages', *NH*, 46 (2009), 219–29

Swanson, Heather, *Building Craftsmen in Late Medieval York*, BP 63 (York, 1983)

Swanson, Heather, *Medieval Artisans: An Urban Class in Late Medieval England* (Oxford, 1989)

Thompson, A. Hamilton, 'The pestilences of the fourteenth century in the diocese of York', *Archaeological Journal*, 71 (1914), 97–154

Thomson, J. A. F., ed., *Towns and Townspeople in the Fifteenth Century* (Gloucester, 1988)

Townend, Matthew, ed., *Wulfstan, Archbishop of York* (Turnhout, 2004)

Tweddle, Dominic, *The Anglian Helmet from 16–22 Coppergate*, AY 17/8 (York, 1992)

Tweddle, Dominic et al., *Anglian York: A Survey of the Evidence*, AY 7/2 (York, 1999)

Twycross, Meg, 'Some aliens in York and their overseas connections: Up to c.1470', *Leeds Medieval Studies*, n.s. 29 (1998), 359–80

The Victoria History of the County of York, ed. William Page, 3 vols (London, 1907–13)

The Victoria History of the County of York: The City of York, ed. P. M. Tillott (Oxford, 1961)

Walker, Simon, *Political Culture in Later Medieval England: Essays by Simon Walker*, ed. M. Braddick (Manchester, 2006)

Walton Rogers, Penelope, *Textile Production at 16–22 Coppergate*, AY 17/11 (York, 1997)

Waterman, D. M., 'Late Saxon,Viking, and early medieval finds from York', *Archaeologia*, 97 (1959), 59–105

Weinbaum, Martin, ed., *British Borough Charters 1307–1660* (Cambridge, 1943)

Wenham, L. P. et al., *St Mary Bishophill Junior and St Mary Castlegate*, AY 8/2 (York, 1987)

White, Eileen, *The St Christopher and St George Guild of York*, BP 72 (York, 1987)

White, Eileen, ed., *Feeding a City: York: The provision of Food from Roman Times to the Beginning of the Twentieth Century* (Totnes, 2000)

Williams, Gareth and Ager, Barry, *The Vale of York Hoard* (London, 2010)

Wilson, Barbara and Mee, Frances, *The Medieval Parish Churches of York* (York, 1998); *'The Fairest Arch in England': Old Ouse Bridge and its Buildings* (2002); *The City Walls and Castles of York* (2005); *St Mary's Abbey and the King's Manor, York* (2009) [AY SS 1, The Pictorial Evidence, fascicules 1–4]

Wilson, Christopher, *The Shrines of St William of York* (York, 1977)

UNPUBLISHED THESES

Bartlett, J. N., 'Some aspects of the economy of York in the later Middle Ages 1300–1550', PhD thesis (University of London, 1958) [London School of Economics theses collection, X29, 075]

O'Brien, D. J. S., ' "The veray registre of all trouthe": The content, function, and character of the civic registers of London and York c.1274–c.1482', DPhil thesis (University of York, 1999)

Rees Jones, S. R., 'Property, tenure and rents: Some aspects of the topography and economy of medieval York', D. Phil. thesis (University of York, 1987)

Picture Acknowledgements

The author and publisher gratefully acknowledge the assistance of the following persons and institutions for providing illustrations, and for their kind permission to reproduce them:

Plates 1, 3, 4, 5, 9, 10, and 16: Professor John Blair
Plates 2a, 6, and 12: York Museums Trust (York Art Gallery)
Plate 2b: Ken Spelman Books
Plates 7 and 8: The Dean and Chapter of York
Plate 11: The Company of Merchant Adventurers of the City of York
Plate 13: The Department of Prints and Drawings, the British Museum
Plates 14 and 15: The Rev. Gordon Plumb

The author is also much indebted to Mr Peter Brown and York Civic Trust for providing him with digital images of several plates, and to Gordon Plumb for the images for Plates 7 and 8.

Index

The following abbreviations are used for office-holders : Abp and bp for (arch)bishop (with dates of episcopate in brackets for archbishops of York); Ald for alderman of York; K for King; M for mayor of York (with dates of mayoralty in brackets); and Q for Queen. Places within the historic county of York are located by riding : ER for East Riding, NR for North Riding, and WR for West Riding.